Our Price
£ 38.00
£ 19.00

CW01457187

BEETHOVEN THE PIANIST

The widely held belief that Beethoven was a rough pianist, impatient with his instruments, is not altogether accurate: it is influenced by anecdotes dating from when deafness had begun to impair his playing. Presenting a new, detailed biography of Beethoven's formative years, this book reviews the composer's early career, outlining how he was influenced by teachers, theorists, and instruments. Skowroneck describes the development and decline of Beethoven's pianism, and pays special attention to early pianos, their construction, and their importance for Beethoven and the modern pianist. The book also includes new discussions of legato and Beethoven's trills, and a complete annotated review of eyewitnesses' reports about his playing. Skowroneck presents a revised picture of Beethoven which traces his development from an impetuous young musician into a virtuoso in command of many musical resources.

TILMAN SKOWRONECK is a postdoctoral researcher at the University of Southampton, and is also a freelance harpsichordist and fortepianist. His main area of interest is the early piano, its construction, and its repertoire. This is his first book.

MUSICAL PERFORMANCE AND RECEPTION
General editors John Butt and Laurence Dreyfus

This series continues the aim of Cambridge Musical Texts and Monographs to publish books centered on the history of musical instruments and the history of performance, but broadens the focus to include musical reception in relation to performance and as a reflection of period expectations and practices.

Published titles

BEETHOVEN THE PIANIST

TILMAN SKOWRONECK

CAMBRIDGE
UNIVERSITY PRESS

CAMBRIDGE
UNIVERSITY PRESS

University Printing House, Cambridge CB2 8BS, United Kingdom

Cambridge University Press is part of the University of Cambridge.

It furthers the University's mission by disseminating knowledge in the pursuit of education, learning and research at the highest international levels of excellence.

www.cambridge.org
Information on this title: www.cambridge.org/9780521119597

© Tilman Skowroneck 2010

This publication is in copyright. Subject to statutory exception and to the provisions of relevant collective licensing agreements, no reproduction of any part may take place without the written permission of Cambridge University Press.

First published 2010

A catalogue record for this publication is available from the British Library

Library of Congress Cataloguing in Publication data
Skowroneck, Tilman.
Beethoven the pianist / Tilman Skowroneck.
p.   cm. – (Musical performance and reception)
Includes bibliographical references.
ISBN 978-0-521-11959-7
1. Beethoven, Ludwig van, 1770–1827.   2. Piano – Performance – History – 18th century.
3. Piano – Performance – History – 19th century.   4. Piano – History – 18th century.
5. Piano – History – 19th century.   I. Title.   II. Series.
ML410.B42S6   2010
786.2092–dc22
[B]
2010000695

ISBN 978-0-521-11959-7 Hardback

Cambridge University Press has no responsibility for the persistence or accuracy of URLs for external or third-party internet websites referred to in this publication, and does not guarantee that any content on such websites is, or will remain, accurate or appropriate.

For Jessica and Lukas

Contents

Acknowledgments

I would like to thank the many people who have contributed to this project.

I am especially grateful to Alf Björnberg, supervisor for my doctoral thesis, for his unfailing helpfulness and good spirits.

This book would not have reached its present state without the support and rigorous reading of Robin Blanton. Robin also provided the right atmosphere for me to concentrate on the final stages of this work. More recently, Susan Blanton and Nicholas Blanton kindly read the final manuscript, for which I am very grateful. Many thanks to David Yearsley and John Koster, who took on the task of reading large parts of an earlier version of this text and helped me to clarify several important points. Some earlier versions of parts of this book were read by Pauline Schenck, Mats Krouthén, Malcolm Bilson, and Michael Latcham, who all helped me to improve my writing.

Special thanks to the participants in the doctoral seminars in musicology at Göteborg University.

Malcolm Bilson has been a friend and critical observer of my playing and writing, and of my skills at presenting papers in public. Through his help I have been able to publish parts of my work, for all of which I am very grateful.

Of the many scholars, musicians, organologists and instrument makers who have helped me with valuable suggestions or in practical matters, patiently answering my many questions and listening to my musings, I especially want to mention Stephen Birkett, Christopher Clarke, Mats d Hermansson, Jean Marc Reichow, Maria van Epenhuysen Rose, Eszter Fontana, Alfons Huber, David Hunt, William Jurgenson, Monika May, Paul Poletti, Siegbert Rampe, and Neal Zaslaw. I am particularly grateful to Michael Latcham, who has generously shared material from his research and commented on my work.

Patricia Stroh at the Beethoven Center San Jose, Nicole Kämpken at the Beethoven-Haus Bonn, and Stephanie Kuban at the library of the Beethoven-Haus Bonn have been particularly helpful and prompt in answering requests.

I am pleased to have been able to reproduce all the excerpts of Beethoven's sonatas from the first editions using the Tecla facsimile edition *The 32 Piano Sonatas*, by kind permission of Tecla Editions (www.tecla.com).

Thanks to the Göteborg Organ Art Center community for inviting me to present and discuss parts of my research at their conferences. Thanks to Cornell University for providing a scholarship for attending the performance practical program in the fall term of 1999, and to the Swedish Royal Academy of Music for a scholarship to cover my expenses during that time.

Many friends and acquaintances have supported my project, helped me to find historical sources and given helpful feedback. Among these are Matthew Bengtson, Hans Davidsson, Geoffrey Govier, Darryl Martin, Ibo Ortgies, Ludger Rémy, Peter Schleuning, Freek Sluijs, and Joel Speerstra. David Pickett spent days copying important material for me that is out of print and I am especially grateful for his help.

Special thanks, finally, to the members of my family. First and foremost for the patience and tolerance of my children, to whom Beethoven is perhaps less important than to me, but who nevertheless were patient and understanding with my project even in difficult times. I especially want to thank my parents, Susanne and Martin Skowroneck both for their support and for their professional advice.

Abbreviations and conventions

AMZ: *Allgemeine musikalische Zeitung*
MGG: *Die Musik in Geschichte und Gegenwart*, edition 1949–1951

References to the "Kafka" sketch miscellany in instances where the date is not crucial are not footnoted and refer to Joseph Kerman, ed., *Ludwig van Beethoven Autograph Miscellany from ca. 1786 to 1799 (The "Kafka" Sketchbook)*. 2 vols., London: The Trustees of the British Museum, 1970.

In order to keep the text readable I have refrained from italicizing certain frequently recurring German terms such as Klavier and Clavier. The capitalization of these terms usually follows the source at hand.

The term *fortepiano* is only one of many historical names for a keyboard instrument with a hammer action. I use this term in the modern way to address any kind of "historical piano," no matter in which tradition or period it was built. This is a necessary shortcut to keep the text readable.

The part of the German and Viennese piano actions that is shaped like a fork in which the hammer pivots is called the *Kapsel* in German. Organologists have chosen various ways of adapting this term to English usage. I have adhered to the German term.

All translations in this book are mine, unless otherwise indicated.

Introduction

This study investigates Beethoven's formative years as a keyboardist and his active career as a keyboard performer, the most important part of which stretches from his youth to the first years of the nineteenth century. Two elements are generally seen as responsible for the end of this career, namely the loss of his hearing and his changing ambitions as a composer. A convenient limit is the turn of the year 1808: Beethoven's last important public appearance as a pianist was on December 22, 1808,[1] and on February 7, 1809, Johann Friedrich Reichardt heard and praised the result of years of hard work by the Streicher piano-building firm: a "perfect" piano that possessed greater sonority and diversity than the earlier Viennese pianos.[2]

If we address Beethoven's keyboard playing and the practice of performing his piano works, one important question is in what way the keyboard tutors of the late eighteenth century fit into the picture. Opinions on this matter vary considerably. The relationship between an eighteenth-century tutor and eighteenth-century performance practice would in any case require careful study. The information we have about Beethoven's relationship to both is even less clear and often contradictory. Apparently even Beethoven's personal opinions about the theorists of his time varied according to the circumstances.[3]

This book is about change: it addresses the changing performance conventions during Beethoven's lifetime, his changing compositional style, his changing keyboard playing, and changes in piano building. I will thus describe Beethoven's pianism as a development, the early stages of which are just as relevant and worth considering as the more famous later developments.

One item that changed just as quickly and radically as Beethoven's composing style for the piano was the piano itself. When considering

---

[1] For some contemporary descriptions of this event, see, for example, Howard C. Robbins Landon, ed., *Ludwig van Beethoven. Leben und Werk in Zeugnissen der Zeit*, Zürich: Universal, 1970, 140–2.

[2] Johann Friedrich Reichardt, *Briefe, die Musik betreffend*, ed. Grita Herre and Walther Siegmund-Schultze, Leipzig: Philipp Reclam jun., 1976, 287.

[3] See, for instance, the anecdote about Beethoven's dislike of voice-leading rules and Marpurg, Kirnberger, and Fuchs in Franz Gerhard Wegeler and Ferdinand Ries, *Biographische Notizen über Beethoven*, Coblenz: Bädeker, 1838, 87.

Beethoven's pianism, one must inevitably make an assessment of the changing instrument. One typical flaw in earlier literature about Beethoven's pianos is the tendency to oversimplify the picture, taking for granted that he always preferred the newest pianos available to him, while the documents sometimes suggest otherwise.

William Newman's article "Beethoven's pianos versus his piano ideals," which appeared in 1970, was a reaction to this tendency. Newman stated that the three "Beethoven pianos" (Érard 1803, Broadwood 1817, and Graf 1825), "partly for the very reason, that they are Beethoven's only extant pianos and partly because they figure specifically more than any other instruments identified with him in the early sources, have been emphasized far beyond their actual musical value to Beethoven."[4] At the same time, however, Newman supported the common view that Beethoven combined a lifelong interest in the developments in piano building with a fundamental dissatisfaction with his instruments.

Ideas from Newman's earlier articles and from his book *Beethoven on Beethoven. Playing His Piano Music His Way*, published in 1988, have found their way into many subsequent studies by other writers.

In the meantime, research about early pianos has flourished and much new organological information has become accessible. While Newman's statement that "new documentary evidence is hard to discover in the oft-combed sources for Beethoven" remains valid,[5] a whole new set of tools has emerged with which to tackle the interpretation of the relevant documents yet again. Instrument makers have, through restoring many antiques and building new pianos after old models, collected an immense body of information about building styles, techniques, and materials. A vehement but informed debate is carried out at the border between organological expertise and opinions and arguments on the aesthetics of sound. In many cases, today's organological knowledge helps us to interpret the available source information about Beethoven's relationship to keyboard instruments and keyboard playing more precisely than only a few decades ago.

Often, however, multiple new plausible interpretations present themselves. Performance practice research has long tended to favor proof and conclusions, and the arguments are often only seen as an instrument to achieve that goal. Beethoven research is no exception in this respect. A case in point is William Newman's and Robert Winter's dispute about Beethoven's trills.[6] Both Newman and Winter strive for a positive confirmation of their hypotheses through argument, but they disagree because

---

[4] William S. Newman, "Beethoven's pianos versus his piano ideals," *Journal of the American Musicological Society* 23/3 (1970): 484.
[5] *Ibid.*
[6] For references and a discussion see Chapter 8.

the source situation is complex and because they attribute a different relevance to secondary knowledge.

Part of the problem in this example may be that a modern effort to bring misty historical information into focus does not always do justice to the historical situation; perhaps it only seems misty because we are lacking some of the information, but perhaps a documented vagueness is the consequence of historical tolerance instead (in the case of the trills, this would be a late eighteenth-century tolerance about various ways to play a trill). In that case, final answers simply fail to describe the historical reality.

For research based on the evidence from Beethoven's music itself, the greatest risk is that we let ourselves be guided by the Beethoven picture of our time. This should be avoided: even if, in acknowledging that the unique cultural relevance of Beethoven reception history is the force that makes Beethoven important today, we end up rejecting Beethoven's own performance practice or the practice of his day, we can nevertheless only gain understanding – even an understanding of the significance of this rejection – if we first acknowledge and accept the historical information.

Whereas a powerfully supported conclusion might have the potential to trigger a specialists' debate, an emphasis on argument greatly enhances the practical usefulness of a performance practice study, especially when a large body of conflicting material is to be considered. Often it is preferable *not* to choose among various competing answers to a question, thus introducing yet another set of constructed Beethovenian truths. I am convinced that using careful discussion as a tool to convey historical likelihood must be preferred to ever so skillfully constructed conclusions. This is the approach I have chosen for this book.

An important stimulus for the artistic aspect of this work was the concert and recording project of the complete Beethoven sonatas on period pianos by fortepianist Malcolm Bilson and six of his former students. The CD set was issued in 1997,[7] and radio broadcasts of a concert series in Utrecht in the Netherlands were distributed around the same time. In the CD set, the use of a total of nine old and new fortepianos (representing Beethoven's possible piano preferences and most of the relevant periods) illustrates the progress of Beethoven's piano style in a most striking manner. The project is founded on the assertion that Beethoven's pianos were part of his reality and hence worth considering. Pianist, recording engineer, and listener are made to share an essential experience: that of the practical and artistic effects of the confrontation of the composer with his pianos. At last, one gets an idea of whether Carl Czerny's 1842 statement that Beethoven's "playing as well as his compositions were ahead of his time, [and] the extremely weak and imperfect fortepianos of that time (until about 1810) often could not yet

---

[7] Claves CD 50–9707/10. The performers are Malcolm Bilson, Tom Beghin, David Breitman, Ursula Dütschler, Zvi Meniker, Bart van Oort, and Andrew Willis.

support his gigantic performance" describes Czerny's actual experience, or is an aesthetic judgment made in hindsight.[8] What is especially successful, in my opinion, is the fact that seven pianists with very different approaches are involved. As a result, the often difficult problems of Beethoven interpretation on the early piano are solved in a variety of ways. With Czerny's words in mind, one might think that the production of expressivity through force is the only true challenge in a confrontation between this repertoire and these instruments. Instead, the recording shows, in a most positive manner, that the realization of awkward technical maneuvers in notated non-accented dynamics, regularity in extended *pp* passages, and polyphonic and melodic clarity, challenge the pianist just as much as the more or less judicious command over the dynamic top of the instrument.

In one area the similarities in these recordings are, however, more striking than the differences: in contrast to the varied approaches to the sonatas from *c.* 1800 onward, the earlier sonatas are presented in a markedly uniform manner. A comparison with the available information about Beethoven's early instruments reveals that the performances of the earlier repertoire are compromised, indeed modernized. For the six sonatas up to the mid-1790s (WoO 47 and Op. 2), a whole range of historically plausible instruments has yet to find its way into the recordings. One wonders whether the pianists on this recording felt that the young Beethoven had access to instruments that are just too archaic to be presentable.

Moreover, if we compare the extensive indications for articulation in the three earliest sonatas (WoO 47) with the recordings of these pieces, we find that their realization has been adapted to Beethoven's later style. The three pianists who perform these sonatas have chosen to approach the passage-work of the outer movements using much more legato than the score suggests. Hence the recordings of these early pieces leave the impression that Beethoven's early notation needs not only interpretation but reworking in order to sound characteristic.

The very fact that the instruments chosen for these early pieces, and the legato touch, are so well suited to some of Beethoven's later works should alert us to the extent of his early development, and to the importance of the young Beethoven's learning and maturing, for our understanding of the performance practice of his works. So, while I was inspired by this project, it also raised questions about the significance of a more detailed approach to Beethoven's early instruments and the performance of his early works.

I should mention some of the key problems regarding the material encountered during my work. The immensity of literature on Beethoven means that it is impossible to consult all of the accessible material. This in itself is no reason for despair. Many areas of information are heavily

---

[8] Carl Czerny, "Erinnerungen aus meinem Leben, 1842," in *Über den richtigen Vortrag der sämtlichen Beethoven'schen Klavierwerke*, ed. Paul Badura-Skoda, Vienna: Universal, 1963, 22.

cross-referenced in the literature and the amount of material that specifically bears on performance practices on early pianos is somewhat less intimidating.

Primary sources have become much more accessible in recent years. Complete critical editions of the letters and the conversation books are available; some important sketchbooks have been published; many autographs and early editions of Beethoven's music have been reprinted in facsimile. Some institutions, such as the Beethoven-Haus in Bonn, have published an enormous amount of source material on the internet.

Most of the anecdotal literature is easily accessible through several well-known compilations, starting with Gerhard Wegeler's and Ferdinand Ries' *Biographische Notizen über Beethoven* from 1838 and culminating in the various editions of Thayer's Beethoven biography, Theodor Frimmel's compilations of material and discussions, and several similar works from the early twentieth century.

In the non-German literature a perennial problem is the translation of primary sources. Beethoven's letters, for example, generate many difficulties of interpretation even in the original language. It is scarcely surprising that, at times, the accepted authorized translations are inadequate as soon as a close reading of the content of a source is required. Sometimes the translations are simply incorrect. This is the reason I have reworked all the translations appearing in this book, with very few exceptions.

Even in the original language, wherever a remark from an original exchange survives on its own, one often needs additional background knowledge for a proper interpretation. In the conversation books, in which everything but Beethoven's words is preserved (with a few exceptions), the difficulty is often not so much the absence of Beethoven's words, but rather our lack of insight into the psychology of the situation. In some cases it is impossible to know whether a writer is making a statement casually, in anticipation of Beethoven's consent, to test his opinion, or even to provoke an argument. The three latter possibilities represent a contemporary's effort to trigger Beethoven's reaction through a remark. Since Beethoven's reaction is lost, such a remark assumes a life of its own beyond the historical moment. Some of the conversation book entries can thus be seen as the embryonic beginnings of Beethoven history writing.

For us who have to rely on the surviving part of this material, the acknowledgment of the historical simultaneity of statement and reaction does not solve the problem of interpretation. Some of the conversation book entries remain, for us, cut off from the Beethovenian reality. An instructive example is a sentence from Carl Czerny's long conversation with Beethoven in August 1823. At one point, Czerny writes, "Of course at that time the instruments were very imperfect."[9] The context (a conversation about the

---

[9] Dagmar Beck, Karl-Heinz Köhler, and Grita Herre, eds., *Ludwig van Beethovens Konversationshefte*, Leipzig: VEB Deutscher Verlag für Musik, 1968–2001, vol. IV, 62.

pianist and composer Moscheles) suggests that Czerny is in fact talking about pianos. This sentence is an almost literal anticipation of Czerny's opinion in 1842 that the earlier pianos were "extremely weak and imperfect."[10] But the context in both quotations is of necessity Czerny's, not Beethoven's. Granted, at any given moment in Czerny's life pianos existed that could justify a definition of earlier pianos as "weak," and there existed (and still exist) examples of pianos of various periods that were and are "imperfect" in some way. Also, the possibility that Beethoven agreed with Czerny certainly needs to be considered. But the option that Czerny perhaps expressed something uncontroversial does not solve the fundamental problem: the quotation from 1823 is, in its value as a source, no different from the 1842 one. That Czerny talks *with* Beethoven in one case and *about* him in the other has no influence on the fact that it is only Czerny who reveals his personal agenda in both these sentences. *Beethoven*'s agenda simply does not appear. So even if the conversation books, as a whole, belong to the primary sources in the narrowest sense, many entries function as a part of the abundant material that is of an anecdotal character.

Apart from the specific and complex case of some conversation book entries, the anecdotal material typically contains contemporary writers' reports about Beethoven's music making, Beethoven's character or appearance, or writers' specific experiences of Beethoven. Many eye-witnesses' reports were written down at a much later date, which presents well-known difficulties in assessing their accuracy and measuring the influence of the reigning zeitgeist. An example is the early romantic belief in aesthetic progress which sometimes influenced contemporary opinions about artistic development, performing style, the composition of piano music, or piano building. The related aspect of personal progress, as has been often observed, frequently caused Beethoven himself to re-formulate and, if necessary, even re-invent his own past – even some of the original material may consequently mirror something that was never really there. There are certainly good reasons for suspecting hidden agendas behind some value judgments in the sources of the time, and hidden value judgments behind some of the surviving factual information.

The possibility of suspicion and hidden agendas opens up a further area of source-critical insecurity. The danger is clear: if it becomes a routine to question the accuracy of the utterances of the past, the documents risk losing their function as documents of a positive character – our whole discussion becomes inherently speculative. The assumption that every historical opinion about Beethoven's playing, music, or style has a hidden meaning would most certainly doom the discussion to non-conclusiveness.

---

[10] A similar remark, but by *Joseph* Czerny, appears even earlier in a conversation book of April 1820: Beck, Köhler, and Herre, eds., *Ludwig van Beethovens Konversationshefte*, vol. II, 37. Joseph Czerny says during a conversation about the Menuetto in the Sonata Op. 2/1 (apparently bars 59–62), "At that time the *Claviere* were worse as well."

The case of Anton Schindler demonstrates, on the other hand, that matters of Beethoven performance practice and biography and a strong personal agenda occasionally *did* coincide. Schindler was most industrious in binding his view of Beethovenian musical expression into a self-glorifying narrative of his closeness to Beethoven, and he falsified and suppressed source information in the process.

Unlike Schindler, Carl Czerny's various texts on Beethoven performance sometimes suffer from a struggle to assume a scholarly attitude and from an effort to combine Beethoven performance with the demands of Czerny's own mid-nineteenth-century musical taste. Additionally, his chronological memory was not always perfect (neither in fact was Schindler's, whose Beethoven biography is full of inaccuracies). However, these flaws are difficulties of systematic writing more than an indication of a personal agenda.

Modern common sense is a doubtful tool for solving the various problems of source evaluation and interpretation. In matters of Beethoven performance practice alone, the evocation of common sense (on both sides) lies behind some of the fiercest controversies. A more useful concept than common sense is contextual verisimilitude. This term encourages a scholarly technique that is based on the idea that a source can reveal a hidden content when it is discussed with such questions in mind that primarily appear relevant in historical contexts and that only secondarily represent the context of a scholar's work.

Working with contextual verisimilitude is a thorny enterprise. We are facing the classic problem that we cannot fully avoid basing our judgment on our own context and common sense. A scholar's goal-oriented mindset could also hamper the creative and playful attitude that could lead to posing perhaps unexpected, but historically relevant questions. The greatest danger, perhaps, is that the interpretation of a source suffers fundamentally from the accidental omission of an important context.

In view of such general and specific complications connected to Beethoven source readings, the traditionally accepted story of Beethoven's dissatisfaction with some or all of his pianos, in whichever argumental framework it may appear, is simply not nuanced enough to match any of the possible emerging realities. Every single Beethoven source that bears on piano playing, piano sound, and piano building involves contexts more complex than the common sense of either fortepiano haters or fortepiano lovers from our time can provide. If the story of Beethoven's relationship to the piano needs to be retold, the story of his relationship to piano playing certainly does. This is the objective of this book.

PART I

Beethoven, his playing, and his instruments

Introduction

The question of how Beethoven, the prophetic composer, was rooted in the musical practices and conventions of the eighteenth century began to interest some authors in the late nineteenth century. In 1881, Franz Kullak investigated the relationship between Beethoven and eighteenth-century keyboard tutors in order to establish guidelines for the performance of Beethoven's trills.[1] In 1888, Theodor Frimmel produced a 62-page essay on Beethoven as a pianist, in which information about Beethoven's musical education and descriptions of his playing alternate with quotations from C. P. E. Bach's *Versuch* on the one hand, and information about Beethoven's various possible keyboard instruments on the other.[2] Frimmel and, later, Ludwig Schiedermair[3] were versed enough in eighteenth-century keyboard treatises to include instruments other than Thayer's ubiquitous "Pianoforte" in their analyses. In his later *Beethoven-Handbuch*, Frimmel gave a detailed overview of the knowledge in his time of Beethoven's various pianos.[4]

After a strong tradition of subjective romantic Beethoven writing, this was a new tendency,[5] in spite of a comparative lack of practical experience on the part of the authors with the performing conventions described in the tutors and with historical instruments.

It was, indeed, not until the 1980s that an increasing number of authors entered the stage who explicitly based their keyboard performance practice studies on their professional experience with historical keyboard instruments.[6] At a time when first-rate institutions have offered complete

---

[1] Franz Kullak, "Über den Triller," in *Beethovens Klavierkonzerte*, Leipzig: Steingräber, 1881, xii–xxviii.

[2] Theodor Frimmel, "Beethoven als Clavierspieler," in *Neue Beethoveniana*, Vienna: Carl Gerold's Sohn, 1888, 1–62.

[3] Ludwig Schiedermair, *Der junge Beethoven*, Leipzig: Quelle & Meyer, 1925.

[4] Theodor Frimmel, *Beethoven-Handbuch*, Leipzig: Breitkopf & Härtel, 1926. Reprint Hildesheim: Olms, 2003.

[5] A typical example of such a romantic approach is Adolf Bernhard Marx, *Anleitung zum Vortrag Beethovenscher Klavierwerke*, ed. Eugen Schmitz, Regensburg: Bosse, 1912.

[6] Examples are: Sandra P. Rosenblum, *Performance Practices in Classic Piano Music*, Bloomington and Indianapolis: Indiana University Press, 1988; Bart van Oort, "The English Classical piano style and its influence on Haydn and Beethoven," DMA thesis, Cornell University, 1993; David Rowland, "Beethoven's pianoforte pedalling," in Robin Stowell, ed., *Performing Beethoven*, Cambridge University Press, 1994; Katalin Komlós, *Fortepianos and their Music*, Oxford: Clarendon Press, 1995.

programs in performance practices for decades, and when the performance of historical music on instruments of historical types has built many successful lifelong careers, it is not arrogant to claim that our experience helps us to understand some of the practical aspects of Beethoven's early musicianship in ways that were inaccessible to earlier scholars – even though the distance from Beethoven has more than doubled since Kullak's or Frimmel's time.

Like their predecessors, modern Beethoven scholars usually rely squarely on the traditional biographical information. Much of this information, especially regarding Beethoven's early years, comes from a small number of compilations of reminiscences that all take a rather associative approach. These sources may not always be correct; the chronology of events is sometimes jumbled, disturbed by the insertion of unrelated blocks of information each with its intact micro-chronology. The quality of information shifts wildly and the evaluation of these sources is often extremely difficult. Consequently, even a well-established part of Beethoven's timeline can be challenged if the sources are subjected to new, careful research.[7]

Most problematic of all, very often a witness would incorporate her or his own evaluation of events into the narrative, thus introducing an interpretation where it is difficult for the modern observer to detect. Having worked with this material for a number of years, and having closely re-read the chronology of events, I hope to bring new insights into this material in the following chapters.

---

[7] See, for example, Jos van der Zanden, "Ferdinand Ries in Wien. Neue Perspektiven zu den *Notizen*," in Ernst Herttrich, ed., *Reihe V Bonner Beethoven-Studien*, Bonn: Verlag Beethoven-Haus, 2005, 191–212.

CHAPTER I

Beethoven's early training

LUDWIG THE ELDER'S AND JOHANN'S PROFESSIONAL TRAINING

The story of music instruction within the Beethoven family is a story of a short but apparently consistent tradition. Ludwig van Beethoven the elder, Beethoven's grandfather, was born in 1712 in Flemish Mechelen as the son of a baker who also traded in various goods.[1] When he was almost six, he was admitted to the choirboy school of the cathedral of St. Rombaut in his hometown, where he stayed until he was thirteen. At that point, in 1725, the cathedral's organist Antoine Colfs took over his education, for payment and the guarantee that "the student was to substitute at the organ at the master's discretion without recompense." Colfs taught Ludwig to play the organ, to accompany, and to play figured bass. At the age of nineteen Ludwig can be found as a singer of the tenor (in the Gregorian sense) at St. Peters in Leuven, where he later became choir director. His subsequent career is one of a fully trained and capable musician.[2]

As far as we can see, Ludwig the elder's musical education was traditional and goal-oriented; it seems to have been well organized and, above all, successful. The contract that informs us about the organ and basso continuo lessons naturally conveys nothing about their spirit or Colf's pedagogical approach, and little about the lessons' actual content. However, the circumstances suggest apprenticeship rather than artistry, tradition rather than novelty, and a blend of learning and professional practice. The education asked for a substantial investment of time and, one would believe, energy from the pupil, as well as a financial investment by his parents.

The concept of investment was carried on in the same tradition when Ludwig the elder, now in service at the Bonn court, had to realize the education of his only surviving child, Johann. Johann van Beethoven

[1] MGG I, 1511. Michiel van Beethoven was also a lace trader. Maynard Solomon, *Beethoven*, New York: Macmillan, 1977, 7, also mentions commercial activities in real estate and as a dealer in paintings and furniture, without a reference.
[2] A transcription of the original documents is printed in Schiedermair, *Der junge Beethoven*, 109–10. See also Alexander Wheelock Thayer, *Life of Beethoven*, ed. Elliot Forbes, Princeton University Press, 1967, 42.

was born in 1739 or 1740. He went to elementary school and to the *Jesuitengymnasium*, where his participation as a singer in a school concert in 1750 is documented.[3] He left school in 1751 or 1752, at the age of twelve or thirteen, to enter service at the Bonn *Hofmusik*. The uncertainty regarding the date results from a mismatch between two petitions from 1756 and 1764, by Johann van Beethoven and Ludwig the elder, respectively.[4] His father had already taught Johann singing and Clavier playing.[5] The 1764 petition informs us that Johann, by about the age of twenty-four, had also achieved some skill in violin playing, but when or where he learned that skill is not recorded in the sources.[6]

The pattern of Johann's education resembles Ludwig the elder's curriculum, with the necessary adjustments to the circumstances in Bonn. Again, it is reasonable to suppose that the musical content of the education was goal-oriented and traditional: his father clearly intended Johann to follow in his footsteps. We can also assume that the content of the music lessons was based on Ludwig the elder's traditional musical background on the one hand, but tailored to meet the requirements of the Bonn court chapel on the other. Similar musicians' careers were certainly not uncommon at that time, as a glance at only a few entries in a music dictionary confirms.

Johann became *Hof Tenorist* in Bonn. There remains some disagreement in the sources about his abilities as a keyboardist: Franz Gerhard Wegeler writes that he was "no Clavier player" at all.[7] Gottfried Fischer's manuscript, however, the single most comprehensive source on Beethoven's family and his early life, contradicts this. Fischer repeatedly mentions that Johann van Beethoven taught Clavier and singing.[8] This report is supported by other testimonies about the circumstances of Ludwig van Beethoven's early music education.

Both Fischer and the above-mentioned petition by his father describe Johann van Beethoven, at the beginning of his professional life, as someone who "performed his duties accurately." He was sufficiently capable and trustworthy to teach "the sons or daughters of the local French, English and Imperial ambassadors, the men and daughters of the nobility, as well as the better citizens." Consequently he had often "more to do than he could cope with."[9]

Nevertheless, in the eyes of Ludwig the elder, the investment in Johann's education may not have paid off as much as expected. Even leaving aside reports that Johann even as a young man was "quite a good wine drinker,"

[3] Schiedermair, *Der junge Beethoven*, 95.   [4] *Ibid.*, 111, 116.
[5] Margot Wetzstein, ed., *Familie Beethoven im kurfürstlichen Bonn. Neuauflage nach den Aufzeichnungen des Bonner Bäckermeisters Gottfried Fischer*, Bonn: Verlag Beethoven-Haus, 2006, 13, orig. 2.
[6] Schiedermair, *Der junge Beethoven*, 44, 95–6 and 116.
[7] Wegeler and Ries, *Biographische Notizen über Beethoven*, 7.
[8] Wetzstein, ed., *Familie Beethoven im kurfürstlichen Bonn*, 42, 55, orig. 17, 18, 22.
[9] *Ibid.*, 41–2, orig. 17.

his career certainly lacked the excellence his father may, for reasons of his own, have desired.[10]

That lack was bound to feed back into Ludwig the elder's own insecurities. His own career had admittedly developed steadily and Wegeler describes him at its end as a well-respected musician.[11] All the same, he had achieved his success and personal status with many pains. He was not appointed Kapellmeister until the age of 49, after 28 years of service at the Bonn court, and then almost by coincidence: On the death of Joseph Zudoli, who had become Kapellmeister in 1753, Ludwig the elder substituted for "more than a year." He was then passed over, "unlawfully" as he himself once expressed it, for the young violinist Touchemoulin and would probably have never gotten his position had not a change of government and the resulting economic measures induced Touchemoulin to quit his post.[12] Unlike many of his contemporaries with comparable backgrounds and careers, Ludwig the elder was not a distinguished composer.[13] Furthermore, the organization of Ludwig's family life – undoubtedly already strained after the early deaths of his first two children – must have completely collapsed at some unknown point when his wife's alcoholism led to her removal to a cloister.[14]

We can glimpse the consequences of this in Ludwig the elder's pronounced need for order and his tendency towards a display of distinction and wealth.[15] In his influential Beethoven biography, Maynard Solomon describes this existence as "carefully ordered, precise, and comfortable," obviously reflecting on its appearance only.[16] However, one may well wonder whether Ludwig the elder found his existence truly "comfortable" or thought of himself as an especially brilliant man; the preserved impression might as well indicate a successful effort to build a façade in order to hide his personal doubts and sorrows.

In an effort to find the reason for Johann's developing alcoholism in his troubled relationship to his father, Solomon repeatedly returns to one of Gottfried Fischer's anecdotes. On one occasion, Fischer relates, Ludwig the elder ridiculed Johann as "Johannes der Läufer" because of his "flighty" spirit that led him to take a series of "small journeys to Köln, Deutz, Andernach, Koblenz, Ehrenbreitstein" when his father was not around.[17] During the incident that Fischer remembers, Ludwig publicly made fun of his son.

[10] *Ibid.*, 14, orig. 3.
[11] Thayer, *Life of Beethoven*, 46; Wegeler and Ries, *Biographische Notizen über Beethoven*, 8.
[12] Schiedermair, *Der junge Beethoven*, 44, 113–14.   [13] Thayer, *Life of Beethoven*, 47.
[14] Wetzstein, ed., *Familie Beethoven im kurfürstlichen Bonn*, 12, orig. 2.
[15] See, for instance, Fischer's description of the household in *ibid.*, 27, orig. 10.
[16] Solomon, *Beethoven*, 6.
[17] Wetzstein, ed., *Familie Beethoven im kurfürstlichen Bonn*, 22, orig. 7.

In his analysis, Solomon writes: "The Fischer memoirs portray a father convinced that his son would never amount to anything, who broadcast this conviction in contemptuous tones."[18] As will be seen later, Johann van Beethoven's actions and lifestyle strongly suggest a conflict-ridden background, so it is admittedly very tempting to construct such an analysis. The interpretation of this isolated incident as a reflection of the *general* family atmosphere is, however, certainly incorrect. On the other hand, it seems safe to accept Solomon's assumption that Johann van Beethoven was, at least professionally, strongly dominated by his father throughout the latter's life. In view of the family circumstances, there is a realistic possibility that, as an only child, Johann's musical education, of which we otherwise know nothing, was accompanied by extensive control.

LUDWIG VAN BEETHOVEN'S EARLY EDUCATION

This consideration becomes important if we try to understand the kind of treatment and education that Johann van Beethoven gave to his son, Ludwig. This education was characterized by violence and harshness, according to all surviving reports. Some of these reports do not mention music at all, which indicates that they reflect very early events. The first historical source known to me which describes the situation dates from November 1800:

I also heard a rather accomplished violinist, with the name Noist, from Bonn, countryman of Betthowen, whom he knew very well. His (Beethowen's) father was, like his son, employed at the chapel of the Elector of Cölln, at whose expense B. made his trip to Vienna. Noist told me that B. was maltreated so horribly by his father, who beat him day after day, and he believes that the peculiar nature of his is only a result of this circumstance.[19]

This description corresponds with Fischer's later observation that the "Beethoven children were not raised gently" and that "the father dealt very strictly with them."[20] Another account, also not related to music, comes from a baker named Krupp, who in 1773 lived in the fourth house to the left of the Beethovens in the Bonngasse: "Especially when he [Johann] had drunk something, he treated his Ludwig roughly and sometimes locked him up in the cellar." This information was also confirmed by another neighbor, Schmitz, across the street.[21]

---

[18] Solomon, *Beethoven*, 11–12.

[19] Letter from Lisette Bernhard to Andreas Streicher, November 6, 1800. Facsimile and transcription in Uta Goebl-Streicher, Jutta Streicher, and Michael Ladenburger, *"Diesem Menschen hätte ich mein ganzes Leben widmen mögen": Beethoven und die Wiener Klavierbauer Nannette und Andreas Streicher*, Bonn: Beethoven-Haus, 1999, 92. Noist was likely related to the bass singer in the Bonn chapel Lucas Carl Noisten.

[20] Wetzstein, ed., *Familie Beethoven im kurfürstlichen Bonn*, 40, orig. 15.

[21] Hermann Deiters and Hugo Riemann, eds., *Ludwig van Beethovens Leben, von Alexander Wheelock Thayer*, 3rd edn., vol. 1, Leipzig: Breitkopf & Härtel, 1917, 135. Quoted after: Wetzstein, ed., *Familie Beethoven im kurfürstlichen Bonn*, 14, n. 47 and 148 for a map.

Soon, however, music lessons were to become a daily routine for Ludwig; all the other witnesses tell us about Johann's harsh conduct toward his son in specific connection with his music lessons. These anecdotes are all, in one way or another, related to the Fischer house in the Rheingasse 966.[22] This means that they could contain first-hand information from at the earliest 1774, apart from possible street gossip from before that time. They describe with certainty the situation after October 1776, when the Beethovens had definitely moved to that address.[23] Thus, at the time of the first reports about Ludwig van Beethoven's music education, he was between four and six years old, and in any case still so small that he had to stand on a little footstool in front of the instrument.[24]

The story of Ludwig van Beethoven's early music education is, as is well known, a sad one. Various witnesses agree that Johann van Beethoven was single-minded and persistent about the lessons, that he punished Ludwig frequently and brutally, beating him to make him practice the Clavier, and that consequently Ludwig could frequently be observed standing at the Clavier and weeping. This would have been in his own room, one of four facing the courtyard, where he was seen by several people, including Beethoven's later friend Franz Wegeler, who, during visits to a schoolmate, could witness the "doings and sufferings of Louis" from the rear of another house.[25]

In the literature we find several attempts to understand why Ludwig was taught music so early and in such a harsh manner. Perhaps typical for the (as he himself admits) unmusical Wegeler, his explanation is not that Johann intended to exploit Ludwig's musical *talent*, but rather his *status* as the eldest son: Wegeler attributes Johann's roughness both to his lack of intellectual or ethical distinction (one should remember that this is a judgment made in hindsight) and to his need "to train the eldest son quickly as an assistant for the education of the others."[26] Wegeler, however, was at best a casual and distant witness of Beethoven's early education and, as such, perhaps not always reliable. On this occasion he seems to have confused Johann's pedagogical goals with what eventually happened in the Beethoven family: on September 20, 1789, Johann van Beethoven, after losing both his voice and his reputation due to his alcohol problems, was

---

[22] Wetzstein, ed., *Familie Beethoven im kurfürstlichen Bonn*, 3, n. 2. The houses were renumbered in 1793. The house numbers given in the literature are often based on the nineteenth-century number-ing and do not concur with the numbers from 1773. See the maps in Wetzstein, ed., *Familie Beethoven im kurfürstlichen Bonn*, 147–53. For Beethoven's various addresses during these years see: Barry Cooper, ed., *Das Beethoven Kompendium*, Munich: Droemer Knaur, 1992, 137; Thayer, *Life of Beethoven*, 56.

[23] Schiedermair, *Der junge Beethoven*, 126 gives 1775/6 as a likely date of the Beethovens' move to the Fischer house.

[24] Wetzstein, ed., *Familie Beethoven im kurfürstlichen Bonn*, 45–6, orig. 20.

[25] Thayer, *Life of Beethoven*, 56–7; Schiedermair, *Der junge Beethoven*, 129–30; Solomon, *Beethoven*, 16–18.

[26] Wegeler and Ries, *Biographische Notizen über Beethoven*, 9.

released from his work by electoral decree, and Ludwig effectively became
the head of the family.[27]

In another mixture of observation and analysis, Gottfried Fischer writes:
"According to his father, he [Ludwig] had not learned much at school, and
that is why his father had placed him so early at the Clavier and instructed
him strictly."[28] Chronologically, this explanation makes no sense (and it
could even indicate that the Fischers did indeed not witness the beginnings
of Beethoven's music lessons): Ludwig Schiedermair suggests that Ludwig
entered school in his sixth or seventh year and stayed until around his
eleventh (even though the exact dates are unknown) because this would
have been typical practice in Bonn.[29] If anything, Ludwig's musical education began together with school, but as mentioned, it may have actually
started even earlier. Thayer, writing before Schiedermair, continues
Fischer's train of thought and also comments on Ludwig's allegedly rudi-
mentary school education: "The father's main object being the earliest and
greatest development of his son's musical genius so as to make it a 'market-
able commodity,' he gave him no other school education than such as was
afforded at one of the public schools."[30] In answer, Schiedermair points out
that providing this kind of school education was scarcely uncommon "even
for the rich" Bonn parents. His conclusion is that Johann simply provided
for Ludwig the same education that he himself had received.[31] This assertion
finds some support in Wegeler's statement that "Beethoven's education
was neither noticeably neglected nor particularly good."[32] A connection
between Beethoven's school career and his early music education is in any
case difficult to establish.

Ludwig the elder died in December 1773. One could, in the light of
the previous discussion about Johann's relationship to his father, accept
Solomon's analysis that "the death of his father brought Johann's hostile
feelings to the surface."[33] As an alternative, one could interpret his court
petition two weeks after his father's death, where he describes himself as
a suitable successor as Kapellmeister, as a naïve attempt to take over
Ludwig the elder's role, that is, to fill his niche as a personality as well
as his court position. This attempt failed when Andrea Lucchesi became
the new Kapellmeister on May 26, 1774. Johann remained court singer
and private music teacher. One of his first tasks after this professional
disappointment was to see to the instruction of his son. To fulfill the
role of Ludwig's teacher, Johann very likely staged a recapitulation of his
own education by his father, both because there was no necessity to

---

[27] Thayer, *Life of Beethoven*, 95; Schiedermair, *Der junge Beethoven*, 192–3.
[28] Wetzstein, ed., *Familie Beethoven im kurfürstlichen Bonn*, 44–5, orig. 20.
[29] Schiedermair, *Der junge Beethoven*, 126.   [30] Thayer, *Life of Beethoven*, 58.
[31] Schiedermair, *Der junge Beethoven*, 128.
[32] Wegeler and Ries, *Biographische Notizen über Beethoven*, 9.   [33] Solomon, *Beethoven*, 11.

invent something different, and in order to prove his own competence as a music-teaching father to himself.

Few eighteenth-century music tutors deal with music teaching for beginners in any detail (with the notable exception of the more important French keyboard schools and, inspired by these, Marpurg in his *Anleitung zum Klavierspielen*). Often the first instruction of the intended reader is assumed to have happened before the advice of the writer is to be considered.[34] Eighteenth-century tutors tell us nothing about the best approach to teaching beginners if the teacher is a parent. Our interpretation of the young Beethoven's education is further complicated because that education does not even represent a "best" pedagogical approach, but just "some" approach in which general pedagogy, music education, and Johann's idiosyncrasies appear all jumbled together. Not surprisingly, the traditional view is that his approach actually *was* a jumble. "Brutal and willful" to Solomon, it gives us today an impression of being methodically unsound in every respect.[35]

One should, however, realize that the elements of intense control, correction, and punishment belonged to the main toolbox of enlightened eighteenth-century German pedagogues, while the concept of pedagogy was becoming a cornerstone of bourgeois identity.[36] Whatever one may think of Johann's rough methods today, they were certainly not unusual. It may perhaps seem that a man who, "especially when he had drunk something," treated his son roughly was acting according to his whim alone. However, a more realistic option is that Johann, a man who was rubbing shoulders with high court officials and distinguished members of the Bonn society, thought of pedagogical strictness as being ambitious and upward-striving, and simply denied that the occasional intensification of such "strictness" due to his alcohol consumption should be worth less. On the basis of the surviving information we simply cannot know with certainty where, in terms of pedagogical awareness, Johann was located on the scale between intuitive brutality and theoretically sanctioned harshness, but his closeness to the latter is by no means unlikely.

---

[34] Pier Francesco Tosi (in Agricola's translation) even proposes that a singer's first instruction should be entrusted to a mediocre musician. (Johann Friedrich Agricola, *Anleitung zur Singkunst 1757*, ed. Thomas Seedorf, Kassel: Bärenreiter, 2002, 1–2.) Quantz is vehemently opposed to such an idea: "Some have the scandalous prejudice that it is unnecessary to have a good master for learning the beginnings." (Johann Joachim Quantz, *Versuch einer Anweisung die flute traversiere zu spielen 1789*, ed. Hans-Peter Schmitz, Kassel: Bärenreiter, 1953, 9.)

[35] Solomon, *Beethoven*, 16.

[36] Katharina Rutschky, ed., *Schwarze Pädagogik, Quellen zur Naturgeschichte der bürgerlichen Erziehung*. Munich: Ullstein, 2001, xxxv–xxxvi. Judged by the practices recommended in some of these sources, Solomon's formulation, "We may surmise that Johann insisted that his harsh methods were merely good pedagogy," sounds almost too careful (Solomon, *Beethoven*, 18).

BEETHOVEN'S EARLY LESSONS – MUSICAL CONSIDERATIONS

In striking contrast to earlier customs in the Beethoven family, Ludwig was not taught to sing. Considering Johann's authoritarian attitude, it seems unlikely that the child's own inclination toward one or the other musical activity was the reason for the choice to instruct him in Clavier and violin playing. But a choice it was, and very likely not a random one. For an explanation, one needs to find reasons much more closely related to the actual situation at the Bonn court than the persistent speculation that Johann van Beethoven was raising, and planning to exploit, a wunderkind after Mozart's example (the story that Beethoven "became known in Bonn as a child prodigy" originates from Johann Aloys Schlosser's 1827 Beethoven biography, but is not backed up by any evidence).[37] Singing had, for both the elder Beethovens, been the basis of their activities at the court. It had helped Ludwig the elder to build a solid reputation as a good musician. But as the circumstances surrounding his Kapellmeister nomination show, this reputation had not prevented him from being temporarily passed over for a younger violin player. Subsequently, Johann saw himself passed over for another instrumentalist: the capable keyboardist and opera conductor Andrea Lucchesi, who became the new Kapellmeister. The new concert master Gaetano Mattioli had much influence as well and earned just as much as Lucchesi.[38] It seems at the very least plausible that Johann van Beethoven simply deemed a court career as an instrumentalist most promising for his son and that he chose such instruments as would provide good chances of a later employment.[39]

The whole setting of Beethoven's early musical education was conflict-ridden. Starting with Johann's unsuccessful Kapellmeister aspirations, several old and new personal frustrations influenced his actions,[40] while the trap of repetition compulsion,[41] as yet another young Beethoven was to be taught music, was wide open. If Johann indeed was also striving for the establishment of "supremacy in the family" through these music lessons, it is doubtful whether he initially understood at all that he had a "supremely gifted" child

---

[37] Johann Aloys Schlosser, *Beethoven: the First Biography [1827]*, trans. Reinhard G. Pauly, ed. Barry Cooper, Portland: Amadeus Press, 1996, 41.

[38] Schiedermair, *Der junge Beethoven*, 46.

[39] This seems more plausible than, for instance, the idea that Johann intended his son to immediately succeed van den Eeden, who in 1775 was around sixty-five years old and had been in court service for forty-eight years.

[40] Solomon mentions, for instance, Maria Magdalena van Beethoven's deep respect for her deceased father-in-law, which made Johann feel "painfully" his "hapless mediocrity."

[41] A Freudian term. Orig. *Wiederholungszwang*. For discussions, see: Alice Miller, *Das Drama des begabten Kindes*, Frankfurt a. M.: Suhrkamp, 1979; Alice Miller, *Am Anfang war Erziehung*, Frankfurt a. M.: Suhrkamp, 1980; Alice Miller, *Du sollst nicht merken*, Frankfurt a. M.: Suhrkamp, 1981.

to guide, as Solomon puts it.[42] That the education of a wunderkind was originally not part of Johann's plan can be seen in his effort to subdue Ludwig's creativity and musical playfulness, as preserved in the following passage from the Fischer memoirs:

Ludwig van Beethoven also [i.e. in addition to Klavier lessons] had daily lessons on the violin.[43] Ludwig was once playing without the music, when his father entered the room, said, what are you again scraping away on such nonsense, you know that I cannot stand that, scrape according to the notes, or your scraping will be of little use. When Johann van Beethoven received visitors, and Ludwig van Beethoven came in, he would usually hang around at the Clavier, playing chords on the Clavier with his right hand, his father said, what are you bubbling now again, go away or I will slap your face. At last, his father began to notice when he heard him play the violin, he played again from his head without the music, then his father came in, don't you ever stop, after all I have told you? He played again, said to his father, but is this not beautiful? His father said, this is only something else, only out of your head, you are not yet ready for such things, practice the Klavier and the violin, [learn] quickly to play the notes correctly, this is more important. After mastering this, you may, and will have to, work sufficiently with your head. But don't concern yourself with this now, you are not yet ready for it.[44]

Gottfried Fischer's musical observations, like this tripartite anecdote, are believed to originate from his elder sister Cäcilie (born in 1762 and around thirteen years old at the time of these events). Cäcilie was in fact Johann van Beethoven's pupil in the fundamentals of singing and Clavier accompaniment, and she had her own opinions about musical matters.[45] This anecdote evidently belongs to the time of Beethoven's early education, when Johann van Beethoven was his only teacher, that is, earlier than any of the incidents when Johann van Beethoven showed off Ludwig's abilities to visitors and during house concerts (see below).

It is easy to name some non-musical reasons for Johann's restrictive attitude in Fischer's three examples: By disregarding the instruction to play from the music and to refrain from "scraping nonsense," Ludwig was disobeying, and thus threatened his father's position as an authority; doing so repeatedly showed stubbornness, which was classed as a "dangerous habit" by eminent pedagogues of the day;[46] Ludwig's

---

[42] Solomon, *Beethoven*, 16.

[43] The rather undisturbed chronology of this section of the Fischer manuscript suggests that this may have happened in 1775 or 1776 and that it was indeed Johann van Beethoven who taught Ludwig the fundamentals not only on the Clavier but on the violin as well.

[44] Wetzstein, ed. *Familie Beethoven im kurfürstlichen Bonn*, 46–7, orig. 21.   [45] *Ibid.*, 42, orig. 18.

[46] In his *Versuch von der Erziehung und Unterweisung der Kinder* from 1748, Georg Friedrich Sulzer ranks stubbornness and disobedience among the first bad habits that children have to be cured of in order to make them into "pliable and good children that afterwards can receive a good education" (Willibald Klinke, ed. *Johann Georg Sulzers Pädagogische Schriften*, Langensalza: Friedrich Mann, 1922). The excerpt dealing with these "Two main tasks of the education of small children" is reprinted in Rutschky, ed., *Schwarze Pädagogik*, 173–6.

insistence on "playing" while his father had decided on "learning" can be seen as a cheeky attempt to upset the division of the day into *Arbeit* and *Vergnügen*; finally, "hanging around" at the Clavier and playing tentative chords to attract attention on the occasion of other grown-ups' visits would be seen, even by the most patient parents of our time, as a trying habit.

Even according to the gentlest music pedagogy at the time, a pupil's auditive inclination to try out sounds and figurations would not have been reason for a teacher to pay special attention. In a paragraph devoted to the negative influence of talent on industry and reflection, for example, Johann Joachim Quantz opposes "disposition," which is innate, and "Wissenschaft" (to be translated as knowledge), which needs to be acquired by way of a good education and an inquisitive mindset.[47] While Quantz earlier emphasizes how essential disposition, or "talent," and "nature's gifts" are if one wants to become a good musician, much of the following text is devoted to the absolute necessity of industry as a good foundation for avoiding becoming a mediocre one.[48] The essence of these ideas, the philosophy of "first steps first," can be found in various forms in music tutors throughout the eighteenth century.

"Mastery of the art of improvisation was the hallmark of the eighteenth-century virtuoso and composer," writes Solomon in his musical analysis of this anecdote, in an attempt to show that Johann's commands do *not* fit into the spirit of the time.[49] However, we witness in Fischer's anecdote the first steps, not in educating a musical genius, but in teaching a court musician *in spe* the fundamentals of his craft. There is no reason whatsoever for expecting a pedagogy that would suit a virtuoso or a composer. Johann was simply guiding, or rather bullying the child along the traditional path of Beethoven music education.

Johann's formulation "[learn] quickly to play the notes correctly" deserves particular attention here. The choice of words is unfortunately somewhat ambiguous. Most likely in the general context it has to do with learning the skill of reading and playing off the score (and with maintaining some discipline during this enterprise) as opposed to "playing out of one's head." "Quickly" is possibly used in the compressed meaning: "Learn to read the notes first; if you do this quickly, you can advance to other things." While lacking all of Quantz's sophistication, Johann's insistence that young Ludwig learn the necessary steps in the right order – so that the effort of learning to play might amount to something of "use" – is thus quite the opposite of a haphazard musical and pedagogical approach.

---

[47] Quantz, *Versuch einer Anweisung die flute traversiere zu spielen*, 12–13.
[48] *Ibid.*, 4–5.   [49] Solomon, *Beethoven*, 18.

VAN DEN EEDEN, PFEIFFER, AND ROVANTINI

Various witnesses describe Ludwig van Beethoven during the last years of the 1770s as "introvert" or "shy and taciturn." He was also "often untidy, indifferent," or even "distinguished by uncleanliness, negligence." The cellist Bernhard Mäurer, who came to Bonn in April 1777, "sometimes sang solfeggios with Beethoven's father, which the latter accompanied. Beethoven and his five-year-old brother were sometimes present and listened quietly. It was not mentioned that Louis played."[50] Evidently, at that time, Ludwig's attempts to attract attention had been successfully suppressed, and Johann did not yet show off his son in any special way – at least not to occasional visitors like Mäurer. One year later, however, Johann deemed Ludwig's musical skills advanced enough to be demonstrated in public. On March 26, 1778, Ludwig shared a public concert in Cologne with one of Johann's pupils, Helene Johanna Averdonck, playing "various *clavier-concerte* and trios." The *Avertissement* for this event informs us that both had been heard at the Bonn court earlier. Seventeen- (or eighteen-) year-old Helene Averdonck is called "Hofaltistin," suggesting that she already had a court position.[51] There are no records of any of these performances, and observers like Mäurer seem to have missed them altogether.

Around the same time, other teachers appeared in Ludwig's life. Gottfried Fischer tells us that Ludwig, under Johann's tuition, advanced far enough to play "neatly" the music that was put in front of him. Johann understood that he "could not bring him much further," and also, he "believed that he [Ludwig] perhaps had a talent to learn to compose music," so "an old master named Santerrini" taught him for a while. However, Johann found this teacher unsuitable and ended the lessons.[52] An actor and singer called Santorini is listed among the participants of the Großmann-Helmuth theater in Bonn.[53]

Beethoven's first external teacher appears to be the almost seventy-year-old court organist Gilles van den Eeden. Van den Eeden is first mentioned in Johann Aloys Schlosser's 1827 biography, albeit surrounded by details about the lessons that cannot be verified from other sources.[54] Wegeler, admittedly uninformed in this particular case, believes in the possibility that Beethoven had lessons with van den Eeden, but is unsure about their content and suggests incorrect dates.[55] The Fischer memoirs, on the other

---

[50] Bernhard Mäurer, according to Otto Jahn's annotations in: Friedrich Kerst, *Die Erinnerungen an Beethoven*, Stuttgart: Julius Hoffmann, 1913, vol. I, 10; Joseph Wurzer in Thayer, *Life of Beethoven*, 58; Wetzstein, ed., *Familie Beethoven im kurfürstlichen Bonn*, 52, orig. 22.

[51] Thayer, *Life of Beethoven*, 57–8.   [52] Wetzstein, ed., *Familie Beethoven im kurfürstlichen Bonn*, 64.

[53] See: *ibid.*, 64, n. 234; Schiedermair, *Der junge Beethoven*, 51.

[54] Schlosser, *Beethoven: the First Biography*, 40–1.

[55] Wegeler and Ries, *Biographische Notizen über Beethoven*, 11.

hand, do not mention the court organist at all in connection with Ludwig's tuition. Anton Schindler, however, refers in his Beethoven biography to Beethoven's own recollections of the organ-playing technique that he learned from van den Eeden.[56] Bernhard Mäurer is confident in this matter as well (but remains otherwise vague, like in his earlier example): "In his eighth year the court organist van der Eeden took him as an apprentice, one did not hear anything about his progress."[57] In view of the uncertainty about Beethoven's exact age at that time, van den Eeden might have become Beethoven's teacher as late as 1780. On the other hand, Mäurer would surely have had opportunities to hear of Beethoven's "progress" by that time. So the lessons with van den Eeden could have begun as early as late 1778, but at the latest in 1780.[58]

There remains some uncertainty about the period, content, and frequency of van den Eeden's lessons. First of all, the Fischer manuscript provides some detailed information about another organ teacher, a Bruder Willibald (Sebastian Koch) from the Franciscan monastery. Willibald was, according to Fischer, well acquainted with Johann van Beethoven, and a respected organ player. He taught Beethoven organ playing and liturgy. As he advanced, he "often used him as an assistant," and he liked and appreciated Beethoven. Subsequent to his association with Koch, Beethoven became friends with the organist of the *Minoritenkirche* and played in the morning mass in that church.[59] Fischer's description of Beethoven's initiatives to search out the possibility of playing on various organs in the town is placed between anecdotes about the fire at the Bonn palace in January 1777 and a lengthy set of miscellaneous anecdotes, but it comes before a passage that describes events after the spring of 1779. This order implies that these initiatives occurred exactly at the time of the supposed influence of van den Eeden.

The period of time that can be concluded from Mäurer's suggestion also coincides with the arrival of Tobias Friedrich Pfeiffer (or Pfeifer), who, according to Mäurer, sang tenor in the theater group of Großmann and Helmuth (the same group that employed Beethoven's later teacher Neefe). The "young" Pfeiffer (his birth date is not given in the literature) was "an accomplished Clavier player and excellent oboist."[60] He quickly became a close friend of the Beethovens. He soon rented a room in their house and taught Ludwig between the spring of 1779 and Easter (March 26) 1780, when he was forced to leave Bonn.[61] Wegeler's suggestion that Beethoven's

[56] Anton Felix Schindler, *Beethoven as I Knew Him*, ed. Donald MacArdle, trans. Constance S. Jolly, London: Faber and Faber, 1966; reprint Dover, 1996, 39.
[57] Kerst, *Die Erinnerungen an Beethoven*, vol. 1, 10. Two of various representations of the court organist's name are van *den* Eeden and van *der* Eeden.
[58] For a discussion of Beethoven's date of birth, see, for example, Solomon, *Beethoven*, 3–4.
[59] Wetzstein, ed., *Familie Beethoven im kurfürstlichen Bonn*, 52–4, orig. 22–4.
[60] Kerst, *Die Erinnerungen an Beethoven*, vol. 1, 10.   [61] Schiedermair, *Der junge Beethoven*, 133.

lessons with van den Eeden only took place after Pfeiffer's departure is, as he admits, only a guess.[62] Mäurer, finally, returns to van den Eeden after discussing Pfeiffer and says that he "remained [Beethoven's] only teacher in thoroughbass and, in his seventies, sent the eleven- or twelve-year-old Beethoven to accompany the mass and other church music in his stead."[63]

In 1801, Lisette Bernhard, a young pianist who knew Beethoven from Vienna, met Tobias Pfeiffer in Düsseldorf. In a letter she writes: "[Pfeiffer] claims that he was Beethoven's master in Bonn. He is said to be a skilful Clavier player and to play the oboe very agreeably. Otherwise, he is a completely uneducated and indecent person."[64] Although Pfeiffer taught Beethoven for only one year, he figures prominently in all the reminiscences. The two reasons for this fact are spelled out in Bernhard's letter: He was a good musician, and his peculiar manners gave people ample reason to remember him as a person. Mäurer famously relates that Pfeiffer taught Beethoven at irregular times, "often" even after the closing hours of the tavern. Nonetheless, Mäurer credits Pfeiffer for recognizing Beethoven's "extraordinary talent."[65] Wegeler describes Pfeiffer's tuition as "far better" than Johann van Beethoven's and he calls him "an excellent artist," and "highly *genial*."[66] The Fischer manuscript is full of anecdotes concerning Pfeiffer, most of which inform us about his personal quirks rather than his music-making. There is, however, a striking agreement between Fischer's memoirs and Wegeler's *Erinnerungen*: Wegeler writes "Beethoven had him to thank for most [of his musical knowledge]," while Fischer, once in the main text and again in the margin of the manuscript, says that Pfeiffer had been "his main master, from whom he received everything."[67]

Beethoven's fourth teacher during this period was Franz Georg Rovantini (born 1757). Rovantini was a son of a cousin of Beethoven's mother. He had returned to Bonn in 1778 after a study trip and lived in the Beethovens' house until his early death in September 1781. Thayer says that according to the Fischer document, Beethoven was among his pupils.[68] The new edition of the Fischer manuscript reproduces a footnote from the previous critical edition that describes Rovantini as Beethoven's first teacher for violin and viola.[69] The circumstances certainly invite the assumption that Rovantini was responsible for this part of Beethoven's education. However, the

---

[62] Wegeler and Ries, *Biographische Notizen über Beethoven*, 11.
[63] Kerst, *Die Erinnerungen an Beethoven*, vol. 1, 11.
[64] Letter to Andreas Streicher, Düsseldorf, November 15, 1801. Facsimile and transcription in Goebl-Streicher, Streicher, and Ladenburger, *"Diesem Menschen hätte ich mein ganzes Leben widmen mögen,"* 101.
[65] Kerst, *Die Erinnerungen an Beethoven*, vol. 1, 10.
[66] Wegeler and Ries, *Biographische Notizen über Beethoven*, 11.
[67] Wetzstein, ed., *Familie Beethoven im kurfürstlichen Bonn*, 65 and, slightly rephrased, 74.
[68] Thayer, *Life of Beethoven*, 61.
[69] Wetzstein, ed., *Familie Beethoven im kurfürstlichen Bonn*, 47, n. 177, identified as quoted from Joseph Schmidt-Görg, ed., *Des Bonner Bäckermeisters Gottfried Fischer Aufzeichnungen über Beethovens Jugend*, Munich / Duisburg: Henle, 1971.

main body of Fischer's text tells us only about daily violin and viola lessons but identifies no teacher.

The previous paragraphs describe the situation according to the few surviving sources. Beethoven biographers have been reluctant to accept some of their claims, to the disadvantage of van den Eeden and Pfeiffer. In the view of many, Christian Gottlob Neefe, who came to Bonn in October 1779, was a much more likely figure to have had a major influence on Beethoven's education than were old-fashioned teachers such as van den Eeden, or erratic, short-term ones such as Pfeiffer. Thayer, for example, finds van den Eeden to be "a totally colorless picture in the history of Beethoven's youth," and believes that Mäurer confused van den Eeden with his successor Neefe, because Neefe later also instructed Beethoven in thoroughbass.[70] This reasoning is weak: Van den Eeden was very likely Beethoven's only thoroughbass teacher at the time Mäurer speaks of. Van den Eeden died in 1782 when Beethoven was eleven-and-a-half years old; it is quite possible that he taught Beethoven in a variety of subjects over an extended period, almost until his death. As to the possible coincidence of van den Eeden's and Pfeiffer's tuition, it could be that Pfeiffer was involved in Beethoven's Clavier lessons during part of the same period that van den Eeden taught him organ playing. Finally, van den Eeden may well – after 1780, when he was in his seventies – have sent Beethoven as a replacement to some of the court services, when his physical condition prevented him from playing himself. Mäurer's only error might have been that Beethoven was actually *younger* than eleven or twelve years.

Moreover, few biographers have been willing to consider Pfeiffer's importance for Beethoven's education. Schindler bases his information about Pfeiffer on Wegeler, whom he dutifully but briefly quotes.[71] Thayer grants Pfeiffer a short paragraph (Solomon does the same later), quoting Mäurer's story about the nocturnal lessons.[72] Paul Bekker supposes that under such circumstances the result of the lessons could scarcely have been fruitful.[73] As an exception, Schiedermair provides lengthy transcriptions about Pfeiffer from the Fischer manuscript. He finds it plausible "that Pfeiffer recognized the unusual talent of his pupil and that the latter really could learn something from him."[74] Theodor Frimmel seconds Thayer's and Bekker's negative opinion in various places. In his entry on Pfeiffer in his *Beethoven-Handbuch*, he strategically edits Fischer's information in support of his view.[75] The fairly recent *Beethoven Kompendium*,[76] finally, does not mention Pfeiffer at all.

---

[70] Thayer, *Life of Beethoven*, 60–1.   [71] Schindler, *Beethoven as I Knew Him*, 39.
[72] Thayer, *Life of Beethoven*, 61; Solomon, *Beethoven*, 17.
[73] Paul Bekker, *Beethoven*, Stuttgart: Deutsche Verlags-Anstalt, 1912, 8–9.
[74] Schiedermair, *Der junge Beethoven*, 133–5.   [75] Frimmel, *Beethoven-Handbuch*, vol. II, 17.
[76] Cooper, ed., *Das Beethoven Kompendium*.

A possible way to disentangle the assignments of Beethoven's various alleged teachers is to understand their different positions in the various musical and social spheres. Beethoven's private keyboard tuition and the making of domestic chamber music belong to a different world than learning to play church organs, which in turn may or may not have had anything to do with the social workings of the Bonn court and with its organist van den Eeden.

In this sense, Pfeiffer could have been a convenient successor for Johann van Beethoven in the domestic sphere, because he was living in the house. Being a good musician and young, he perhaps was familiar with the newest trends of musical fashion, which could have made him especially interesting for the Beethovens.

Returning to the matter of church organs, another piece of circumstantial evidence makes it likely that the chronological placement of the information about Beethoven's organ playing in the Fischer manuscript is correct: during the fire in 1777, the organ in the electoral chapel at the Bonn court was destroyed and the new one was "very small and a temporary solution."[77] It was therefore necessary for Beethoven to learn organ playing in another place. If van den Eeden was truly conscientious in teaching Beethoven, he would in fact have been the first person to suggest this. In order to gain access to church organs, Beethoven naturally had to become associated with their organists in one way or another. All this was bound to happen at the same time as he was taught by van den Eeden. To involve Brother Willibald in his tuition would have been sensible because he was a renowned organist, he could teach Beethoven the liturgy and he could use him as an assistant, providing practical training in the craft (much in the spirit of the Beethoven family tradition).

About van den Eeden, finally, we know too little to decide whether he was a brilliant teacher or not. Having been a lifelong colleague of Beethoven's grandfather, he was very likely a close acquaintance or perhaps even a friend to the Beethovens. He was in any case very well suited to initiate Beethoven in the ways of keyboard service at the Bonn chapel and to introduce him to court life in general. So to employ him as a teacher might have been a political choice as well as a musical one.

BEETHOVEN'S CLAVIER

In addition to the search for Beethoven's most influential teacher, a favorite question concerns the most likely keyboard instrument for Beethoven's

---

[77] Christian Gottlob Neefe, "Christian Gottlob Neefens Lebenslauf von ihm selbst beschrieben. Nebst beigefügtem Karakter," in *Die Sammlung der UB Kiel*, Bonn, 1782 and 1789, 17 in the manuscript. The manuscript of Neefe's autobiography is available under the tab "fasz.11" at www.uni-kiel.de/ub/Nachlass/Cramer/ (last accessed March 2, 2009).

early tuition. Apart from the organ, the term Clavier, or Klavier, is used throughout the documents dealing with this period. This allows both a general interpretation as "keyboard instrument" and a specific one as "clavichord." Schlosser describes van den Eeden as court organist and "the best Klavier player in Bonn."[78] Thayer interprets Schlosser's apparent failure to distinguish between "Klavier" and "organ" as follows: "Schlosser does not say that [Beethoven's] instruction was on the organ and it is unlikely that the boy, who was destined for a more systematic instruction in pianoforte playing, was put at the organ at so early an age." He concludes: "It is our conjecture that van den Eeden taught the boy chiefly pianoforte playing, being a master in that art; but his influence was small."[79]

In 1888, Frimmel assumed a more historically realistic perspective by suggesting that in his youth, Beethoven possibly still played on clavichords and harpsichords.[80] A few decades later, Schiedermair wrote in the same spirit that the instrument for Beethoven's lessons was "probably at first still the old clavichord ... but quite soon also the pianoforte."[81] Thus a typical eighteenth-century situation in the Beethoven household was accepted early on in German Beethoven scholarship. Elsewhere, it took a long time for a full acceptance of the idea that the clavichord or the harpsichord had some relevance for the young Beethoven.

The various English translations of "Clavier," for example, remained conservative for a long time. It may not be surprising that Thayer, writing in the nineteenth century, translated most – not all – occurrences of the word "Clavier" into "pianoforte." But even the Beethoven entry in the 1980 edition of *The New Grove Dictionary of Music and Musicians* puts "piano" in place of Clavier.

Obviously, we cannot decide about the keyboard instruments of Beethoven's youth without considering the typical conditions of the period and Beethoven's specific circumstances. This realization lies behind the statements of Frimmel and Schiedermair. Thayer's opinion, based on the outdated assumption of fortepiano dominance in Germany before the 1780s, would not need to be mentioned at all, were it not that the implication of a "destination" for Beethoven's training still persists in Beethoven scholarship as well as the myth about his preferred or "intended" instruments.

Our unease with the ambiguous term "Clavier" is probably not only the result of our *own* desire to know the whole story: we also suspect that the

[78] Translation from Schlosser, *Beethoven: the First Biography*, 40, except for taking the word Klavier from the original. Many thanks to Patricia Stroh of the Beethoven Center in San Jose, California, for providing the original text. Schlosser is the only one of the relatively early commentators who might be confusing van den Eeden and Neefe when he writes: "Being both organist and a member of the Elector's court chapel, he was very busy; moreover he needed to earn additional income by giving lessons. This left little time for Ludwig's instruction." Schlosser, *Beethoven: the First Biography*, 41.
[79] Thayer, *Life of Beethoven*, 60–1.   [80] Frimmel, *Neue Beethoveniana*, 23.
[81] Schiedermair, *Der junge Beethoven*, 159.

term hampers our access to opinions about, and preferences for, the specific instruments that actually existed *at the time.*

Opinions about the matter did, in fact, exist. In 1781, Johann Nicolaus Forkel commented upon the exclusive use of "Clavier" in musical editions:

> The mere use of the word Clavier does not suggest anything and it is indeed careless and odd that a composer so often writes: "Sonatas for Clavier," without indicating at the same time to which species they really belong. Because it makes a difference whether I compose for harpsichord [*Flügel*], fortepiano or clavichord; each composition for each of these instruments must have its different character.[82]

In order to make his point, Forkel tactically omits what was probably the most important reason for that so-called carelessness: narrowing down the choice of keyboard instrument was unwise if a composer wanted to sell his music to a large community of keyboard amateurs.

Apart from this, Forkel tells us that there was not always a pre-understood context available to guide even an eighteenth-century "Kenner" of music as to whether Clavier meant specifically clavichord or was being used in a generic sense. Obviously neither the typical keyboard composer nor the public bothered too much about such a distinction. In fact, this indifference concerned the actual use of the instrument. While Forkel asks for the recognition of the harpsichord, the fortepiano, and the clavichord as aesthetically distinct instruments, the average amateur simply played keyboard music on some keyboard instrument. This indifference in musical practice would explain the indifferent use of terminology in the early Beethoven sources.

However, there can be little doubt that a typical instrument for the keyboard lessons of a talented child, in a German city around 1777 with teachers all born in the first half of the eighteenth century, would have been the clavichord; it is the most probable instrument of Beethoven's early years. Eighteenth-century authors agreed on the merits of instruction on the clavichord. For example, C. P. E. Bach wrote in his *Versuch* in 1753:

> Every *clavierist* should have a good harpsichord and also a good clavichord to be able to play all kind of pieces alternately. Whoever can play on the clavichord in a good fashion will be able to do the same on the harpsichord, but not the reverse. So one must use the clavichord to learn the right expression and the harpsichord to strengthen the fingers.[83]

Jakob Adlung's view, published six years after his death in 1768, is similar:

> [The clavichord] has the advantage that one does not need to annoy oneself with [the replacing of] quill plectra, they [*sic*] also keep the tuning better ... This is why

---

[82] Johann Nicolaus Forkel in *Musikalischer Almanach für Deutschland auf das Jahr 1782*, Leipzig, 1781, 82, quoted in Siegbert Rampe, *Mozarts Claviermusik. Klangwelt und Aufführungspraxis*, Kassel: Bärenreiter, 1995, 20.

[83] Carl Philipp Emanuel Bach, *Versuch über die wahre Art, das Clavier zu spielen*, ed. Lothar Hoffmann-Erbrecht, Leipzig: Breitkopf & Härtel, 1957, 10–11.

they are used for teaching: because anyone who has learned on it can also play on organs, harpsichords etc.[84]

In 1773, Charles Burney reported:

I went to Mr. L'Augier's concert, which was begun by [a] child of eight or nine years old ... who played two difficult lessons of Scarlatti, with three or four by M. Becke, upon a small, and not good Piano forte. The neatness of the child's execution did not so much surprise me, though uncommon, as her expression. All the *pianos* and *fortes* were so judiciously attended to; and there was such shading off some passages, and force given to others as nothing but the best teaching, or greatest natural feeling and sensibility could produce. I enquired of Signor Giorgio, an Italian, who attended her, upon what instrument she usually practised at home, and was answered, 'on the clavichord'. This accounts for her expression, and convinces me, that children should learn upon that, or a Piano Forte very early on, and be obliged to give an expression to lady Coventry's Minuet, or whatever is their first tune; otherwise, after long practice on a monotonous harpsichord, however useful for strengthening the hand, the case is hopeless.[85]

Daniel Gottlob Türk, finally, writes in 1789:

For learning, the clavichord is undeniably most suitable, at least in the beginning; because no other keyboard instrument is more suited for achieving subtlety of expression. Later, it is an advantage if one can have a harpsichord or a good fortepiano as well; because the fingers achieve more strength and elasticity by playing on these instruments.[86]

In these examples, the clavichord gets credit as a pedagogical device rather than an aesthetic one. There will be more to say about the favorite instrument of the German *Empfindsamkeit* further below. It is, in any case, overwhelmingly documented that the clavichord was, more than any other keyboard instrument, ubiquitous in the musical Germany of the eighteenth century. The Fischer house that the Beethovens occupied was no exception. As mentioned above, Johann van Beethoven taught Cäcilie Fischer in singing and accompanying herself. She advanced far enough to "sing from the music and also play it neatly on the Klavier." In fact she made such musical progress that both Johann van Beethoven and Pfeiffer tried to persuade her to become a professional singer, which she declined; but in order to master the "songs that were difficult to sing and difficult to play, she exercised them so long that she was able to sing and play them correctly." [87] In view of such diligence and relative success, it would in fact seem that the Fischers had their own Clavier for her daily practice.

---

[84] Jakob Adlung, *Musica Mechanica Organoedi*, ed. Christhard Marenholz, Kassel: Bärenreiter, 1931, part II, 144.

[85] Charles Burney, *Tagebuch einer musikalischen Reise, transl. C.D. Ebeling 1772*, ed. Richard Schaal, Wilhelmshaven: Heinrichshofen, 1975, 96. English original from Komlós, *Fortepianos and their Music*, 134–5.

[86] Daniel Gottlob Türk, *Klavierschule 1789*, ed. Erwin R. Jacobi, Kassel: Bärenreiter, 1967, 11.

[87] Wetzstein, ed., *Familie Beethoven im kurfürstlichen Bonn*, 42, orig. 18. See also 65, orig. 35.

Regarding Beethoven's Clavier, we get an unexpected snippet of information from Carl Czerny. Czerny remembers Beethoven telling him that, "in his youth, he had practiced enormously, often until long after midnight."[88] This description may not tell us when all this happened, but it suggests that Beethoven practiced in his own room and this does give an indication of his practice instrument. One has to imagine a house where the second floor was rented by a musician's family with three children, a maid, and one or two permanent houseguests. The family of the landlord lived on the first floor. The clavichord would have been the only keyboard instrument to allow for a practice routine like Beethoven's. Any other instrument would inevitably have been too loud; Beethoven's playing would have led to a constant struggle with the other inhabitants of the house, and the information about this would have found its way into the surviving documents.[89]

One set of anecdotes from the Fischer manuscript describes music making in the Beethoven house that in fact could be heard in the street, causing people to stop and listen, and to praise the beautiful music. At one point, Fischer talks about Tobias Pfeiffer playing the flute and Beethoven improvising at the Klavier. Later on, he rewrites the passage and says that Beethoven played the Klavier, Pfeiffer the flute, and Rovantini improvised on the violin.[90] This must have been a typical situation ("Whenever the three happened to come together") from the time between the summer of 1779 and Easter 1780 (i.e. during Pfeiffer's stay in Bonn). Most probably these chamber music sessions indeed took place during the summer or early autumn of 1779, if one assumes that the windows in the house were open on such occasions. From these anecdotes we learn that there must have been another keyboard instrument in the house at that time besides the clavichord presumably in Ludwig's room, one that stood in one of the "two big rooms towards the road." This instrument, "Johann v. Beethoven's Klavier," which had to be tuned by the organist Mombauer,[91] was loud enough to function in chamber music and to be heard in the street. Later still, just before the Beethovens moved out of the Fischer house in 1787, the constant music making had become a problem for the landlord: At that time, a Klavier at the front stood right above the bedroom of the Fischers. Whether this was the same instrument as in 1780, or a new one, is not known. It was in any case loud enough to disturb old "Master Fischer," who

---

[88] Carl Czerny, "Anekdoten und Notizen über Beethoven 1852," in *Über den richtigen Vortrag der sämtlichen Beethoven'schen Klavierwerke*, ed. Paul Badura-Skoda, Vienna: Universal, 1963, 22.

[89] In a recent essay, Siegbert Rampe mentions a travel clavichord by Otto Joachim Tiefenbrunn, which according to oral tradition was owned by Beethoven. Siegbert Rampe, "Beethovens Klavier – Klangwelt und Aufführungspraxis," in Wolfram Steinbeck and Hartmut Hein, eds., *Beethovens Klaviermusik. Das Handbuch*, Laaber, in preparation (copy provided by the author, 3).

[90] Wetzstein, ed., *Familie Beethoven im kurfürstlichen Bonn*, 68, orig. 38, and 73–4, orig. 42.

[91] *Ibid.*, 79–80, orig. 46.

was a baker and had to begin his work very early in the morning, in his afternoon sleep.[92]

We do not know what kind of instrument Johann van Beethoven's Klavier was. It seems unlikely that it was a new fortepiano: the Fischers already mention a Klavier of some kind in the household of Johann van Beethoven's father.[93] Johann van Beethoven most likely inherited this very instrument. For a court singer and private music teacher there would have been no real reason to buy a large new instrument when he already owned a keyboard instrument, at a time when the fortepiano was not yet universally accepted. Another question is whether Johann actually had the means to obtain an expensive instrument of a new kind, such as a fortepiano.[94] The title of Beethoven's first surviving work (the Dressler variations, WoO 63 from 1782): "Variations pour le Clavecin sur une Marche de Mr. Dresler composées et dediées à son Excellence Madame Comtesse de Wolfmetternich née Baronne d'Assebourg par un jeune amateur Louis van Beethoven agé de dix ans," as well as the total absence of any dynamic signs in these variations, suggest that they were written with a harpsichord in mind. Whether Johann's Klavier was a harpsichord or not remains nevertheless a guess.

The discussion about Beethoven's domestic keyboard instruments distracts from the one instrument of his ambition, both musically and professionally, that stands out as relevant from his own perspective at the time: the organ. Perhaps he did like, and was inspired by, the organ more than other instruments. Moreover, practicing in various churches gave Ludwig an opportunity to learn music away from the immediate and permanent control he experienced at home. Domestic Clavier playing, although less conspicuously audible than his violin or viola studies (again assuming the clavichord), did not provide this sort of freedom. On the other hand, one wonders how many opportunities Beethoven would have had to play organs outside the church services. This would even have been a financial problem, because the people who worked the bellows had to be paid.

FIRST SUCCESS

Pfeiffer departed from Bonn in the spring of 1780. Mäurer – clearly better informed this time – writes that Beethoven's "exalted" father at this point suddenly recognized his son's talent and "invited everyone" to admire him. According to Fischer's account, curious music lovers would frequently come and ask to hear the young Beethoven "in a little concert," especially when Ludwig also became known as a composer (that is, in 1782 at the

---

[92] *Ibid.*, 114, orig. 62.   [93] *Ibid.*, 7, orig. 1.
[94] This aspect has already been discussed briefly in Frimmel, *Neue Beethoveniana*, 24.

earliest). Johann van Beethoven would then try to arrange a private concert with local musicians.

A long passage in the Fischer manuscript deals with three consecutive trips made by Johann van Beethoven, Rovantini, and Ludwig. These most likely took place during the summer of 1781, just after Beethoven's school attendance had come to an end.[95] The company had been invited to two of the twelve destinations. In the period between these invitations, they made a round trip to various old acquaintances of Johann van Beethoven and the Fischer family, and to others who were "equipped with [a] Clavier." Fischer uniformly characterizes ten of the hosts as "great music lovers" and relates that the party received "many honors." Clearly the whole trip was devised as a promotion tour with the objective of receiving such honors.

The circumstances suggest that Johann van Beethoven finally, in the summer of 1781, showed off his son to the musical world around him. Whether or not Johann was beginning to see the possibility of actually exploiting Ludwig's talent is, however, unclear. Johann was in any case too late: the teenager Ludwig was not at all keen on the sudden attention. Mäurer mentions Beethoven's indifference to praise and explains that Ludwig "removed himself in order to practice alone, preferably when his father was not at home."[96] In a similar vein, Fischer writes that Ludwig had his "happiest hours when he was excused from the company of his parents, which was seldom the case."[97] These descriptions show that the thing that Beethoven seemed to have loathed most about the domestic musical situation remained unchanged during the period of Johann van Beethoven's domination: the element of control and exposure. It makes little difference whether a child gets excessive attention through harsh criticism and unjust punishment, or by means of exaggerated praise. It may indeed have been especially confusing that the same father in close succession assumed both attitudes. Beethoven's difficulties in acknowledging his public's praise in a graceful and unforced manner are documented throughout his life, as is his pronounced reluctance to play anything upon request. It is clear that this behavior pattern has its origins in these early days.

Following his initial musical success, Beethoven soon learned to see himself not as a talented youngster, but rather as a capable young adult. Thayer records an anecdote about the organist of the *Münsterkirche*, Zenser. When Beethoven brought him some compositions of his own, he said: "Why, you can't play that, Ludwig," to which the latter replied, "I will when

---

[95] Wetzstein, ed., *Familie Beethoven im kurfürstlichen Bonn*, 90–2, orig. 52–4 and n. 344 and 355. The trips happened during the musicians' vacation while the Elector stayed in Westphalia, which was in the summer of 1781. The year can also be established backwards from Rovantini's death on September 9, 1781.

[96] Kerst, *Die Erinnerungen an Beethoven*, vol. I, 10.

[97] Wetzstein, ed., *Familie Beethoven im kurfürstlichen Bonn*, 75–6, orig. 44.

I am bigger."[98] If there is any substance to this anecdote at all, the event must also belong to the time around 1780. Later, Beethoven would surely have brought his compositions to Neefe instead. Fischer describes how Beethoven suddenly "adopted a totally and completely different attitude" and "attached much importance to being treated respectfully." Fischer mentions Rovantini before and after this quotation, which suggests again that he is addressing the time before Rovantini died in September 1781. Beethoven now received the uniform of the court musicians, and he is reported playing together with Rovantini and his father at court and in various other professional circumstances, such as "Komedi" performances at the Poppelsdorfer castle.[99] His prior negligence, indifference, and untidiness were replaced by an attempt to appear mature.[100]

It is impossible to know exactly when and how Beethoven took his development into his own hands, and how Johann van Beethoven's influence changed during this process. Somewhat awkwardly, Fischer twice uses a phrase about how Beethoven "now believed that he was equal to his father in music," but he is silent about the consequences this "belief" may have had for their personal relationship.[101] We do get the impression that Beethoven tried to use his early introduction at the court as a chance to exhibit his musical talent in his own way. Mäurer relates, for instance, how the eleven- or twelve-year-old Beethoven (he was actually ten or eleven) substituted for van den Eeden at the Bonn chapel and on one occasion surprised everyone with his abilities, so that "one was bound to think that he had [previously] restrained himself on purpose."[102]

---

[98] Thayer, *Life of Beethoven*, 62.
[99] Wetzstein, ed., *Familie Beethoven im kurfürstlichen Bonn*, 75 and 87, orig. 44 and 50.
[100] See also Solomon, *Beethoven*, 25–6. As I will discuss below, the description of Neefe as "pivotal" in this development is problematic for several reasons.
[101] Wetzstein, ed., *Familie Beethoven im kurfürstlichen Bonn*, 62 and 64, orig. 32 and 34.
[102] Kerst, *Die Erinnerungen an Beethoven*, vol. I, 11.

CHAPTER 2

Beethoven the pianist

CHRISTIAN GOTTLOB NEEFE: THE
TRADITIONAL PICTURE

Christian Gottlob Neefe came to Frankfurt in May 1777, to conduct the orchestra of Seyler's theater company. He worked there for two and a half years, conducting operas "which, in turn, were presented in Frankfurt, Mainz, Kölln, Hanau, Mannheim and Heidelberg."[1] In August 1779, Seyler went bankrupt and fled from Frankfurt; his company continued playing for a while "to earn the means of leaving the city," but in October its members dispersed.[2] Neefe went to Bonn to join the *Nationalbühne* of Großmann and Helmuth, who, too, had both previously been members of Seyler's company. This theater had been opened at the request of Elector Maximilian Friedrich in November 1778.

On February 15, 1781, Neefe's name appears for the first time in the Bonn court documents. On that date, "on the recommendation of the reigning minister Count von Belderbusch and of Countess von Hatzfeld," an official decree pronounced him "candidate for the office of court organist in Bonn."[3] It is not known when Ludwig van Beethoven's lessons with Neefe began. Thayer writes: "It would create no surprise should proof hereafter come to light that this change [of teacher] was made even before the issue of the decree of February 15, 1781."[4] In the same vein, Schiedermair supposes the lessons to have begun around 1780, after Tobias Pfeiffer had left Bonn.[5]

Born in 1748, half a generation younger than C. P. E. Bach, well educated, intelligent, and an articulate writer, Neefe was an excellent example of the enlightened musician of the late eighteenth century. As he writes in his autobiography, he was largely self-taught as a keyboard player, using Marpurg's and C. P. E. Bach's methods.[6] While he was still at school,

---

[1] Neefe, "Christian Gottlob Neefens Lebenslauf," 13.   [2] Thayer, *Life of Beethoven*, 30.
[3] Neefe, "Christian Gottlob Neefens Lebenslauf," 16. See also Thayer, *Life of Beethoven*, 25.
[4] Thayer, *Life of Beethoven*, 64.   [5] Schiedermair, *Der junge Beethoven*, 157–8.
[6] See Neefe, "Christian Gottlob Neefens Lebenslauf," 2a of the manuscript. Neefe first describes his initial lessons in keyboard playing – hampered by the lack of "better masters" and money, and by the long traveling distance – with a number of teachers. Neefe continues, "I learned the best part afterwards, from Marpurg's *Anleitung* and C. P. E. Bach's *Versuch*," without providing more detail.

35

however, he also wrote to Johann Adam Hiller for instruction in composition. When he moved from his native Chemnitz to Leipzig, he became friends with Hiller, and after completing his law studies, he apparently received tuition and professional support from his friend and teacher in every way:

He recommended me as music teacher in various distinguished houses, accepted me as an assistant for his operetta *Der Dorfbarbier* and for his weekly *musikalische Nachrichten und Anmerkungen*, and thus he introduced me to the musical world. He helped to get some of my subsequent works printed, and thus increased my income. Some songs of the Dorfbarbier, various small pieces in his weekly N[achrichten] u[nd] A[nmerkungen], three operettas ... and the Klavier sonatas that are dedicated to C. P. E. Bach were composed and printed entirely under his supervision.[7]

Neefe possessed musical experience, personal discipline and general knowledge, and he had a keen interest in the philosophy of the day, so it is no surprise that Beethoven's biographers have given him a prominent position. Especially striking in Neefe's career is the similarity between the support he received from Hiller and the encouragement he himself later gave to Beethoven. In his famous letter to Carl Friedrich Cramer's *Magazin der Musik* (March 2, 1783, published on March 30), in which he describes Bonn's musical life, Neefe himself gives us the details:

Louis van Betthoven, son of the above-mentioned *tenorist*, a boy of 11 years, and of a very promising talent. He plays the Klavier with much skill and power, reads excellently at sight, and he plays the greater part of the Well-Tempered Clavier by Sebastian Bach, which Mr. Neefe has given him to play, which says it all ... Mr. Neefe has also, as far as his other duties permitted, given him some instructions in thoroughbass. Now he trains him in composition and has, for his encouragement, arranged for nine variations on a march for Clavier by him to be engraved in Mannheim.[8]

This passage shows in a snapshot how Neefe had thus far supported the talented young man, in whom he clearly was genuinely interested. Beethoven's gratitude for this support is evident in an excerpt from a letter he wrote to Neefe, perhaps in connection with his departure from Bonn in October 1792. The fragment survives in a newspaper article from 1793 about Beethoven's study trip to Vienna (Beethoven is said to be "Now beyond doubt one of the foremost Klavier players"). The editor honors Neefe with the assertion that Beethoven was "indebted to Neefe for part of his development," and cites the following passage from Beethoven's letter, which clearly was provided by Neefe:

[7] *Ibid.*, 10b. and 10c.
[8] Carl Friedrich Cramer, *Magazin der Musik 1783–1787*, Hildesheim: Olms, 1971–1974, 394–5.

I thank you for the advice which you have very often given me for the progress of my divine art. If I ever become a great man, you will have a part in this; this will please you all the more, because you can be assured ...[9]

A consideration of Neefe's actual influence on Beethoven is of great importance in establishing Beethoven's relationship to several of the musical traditions or stylistic trends of his time. The tradition of emphasizing Neefe's role dates back at least to Thayer, where it is an explicit response to a problematical passage in Wegeler's *Erinnerungen*, as well as an implicit one to Schindler's muddled evaluation of Wegeler's account.[10] Wegeler, who says that he made Beethoven's acquaintance in 1782, claims that Neefe had "little influence" on Beethoven's education, and that Beethoven "even complained about Neefe's too severe criticism."[11] Thayer judges, "The first of these assertions is obviously an utter mistake," and he adds a lengthy passage about the possible content of Beethoven's lessons with the "zealous Bachist."[12]

Ludwig Schiedermair portrays Neefe's own life and musical preferences, and especially his admiration of C. P. E. Bach and his *Versuch*, in much the same vein. This assemblage of facts subsequently forms the basis of several long passages of free association about the possible content of Beethoven's tuition (about which, in fact, only the 1783 quotation from Cramer's *Magazin* gives any particulars). Neefe is here assigned the role of "Lehrmeister" (the word is emphasized in the text), the implication being that he, in an intensive course of study, and with great personal devotion, taught Beethoven not only music but all of his aesthetical and philosophical values.[13]

This picture is handed down in the vast majority of publications about Beethoven on every level. In the face of Thayer's and Schiedermair's vehemence, it seems indeed that Wegeler was mistaken. There are a few possible explanations for this, to which I will return below. Nevertheless, the canonical picture is not without its own problems: the suggested period of time and the intensity of the tuition, as well as Beethoven's attitude in receiving it, deserve a closer look.

A LOOK AT NEEFE'S AND BEETHOVEN'S CALENDARS

The two famous passages about Neefe and Beethoven are the only existing documents that inform us about a teacher–pupil relationship of any sort between Neefe and Beethoven, apart from Wegeler's recollection. The

[9] Here ends the fragment of Beethoven's letter (or perhaps personal note) to Neefe. It is, in this form, part of an article in the *Berlinische Musikalische Zeitung*, October 26, 1793. Ludwig van Beethoven, *Briefwechsel Gesamtausgabe*, ed. Sieghard Brandenburg, vol. 1, Munich: Henle, 1996, 11.
[10] Schindler, *Beethoven as I Knew Him*, 39f.
[11] Wegeler and Ries, *Biographische Notizen über Beethoven*, 11.   [12] Thayer, *Life of Beethoven*, 64–5.
[13] Schiedermair, "Christian Gottlob Neefe," in *Der junge Beethoven*, 140–62.

window through which we see Neefe providing Beethoven with a regular tuition is, in fact, very small. Other documents, even Neefe's autobiography, usually mention Beethoven as Neefe's assistant, either temporary (from 1782), or permanent (from 1784). Besides these sources, Gottlieb Fischer lists Neefe and his wife among the friends that often visited the Beethovens, but he mentions no date or period of time.[14]

In the following, I will present a schedule of Beethoven's lessons with Neefe, based on Wegeler's and Neefe's descriptions, and on a comparison between Beethoven's and Neefe's activities after the latter arrived in Bonn. The fact that Neefe himself provided the only passages which describe him as Beethoven's teacher and mentor should not be seen as problematic. His sincerity and modesty speak clearly from all his writings and actions. In his own words, he was indifferent to "status and title," but he "always loved honor and it [was] the driving force for many of [his] actions."[15] To meet these standards it would have been out of the question to modify the facts for his own sake, while it would, on the other hand, have been careless not to state his role in Beethoven's education (since this was a matter of his honor).

As discussed earlier, during the winter of 1779–80, Beethoven probably had lessons with Pfeiffer and van den Eeden. He was also still attending school. Neefe, on the other hand, had just become "Musickdirecktor." His wife had joined the theater company as an actress. The theater season of that year opened on December 3, with a welcome program for the returning Elector that featured music by Neefe and other composers.[16] One of Neefe's first tasks was to "fill the gaps" and "put the opera on a better foundation." At the same time, he had his mind set on his long-standing plan to return to his native Saxony. Until mid-January 1780 he fought unsuccessfully for his right to leave Bonn, but his plan was successfully thwarted by his employers Großmann and Helmuth, who needed Neefe in Bonn.[17] It should also be mentioned that between their marriage in May 1778 and September 1782, the Neefes had six children, of whom two died. Even if one assumes that they had one or more pairs of twins (otherwise a child was born in the Neefe house every nine months), their family life must have required a lot of energy. Perhaps this is what leads Neefe to state somewhat defiantly in his autobiography: "I do not gladly let matters of [my] marriage, or friendship, disturb me in my general duties."[18]

Between March 16 and the beginning of April 1780, the theater company was in Frankfurt. Neefe was back in Bonn during April and May. This was immediately after Pfeiffer had left Bonn, but it is doubtful whether Neefe,

---

[14] Wetzstein, ed., *Familie Beethoven im kurfürstlichen Bonn*, 127, orig. 69.
[15] Neefe, "Christian Gottlob Neefens Lebenslauf," 20a.   [16] Thayer, *Life of Beethoven*, 30.
[17] Neefe, "Christian Gottlob Neefens Lebenslauf," 14–15a. See also Thayer, *Life of Beethoven*, 30, and the transcription of a letter from Neefe to Helmuth in Schiedermair, *Der junge Beethoven*, 144–5.
[18] Neefe, "Christian Gottlob Neefens Lebenslauf," 20.

during the preparation of the seven different programs that were performed up until the close of the season, had any time to spare for Beethoven.[19] Between the beginning of June and the end of September, the company was traveling.[20]

Compared to the preceding season, the winter season (1780–81) at the theater was somewhat less active. Neefe indicated his interest in the position of organist in the court chapel in the spring of 1781. In the eyes of court habitués, the services of the aging van den Eeden had become unsatisfactory. Neefe was supported by the very influential Count von Belderbusch and Countess von Hatzfeld. On February 15, 1781, Neefe was declared a candidate for court organist. However, this had no far-reaching immediate consequences, as Neefe traveled again with Großmann and Helmut during the entire summer, leaving Bonn on April 17 and returning on September 29.[21]

Mäurer and Fischer remember Beethoven appearing at court around 1781, playing in performances like the "Komedi" and substituting for van den Eeden in the court chapel. Neefe must have been acquainted with the Beethovens by that time. But before he took a personal interest in the organist's position and thus came close to the Beethovens' sphere of work (or perhaps to Ludwig's ambitions), the likelihood of any intense musical or professional contact seems rather small.

Mäurer remembers that Beethoven presented "his first attempt at composition" in January 1781. This was a funeral cantata for the English envoy George Cressener. The music director Lucchesi was asked to correct the piece and it was later performed.[22] The lack of corroboration for this story, including the fact that no cantata of this kind is preserved, cautions against drawing too far-reaching conclusions from it. Nevertheless, Mäurer is clear enough in mentioning Lucchesi; it would seem, therefore, that in early 1781 the person who corrected Beethoven's attempts at composition was not yet Christian Gottlob Neefe. On the other hand, the theater had no performances with music between February 21 and April 17, 1781, so Neefe might have had time to spare in these weeks, perhaps even to teach Beethoven.

After his usual active summer away from Bonn, Neefe's workload over the whole year between the autumns of 1781 and 1782 can be measured by the fact that, up until the summer of 1782, the orchestra rehearsed seventeen new musical dramas, including three by Neefe.[23] On June 19, 1782, van den Eeden's funeral was held, and Neefe became the "true court and court chapel organist." Nevertheless, he departed again for summer tours on June 20 and he was away until October. His duties as court organist were

[19] Thayer, *Life of Beethoven*, 30.   [20] Schiedermair, *Der junge Beethoven*, 145.

[21] Neefe, "Christian Gottlob Neefens Lebenslauf," 16–16a; Thayer, *Life of Beethoven*, 31.

[22] Kerst, *Die Erinnerungen an Beethoven*, vol. I, 11. Mäurer says that Lucchesi did not correct the piece since he did not understand it, but he performed it nevertheless.

[23] Thayer, *Life of Beethoven*, 31.

entrusted to a "Vikar." On September 30, 1782, while still in Frankfurt, Neefe concluded the first part of his autobiography with this very piece of information.[24] This "Vikar" has since been identified as the eleven-year-old Beethoven.[25]

Little is known of Beethoven's activities during the same season. His alleged violin teacher Rovantini died on September 9, 1781, at the age of twenty-four. Neefe's appointment suggests that, as early as the spring of 1781, van den Eeden was unable to perform his duties on a regular basis, which makes it even less probable that he taught Beethoven in the subsequent autumn of 1781. This is the point in history where we can suppose that Beethoven needed a new outlook. It is therefore likely that Neefe became Beethoven's teacher during the winter season of 1781–82. On the other hand, it is slightly confusing that Neefe does not name Beethoven in his autobiography when he speaks of his "Vikar" in September 1782, having taught him perhaps for the best part of a year. In his letter to Cramer's *Magazin* from early 1783, he is full of praise for Beethoven. So why did he, half a year earlier, merely refer to a "Vikar"? There is no certain answer to this question, but the formulation rather suggests that at that point Beethoven did not yet have a prominent place in Neefe's life.

During the winter of 1782, Neefe prepared his extensive report for Cramer's *Magazin* from which I have quoted above. In a letter to Cramer dated December 24, 1782, he also mentions that "the pressure of so many mechanical tasks at the theater" prevented him from composing a piece for Cramer, which is referred to as "an old debt" but is nevertheless "a task I would have preferred."[26] Neefe's workload during this time is also evident when he describes how he taught Beethoven "as far as his other duties permitted."

On April 26, 1783, the *Kapellmeister* Andrea Lucchesi and the *Konzertmeister* Cajetano Mattioli went on a journey to Italy, and Neefe stood in as *Kapellmeister* for the church music, taking on yet more tasks.[27] The twelve-year-old Beethoven is said to have helped as a "cembalist" in the orchestra.[28] The strain on Neefe during the 1783–84 season was probably even more extreme. A notice by Graf Salm (the content of which is based on Beethoven's lost petition for a salary increase) from February 23, 1784 retrospectively credits Beethoven for his efforts as an assistant. "After a preliminary adequate examination," writes Salm, Beethoven has shown "ample capability for the court organ, which he has frequently played during the often recurring absence of the organist Neffe, at opera rehearsals or otherwise, and will continue to do in similar cases."[29]

---

[24] Neefe, "Christian Gottlob Neefens Lebenslauf," 16a.   [25] Thayer, *Life of Beethoven*, 65.
[26] Reprinted in Schiedermair, *Der junge Beethoven*, 72.
[27] Neefe, "Christian Gottlob Neefens Lebenslauf," 17.
[28] Thayer, *Life of Beethoven*, 68. "Cembalist" appears in quotation marks all over the literature, but I have not found an original document containing this term.
[29] Beethoven, *Briefwechsel*, vol. 1, 4.

In a letter from January 20, 1784, Neefe confirms this information. He writes, "In the year 1783 Beethoven, then still small, later so great [received] only 48 Cologne Guilders for playing the organ in the court chapel."[30] Beethoven's development was now apparent in his compositions (after the initial Dressler Variations, he composed three sonatas and four small works during 1783, of which all but one fugue were directly published). Additionally, he was now beginning a professional performer's career and took the role of deputy organist ever more seriously. At the same time, Neefe's slightly ironic formulation "so great" conveys, in its context, estrangement rather than admiration. Apparently, the thirteen-year-old "great" Beethoven was now established and did not need to be taught any more.

Following the death of Elector Maximilian Friedrich on April 15, 1784, Neefe's position at the Bonn court became endangered due to personal intrigues. This development directly strengthened Beethoven's position, and one can assume that one consequence was a temporary detachment between Neefe and Beethoven.[31] Already in the February of that year, Graf Salm described Beethoven in the abovementioned notice as a "frequent" substitute during Neefe's absence. The second of three *pro memorias* that were assembled for the information of the new Elector Maximilian Franz contains a description of Neefe as "not very well versed on the organ, also a foreigner with no merits at all and of Calvinistic religion." An entry on Beethoven follows, presenting him as "of good ability, still young, of good and quiet conduct and poor."[32] One passage in the third report reveals that these descriptions were part of a plan to promote Beethoven: "If Neefe were to be dismissed, another organist would have to be appointed, who if he were to be used only in the chapel could be had for 150 florins, the same is small, young and a son of one of the court musici, and when it has been necessary has already filled the place for nearly a year [*sic*] very well."[33] A pay list from June 23 lists Beethoven next to Neefe with a salary of 150 florins.[34]

In a lengthy letter to Großmann from July 23, Neefe describes how his friends successfully convinced him not to resign and to wait instead until the truth came to light to "put shame on the slanderers." On January 19, 1785, Neefe was still waiting for the situation to improve. Commenting on the fact that the news was spreading that he was forced to teach six hours each day, he writes in another letter to Großmann: "Betthoven will be most happy of all, but I doubt nevertheless that he will truly profit from this [circumstance]."[35]

---

[30] Letter from Neefe to Assessor Kummer, Bonn, January 20, 1784. Beethoven-Haus Bonn, NE 224.
[31] See Thayer, *Life of Beethoven*, 78–9, and Schiedermair, *Der junge Beethoven*, 166–7.
[32] Schiedermair, *Der junge Beethoven*, 57.   [33] Quoted from *ibid.*, 166.
[34] Thayer, *Life of Beethoven*, 79; Schiedermair, *Der junge Beethoven*, 167.
[35] Schiedermair, *Der junge Beethoven*, 146–8.

The complete meaning of Neefe's allusions remains hidden. It seems, for instance, unlikely that he thought Beethoven was happy because Neefe was forced to give private music lessons against his will. It is, however, clear that Neefe (as Beethoven's former teacher) doubted that the situation was doing Beethoven much good, musically speaking. It is also clear that Neefe had no influence on Beethoven whatsoever during his time of absence from the Bonn court. On February 8, 1785, Neefe's former allowance was restored.[36]

WHAT NEEFE TAUGHT BEETHOVEN

So far, we have only learned something about the possible extent of Beethoven's lessons with Neefe, but nothing about the lessons themselves. A closer look at Neefe's 1783 letter to Cramer's *Magazin* reveals certain subtleties that further help us to understand the duration and the content of Beethoven's tuition.

Neefe's use of present and past tense indicates that he is describing a development and not a static situation: Neefe *has* given Beethoven instruction in thoroughbass and he *has* given him the *Well-Tempered Clavier* to play. *Now* Neefe is training him in composition, while he *has already* initiated the publication of the variations.

We also get some information about the intensity of the various elements of this tuition: thoroughbass, composition and Clavier playing. Neefe spent time teaching Beethoven thoroughbass only "as far as his other duties permitted." But he mentions no such reservation when he talks about teaching Beethoven composition, which is, as we have seen, an ongoing project at the time of the article. On the contrary, in spite of his many obligations, he has *in addition* arranged for the publication of the variations as an encouragement. Finally, Neefe does not actually mention giving Beethoven any keyboard instruction at all. He merely states his interest in Beethoven's talent and that he gave him Bach to play.

In fact Neefe does not suggest that he is a good player *because* he gave him Bach to play, but that he is already accomplished enough to play it. However, Beethoven needed training in thoroughbass for a short while. But "some instructions" were sufficient and were clearly discontinued in favor of the composition studies. In composition, finally, Beethoven still needed to be "trained" and "encouraged" at the moment of writing.

Apparently, Neefe concentrated his efforts chiefly on teaching Beethoven in composition, and this tuition was in its most intense phase at the time when Neefe prepared his article, probably during the winter of 1782–83. The timetable of Beethoven's development indicates that he was already (or rapidly becoming) a very advanced keyboard player when Neefe entered his world. Considering that his playing skills at that time were very likely the

---

[36] Thayer, *Life of Beethoven*, 79.

cause of Beethoven's growing self-esteem (rather than his compositions), it is unlikely that he saw himself in need of any more keyboard lessons after a certain point. The lack of detail in Neefe's letter suggests that, by 1783, any keyboard tuition by Neefe (if it ever took place) belonged to the past.

One problem still to be solved is the discrepancy between Wegeler's account and Neefe's letters from 1783 and 1792. The passage from Wegeler about the content and influence of Neefe's tuition runs as follows:

> The musician Neefe, who was initially employed as director of music in Großmann's theater company, later as court organist, and who also had a name as a composer, had little influence on the tuition of our Ludwig; the latter even complained about Neefe's too severe criticism of his first attempts in composition.[37]

Beethoven's complaints were very likely something Wegeler actually observed in person soon after he met Beethoven in 1782,[38] for the word "klagte" in the German original typically describes someone's discontent with an ongoing situation. If we accept Beethoven's complaints as a fact, they could well have caused Wegeler, an unmusical onlooker, to misinterpret and underestimate Neefe's overall influence. Wegeler shows elsewhere that he was not too well informed about the Bonn court music. By asserting, for example, that other duties did not hinder Neefe ("who was in good health") from playing the organ himself, Wegeler disregards Neefe's involvement at the theater as well as his role of temporary *Kapellmeister* in 1783. Wegeler's explanation that Beethoven's appointment as deputy organist was probably only a pretext made by the Elector for supporting Beethoven financially is pure speculation. His final claim that this act of charity was the work of Count Waldstein is simply incorrect because Waldstein did not arrive in Bonn until 1788.[39] The whole presentation shows that Wegeler was only scantily informed about the music at the court chapel and that he remembers the succession of events imprecisely, while perhaps also being uninterested in Neefe as a person.

Around 1792, when Beethoven wrote to Neefe to thank him for the "advice" which he "very frequently" gave him for his musical progress, he no longer held a grudge against his strict teacher. Whereas Wegeler describes the situation at one particular moment, Beethoven in his later letter gratefully sums up the *entire* time of his and Neefe's acquaintance. However, it is also clear that Beethoven understood his influence as a whole as being frequently given "advice" rather than, for example, instruction or lessons.

---

[37] Wegeler and Ries, *Biographische Notizen über Beethoven*, 11.
[38] This date from Wegeler's preface has been questioned because Wegeler says that he met Beethoven when he "already was an author." If one reads "author" as "composer" this should not be problematic. See also Schiedermair, *Der junge Beethoven*, 175–6, and Frimmel, *Beethoven-Handbuch*, vol. II, 408.
[39] Wegeler and Ries, *Biographische Notizen über Beethoven*, 12–13.

This again suggests that Neefe's tuition was perhaps rather informal at times.

The only early publication to fill in the gaps in our knowledge about Neefe's lessons is Johann Aloys Schlosser's Beethoven biography from 1827. This work has always occupied a difficult position as a source because it is full of factual errors and owes much of the correct part of its content to citations from other written sources. While Barry Cooper, the editor of the 1996 English translation, finds the traditional criticism of Schlosser's book "at times overstated," no one can overlook Schlosser's tendency to fill in gaps in his information with pure conjecture.[40] This is especially problematic when he describes events that are otherwise not documented. The whole passage about Neefe's tuition is an example: "The Elector [Maximilian Friedrich]," writes Schlosser, "instructed Neefe to consider young Beethoven's musical education one of the most important assignments. This pleased Neefe, who had already noted the talents of his future pupil. He was glad to do everything possible for him, especially since Ludwig was very fond of him and tried to please him by showing great industry."[41]

It is hard to know what to make of Schlosser's statement. There is, of course, no doubt that Neefe acknowledged Beethoven's talents. But we can conclude from the previous three sections that only little is known of what, when, and how intensely Neefe taught Beethoven. Less still is known of Neefe's personal closeness to Beethoven, or about the attitude with which Beethoven received this tuition. Nothing, finally, tells us about the older Elector's interest in Beethoven. Schlosser would be totally alone in his assertions were it not for the fact that much of the later evolving, now canonical, account of these matters seems to be inspired by similar ideas of what very likely happened, or even what most desirably ought to have happened.

It is certainly compelling to think that Neefe, given the opportunity, exposed Beethoven to the full essence of his knowledge, aesthetic outlook, and philosophy. In the same manner it is tempting to believe that Neefe's initiative to give Beethoven Bach's music to play was an element in a complete course of keyboard playing. Both can certainly not be excluded, but it is important to realize that our information about these matters is substantially less precise than any of the major Beethoven biographies suggest.

THE INTRODUCTION OF FORTEPIANOS IN BONN

During the 1780s, Beethoven engaged in various kinds of musical activities: playing at court (using the small organ there and perhaps a harpsichord for

---

[40] Schlosser, *Beethoven: the First Biography*, 14.   [41] English translation from *ibid.*, 47–9.

continuo), playing organs in churches (although this may have been earlier, as described above), composing and playing solo on the Clavier in various circumstances, and, eventually, playing the viola in the reinstated court orchestra. At the same time, Bonn's music world, and Beethoven with it, adapted to the latest fashion in keyboard instruments.

Despite the lack of documentation of the extent of Neefe's influence on Beethoven, we know that they had *some* kind of exchange about keyboard playing besides organ playing. It is, therefore, interesting to review briefly how Neefe's own taste in keyboard instruments developed.

Neefe was an admirer of C. P. E. Bach. In Bonn, his affinity with *Empfindsamkeit* and the clavichord as a medium for expressing the intense and spontaneous had given way to a curiosity about new developments. Schiedermair says that Neefe at one point even became an agent for the fortepianos and clavichords of Friederici and other renowned masters.[42] In his letter to Cramer's *Magazin der Musik* from March 2, 1783, in which he mentions the young Beethoven, Neefe provides an extensive description of the musical life in Bonn. Interestingly, he departs from the generalized use of the term *Clavier* whenever he mentions keyboard instruments of special interest. This is, for example, the case with the collection of five harpsichords ("Flügel") from between 1646 and 1664, and a clavichord (which he in fact calls "Clavichord" and not "Clavier") owned by the music enthusiast Hofkammerrath von Mastiaux.[43]

Neefe also mentions thirteen amateurs (including Beethoven and six other talented youngsters), nine of whom played Clavier at varying levels. Only two people either owned a fortepiano worth mentioning or were able to master it. One was Mastiaux, who had a "large *Hammerclavier* in the shape of a pyramid" in his collection. This was part of a yet unfinished combination instrument. It still had to be completed with a pedalboard, a glockenspiel and a stop of pipes. The other was Countess von Hatzfeld, whom Neefe describes explicitly as a brilliant fortepiano player.

Also mentioned in Neefe's letter are a number of inventions by the maker of Mastiaux's brand-new combination instrument, one Gottlieb Friedrich Riedlen. Riedlen (b. 1749) was in Neefe's opinion a "skilled *mechanicus*" who, apart from building "quilled harpsichords [*Flügel*] of the ordinary kind," appears to have been very keen on innovation and experiment. That he experimented with metal harpsichord plectra may not seem very extraordinary in comparison with his invention of a "means to let most Clavier-instruments stay in tune, even though the climate has a strong influence on

---

[42] Schiedermair, *Der junge Beethoven*, 69.
[43] One instrument not mentioned is the Clavier with thirty *Veränderungen* which the Regensburg instrument maker Franz Jakob Spath presented to the Bonn Elector in 1751. Possibly it was destroyed in the fire of 1777. Michael Latcham, "Franz Jakob Spath and the Tangentenflügel, an eighteenth-century tradition," *Galpin Society Journal* 57 (2004), referring to Jakob Adlung, *Anleitung zu der musikalischen Gelahrtheit*, Erfurt: 1758, 576–7.

the strings," or "an instrument on which everything that is played by the
player is, during the playing, printed out in music by means of a special
mechanism."[44] Of a more serious character were probably the remaining
three *Instrumente*:[45] one with "hammers of a new invention from which the
player may expect nothing but satisfaction," another kind, also newly
invented, with quills and hammers, and an "instrument with gut strings
with which one can make the impression of two violins, viola, cello, double
bass, and the flute with all ease."[46]

It seems that Neefe was less biased against such instruments than was
Cramer, the editor of the *Magazin der Musik*. Although, during the course
of 1783, Cramer let various instrument builders advertise in his magazine,[47]
reviewed the work of especially talented builders,[48] and personally contributed a lengthy report about a *Bogenhammerclavier*,[49] at the end of the same
year he lost patience with all new fashions in instrument building and
wrote:

It is indeed a sad thing for music to find this sort of instrument [the fortepiano] to
be dominating whole nations, and even in Germany, the real home of the Clavier
[clavichord], and to find, especially in the southern parts, twenty good pianofortes,
fortpiens, clavecin-royals, and whatever else this kind of *Hackbrett* is called, for every
single tolerable Clavier.[50]

We need not concern ourselves with Cramer's objections against changing
fashion; what is important here is that the tide was definitely turning.
Especially in southern Germany, fortepianos were replacing clavichords in
ever larger numbers. Equally clear is that in 1783 the situation in Bonn can
still be safely described as fairly provincial.[51] This is not so surprising. The

---

[44] In Boßler's *Musikalische Real-Zeitung*, no. 3, July 16, 1788, a reader inquired about the nature of this
interesting instrument. An answer appeared in no. 20, November 12, 1788: "Mr. Riedlen has indeed
claimed to have made such an instrument, and that is why he had it announced in 'Cramer's
Magazin,' but as long as he was in Bonn, he never made it. He moved from there almost three years
ago, but nobody knows where he lives now." Heinrich Philipp Boßler, *Musikalische Real-Zeitung für
das Jahr 1788*, Hildesheim: Olms, 1971, 24 and 160.

[45] Unlike *Clavier*, *Instrument* is used sometimes for various keyboard instruments with experimental
actions. Those with plain hammer actions normally were called *Hammerclavier* or *fortepiano*.

[46] Compiled from Neefe's letter "Nachricht von der churfürstlich=cöllnischen Hofcapelle zu Bonn und
anderen Tonkünstlern daselbst," written on March 2, 1783, published on March 20. Cramer,
Magazin der Musik, 377–96.

[47] The Schleswig builder Jürgensen, for instance, offered a "Clavecin Royal" which he claimed was of his
own invention (the *Clavecin Royal* was actually a concept of J. G. Wagner from Dresden) and a
"Bellsonoreal" which could imitate all possible kinds of instruments. *Ibid.*, 661–2.

[48] Such as the Kassel court organ builder Wilhelm, who built square pianos of high quality after English
models. *Ibid.*, 666.

[49] *Ibid.*, 654–61. The concept may have resembled the gut-strung instrument by Riedlen mentioned
above.

[50] *Ibid.*, 1246–7. Also discussed in Komlós, *Fortepianos and their Music*, 5 (as this text partly uses very
detailed and specific vocabulary like *Clavecin Royal*, my interpretation of *Clavier* as *Clavichord*
deserves no further explanation in this case). Obviously, Cramer regretted the decline of the
clavichord as an "institution," even though the fortepianos that started to be fashionable in southern
Germany were "good" and some clavichords were merely "tolerable."

[51] See also the discussion in Frimmel, *Neue Beethoveniana*, 24–6.

earliest-known so-called German, or *Prellzungen*, piano action by Johann Andreas Stein, for example, was made as late as 1781.[52] It is in fact plausible that fortepianos of a quality to satisfy professional musicians or advanced *Liebhaber* appeared in Bonn only shortly before Neefe wrote about them in 1783.

Only four years later, the new trend had definitely arrived in Bonn. On April 8, 1787, Neefe sent another, much shorter letter to Cramer's *Magazin* in which he wrote:

The love of music is increasing greatly among the inhabitants. The Clavier is especially liked; there are here several *Hämmerclaviere* by Stein of Augsburg and other equivalent instruments.[53]

A list of nine countesses devoted to this instrument accompanies this notice. Apart from that, Beethoven, the four Mastiaux sons, the children of the *Kapellmeister*, and one young baron are mentioned as Clavier players (the list closes with "etc."). A comparison of Neefe's two letters shows clearly enough that good fortepianos such as the ones by Johann Andreas Stein, which soon became important for Beethoven's early career as a keyboard virtuoso, came to Bonn after 1783 and before 1787.

Beethoven soon found his own ways to introduce himself to the musical scene described by Neefe in 1783. His association with the household of the widow von Breuning (he soon became Clavier teacher for the two children and took part in the musical activities of the house) is but one example of his various connections. The Beethovens were close to most amateur musicians among the officials at court. Some of these were extraordinarily active. Mastiaux, a devotee of Joseph Haydn, organized house concerts in his concert hall once a week during the winter and had, apart from his many musical instruments, a huge collection of music scores. Beethoven was good friends with one of his five children, Caspar Anton, a fine Clavier player. Countess von Hatzfeld, a niece of the Elector, later received the dedication of Beethoven's "Venni Amore" variations (WoO 65), composed between 1788 and 1791.

Naturally, the arrival of any new fortepiano in these circles would soon have come to Beethoven's attention. Once he had started to take part in public performances himself, there would have been ample opportunity for Beethoven to become acquainted with the fortepiano. We can therefore assume that his association with the clavichord became less important at this stage. It is also evident that Beethoven never had much interest in the

---

[52] Claviorgan, Stadsmuseet in Gothenburg, former Göteborgs Historiska Museums kulturhistoriska samling inv. no. GM: 4478. See also Michael Latcham, "Mozart and the pianos of Johann Andreas Stein," *The Galpin Society Journal* 51 (1998): 114–53, and Michael Latcham, "Mozart and the pianos of Gabriel Anton Walter," *Early Music* 25/3 (1997): 382–400.

[53] Cramer, *Magazin der Musik*, 1386. Neefe uses "Clavier" here evidently as "keyboard instrument" and "Hämmerclaviere" to specify which kind.

Example 2.1. Concerto in E flat major WoO 4, mvt. 1, Allegro moderato, bars 95–6[54]

clavichord as a special expressive medium after the fashion of the North German School, even though it must have been the tool for his daily practice for quite some time.

Beethoven's experience with the fortepiano can be traced in documents going back to 1783. During the late autumn of that year, he traveled with his mother to Rotterdam and played "a great deal in great houses, astonished people by his skill and received valuable presents."[55] On November 23, he performed on the "forte piano" at the court in The Hague, in a concert where Carl Stamitz played the viola. Apparently Beethoven, and probably Stamitz too, played solo concerti. There was an orchestra present, and Beethoven's payment was sixty-three guilders, that of Stamitz fourteen, while the other musicians involved received only seven guilders.[56] What music Beethoven played is not known.

The surviving copy of the keyboard part of Beethoven's 1784 Piano Concerto in E flat major (WoO 4) is not in his hand but bears a title written by him: "Un Concert pour le Clavecin ou Forte-Piano Composé par Louis Van Beethoven agé douze ans" (the age is wrong: he was thirteen years old). The keyboard part itself is headed with the word "Cembalo," and at least one passage in the first movement, with crossing sixteenth-note passages in both hands, looks as if it is inspired by the possibilities of a two-manual harpsichord (bar 96 in Example 2.1).

On the other hand, the solos in this concerto are marked with the dynamics *f*, *fp*, *p* and *pp* (sometimes in quick alternation), which would have been impossible to realize properly on a harpsichord. In addition, at three points in the first movement a "*cresc*" is indicated, as in the following example from bar 82 of the first movement (Example 2.2).

---

[54] Reproduced with the kind permission of the Staatsbibliothek zu Berlin – Preussischer Kulturbesitz. Musikabteilung mit Mendelssohn-Archiv. Mus.ms.autogr. Beethoven Artaria 125.

[55] Thayer, *Life of Beethoven*, 63, quoting a recollection by Widow Karth, a former neighbor of the Beethovens.

[56] Luc van Hasselt, "Beethoven in Holland," *Die Musikforschung* 18 (1965): 182–3. A surviving bill shows that nine of the listed musicians received seven guilders each and one three guilders. Since the regular court musicians would not appear on such a bill, van Hasselt assumes that the orchestra was bigger than the ten listed musicians, perhaps even "about twenty."

Example 2.2. Concerto in E flat major WoO 4, mvt. 1, Allegro moderato, bars 82–3[57]

The second example definitely indicates that the instrument Beethoven had in mind for this concerto was a fortepiano, and that the interlinked sixteenth notes of the first example were meant to be a virtuosic display on one keyboard. This is important because Beethoven's interest in playing the fortepiano is otherwise not documented earlier than the descriptions of his playing from 1791 and some of his musical sketches from around the same time. Both will be discussed further below.

The title pages of Beethoven's early compositions, whether autographs or printed, give no evidence of his interest in the fortepiano.[58] As Forkel's criticism from 1781 makes clear, printed editions of keyboard music often *did* contain conservative or vague indications, simply because this would ensure their appeal to all the *Clavierliebhaber*, no matter which variety of instrument they played. The printed editions of Beethoven's early keyboard works are no exception. For example, the variations WoO 63 are for "clavecin," the title page of the Sonatas WoO 47 indicates "Klavier" (while, above the first sonata, "Cembalo solo" is written). The two rondos and songs from Boßler's "Blumenlese" (WoO 48, 49, and 107, all from 1782, and WoO 108 from 1784) bear no separate indications as they are part of a large compilation of compositions called "Blumenlese für Klavierliebhaber." Only the four-hand variations WoO 67 from 1792 are for "Piano Forte."

In the autograph sources, too, Beethoven's instrument indications are conservative. In the early chamber music with keyboard, for instance, he uses various words for the harpsichord. Thus, the title of the three piano quartets WoO 36 (1785) bears the indication "clavecin" and the keyboard part is consistently marked "cembalo." The title of the woodwind trio WoO 37 (after 1785) indicates "clavicembalo."[59] Three pieces are linked to the organ: the 1782 fugue WoO 31 (which Gustav Nottebohm believed Beethoven

---

[57] Reproduced with the kind permission of the Staatsbibliothek zu Berlin – Preussischer Kulturbesitz. Musikabteilung mit Mendelssohn-Archiv. Mus.ms.autogr. Beethoven Artaria 125.

[58] In an earlier publication, Tilman Skowroneck, "Keyboard instruments of the young Beethoven," in *Beethoven and His World*, ed. Scott Burnham and Michael Steinberg, Princeton: Princeton University Press, 2000, 161, I believed it was possible to discern a tendency in the title pages, based on secondary source research. However, a renewed examination of facsimiles of the early editions and manuscripts reveals no such tendency. My thanks to Barry Cooper for drawing my attention to the problem.

[59] Georg Kinsky and Hans Halm, *Das Werk Beethovens: Thematisch-Bibliographisches Verzeichnis*, Munich: Henle, 1955, 480.

to have played at his audition for the post of second organist),[60] and the two preludes Op. 39, which are possibly from 1789.[61] The autograph of two sonata movements from around 1790 (WoO 50) has no indication. Finally, the sketches for the "Venni amore" variations WoO 65 bear the inscription "orgelVariationen," whereas in 1791 they were published for "Clavier ou Pianoforte."[62] Beethoven later played them on a fortepiano. Other sketches (for example, the sketches for a concerto in A) bear no indication at all, or they have indications such as "cembalo" or "clavicembalo," for example, the E minor *Romanze* for flute, bassoon, and keyboard instrument, and the Concerto Op. 19. This concerto, which Beethoven played in various forms in concerts during his first Viennese years, was definitely performed on fortepianos.

Beethoven's occasional use of a term that indicates the harpsichord in pieces that are unequivocally meant for the fortepiano (such as the Concerto WoO 4), or that Beethoven reportedly performed on a fortepiano (such as the Concerto Op. 19), shows that in these cases, he was indicating obbligato and soloistic keyboard parts, but not specifically the instrument. His indications probably represent a conservative usage of terminology rather than a conservative choice of instrument.

There is no surviving piano known to have been played or owned by Beethoven from before 1803, with one possible exception. During his first stay in Vienna, approximately between April 7 and 20, 1787,[63] Beethoven is thought to have played for Mozart and perhaps also to have taken some lessons from him.[64] The most trustworthy version of this story probably comes from Otto Jahn, who, on the word of a "good source" in Vienna, says that Beethoven was "taken to Mozart" and was asked to play for him.[65] If this is accurate, he would have played on Mozart's own fortepiano, an instrument attributed to Anton Walter (1782) which is preserved and playable today. This instrument normally stood in Mozart's study and was transported to all his concerts.[66] There are no reports of major public appearances by Mozart for the period when Beethoven was there, so the instrument was probably in

---

[60] Thayer, *Life of Beethoven*, 68.

[61] The indication in their first edition (Hoffmeister and Kühnel, 1803) is "pour le Fortepiano ou l'Orgue."

[62] Joseph Kerman, ed., *Ludwig van Beethoven Autograph Miscellany from ca. 1786 to 1799 (The "Kafka" Sketchbook)*, London: The Trustees of the British Museum, 1970, vol. i, f. 123v.; Kinsky and Halm, *Das Werk Beethovens*, 513.

[63] Dates according to Eduard Panzerbieter, quoted by Elliot Forbes in Thayer, *Life of Beethoven*, 87.

[64] The circumstances are somewhat unclear. Schindler (Schindler, *Beethoven as I Knew Him*, 46) and Otto Jahn (quoted, for example, in Kerst, *Die Erinnerungen an Beethoven*, vol. 1, 14) agree that Beethoven played for Mozart to the latter's acclaim. Ferdinand Ries even writes in 1838 that Beethoven received "some tuition" (Wegeler and Ries, *Biographische Notizen über Beethoven*, 86). See the discussions in Thayer, *Life of Beethoven*, 87, and Schiedermair, *Der junge Beethoven*, 182–7.

[65] Interpreting the words "taken to" literally, Beethoven would have met Mozart in his house. Schindler, on the other hand, says that the encounter took place in the rooms of Emperor Joseph. This is unlikely because Joseph left Vienna on April 20.

[66] Letter from 1855 by Carl Mozart in Wolfgang Amadeus Mozart, *Briefe und Aufzeichnungen*, ed. Ulrich Konrad, vol. vi, Munich: Deutscher Taschenbuch Verlag, 2005, 665.

Mozart's home.[67] Since Beethoven seems to have greatly impressed Mozart with his playing, we can assume that he was well acquainted with fortepiano playing at that time, providing the story is true.

On his way back from Vienna, Beethoven stayed in Augsburg with the family of Joseph Wilhelm von Schaden. Anna (Nanette) von Schaden, who showed "admirable skill on the Piano forte," was a close friend of Nannette Stein, the daughter of piano builder Johann Andreas Stein, who at the time had become a celebrity among instrument makers.[68] An entry by Nannette Stein in a conversation book from September 1824 suggests that, during his stay in Augsburg, Beethoven visited Stein's workshop and played his instruments.[69]

One of Thayer's sources from the Bonn years, the Widow Karth, remembered that Beethoven's patron Count Waldstein had given him a fortepiano as a present some unknown time after his arrival in Bonn in 1788.[70] The story of Waldstein's present is inconclusive in many ways. It is sometimes suggested in the literature that this piano was also by Stein, but there is nothing to substantiate this claim.[71] The instrument must have stayed in Bonn when Beethoven moved to Vienna, because once in Vienna, he immediately took steps to rent a grand piano.[72] One possibility is, of course, that upon his departure Beethoven returned it with gratitude to Waldstein, in anticipation of the vast offerings of the *Klavierland* Vienna. But perhaps it was not an exceptionally valuable or outstanding instrument at all. In fact we do not even know whether it was a square piano or a grand piano (for other reasons, the notion that Beethoven would have accepted a very expensive instrument is debatable as well).[73]

Sometime during the period 1790–92 (probably in 1792), there was a fortepiano with knee levers for the damping mechanism at the chapel of the Bonn court. On one page of the Kafka sketch miscellany, two distinct sets of Beethoven's sketches for a piano accompaniment for Jeremiah's lamentations, to be performed on a Klavier (instead of the organ) during Holy Week in one of these years, are preserved.[74] These sketches contain an

[67] Howard C. Robbins Landon, ed., *Das Mozart-Kompendium*, Munich: Droemer Knaur, 1990, 36.

[68] See Goebl-Streicher, Streicher, and Ladenburger, *"Diesem Menschen hätte ich mein ganzes Leben widmen mögen,"* 63, and Paul von Stetten, *Kunst-, Gewerb- und Handwerks-Geschichte der Reichs-Stadt Augsburg*, vol. II, Augsburg: 1788, 319–20. Available at www.bibliothek.uni-augsburg.de/de/dda/dr/oew/we_01107–01108/index.html (last accessed March 2, 2009). My thanks to Robin Blanton for pointing out this resource.

[69] Beck, Köhler, and Herre, eds., *Ludwig van Beethovens Konversationshefte*, vol. VI, 321; see also Thayer, *Life of Beethoven*, 88.

[70] Thayer, *Life of Beethoven*, 94.

[71] See Frimmel, *Neue Beethoveniana*, 23; Bekker, *Beethoven*, 109; and William Newman, *Beethoven on Beethoven. Playing His Piano Music His Way*, New York: Norton, 1988, 50.

[72] See Chapter 3.

[73] Solomon, *Beethoven*, 63–4, provides a discussion of Beethoven's ambivalent attitude toward financial or material support and his general inability to show his gratitude.

[74] For a discussion of the ink types and dates, see Barry Cooper, "The ink in Beethoven's 'Kafka' sketch miscellany," *Music and Letters* 68 (1987): 322. I am grateful to Barry Cooper for informing me about this specific reference to the "*Jeremiah*" sketches in his article. See also Douglas P. Johnson, *Beethoven's Early Sketches in the "Fischhof Miscellany": Berlin Autograph 28*, Ann Arbor: UMI Research Press, 1980, vol. I, 251.

"oom-pah-pah-pah" bass figure with thick *crescendo–decrescendo* hairpins and the written addition "mit dem Knie," meaning that the player should lift the damping during the "pahs" with his knee.[75] This feature points to a grand piano of the newer kind, such as Stein and some Viennese piano builders were making.

Some sketches from the Kafka miscellany that might date from around the same time contain quite extreme dynamic markings which also suggest the use of fortepianos. For example, one exercise that appears on f. 88r. together with sketches for the cantata WoO 88 from October 1790 (lines 10/9; 11/9, continued on lines 12; 13) is marked *crescendo* (plus hairpin) *ff*, *fff*, *sf* (*decrescendo* hairpin) *p*, *pp*. This exercise may, however, stem from a later date since it is written in another ink than the cantata, as even the monochrome facsimile of this page shows.[76] The appearance on the page also suggests that they were written later than the cantata sketches, making use of empty space on the page. As another example for sketches that contain extreme dynamics, the keyboard part in a sketch for the choir "Der freie Mann" WoO 117 from 1792 shows an alternation of *ff* and *sf* and ends *fff* (f. 61r).[77]

Anton Reicha, who became Beethoven's friend after arriving in Bonn in 1785, relates that Beethoven performed a Mozart concerto at the court. The details leave no doubt that this performance was on a fortepiano.[78] This fits well with the description in Boßler's *Musikalische Korrespondenz* No. 28 from July 13, 1791: "Hr. Ludwig von Beethoven plays Klavier concertos and Hr. Neefe accompanies at court, in the theater and in concerts."[79]

During a trip to Mergentheim with the court orchestra, also in 1791, Beethoven visited the keyboard virtuoso Franz Xaver Sterkel in Aschaffenburg and played on his Klavier (as will be discussed in more detail below). Sterkel owned a Stein grand piano ("Flügel") which had been sent to him on February 20, 1783.[80]

---

[75] Kerman, ed., *Ludwig van Beethoven Autograph Miscellany from ca. 1786 to 1799 (The "Kafka" Sketchbook)*, vol. 1, f. 96r.

[76] Cooper identifies it as the same ink that is used in the second set of "Jeremiah" sketches. Cooper, "The ink in Beethoven's 'Kafka' sketch miscellany," 323, 327.

[77] The page numbers refer to Kerman, ed., *Ludwig van Beethoven Autograph Miscellany from ca. 1786 to 1799 (The "Kafka" Sketchbook)*, vol. 1. The chronology of the early sketches from Bonn is discussed in the notes of vol. 11 of the same work, in Johnson, *Beethoven's Early Sketches in the "Fischhof Miscellany,"* vol. 1, 219–25, and in Cooper, "The ink in Beethoven's 'Kafka' sketch miscellany." In his appendix, Cooper conveniently provides the dates, paper sorts, and ink sorts in one table.

[78] Jacques-Gabriel Prod'homme, "From the unpublished autobiography of Antoine Reicha," *Music Quarterly* 22/3 (1936): 351.

[79] Kerst, *Die Erinnerungen an Beethoven*, vol. 1, 15. Thayer's interpretation that Beethoven was "being made court pianist" (Thayer, *Life of Beethoven*, 107) suggests an actual position and appears unfounded.

[80] Goebl-Streicher, Streicher, and Ladenburger, *"Diesem Menschen hätte ich mein ganzes Leben widmen mögen,"* 55.

On the same journey, he encountered Carl Ludwig Junker, who then wrote a lengthy article describing Beethoven's playing as brilliant and idiosyncratic in a most positive way. Junker relates that Beethoven refused to perform in public because the instrument on that occasion was a Flügel by Spath, and in Bonn Beethoven was "accustomed only to play upon one by Stein."[81]

From all this it is clear that, during Beethoven's last years in Bonn, the fortepiano became well established both in the local musical scene and in Beethoven's personal practice. In the following section, I will explain how Reicha's recollection, and the information and anecdotes from the Mergentheim trip, relate to Beethoven's playing style at that time. I will also discuss the characteristics of the instruments in question.

A SUITABLE TOUCH – EXPLORING A NEW INSTRUMENT

In 1825, Beethoven told the visiting organist Karl Gottlieb Freudenberg: "I, too, played the organ often in my youth, but my nerves could not endure the force of this huge instrument. If an organist is master of his instrument, I rank him highest among the virtuosos."[82] In 1790 or 1791, Beethoven could evidently still endure the force of the "Rieseninstrument," as an anecdote related by Professor Wurzer (Beethoven's former classmate) suggests. A group of friends had talked Beethoven into trying out the organ in the freshly renovated church of Marienforst near Godesberg, and with "his great good nature" he "soon" yielded to the request.[83] He then improvised on themes given to him by the company. His playing greatly moved his friends and some "simple workers" who were busy cleaning the church.[84]

A cluster of reports from the early 1790s and their discussions in the literature have created the impression that playing the organ and performing on the fortepiano did not go together very well for Beethoven. That Beethoven's keyboard technique at least once led to complications during a concert is evident from Reicha's aforementioned description of Beethoven performing a Mozart concerto at the Bonn court:

One evening when Beethoven was playing a Mozart piano concerto at the Court, he asked me to turn the pages for him. But I was mostly occupied in wrenching out the strings of the piano, which snapped, while the hammers stuck among the broken strings. Beethoven insisted upon finishing the concerto, so back and forth I leaped, jerking out a string, disentangling a hammer, turning a page, and I worked harder than did Beethoven.[85]

[81] Kerst, *Die Erinnerungen an Beethoven*, vol. I, 17.   [82] *Ibid.*, vol. II, 114.
[83] In this anecdote there is no evidence of Beethoven's reluctance to play on demand. At the time, apparently, a request from a group of friends of his age did not trigger any negative reactions.
[84] Kerst, *Die Erinnerungen an Beethoven*, vol. I, 14.
[85] Translation from Prod'homme, "From the unpublished autobiography of Antoine Reicha," 351.

As has been pointed out above, Reicha's arrival in Bonn in 1785 allows us to date this incident to some time between that year and 1792, when Beethoven left Bonn.[86] Of course, without knowing more about the circumstances, it is impossible to draw definite conclusions about Beethoven's playing technique. Modern experience of playing early forte-pianos with strings that have been produced in our time suggests that it is extremely hard to break the strings in such instruments by playing without first damaging parts of the action.[87] Also, the sound of any kind of early piano would become very ugly long before a string actually broke.

Such modern experience cannot, however, be transferred to the historical situation without further consideration. The inevitability of string breakage, especially as a consequence of excessive pounding, must have been a major issue at the time, since it is mentioned in various manuals about tuning and instrument maintenance from around 1800.[88] From these sources it becomes very clear that historical stringing and modern replacement materials cannot be directly compared.[89]

String breakage in early pianos could occur in areas where the tension is closest to the breaking point of the strings. It could also result from structural weaknesses in some of the handcrafted strings. Such structural weaknesses usually reveal themselves when other conditions change: on the first few occasions when a new instrument is used for a whole performance, after an instrument has been tuned up (for instance, to match the pitch of an orchestra), or in reaction to climatic changes caused by, for instance, sudden drafts, candles, or the audience. The rise in pitch caused by the increase in humidity and drop in temperature associated with a sudden thunderstorm in an environment with large single-pane windows might, for example, cause the most critical strings of an instrument to snap spontaneously if the instrument was already tuned relatively high.[90]

---

[86] Tia DeNora has mistakenly suggested that this incident took place 1795 in Vienna (Tia DeNora, *Beethoven and the Construction of Genius*, Berkeley: University of California Press, 1995, 175). In 1795, Reicha lived in Hamburg. He arrived in Vienna from Paris in October 1802 (Beethoven, *Briefwechsel*, vol. 1, 151, n12). See also Olga Šolotová, *Antonín Rejcha*, trans. Deryck Viney, Prague: Supraphon, 1990, 12.

[87] This observation refers to the kinds of strings usually found in modern copies of historical pianos. Such strings are made of soft metal and have properties that (up to a certain level) are comparable with historical strings. However, they are produced to more regular standards than some historical strings.

[88] See, for example, Andreas Streicher, *Kurze Bemerkungen über das Spielen, Stimmen und Erhalten der Fortepiano, welche von Nannette Streicher, geborene Stein in Wien verfertiget warden 1801*, The Hague: Lelieveld, 1979, 10, 21, 23–4; the elaboration of Streicher's book in Johann Lorenz Schiedmayer and Carl Dieudonné, *Kurze Anleitung zu einer richtigen Behandlung der Forte-Pianos 1824*, Tübingen: Gulde-Verlag, 1994, 31, 38, and 50; and Joseph Gall, ed., *Clavier–Stimmbuch, oder deutliche Anweisung wie jeder Musikfreund sein Clavier–Flügel, Fortepiano und Flügel–Fortepiano selbst stimmen, reparieren, und bestmöglichst gut erhalten könne*, Vienna: Carl Kupffer, 1805, 119–20.

[89] The majority of historical strings that have remained in the instruments are safe today. Any uneven or otherwise faulty old string has had the opportunity to break at any moment during the past centuries. Surviving original strings are bound to represent the very best standard of historical strings.

[90] Based on personal experience. My thanks also to Paul Poletti for sharing with me his research on scaling and string breakage in early pianos.

Another possibility is that Beethoven indeed played too loudly, or was carried away by his temperament, or was especially tense because he was performing a concerto at the court.

Finally, it is not entirely clear from Reicha's story just how serious the trouble actually was. Disentangling broken strings during an ongoing performance is an intricate maneuver to be performed quickly; this consideration, along with the obvious pleasure Reicha has in telling this story, might well suggest that it reflects Reicha's involvement rather than the actual number of broken strings. The fact that Beethoven played on suggests that this number may have been lower than Reicha implies.

The assumption that the young Beethoven indeed had a heavy touch during a certain period helps to explain a famous but contradictory passage by Wegeler. Wegeler retells an anecdote about Beethoven's visit to Abbé Franz Xaver Sterkel in Aschaffenburg. This event took place during the Bonn orchestra's journey to Mergentheim in the late summer of 1791. Besides Wegeler's version, which is based on an otherwise unknown verbal account by Franz Ries, there is also a firsthand account of the event from Nikolaus Simrock, who was, like Ries, present on the occasion.[91]

After playing for his visitors, Sterkel asked Beethoven to play some of his newly published Righini variations (WoO 65). Sterkel could not find the music and Beethoven was forced to play from memory, which he initially refused to do. When it became clear that Sterkel suspected him of being unable to play the variations, he finally played. Both versions of the story agree upon his ability to play the music from memory, to add a few improvised variations, and also to imitate the elegance and ease of Sterkel's playing, as Wegeler says, "to the greatest surprise of the listeners." Simrock explains the "amazement" of the Bonn musicians present from the fact that they had never heard Beethoven play in this way earlier.

At the beginning of Wegeler's account, however, we find a comment that seems altogether irreconcilable with Beethoven's ability to adjust his playing spontaneously to Sterkel's elegant manner:

Beethoven, who until then had not heard any great, outstanding Clavier player, did not know the finer *nuances* in the treatment of the instrument; his playing was rough and hard.[92]

The literature has been oddly forgiving regarding the obvious incompatibility of this statement with, on the one hand, the known facts (Beethoven had, before 1791, already visited the Netherlands and Vienna, and a common assumption in the literature is that he had certainly already heard other famous keyboard players) and, on the other, the content of the anecdote

---

[91] Kerst, *Die Erinnerungen an Beethoven*, vol. 1, 19; Wegeler and Ries, *Biographische Notizen über Beethoven*, 17.
[92] *Ibid.*

itself. Schiedermair adds an editorial question mark to the claim that Beethoven had not heard a great Clavier player and an exclamation mark after "hard."[93] Thayer leaves the sentence uncommented upon,[94] while Schindler mentions another contrast: that between Beethoven's flexibility on this occasion and two accounts of Beethoven's later inability to "adopt another pianist's style" (referring to characterizations by John Cramer and Cherubini that date from 1799 and 1805 respectively).[95] Newman acknowledges the contradiction in passing.[96] Frimmel writes, "These reliable details from Wegeler reveal that his playing then, that is in his twenty-first year, was only agreeable by way of exception, but usually rough and harsh, and hence agreed with his general disposition."[97] Finally, Siegbert Rampe accepts Beethoven's technical flexibility in this anecdote as a part of Beethoven's general disposition and describes his "characteristic heavy touch" as a deliberate means to "expand the fortepiano tone to its limits and beyond."[98]

In an earlier attempt to interpret Wegeler's comment, I have, by contrast, suggested that he might have been wrong about the chronology and that "the testimony about his rough playing simply found its way into the wrong story."[99] A close examination of the narrative technique in the anecdotes further strengthens this assumption. The intended climax of the story is, evidently, the "greatest surprise" or the "amazement" of the listeners, who "had never heard Beethoven play in this way earlier." In order to make this effect even clearer, Franz Ries apparently inserted a description of his own about the "rough" playing style the Bonn musicians otherwise knew from Beethoven. In retelling Ries's version, Wegeler simply omits to forge a convincing logical connection between his first sentence and the following anecdote: the point of the story was the *very fact* that Beethoven suddenly and unexpectedly displayed qualities that (indeed) seemed altogether incompatible with his usual ways. Ries's (or Wegeler's) explanation for Beethoven's "rough" playing is probably truthful, but it belongs to a time before the late summer of 1791 and the words "until then" are simply inexact.

Schindler explains the whole in the following way: "Beethoven himself blamed the harshness of his touch at that time on his constant playing of the organ."[100] Unfortunately, Schindler does not make it at all clear whether he actually talked with Beethoven about his performance at Sterkel's in particular (in which case it would have been Beethoven himself who told Schindler all the circumstances, since both Wegeler's and Simrock's

---

[93] Schiedermair, *Der junge Beethoven*, 213.   [94] Thayer, *Life of Beethoven*, 103.
[95] Schindler, *Beethoven as I Knew Him*, 43.   [96] Newman, *Beethoven on Beethoven*, 80.
[97] Frimmel, *Neue Beethoveniana*, 20.
[98] Rampe, "Wiener und Englische Mechaniken," in "Beethovens Klavier – Klangwelt und Aufführungspraxis" (copy provided by the author).
[99] Skowroneck, "Keyboard instruments of the young Beethoven," 164.
[100] Schindler, *Beethoven as I Knew Him*, 44.

versions became known to the public only after Beethoven's death), or whether he just combined his recollection of a remark by Beethoven with this particular story, which he had read in Wegeler's book.

Whatever the correct explanation for Wegeler's comment may be, it is obvious that in the late summer of 1791 Beethoven's technique was not rough any more, or at least not necessarily *only* rough, and that this development was quite remarkable even to musical observers. A well-known description of Beethoven's playing later during the same journey was written by Carl Ludwig Junker in the November of that year. Here we also find the first evidence of Beethoven's interest in the quality of keyboard instruments (Junker had listened to rehearsals and concerts of the musicians of the Bonn court chapel during their stay at Mergentheim, on October 11 and 12, 1791):

I also heard one of the greatest Klavier players, the dear, good Bethofen, some compositions by whom appeared in the Speier Blumenlese in 1783, written in his eleventh year. True, he did not perform in public, perhaps because the instrument was not to his taste. It was a Flügel by Spath and in Bonn he is accustomed only to play upon one by Stein. Yet, to my far greater pleasure, I heard him extemporize, I was even invited to give a theme for him to vary. One can, I believe, safely measure the virtuosity of this kind, quiet man by the sheer inexhaustible wealth of his ideas, by the completely personal kind of expressivity of his playing and by the dexterity of his playing. So I cannot imagine what could prevent him from achieving the greatness of a true artist. I have heard Vogler on the fortepiano … often and for hours at a time, and always admired his exceptional skill, but Beethoven is, apart from his skill, more speaking, more significant, more expressive, in a word more for the heart: that is, [just as] good an adagio player as an allegro player. Even all the outstanding members of this orchestra [the Elector's orchestra] are his admirers and are all ears when he plays. But he remains modest and free from all pretension. Nevertheless he confessed that, during the journeys that the Elector had enabled him to make, he had seldom found in the playing of the most famous Klavier players what he supposed he had a right to expect. His playing differs so much from the usual way of treating the Klavier that it seems as if he has made his own path towards the perfection he has now reached.[101]

It has been observed that, when writing his article, Junker "had much to gain from being impressed and absolutely nothing to gain from criticizing." His enthusiastic report was perhaps even an attempt to "depict himself close to court society."[102] We should, therefore, especially appreciate the fact that most of the details in his account agree with other descriptions of Beethoven's character and playing from that time: for example, his unwillingness to play upon request is also evident in the Ries/Simrock anecdote.

---

[101] Carl Ludwig Junker in Boßler's *Musikalische Korrespondenz* 47, November 23, 1791, quoted in Kerst, *Die Erinnerungen an Beethoven*, vol. I, 17–19. William Newman erroneously writes that Beethoven rejected the Spath Flügel and preferred Stein's fortepianos in 1783 (Newman, "Beethoven's pianos versus his piano ideals," 486, and Newman, *Beethoven on Beethoven*, 50).

[102] DeNora, *Beethoven and the Construction of Genius*, 68–9.

This idiosyncrasy was to become constant in later years; the only interesting element here is that his reason for not playing in public was the instrument. His early skill in improvising with dexterity and imagination is documented in Wurzer's account mentioned above. In another early description, Wegeler relates how Beethoven, at the von Breunings', was asked to characterize various well-known persons through his playing.[103] The two versions of the Sterkel anecdote also support his ability. While as a youngster he could be "stubborn and unfriendly" in private,[104] by 1784 the above-mentioned *pro memoriam* of the Bonn court attested to his "good and quiet conduct" in public, which matches well with Junker's characterizations "dear," "good," "kind," and "quiet." The only real disagreement (with Wegeler's account) has to do with Beethoven's travels and his having heard other famous keyboardists.

There is every reason to believe that the new information contained in Junker's text is accurate as well. Most interesting is the fact that Beethoven, at twenty, already played markedly differently from other fortepianists in a *positive* sense and that he thought about playing in a different way from others (his disapproval of the usual manner of treating the fortepiano recurs in his correspondence with Andreas Streicher in 1796, which is discussed below).

Taken together, the evidence of Wegeler's, Simrock's, and Junker's anecdotes suggests that Beethoven, in the fall of 1791, had recently been making deliberate efforts to improve his technique of playing, specifically, the fortepiano. These efforts, which can be clearly seen in connection with (or were perhaps even directly inspired by) Stein's pianos (on which he was "accustomed to play"), and which perhaps also related to some of the surviving early sketches of technical exercises, bore fruit quickly enough to surprise even the musicians that knew Beethoven well.[105]

SPATH'S AND STEIN'S KLAVIERE

Beethoven's refusal to perform on a Spath instrument deserves a short discussion. Franz Jacob Spath from Regensburg (1714–86) was especially known for his *Tangentenflügel* (a term only employed from around 1790).[106] These instruments have an action different from the clavichord, harpsichord, and fortepiano (see Figure 2.1). Upon depressing the key, a wooden strip not unlike a harpsichord jack[107] is propelled by means of an intermediate lever upward to the string. It strikes the string, allowing for dynamic variation, and then immediately falls back.

---

[103] Wegeler and Ries, *Biographische Notizen über Beethoven*, 20.   [104] *Ibid.*, 10.
[105] For another discussion of these sketches, see Rosenblum, *Performance Practices in Classic Piano Music*, 204–9.
[106] See Latcham, "Franz Jakob Spath and the Tangentenflügel, an eighteenth-century tradition." The issue of the missing umlaut in historical references to Spath (who today is often called Späth) is briefly addressed in this article.
[107] The term "tangent" was occasionally used for harpsichord jacks too.

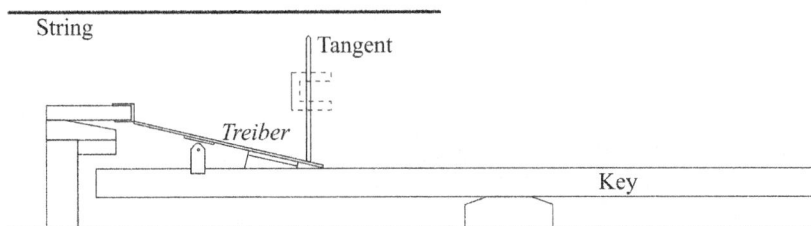

Figure 2.1. Diagram of a tangent action[108]

The top of the tangent is usually not covered with leather like most piano hammers, producing a sound not unlike a large clavichord. However, the surviving instruments have at least four stops that allow for a whole range of variations in timbre. Such variations are to be seen as integral to the instrument's concept.[109]

We cannot be completely certain that the rejected Flügel had such a tangent action.[110] Spath was known for making a variety of keyboard instruments.[111] It is perhaps *likely* that the Mergentheim Flügel was such an instrument, but even so, it is impossible to trace the exact nature of Beethoven's problems. Since Beethoven did agree to improvise on the Spath, it is possible that it was simply acoustically unsuited for a performance for a larger audience. The *c.* 1785 Spath & Schmahl *Tangentenflügel* in the National Music Museum in Vermillion is a perfectly good match for the medium-sized hall at the museum, but if played in a large hall with a high ceiling it would probably sound very soft.[112] Another significant difference between Stein's *Hammerflügel* and Spath's *Tangentenflügel* is the dynamic control for the player: while a good tangent action can be even and pleasant enough to be played with confidence, it also has a tendency to be unresponsive at lower dynamic levels. Stein's action, by contrast, was designed to give the player the utmost control down to very soft levels; a well-regulated Stein action is in this respect definitely superior.[113]

---

[108] Dampers and other parts of the construction omitted. This drawing is based on Christo Lelie, *Van piano tot forte*, Kampen: Kok Lyra, 1995, 80, and Rosamond E.M. Harding, *The Piano-Forte*, 2nd ed., London: Heckscher & Co., 1933 and 1978, 50, but is not to scale.

[109] Latcham, "Franz Jakob Spath and the Tangentenflügel, an eighteenth-century tradition," 156–63.

[110] This is also the case with the preference Mozart expressed for Stein's instruments instead of Spath's in his letter from October 17, 1777. Mozart, *Briefe und Aufzeichnungen*, vol. II, 68.

[111] The National Music Museum in Vermillion, South Dakota, owns a short-scale grand piano by Frantz Jacob Spath from 1767 (Cat. No. NMM 13010) which is equipped with a simple hammer action (*Stoßmechanik*) without an escapement. See also Latcham, "Franz Jakob Spath and the Tangentenflügel, an eighteenth-century tradition," 154.

[112] Cat. No. NMM 4145.

[113] My thanks to John Koster from the National Music Museum in Vermillion, South Dakota, for allowing me to play on the *c.* 1785 *Tangentenflügel*, and to Mats Krouthén of the Ringve Museum in Trondheim, Norway, and the Gothenburg *Stadsmuseum* for letting me examine the actions of their Stein grand pianos.

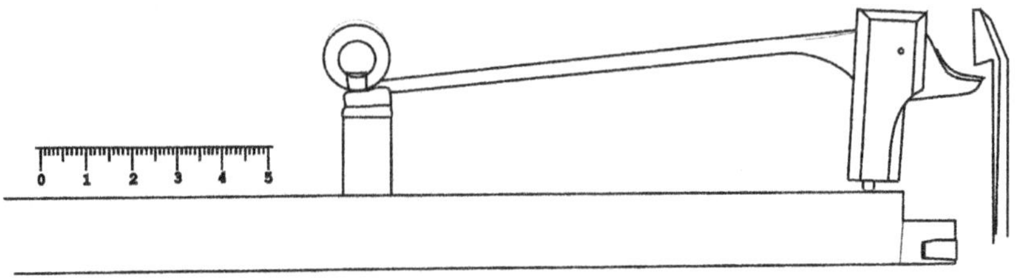

Figure 2.2. Stein Phase II action (Gothenburg claviorgan)

From a modern standpoint, in a world of standardized piano keyboards, it would certainly seem logical that Beethoven hesitated to play in public on an instrument that was quite different from the ones he knew well. My suggestion that during this period he was actively (and apparently self-consciously) working to improve his fortepiano technique would fit such an explanation well. But it is impossible to assess what degree of variety in keyboard instruments was acceptable, even to an ambitious young player, at a time when typical keyboardists were accustomed to moving freely between harpsichords, organs, clavichords, and fortepianos of various kinds.

While little can be said about the Spath Klavier in Mergentheim, more is known about the characteristics of Johann Andreas Stein's fortepianos during the 1780s, to which Beethoven had access in Bonn.[114] Sixteen of Stein's fortepianos from 1781 onwards still exist. This may represent about three percent of Stein's total output. Some of the instruments have been restored to playing condition.

Organologist Michael Latcham has divided the surviving Stein pianos into three phases.[115] The second phase, *c.* 1781–83, is certainly of interest here. It is represented by six surviving instruments. Instruments of this type would have been in circulation even after Stein changed the design of his action at some time during 1783. As mentioned above, for instance, Franz Xaver Sterkel had owned a Stein Flügel since the spring of 1783, on which Beethoven quite probably played in 1791.

The German action (*Prellzungenmechanik*) of Stein's Phase II instruments featured wooden Kapseln, hollow, round, wooden hammer heads[116] that are glued to the hammer shanks and secured by thin strips of leather, and no hammer checks. These hammers were, as far as is known, originally covered with one layer of leather (Figure 2.2).

---

[114] Many modern Stein "copies" have modified actions that do not possess the properties of the originals.

[115] See Latcham, "Mozart and the pianos of Johann Andreas Stein," 122–3. The three phases are discussed in detail on pp. 136–43 of the same article.

[116] Described as "ring shaped cores of barberry wood" in John Koster, *Keyboard Musical Instruments in the Museum of Fine Arts, Boston*, Boston: Museum of Fine Arts, 1994, 134. The specification "cane" or "bamboo" for the hammers that can sometimes be found does not apply to the instruments in Gothenburg, Boston, and Trondheim. These hammers all have annual rings.

Stein's third phase (1783–92) is represented by ten surviving grand pianos. Here too, the Kapseln are wooden and there are no checks. The hammers in these instruments are solid, club-shaped and were, as Latcham suggests, covered with one or two layers of leather.[117] The stringing, the internal construction, and the design of the hammer escapement also differ from those in earlier instruments.

Of all these details, those that bear upon the sound character of the instrument and its responsiveness to various styles of playing are of most interest here. One central item in the discussion of sound is the covering of the hammers. Hammer leathers have been replaced as a matter of maintenance on most historical pianos. While doing so, an upgrade of the sound character was often attempted. During this process, some of the original materials may have been removed. This has inspired a very careful approach among organologists and restorers in the field: the idea of using less, or even no, leather on early piano hammer heads is beginning to be accepted as a true possibility for the sound world of the late eighteenth century, even for instruments other than the *Tangentenflügel*.

Depending on the construction of a piano and the dimensions of the hammers in relation to the stringing, bare or almost bare hammers can produce timbres roughly covering the range between the sound of a clavichord and that of a hammered dulcimer.[118] Michael Latcham has argued that instruments with bare hammers often had devices to alter the timbre, as in the case of Spath's *Tangentenflügel*.[119] One important feature of Stein's pianos is that there are generally no such *Veränderungen*, apart from a knee lever to lift the damping.[120] Only the two earliest Stein instruments, the 1777 so-called *Vis-à-vis* (with bare wooden hammers) and the 1781 claviorgan in Gothenburg, have original moderators (a register where a layer of cloth is inserted between the hammer and the string).[121]

The Gothenburg claviorgan hammers feature a layer of leather of graduated thickness (below two other, probably unoriginal, layers) that matches the rather firm original beak leather, and that therefore also seems original despite the confusing fact that it was detached and re-glued for an unknown reason some time *after* the other layers were mounted.[122] The thickness is around 1.5 mm at FF and *c.* 0.5 mm from d' upwards. The hammer leathers

[117] Latcham, "Mozart and the pianos of Johann Andreas Stein," 141, 143.

[118] See Bram Gätjen, "Das Hammerklavier – akustisches Bindeglied zwischen Clavichord, Cembalo und modernem Flügel? Untersuchungen zur Wechselwirkung zwischen Hammer und Saite," in Monika Lustig, ed., *Zur Geschichte des Hammerklaviers*, Institut für Aufführungspraxis Michaelstein, 1993.

[119] See Michael Latcham, "Swirling from one level of the affects to another: the expressive Clavier in Mozart's time," *Early Music* 30/4 (2002): 512–13.

[120] The 1781 claviorgan has hand stops instead of knee levers for the dampers, clearly because the organ case is in the way, and because the feet are already operating the bellows.

[121] Latcham, "Franz Jakob Spath and the Tangentenflügel, an eighteenth-century tradition," 152, esp. n. 15.

[122] The first layer matches the beak leather perfectly under ten-times magnification.

in another 1783 (Phase II) instrument are similar in thickness, but made from "compact, fine-textured chamois leather."[123] Even after Stein began to use solid hammer heads and two layers of leather, these were, by comparison with most later fortepianos, very thin.[124] The sound that these pianos produce is considerably brighter than the average sound that has become customary in the fortepiano playing of our time. On the instrument in Gothenburg a few test chords are playable with a regulated action and proper stringing. The touch feels very precise and quite light, but in comparison with other historical pianos from the Viennese tradition not surprisingly so; the tone is brilliant but pleasant and the treble sustain is astonishingly good. The 1783 Trondheim piano is not kept in a playing condition.[125] Phase III pianos with solid hammers could produce somewhat more volume than the earlier instruments.[126]

The special feature in Stein's actions that generated some historical discussion and has strongly influenced modern opinion is the absence of a hammer check in his instruments. Such a device has the function of catching the hammer on its return from the attack, preventing it from hopping up and striking the string again. A detailed discussion about the function of the check is part of my further comparison between Walter's and the Geschwister Stein fortepianos.[127] Here it suffices to say that, in newly regulated instruments, this particular characteristic of Stein's design would not have been seen as problematic, nor would it have been outdated in 1791. Instruments with similar actions were built until after 1800, and their regulation is still described in some detail in an owner's manual from 1814.[128]

If by 1791 Beethoven was indeed used to playing on a piano by Stein, the clavichord and the harpsichord evidently belonged to his musical past at this point. After 1783, Stein's fortepianos displayed one consistent feature, which is that one basic timbre is supplied by the builder whereas tonal variation is to be achieved by the touch of the player, aided by a very carefully crafted action; Beethoven had not simply become acquainted with some piano, he had gotten used to that particular concept. This link between instrument and player finds its modern counterpart among brand-oriented concert

---

[123] Latcham, "Mozart and the pianos of Johann Andreas Stein," 138. Satisfyingly, Latcham can report that the original leather, which today is covered by another, newer top layer, originally "has been in contact with strings."

[124] See the pictures in *ibid.*, 143, and especially in Latcham, "Swirling from one level of the affects to another," 510. Although no measurements are provided with the latter picture, careful comparison with my material suggests that the layer of the 1788–1 hammer that is shown had a leather layer only slightly thicker than 1 mm.

[125] A recording made between 1975 and 1979 (Klaverinstrumenter på Ringve Museum, RMCD 60. 001) is not very conclusive. The recording technique is unflattering and the instrument was not very well regulated at the moment of the recording. The unequal and too heavy stringing and partly unoriginal leathering in the instrument's present state further explain the poor sound.

[126] Latcham, "Mozart and the Pianos of Johann Andreas Stein," 151.   [127] See Chapter 3.

[128] Schiedmayer and Dieudonné, *Kurze Anleitung zu einer richtigen Behandlung der Forte-Pianos*, 64.

pianists. In terms of late eighteenth-century Clavier playing, however, it must have been a novelty.

Our excitement about the connection between Stein's fortepianos and Beethoven should not blind us to the fact that the instruments under discussion have sound properties that, in comparison with the ubiquitous modern *c.* 1800 Anton Walter copy, might be called archaic. Stein's instruments are brilliant and responsive; they react well to impulsive attacks, but not to weighty pounding; they sound elegant but never massive. Considering the future of Beethoven's piano writing, they do, however, lack certain possibilities. They were nevertheless important for him during the time he shaped his personal playing style. If we regard them as made to fit the requirements of their time, they were among the best available, and Beethoven was, like everyone else, certainly aware of this.

To summarize, it is possible to establish with some certainty that 1791 was the decisive year for Beethoven's development, from an enthusiastic and virtuosic player of various keyboard instruments (especially the organ) whose playing sometimes lacked sophistication, to a fortepianist with a large expressive range. Although his private instrument of that time is not known, circumstantial evidence suggests that his new skills are closely connected to the possibilities of the pianos of Johann Andreas Stein. To the modern listener, Stein's pianos perhaps do not stand out as a typical medium for Beethovenian power; they sound elegant and have an action that reacts to the subtlest differences of touch. It is, however, clear that Beethoven was used to Stein's instruments at that time and that he was reluctant to take the risk of performing on instruments of another builder, such as Spath. The harpsichord and the clavichord were definitely things of the past when Beethoven made his decisive move to Vienna.

CHAPTER 3

Beethoven's first decade in Vienna

THE FIRST YEAR

Beethoven's first year in Vienna is in fact not very well documented. We do know that he had financial troubles after the death of his father on December 18, 1792, when he had to ensure that he received his rightful salary from Bonn.[1] A late source, addressing his first months in Vienna, says that he generally had "a miserable time."[2] Anton Schindler writes that, upon his arrival, Beethoven carried letters of introduction from the Elector Max Franz to various prominent persons in Vienna. He claims that Baron van Swieten became one of Beethoven's first and most influential friends, even though Beethoven's connection to the Lichnowsky family was "the most important" one, but gives no exact dates for Beethoven's introduction in these circles.[3] Theodor Frimmel suspects that it was Count Waldstein (and not the Elector) who helped to "open all the doors" to Beethoven, since he was acquainted with "almost all the high nobility of Austria."[4]

It is, in any case, impossible to create a detailed account of Beethoven's activities based on the scanty material dating from the first year. However, one can establish a chronology of the information that has to do with his keyboard playing and his first musical contacts. Beethoven's first year unfolds as follows.

By the time Beethoven moved to Vienna in November 1792, he no longer considered any keyboard instrument other than a fortepiano suitable for his private use. On page three of his diary from that time, in the midst of other entries from his first weeks in Vienna, we find two addresses that correspond to two advertisements in the *Wiener Zeitung* from November 10, 1792.[5] One of these advertised a "very beautiful fortepiano with two mutations."

---

[1] See his calculations and comments in his diary p. 5v. from December 1792, Dagmar von Busch-Weise, "Beethovens Jugendtagebuch," *Studien zur Musikwissenschaft* 25 (1962): 73, and the letter to the Elector Max Franz from April 1793 (Beethoven, *Briefwechsel*, vol. 1, 12).

[2] Karl Holz according to Otto Jahn, Thayer, *Life of Beethoven*, 258.

[3] Schindler, *Beethoven as I Knew Him*, 48–9.

[4] Frimmel, *Beethoven-Handbuch*, vol. 11, 398. See also Thayer, *Life of Beethoven*, 160–1.

[5] Busch-Weise, "Beethovens Jugendtagebuch," 85, n. 35. Compare with Richard Maunder, *Keyboard Instruments in Eighteenth-Century Vienna*, Oxford: Clarendon Press, 1998, 170, entry for October 17 and second entry for November 10.

Beethoven crossed out this address. The other advertisement by an instrument dealer (whose name recurs in the *Wiener Zeitung*, but who has not been identified)[6] offers "two large *forte piano*." The maker (or makers) of these instruments and the persons who placed the advertisements are not known. We also know nothing about the instrument Beethoven eventually obtained, but it is evident that he was interested in "large fortepianos." On the next page of his diary (5r.) and the two following pages there are three entries of 6 *Gulden* and 40 *Kreuzer*, two of which are marked "Klawier." One of these stands before an entry from December 12, 1792, and two come after that date. This amount is small in comparison with other amounts on these pages; boots cost 6 *Gulden* (5v.) and the house rent 14 *Gulden* (6v.). The most logical explanation, particularly in the light of Beethoven's economic situation in his early time in Vienna, is that he initially rented an instrument.

An early anecdote about Beethoven's musical activity comes from the composer Johann Schenk; the story also involves the Klavier virtuoso Abbé Gelinek and Baron van Swieten. Schenk first heard from Gelinek that Beethoven was making slow progress in his studies with Haydn, and that van Swieten had seriously advised Beethoven to take further counterpoint studies elsewhere. Beethoven then met Schenk at Gelinek's residence and improvised for him, whereupon Schenk agreed to help Beethoven and to correct the faulty counterpoint exercises behind Haydn's back.[7] Unfortunately, this otherwise quite detailed story has some serious chronological flaws that have been frequently discussed in the literature. Schenk's indication of the date (July 1792) is obviously wrong because Beethoven did not arrive in Vienna until later; from his statement that Beethoven had already worked with Haydn for "more than six months" it seems that these events cannot have taken place before the late spring of 1793. However, the secret tuition ended in mid-June of that year: Schenk quotes a letter from Beethoven which he wrote before traveling to Eisenstadt on June 19, 1793. In this letter, Beethoven thanks Schenk for what he has done for him and promises to compensate him.[8] On the one hand, Schenk's reference to this trip makes it seem even less likely that he simply remembers the wrong year and the correct month (July), but on the other hand, it seems curious that the tuition should have begun in May (i.e. six months after Beethoven's arrival) and lasted only one month.[9]

Whatever the exact chronology in this anecdote, we can establish that the Beethoven–Gelinek piano duel famously described by Carl Czerny took place before Beethoven's encounter with Schenk. Czerny writes that he "still remembers" how Gelinek was invited one evening to compete with an

[6] Maunder, *Keyboard Instruments in Eighteenth-Century Vienna*, 236.
[7] Kerst, *Die Erinnerungen an Beethoven*, vol. 1, 25–8. See also Schindler, *Beethoven as I Knew Him*, 53–4.
[8] Beethoven, *Briefwechsel*, vol. 1, 14.   [9] See also Thayer, *Life of Beethoven*, 142–3.

unknown pianist, who outplayed him with his improvisations and with his compositions. This pianist was Beethoven, "A small, ugly, dark, and stubborn-looking young man who had come from Germany a few years before at Lichnowsky's request to study with Haydn, Albrechtsberger, and Salieri."[10] Typical for Czerny is his failure to distinguish here between his own recollection and information he collected at a later time (which is of varying correctness): it was not Lichnowsky who brought Beethoven to Vienna; the comment "a few years before" suggests too late a date, as do the names of Albrechtsberger (who taught Beethoven in 1794) and Salieri (who taught him around 1800).[11] Even if Schenk was indeed mistaken by a whole year and met Beethoven only in July 1793, this still means that Beethoven knew Gelinek before that date; if Beethoven was "unknown" to Gelinek at the time of their duel, one can suppose that Czerny's anecdote refers to events of early 1793 at the latest. So, in spite of his claim, it is unlikely that Czerny personally recalled this incident, since he was born in 1791; the story must have belonged to the family repertoire.

From Schenk's anecdote we can conclude that Baron van Swieten took an early interest in Beethoven's progress in his counterpoint studies. In view of the close connection between van Swieten and Haydn, this is not surprising. In the autumn of 1793, there is actual evidence of closer contact between Beethoven and van Swieten: in a column of his diary headed with the words: "Counted from the first of November," Beethoven noted that he had eaten at van Swieten's and paid the doorkeeper 4 *Kreuzer*.[12]

A more actively musical connection may have been Beethoven's acquaintance with Baron Nikolaus Zmeskall, whom he knew in June 1793, as is apparent from a letter to Zmeskall dated June 18, 1793,[13] and who soon became a close friend. Zmeskall was a good violoncellist.

In a conversation book entry from March 1820, an unknown person recalls one circle that "frequently" gathered "more than twenty-five years ago." Including the writer and Beethoven, there were eight people who "made music, ate supper and had punch" ("musizirt & soupirt & poun-schirt"), after which Beethoven "often" entertained the group on the writer's "P.[iano]f.[orte]."[14]

For such appearances he naturally used the fortepiano provided for the occasion. After 1790, the fortepiano had definitely replaced the harpsichord (and the clavichord) in Vienna. The list of musical professionals and

[10] Czerny, "Erinnerungen aus meinem Leben," 10.   [11] Cooper, ed., *Das Beethoven Kompendium*, 61.
[12] Busch-Weise, "Beethovens Jugendtagebuch," 75, 9v. The year can be established from Beethoven's entry a few pages later: "We are in the month of December. Thursday was the fifth." December 5, 1793 was a Thursday. Busch-Weise, "Beethovens Jugendtagebuch," 76, 11r.
[13] Beethoven, *Briefwechsel*, vol. 1, 13.
[14] Beck, Köhler, and Herre, eds., *Ludwig van Beethovens Konversationshefte*, vol. 1, 372–3. The commentary identifies the singer Johann Michael Vogl, who later became famous as an interpreter of Schubert's songs, and the music scholar Raphael Georg Kiesewetter as members of this group.

amateurs in Johann Ferdinand von Schönfeld's *Jahrbuch der Tonkunst* (1796) gives us an idea about the extent of the fortepiano's acceptance.

Disregarding recurrences within families, von Schönfeld lists forty-eight players of the fortepiano specifically, eighteen players of the Klavier, two owners of a Flügel,[15] and three fortepiano builders.[16]

In the first half of 1793, some unidentified well-wishers were taking an interest in Beethoven's progress as a publishing composer. In a letter of November 17, 1793 to Eleonore von Breuning, Beethoven excuses himself for dedicating to her only the variations WoO 40 (for violin and piano), whereas she deserved a greater work. These variations had been published by Artaria in Vienna in the previous July, after "I was harassed into publishing this little piece," as Beethoven says.[17]

Finally, no contact at all with Count Carl von Lichnowsky can be safely established during Beethoven's first year in Vienna. However, Wegeler, who arrived in Vienna in October 1794, remembers that he found Beethoven living at Lichnowsky's.[18] A letter from van Swieten dated December 15 [1794] indeed gives Beethoven's address as "in der Alstergasse N° 45 bey dem Hn. Fürsten Lichnowski."[19]

TOWARD A PROFESSIONAL CAREER

Beethoven's main professional concern during his first years in Vienna was apparently the competition with the Viennese *Klaviermeister*. A year after the Schenk episode, Gelinek and Beethoven had some disagreement, the cause of which Schenk does not remember. Wegeler provides a possible explanation: according to Beethoven, "H[err] Ab[bé] G[elinek]" always took quarters near to him so that he could spy on his playing.[20] Wegeler mentions this circumstance to explain another passage in Beethoven's letter to Eleonore von Breuning: excusing himself for the difficult coda in the variations (the coda contains 30 bars altogether, with difficult double trills and "Beethoven trills"[21] alternating in both hands) Beethoven writes:

I would never have written something like this, but I had already noticed that now and again there was someone in Vienna who, when I extemporized of an evening, would often write down many of my specialties the next day and would boast about them. Since I foresaw that such things soon would be published, I wanted to

---

[15] One of the two is Joseph Anton Steffan, "a master who now has been overtaken by the taste of his time" (Johann Ferdinand von Schönfeld, *Jahrbuch der Tonkunst von Wien und Prag 1796*, Katzbichler: Munich, 1976, 58). Steffan owned a harpsichord, a clavichord, and two violins (Maunder, *Keyboard Instruments in Eighteenth-Century Vienna*, 233).

[16] In five cases in von Schönfeld's list, I have used information about fortepiano ownership from other sources.

[17] Beethoven, *Briefwechsel*, vol. 1, 17.

[18] Wegeler and Ries, *Biographische Notizen über Beethoven*, 28.   [19] Beethoven, *Briefwechsel*, vol. 1, 27.

[20] Wegeler and Ries, *Biographische Notizen über Beethoven*, 59–60.

[21] That is, a trill and a melody to be played simultaneously in one hand.

anticipate them. There was also another reason, namely to embarrass the *Klawiermeister* from here, some of whom are my deadly enemies, and so I wanted to take my revenge in this fashion, because I knew that sometime they would be given the variations to play, and then these gentlemen would give a bad performance.[22]

Competition with a whole group of keyboard professionals was a completely new situation for Beethoven. From the Bonn years, his (friendly) encounter with Sterkel is the only known occasion where he compared skills with another virtuoso.

It is no exaggeration when Beethoven identifies the awkward trills in the coda of WoO 40 as one of his "specialties" of that time: from 1793 alone there survive at least ten pages of sketches that contain around eighteen examples of material with simultaneous trills and melodies for one hand (or trills that acoustically suggest that effect) and cadential triple trills.[23] This rather high concentration coincides with a flood of sketches with technical exercises or pianistic patterns of various kinds that survive from around the same time. There can be no doubt that Beethoven, at the time of this letter, had accepted the challenge of competition and was honing his skills as a fortepiano virtuoso. Doubtless too, he had the opportunity to demonstrate these skills for listeners; despite the fact that most of the evidence is indirect, it is clear that by 1793 at the latest he had begun to present himself in Viennese musical circles and at the soirées of the nobility.

In March 1794, the Elector Max Franz terminated his payments to Beethoven,[24] who now needed to live on his reputation in Vienna alone. A larger amount of miscellaneous information survives regarding his activities as a pianist from this time, but the information about his tool for these activities, the fortepiano, is still inconclusive.

We know that in the summer of 1794 Beethoven asked Zmeskall to rent a summer residence, including Zmeskall's piano, but what sort of piano this was is not known.[25] Wegeler had a Klavier at his home and he describes how Beethoven sometimes improvised on it, but again, what kind of instrument it was is not known.[26] One can also be sure that Beethoven had free access to Prince Lichnowsky's piano (or pianos) during the period between *c.* 1794 and 1795, when he was a permanent guest in Lichnowsky's palace. Prince

[22] Beethoven, *Briefwechsel*, vol. I, 18.
[23] I am counting here examples from the editions of the "Kafka" and the "Fischhof" sketch miscellanies: Kerman, ed., *Ludwig van Beethoven Autograph Miscellany from ca. 1786 to 1799 (The "Kafka" Sketchbook)*, and Johnson, *Beethoven's Early Sketches in the "Fischhof Miscellany."* Complex trill textures appear in single fragments, cadenza sketches and one sketch of a left-hand trill from the WoO 40 coda. Johnson believes that some of the cadenza sketches are to be seen in connection with a projected or unknown performance of Op. 19 in or around 1793 (Johnson, *Beethoven's Early Sketches in the "Fischhof Miscellany,"* vol. I, 88 and 113). Examples can be found in Vienna A11 (1792, transcribed in Johnson, vol. II, 4); Kafka 39v., 41r., 46r., 51r.–v., 53r., 89v., 98r., and Fischhof 6r. (all 1792; see the respective facsimile pages in Kerman's publication, and Johnson, vol. II, 123); Paris Ms 7or. (1793–94, in Johnson, vol. II, 89).
[24] Thayer, *Life of Beethoven*, 137.   [25] Beethoven, *Briefwechsel*, vol. I, 25.
[26] Wegeler and Ries, *Biographische Notizen über Beethoven*, 19.

Lichnowsky was, like his wife and his brother Moritz, a good fortepiano player himself.[27] I have not found any information about Lichnowsky's instrument or instruments from the time before 1803.

Nor do we know the name of the builder of the pianos used in Beethoven's concerts on March 2, 1795, at Prince Lobkowitz's residence; March 29, 30, and 31 in the Burgtheater; April 23 at Count Razumowsky's residence; and December 18 and January 8, 1796, in the Kleiner Redoutensaal.[28] At the first of the Burgtheater concerts, Salieri conducted and Beethoven performed a "new concerto on the Piano-Forte" (possibly the third version of Op. 19),[29] and "earned the undivided applause of the audience."[30] In the second concert, he improvised. The third concert on March 31 was a performance of Mozart's *La clemenza di Tito* arranged by Konstanze Mozart. After the first part, Beethoven played a concerto by Mozart. Had Beethoven not played on the two preceding evenings on the same stage on his own behalf, one might be tempted to conjecture that he performed the Mozart concerto on Mozart's piano. At some point, possibly during the 1790s, this instrument was refurbished by its builder Anton Walter, after which, in terms of its general construction, it would have been fairly up-to-date.[31] But there is no evidence for or against such an assumption. On December 18, 1795, Beethoven participated in Haydn's Akademie, and on January 8, 1796, in a concert by the singer Maria Bolla where he again played a concerto, which could already have been Op. 15.[32]

The only anecdote from these years that names Beethoven in connection with any piano builder comes from the diaries of Karl Friedrich Kübeck von Kübau. Von Kübau relates how he met Beethoven at the home of a "family M...r,"[33] who had a "new instrument, a fortepiano, made by Mr. Walter." Beethoven, he writes, "mastered the instrument enchantingly for half an hour." It is not entirely clear if the instrument was actually new, or just

[27] *Ibid.*, 28; Cooper, ed., *Das Beethoven Kompendium*, 57; Schönfeld, *Jahrbuch der Tonkunst von Wien und Prag*, 41.

[28] These dates are compiled from Leon Plantinga, *Beethoven's Concertos*, New York: Norton, 1999, 49 (partly based on Mary Sue Morrow, *Concert Life in Haydn's Vienna: Aspects of a Developing Musical and Social Institution*, Stuyvesant, NY: Pendragon Press, 1989, 387–8), and Thayer, *Life of Beethoven*, 175.

[29] There has been some disagreement about which of the first two concertos Beethoven played. Leon Plantinga argues for Op. 19, Plantinga, *Beethoven's Concertos*, 60, 64.

[30] *Wiener Zeitung* April 1, 1795, quoted after Robbins Landon, ed., *Ludwig van Beethoven. Leben und Werk in Zeugnissen der Zeit*, 44.

[31] See Latcham, "Mozart and the pianos of Gabriel Anton Walter," 388–91. Latcham explains that these changes could date from any point between 1790 and 1810.

[32] For a discussion of the sketches and dates of Op. 15, see Plantinga, *Beethoven's Concertos*, 62–5.

[33] Robbins-Landon identifies M...r as the actor Johann Friedrich Müller, who lived in the same large building, the "Bürgerspital," as did von Kübau's aunt, who introduced him to the M...r family. Slightly different excerpts from von Kübau's memoirs are reproduced in Frimmel, *Beethoven-Handbuch*, vol. I, 309; Kerst, *Die Erinnerungen an Beethoven*, vol. I, 68–71; and Robbins Landon, ed., *Ludwig van Beethoven. Leben und Werk in Zeugnissen der Zeit*, 51–2.

unfamiliar to the fifteen- or sixteen-year-old Kübeck, who was used to a "Flügel."[34]

BEETHOVEN ON PIANO PLAYING

Beethoven's relationship with many of the Viennese *Klaviermeister* and composers remained strained. Around 1800, the eminent composer Leopold Kozeluch threw the score of the C minor Piano Trio on the ground when Johann Nepomuk Dolezalek played it for him.[35] In a letter from 1812, Beethoven called Kozeluch, as a composer, "miserabilis."[36] In contrast, Beethoven maintained a friendly relationship with Andreas Streicher. Streicher was a composer, fortepianist, and piano teacher, and in the late 1790s became the business secretary of the piano-building firm of his wife Nannette and her brother Matthäus Andreas Stein.[37] Streicher's position in Vienna and his relationship to Beethoven require a detailed discussion, especially because Streicher, in 1796, received two letters from Beethoven that deal with matters of fortepiano playing and fortepiano tone. Let us first look at the circumstances that led to their acquaintance.

After the death of Johann Andreas Stein in 1792, his children Nannette and Matthäus Andreas Stein took over his piano-building firm under the name "Geschwister Stein." On October 9, 1793, Nannette wrote to her future husband, Andreas Streicher, from Vienna, where she was, with her brother, preparing to move their firm and obtaining the required official permission. According to Nannette the prospects for Streicher in Vienna were the best in the world. Haydn and Leopold Kozeluch in particular were complimentary about Streicher's Klavier music, which Nannette had performed the previous day at a private *Academie*. "A certain *Baronesse*" had already signed up on behalf of her daughter for Klavier tuition.

The Streichers, now married, moved to Vienna in July 1794.[38] Andreas Streicher, thirty-two years old, was immediately accepted as a new and fashionable *Klaviermeister*. Von Schönfeld writes:

Streicher. Vienna has made a new and definitely positive acquisition in this man. He has only recently arrived from Munich. His compositions are rich, pleasant, and very elegant, very popular abroad, but not yet familiar here. They are especially suited for the fortepiano and they will grant our dilettantes no little pleasure. He himself plays really excellently and knows how to treat this instrument very

---

[34] Frimmel, Kerst, and Robbins-Landon all indicate April 1796 for the succession of diary entries that deal with Kübeck's first encounters with Beethoven. However, Beethoven was already in Prague in February 1796. Kübeck's encounter with Beethoven must therefore have taken place in another year.

[35] Kerst, *Die Erinnerungen an Beethoven*, vol. II, 191.

[36] Letter to George Thomson, February 29, 1812. Beethoven, *Briefwechsel*, vol. II, 247.

[37] See Goebl-Streicher, Streicher, and Ladenburger, *"Diesem Menschen hätte ich mein ganzes Leben widmen mögen,"* 12–13.

[38] *Ibid.,* 34.

beautifully. He plays with great skill and velocity, but in doing so, he never neglects the purest clarity and the most precise expression. He will certainly be welcome to all those music lovers who favor music for the heart, and he is perhaps the only one who at teaching can replace Kozeluch.[39]

Schönfeld writes elsewhere that Kozeluch had been the crucial figure in making the fortepiano popular; he was the archetypal Viennese *Klaviermeister*.

In 1795, when Schönfeld collected information for his book,[40] Streicher had been in Vienna for about one year. For a newcomer, he was very well received indeed. In a few years' time, he was able to count some of the most talented Viennese dilettantes among his pupils, including the Gräfin von Schönfeld (who earlier had been Kozeluch's pupil).[41] The firm of Geschwister Stein established itself just as rapidly and von Schönfeld also wrote an enthusiastic report about the Stein pianos.[42]

At the same time Beethoven was becoming extremely busy composing, playing, and publishing. In August 1794, in a letter to the publisher Nikolaus Simrock, he had to excuse himself for neglecting to correct the proofs of the Variations WoO 67 because of "überhaüfter [*sic*] Geschäfte," that is, piled-up work.[43] While working on the trios Op. 1 and the piano Sonatas Op. 2, he took lessons with Johann Georg Albrechtsberger, which he apparently took more seriously than Haydn's tuition. At the same time he was preparing for his first public appearance. During this period, we know of no contact with the Streichers, although this can certainly not be excluded and is perhaps even likely, since Beethoven knew both the Streichers from earlier.[44]

In February 1796, Beethoven was in Prague, heading for Dresden, Leipzig, and Berlin. He did not return to Vienna until at least mid-July of that year. Beethoven's friends from Bonn, Stephan and Lorenz von Breuning, saw him shortly after his return. Stephan wrote that Beethoven indulged in "surges of his friendship" and that he had become more "convinced of the rareness of the value of good friends." Both agreed that

[39] Schönfeld, *Jahrbuch der Tonkunst von Wien und Prag*, 59–60.

[40] See *ibid.*, *Nachwort* by Otto Biba.

[41] *Ibid.*, 54–5. See also Michael Ladenburger's contribution in Goebl-Streicher, Streicher, and Ladenburger, *"Diesem Menschen hätte ich mein ganzes Leben widmen mögen,"* 35–40.

[42] The firm maintained the name "Geschwister Stein" until 1802. See Michael Latcham, *The Stringing, Scaling and Pitch of Hammerflügel Built in the Southern German and Viennese Traditions 1780–1820*, Munich/Salzburg: Katzbichler, 2000, vol. 1, 5.

[43] Beethoven, *Briefwechsel*, vol. 1, 25.

[44] As discussed in Chapter 2, Beethoven very likely met Nannette for the first time in Augsburg in the spring of 1787. Andreas Streicher, on the other hand, wrote in 1802 that he had already known Beethoven for 14 years – it is unknown whether he also first met Beethoven in Augsburg in 1787 but had lost count of the precise number of years, or somewhere else. Wilhelm Lütge suggests Mannheim. Wilhelm Lütge, "Andreas und Nanette Streicher," in *Der Bär (Jahrbuch von Breitkopf & Härtel)* (1927), 56. See also Goebl-Streicher, Streicher, and Ladenburger, *"Diesem Menschen hätte ich mein ganzes Leben widmen mögen,"* 34.

Beethoven had, during his journey, become "somewhat more solid," and
that he had improved his judgment of human nature.[45]

In the spirit of just such a "surge" of friendship, Beethoven wrote to
Andreas Streicher sometime between the second half of July and September
1796, just before he was able to give him his new permanent address in
Vienna:

Dear Streicher!

I really must apologize for answering your very friendly letter so late ... to tell the
truth, I was prevented by my work piling up. Your young pupil, dear St., moved me
to tears when she played my adagio and astonished me besides. I wish you luck that
you are so fortunate as to be able to demonstrate your insights to such a talented
pupil, and I am equally glad of the fact that the dear little [girl] with all her gifts has
gotten you as a master. Truly, dear Streicher, for the first time I dared to listen to
my *Terzett* in performance, and this will really make me compose more for the
Klavier than before; I will be content [even] if only few [should] understand me.
Until now, the way people play the Klavier certainly still makes it the most
uncultivated of all instruments; one often believes one hears only a harp, and I
am glad that you are one of the few who understand and feel that, if one can feel,
one can also sing on the Klavier. I hope the time will come when the harp and the
Klavier will become two totally different instruments. By the way, I believe that you
can let the little one play anywhere, and, between us, she would put some of our
ordinary conceited hurdy-gurdy men to shame.

One more thing: I hope you will not take offence, dear St., if I take just a little
interest in her education? That is, that I am only concerned about her progress
because, without wanting to flatter you, I would not know what to tell her any
better than you. Just let me contemplate her progress and encourage her. Farewell
now, dear Streicher and remain my friend as I am wholly

Your true friend   L. v. Beethoven

[Postscript] I hope to be able to visit you soon and then I will let you know my
house number; my regards to your dear wife.[46]

This famous letter serves various purposes: Beethoven's wish to re-establish
contact with his friend shortly after returning from a long concert tour is, for
instance, immediately apparent. Perhaps the most noticeable feature of the
letter is the flattering vocabulary; one might wonder how good the relationship between the two men really was if Beethoven needed so many words to
affirm it. This tone can be partly explained by Beethoven's apparent fear
that his interest in Streicher's pupil might be taken as interference. But there
may be another explanation for Beethoven's effusive style.

Streicher's gifted pupil was probably the twelve-year-old Elisabeth
(Lisette) von Kissow (later Bernhard) from Augsburg, who had followed
her teacher to Vienna.[47] Soon after Beethoven's Sonatas Op. 2 were
available (they were advertised on March 9, 1796), Streicher encouraged

---

[45] Letter from Stephan von Breuning on November 23, 1796. Reprinted by Wegeler and Ries,
   Biographische Notizen über Beethoven, Nachtrag 20.
[46] Beethoven, *Briefwechsel*, vol. I, 32.   [47] *Ibid.*, 32–3, n. 3.

her to play these new pieces, "which the ladies did not want to play because they found them too difficult and incomprehensible." She subsequently played "these and other works by Beethoven with such skill that she was invited to the private musical entertainments at Lichnowsky's and Rasumowsky's residences." There she met Beethoven, who showed an interest in her playing and progress.[48] Beethoven's letter suggests that, at one such soirée, Lisette played, perhaps among other pieces, an adagio from a piano trio.[49]

Lisette Bernhard's recollection that "the ladies" found the Sonatas Op. 2 technically and musically difficult certainly rings true, although Ferdinand Ries writes in retrospect that they immediately "caused a big sensation." Although we cannot know in detail how the Viennese fortepiano teachers and amateurs reacted to the publication of the new works, it is quite possible that Beethoven had not heard the piece in question performed before young Lisette played it for him.

Beethoven's curious blend of criticism of other pianists ("uncultivated") with self-criticism ("for the first time I dared to listen …") was in fact his extended concern. A famous entry from June 2, 1804, in the "Leonore" sketchbook carries a similar message: "The finale always simpler, all Klavier music as well. God knows why my Klavier music still makes the worst impression on me, especially when it is played badly."[50]

Interpreting Beethoven's letter as merely flattering would obscure its main objective, which is to show Beethoven's gratitude to Streicher. In the context of jealousy from other pianists, and in view of Beethoven's reluctance to listen to his works in anticipation of yet another "uncultivated" rendering, Streicher's initiative to give Beethoven's works to his talented pupil must have been a truly encouraging move. The fact that Lisette von Kissow also played them well was naturally reason enough to "move him to tears." In this light, the whole letter stands out as a sincere and straightforward document to Beethoven's feelings. Thus encouraged, he felt safe to add the passage about the uncultivated ways of other fortepianists. Beethoven *knew* that Streicher was on his side in this matter.[51]

This letter has frequently encouraged an interpretation of Beethoven's "harp" as his implicit criticism of the fortepiano.[52] But Beethoven addresses Streicher here exclusively as a piano teacher, and the letter is free of any

---

[48] Elisabeth Bernhard was interviewed by Ludwig Nohl in 1864; the text is reprinted in Kerst, *Die Erinnerungen an Beethoven*, vol. 1, 23–5.

[49] Beethoven, *Briefwechsel*, vol. 1, 33, n. 4 and 5.

[50] Quoted after Uli Molsen, *Die Geschichte des Klavierspiels in historischen Zitaten*, Balingen: Uli Molsen, 1983, 63. See also Thayer, *Life of Beethoven*, 380.

[51] I previously presented a slightly different interpretation of Beethoven's motives in this letter. See Skowroneck, "Keyboard instruments of the young Beethoven," 169.

[52] See Eszter Fontana, "Ein Geschenk für Beethoven," in *Musikästhetik und Analyse, Festschrift W. Seidel zum 65. Geburtstag*, Laaber, 2002, 270, and Hans-Werner Küthen, "Ein verlorener Registerklang. Beethovens Imitation der Aeolsharfe," *Musik & Ästhetik* 34 (April 2005): 83.

allusions to piano building. A person "who can feel" can also "sing" on the Klavier; so it is the fault of the player if the Klavier sounds like a harp.[53]

Streicher presented his own thoughts on the fortepiano and fortepiano playing in his booklet of 1801, which was given to every new owner of a piano built by Geschwister Stein (later Nannette Streicher).[54] Even if its style is not unlike modern owners' manuals, the text is well worked out and reflects genuine conviction. Streicher's choice of words is strikingly similar to Beethoven's:

It is a pity that, even though so many play the fortepiano, so few try to treat it according to its true nature. Nothing is more common than to hear this resourceful instrument *ill-treated* in such a way that it can often make no better effect than a tinkling harp or a miserable *Hackbrett* [hammered dulcimer].[55]

On producing a singing tone on the piano, Streicher has this to say:

[The good player] knows how to let every tone *sing* without straining his instrument, *because he touches every key appropriately.*[56]

Thus Beethoven and Streicher agreed that it was the player's responsibility to learn to make the piano "sing" and to avoid letting it sound like a "tinkling harp." At this point, we may conclude that the contact between Beethoven and Streicher was not merely polite but genuinely friendly, and that it was based on shared musical opinions.

BEETHOVEN ON FORTEPIANO SOUND

A few months later, in November 1796, Beethoven wrote again to Streicher. This time he did give his opinion about an instrument. Beethoven had borrowed a piano from the Geschwister Stein firm for a concert in Pressburg (some 50 km from Vienna) that apparently had the double function of promoting both Beethoven and the instrument:

Dear Streicher!
I received your fortepiano the day before yesterday. It is really marvelous, anybody else would like to have it for his own, and I – you may laugh, but I would have to lie if I didn't tell you that it is too good for me, and why? – because it deprives me of the freedom to create my own tone. Besides, this shall not hinder you from making all your fortepianos in the same way; there will not be many others found with the same idiosyncrasies. Wednesday the 23rd will be my *Akademie*. If Stein [Streicher's

---

[53] Beethoven would have rejected any piano that frustrated the efforts of this "feeling" and "singing" pianist. So *indirectly*, his expectations of a good fortepiano are clear even in this letter. However, this is no inherent criticism of the fortepiano as such.

[54] Streicher, *Kurze Bemerkungen*.

[55] *Ibid.*, 3–4. Original italics. John Koster has pointed out that Streicher might be alluding to a folk harp with brays.

[56] *Ibid.*, 17.

brother-in-law Matthäus Andreas Stein] wants to come, he is cordially welcome, he can certainly sleep at my place.

Regarding the sale of the fortepiano, I already had the idea before you did, and I will certainly try to carry it out. I thank you from the bottom of my heart, dear St[reicher], for your kindness in accommodating me; I only wish to be able to repay some of your kindness, and hope that you are convinced, even if I do not tell you so here, of how much I wish the merits of your instruments to be recognized here and elsewhere, and how much I want you always to think well of me and regard me

as your loving and warm friend   Beethoven

Preßburg, Nov. 19, 1796 *post christum natum*

[Postscript] Many regards to your wife and to the bride and bridegroom. [Matthäus Andreas Stein had married seven days earlier][57]

Beethoven's wish, in this letter, to "create his own tone" (which in itself is somewhat of a novelty in terms of the keyboard playing of the time) carries a clear note of criticism. Nevertheless, he borrowed this fortepiano from Streicher for his *Akademie* and had apparently agreed to promote the sale of this instrument. If this indeed was the agreement, Streicher would not have expected Beethoven to have the fortepiano "for his own," and one wonders why Beethoven even mentions that option.

Beethoven's explicit statement that his criticism should not prevent Streicher from building "all his instruments" in the same way because he wishes their quality to be universally recognized may indeed seem "enigmatic."[58] The logical explanation for this remark is that Beethoven welcomed these instruments in general, but nevertheless had other personal preferences.

The Stein/Streicher firm did indeed not change the basic design of their pianos for years to come. Although the quality of the work itself was widely recognized as impeccable, their construction remained largely based on the design of Johann Andreas Stein, which at that time was becoming conservative. Beethoven, on the other hand, owned a fortepiano built by Anton Walter at the end of 1799. Does the Pressburg letter indicate that Beethoven was already contemplating alternatives to the Streicher/Stein model in 1796? In the following sections, I will discuss this question in more detail.

TWO VIENNESE SCHOOLS OF FORTEPIANO BUILDING AND FORTEPIANO PLAYING

Beethoven's letters to Streicher in 1796 are his only utterances from this time about pianism and the fortepiano. However, they stand side by side without really connecting: the first one deals with playing the fortepiano and the second with the properties of one particular instrument. The missing information in Beethoven's letters – how the instruments and

---

[57] Beethoven, *Briefwechsel*, vol. 1, 33.
[58] Newman, "Beethoven's pianos versus his piano ideals," 487.

the particular playing styles connected – is preserved in other Viennese documents of the time.

It is again von Schönfeld who describes Geschwister Stein's and Anton Walter's fortepianos as belonging to two distinct traditions and so helps us to understand that we are indeed contemplating two alternatives:

… we have, in a manner of speaking, two original instrument builders, that is, Walter, and [Nannette] Streicher; all the others imitate either the former or the latter; Walter especially has very many initators, since some of them come from his school.[59]

The third builder named in this text is Johann Schanz, who according to Schönfeld built copies of Stein's instruments. This characterization is not supported by Schanz's surviving instruments.[60] Schönfeld was perhaps not used to a careful analysis of fortepiano construction. But regarding the instrument's properties, his observations are acute, and he makes a special point about the connection between piano design and the various manners of playing:

Since we now have two "original" instrument builders, we also divide our fortepianos in two groups: those of Walter and those of Streicher. Upon careful observation, we can divide our greatest pianists into two groups as well. One of these groups loves a great feast for the ear, that is, it likes enormous noise; consequently it plays very sonorously, extremely quickly, studies the trickiest passages, and the quickest octave leaps. This demands force and strong nerves; in exerting these, one is not capable of achieving a measure of moderation, so one needs a fortepiano whose tone does not jangle ["dessen Schwebung nicht überschnapt"].

For virtuosos of this kind we recommend a fortepiano of Walter's kind. The other group of our great pianists seeks nourishment for the soul and likes not only precise, but also sweet, melting playing. These players cannot choose a better instrument than one of Streicher's, or the so-called Stein model.[61]

Schönfeld's central claim is that the group of powerful pianists should use the Walter model, because the tone of other instruments (i.e. of Streicher's model) starts to jangle if the pianist plays without "a measure of moderation." The use of "Schwebung" for a wider range of meanings than the literal "beat" of a frequency is not uncommon in historical texts. In this example it clearly means "tone". "Überschnappen," on the other hand, (which literally translates as "flipping over") can perhaps only be understood properly by anyone who has actually tried to force the tone of a historical piano beyond its limits: the strings react to an overly forceful blow with an impure sound. The tone declines faster, and it sounds harsh and gives an

---

[59] Schönfeld, *Jahrbuch der Tonkunst von Wien und Prag*, 90.
[60] Evidence for this fact is presented throughout Latcham, *The Stringing, Scaling and Pitch of Hammerflügel*.
[61] Schönfeld, *Jahrbuch der Tonkunst von Wien und Prag*, 90–1.

impression of being off pitch. Another consequence of a forceful blow might be that the hammer strikes the string several times. In practice, either of these effects would sound similar in terms of a disturbance of the musical flow, hence my translation as "jangle."

In his manual, Streicher confirms that the Stein/Streicher fortepianos required "a measure of moderation":

Strong pounding (which cannot but spoil any fortepiano) in any case gives far less tone than is generally believed, because each string can only give a certain degree of volume. If one wants to further increase this volume by a vigorous attack, [the string] will begin to vibrate in an unnatural way.[62]

Streicher's formulation that corresponds with von Schönfeld's "überschnappende Schwebung" is unambiguous: a vigorous attack makes the string sound unnaturally without further increasing the tone volume.

Modern knowledge about the construction of surviving Viennese fortepianos from around 1800 has made it easier to understand these descriptions. Some general differences between the Stein/Streicher forte-pianos of the last decade of the eighteenth century and those by Walter concern the weight of the moving parts of the action and the strings. The Streicher firm retained the wooden Kapseln, thin hammer shanks, and light hammers of Stein's original construction (this is why I occasionally refer to features of Stein's instruments). Walter, on the other hand, used brass Kapseln and – eventually – heavier hammers. Walter's strings were generally thicker than Streicher's and the treble of his instruments from around b′ was triple-strung.[63]

One difference that to some degree helps to explain the characterizations given by Schönfeld and the caution recommended by Streicher regarding "pounding" is the absence of a hammer check in Stein's instruments. As mentioned in Chapter 2, a check catches the hammer on its return from the attack, preventing it from striking twice. It has frequently been argued that rebounding hammers would be the *normal* result of forceful playing on checkless fortepianos.[64] Von Schönfeld's "überschnappende Schwebung" may well be an attempt to describe this effect.

The usual belief has been that the German action relied on the absorbent quality of the material that covered the hammer rest, on some friction at the hammer pivots,[65] and most importantly, on the pianist's ability to play in a

---

[62] Streicher, *Kurze Bemerkungen*, 10.
[63] Michael Latcham, "Alternatives to the modern piano for the performance of Mozart," paper presented at the Institut für Aufführungspraxis, Michaelstein, 1992, 12, later reworked in various articles by the same author and presented in a condensed form in Latcham, *The Stringing, Scaling and Pitch of Hammerflügel*, vol. 1, especially 10–25.
[64] See Michael Latcham, "The check in some early pianos and the development of piano technique around the turn of the 18th century," *Early Music* 21/1 (1993): 28–42, and Latcham, "Mozart and the pianos of Gabriel Anton Walter."
[65] See Latcham, "Mozart and the pianos of Johann Andreas Stein," 139–40, and Latcham, *The Stringing, Scaling and Pitch of Hammerflügel*, vol. 1, 10.

manner appropriate to the piano. Recent research by Stephen Birkett, who has been working with high-speed imaging of various fortepiano actions, has shown that the Stein-type piano actions absorb the energy of the returning hammer in several other ways: "In effect, the flexible hammer shank acts as a check to dissipate the energy of the returning hammer as it flies off the string. The flex also moves the effective escapement point into the string, further enhancing the subsequent loss of energy."[66]

According to Birkett's analysis, a Stein action should be set up with minimal friction at the hammer pivots.[67] His conclusion is, "When set up properly, a Stein action without backcheck cannot be made to double strike even if you try."[68]

One could, however, imagine slight deviations from the optimal action set-up in instruments that are in constant use; it is hard to believe that every Stein/Streicher fortepiano in Vienna around 1800 was optimally set up within very close margins. The few playing hammers in the Gothenburg Stein which are regulated reasonably well, for example, *do* rebound when played very forcefully. But the sound thus produced is plainly not optimal: it assumes a forced, twanging, and out-of-tune quality. This observation corresponds with Streicher's and Schönfeld's descriptions.

The thicker strings and the triple-strung treble made it possible to play on Walter's instruments more loudly without forcing the tone. The hammer rests absorbed only a little of the hammer's return energy, and the friction of the hammer axle bearings in the brass Kapseln was minimal. Thus, the check to prevent the hammer from bouncing up became an integral part of Walter's whole concept. Doubtless, the realization of some of Beethoven's specialties is facilitated by these instruments. It is, for instance, easier to give long *fortissimo* passages (such as the closing formula in the first movement of his Sonata Op. 2/3) the impression of a fully engaged classical orchestra if one does *not* have to think about the limits of the instrument. Furthermore, a neat execution of Beethoven's *sforzati* is much easier with such an action.

But Walter's piano action was not universally seen as an improvement. Von Schönfeld's description of the development of tone characteristics in Walter's fortepianos identifies some of the problems in these instruments:

[Walter's] fortepianos have a full bell-like tone, a clear attack, and a strong, full bass. At first the tone is somewhat dull, but if one has played for some time it becomes very clear, especially in the treble. If they are played very much, the tone soon becomes sharp and iron-like, which can be corrected by re-leathering the hammers.[69]

---

[66] Stephen Birkett, University of Waterloo, personal communication, and on the Yahoo fortepiano list at: launch.groups.yahoo.com/group/fortepiano/message/6120 (last accessed March 2, 2009).

[67] Even the 1824 fortepiano manual by Schiedmayer and Dieudonné, which contains a maintenance description for German actions, leaves no doubt that axle friction was undesirable. Schiedmayer and Dieudonné, *Kurze Anleitung zu einer richtigen Behandlung der Forte-Pianos*, 64.

[68] Stephen Birkett, personal communication.

[69] Schönfeld, *Jahrbuch der Tonkunst von Wien und Prag*, 88.

To Streicher the ideal fortepiano tone should resemble wind instruments (I will return to this detail below), and even he comments upon an "iron" tone, though without actually naming Walter.[70]

The "iron" tone that Schönfeld and Streicher describe is caused by a change in the density of the leather hammer covering as a result of playing.[71] Clearly, the covering of Walter's hammers wore out rather quickly. Perhaps the type of leather Walter was using was less durable than Geschwister Stein's. Streicher's explanations suggest, additionally, that the louder-playing pianists associated with Walter wore his instruments out at a quicker pace. This passage helps to explain why Streicher, as quoted earlier, believed that strong pounding would spoil *any kind* of fortepiano.[72]

To summarize, we can state that Geschwister Stein maintained a conservative action design not because of a lack of innovative fantasy. The Stein action was the result of a carefully judged balance of interactive mechanical elements and was perfectly suited to the performance aesthetics deemed desirable by competent observers like Streicher. Streicher did not merely regard the lighter action as sufficiently efficient.[73] His words also suggest that Geschwister Stein consciously refrained from changing it in a way that would tempt pianists to exceed the limits of their instruments and thus jeopardize their durability. His description of the string that starts to vibrate in an unnatural way clearly indicates his opinion about these limits. The pianist was not even to go so far as to let the hammers bounce twice, because the limit of the strings was reached at lower dynamic levels.

BEETHOVEN'S "OWN TONE"

One could believe that Beethoven belonged to Schönfeld's group of powerful pianists who liked "enormous noise," played "very sonorously," and "extremely quickly."[74] In his manual, Streicher offers a caricature of a (fictional) pianist for whom the Stein/Streicher fortepianos would be unsuitable:

---

[70] Streicher, *Kurze Bemerkungen*, 12–13.

[71] See Gätjen, "Das Hammerklavier – akustisches Bindeglied zwischen Clavichord, Cembalo und modernem Flügel?"

[72] Another reason why pounding should be avoided is that the parchment attachments of the escapement hoppers are difficult to replace. Schiedmayer and Dieudonné, *Kurze Anleitung zu einer richtigen Behandlung der Forte-Pianos*, 72–3.

[73] The lower string tension in his fortepianos enabled Streicher to retain a lighter soundboard ribbing than Walter. This resulted in better resonance, partly compensating for the disadvantages of the lighter stringing.

[74] This opinion is expressed in Michael Latcham, "The development of the Streicher firm of piano builders under the leadership of Nannette Streicher, 1792–1823," in Beatrix Darmstädter, Rudolf Hopfner, and Alfons Huber, eds., *Das wiener Klavier bis 1850*, Tutzing: Schneider, 2007, 43–71; copy provided by the author, 25, "Beethoven" section.

A player with the reputation that "he plays extraordinarily, such as you have never heard," sits down (or *throws* himself) at the fortepiano. His very first chords are given with such strength that one wonders whether he is deaf, or thinks that his audience is. With the movements of his body, arms, and hands, he seems to want to make us understand how difficult is the *labor* that he undertakes. He becomes excited and treats his instrument like one bent on revenge, who has got hold of his arch-enemy and is about to torture him to death slowly, with cruel enjoyment. He wants to play *forte*, but since he has already exaggerated [the tone] at the beginning, it is no longer possible to produce more sound. *So he pounds*, and now the abused strings go out of tune, some of them fly among the listeners, who hastily retreat in order to protect their eyes. This note is marked *sforzato*! Luckily, the hammer and the string still hold. But hear how the tone grinds, how painful it is to the ear! He transforms passionate fire into anger and he expresses soothing feelings by *cold playing*. Since he exaggerates everything, it is natural that, when expressing the sensation of pain, he makes the fortepiano squeal and howl, and during quick and joyful melodies beats the keys and hammers into lameness ...

Exhausted, spent, as if he has been trying to uproot oak trees, he finally rises and leaves the poor fortepiano (for which its owner was trembling at every note) in a state which could not have been worsened by the fury of a barbarian. One is lucky if the damage can be mended with half a dozen strings, and if broken hammers and keys do not lie scattered about.

If he notices the bad impression [he has made] on the listeners (could anyone admire him [after all this]!), he is courteous enough to blame the instrument, on which one cannot play with fire and expressivity.[75]

This passage has occasionally been interpreted as a caricature of Beethoven's playing.[76] But von Schönfeld's "Walter" pianist, Streicher's string-breaking keyboardist, and Beethoven cannot belong to one and the same group. Schönfeld's description of the pianist who "wants to stimulate the ear" suggests labor: he "studies the trickiest passages, and the quickest octave leaps. This demands force and strong nerves; in exerting these, one is not capable achieving a measure of moderation." No such labor is implied by his description of Beethoven as "a musical genius who chose to live in Vienna two years ago. He is commonly admired because of his particular speed and because of the extraordinary difficulties which he executes so very easily."[77]

The "piano strangler" (*Clavierwürger*), as Streicher calls his amateur figure, definitely does not execute "extraordinary difficulties" easily. We have also seen that Beethoven's interests went well beyond the execution of difficult passages with ease. "If one can feel, one can also sing on the Klavier," he wrote, showing his sympathies with Streicher's ideal. Beethoven's letters to Streicher give an impression of a cherished but slightly formal friendship, maintained with special care. I have not encountered a single formulation about Beethoven in Streicher's correspondence that conveys anything other than respect and, occasionally, tolerance. Considering this

---

[75] Streicher, *Kurze Bemerkungen*, 20 and 23–4.
[76] See, for example, DeNora, *Beethoven and the Construction of Genius*, 133–4.   [77] *Ibid.*, 7.

relationship, we can safely assume that the difference between Beethoven and *serious* contemporary pianists depended upon other characteristics, or rather qualities, than those which Streicher caricatured.

Returning to Beethoven's Pressburg letter, we can now try to define the limits he was willing to observe in 1796 and the particular character of his preference. As discussed earlier, Beethoven was well acquainted with Stein's pianos. There can be no doubt that he knew very well what features he would encounter in such an instrument. Since he himself took the initiative to borrow a Geschwister Stein piano for his Pressburg concert, its action cannot have presented a problem for him. To perform on this instrument did not frustrate his expressive ambitions more substantially than is reflected in his letter. If Beethoven, in Schönfeld's terms, was a pianist of "force and strong nerves," he was certainly also capable of "a measure of moderation" when necessary to perform on an instrument of a type that would otherwise have started to "jangle."

We can, therefore, suppose that the Stein action was not the essential reason for Beethoven's criticism, but that he was addressing some aspect of the sound properties of the instrument. If we again compare Beethoven's opinion with Streicher's booklet from 1801, a subtle discrepancy of philosophy between the two indeed becomes apparent. Streicher writes:

Although some people believe that it [the piano] must be far inferior to other instruments *with regard to expressive playing,* such an accusation refers only to fortepianos *that have an inflexible tone, an extremely heavy-to-play keyboard and an action which does not support the movement of the fingers.*[78]

Thus far, Beethoven would have agreed with Streicher. A bad piano is an obstacle to a good performance. However, after a passage about the basic principles of a piano action, Streicher continues:

But even the best action can but *prepare a good touch.* It can only *make it possible and easy* for the player *to touch in such a way* that the tone produced is exactly of the character desired by the music or his feeling. It is *his* task to enliven the action. *He alone* is responsible if his instrument makes a better or worse impression.[79]

Here, Streicher clearly wants to describe a situation where a player has to live up to the possibilities of a good piano. This point is so important that he returns to it later on:

If the separate tones, as well as those played simultaneously, are to please or move, they should as much as possible resemble those of the best wind instruments …

On a fortepiano by Stein, the tone is formed entirely according to this ideal and also everything that the player needs for any sort of musical execution is already prepared in its keyboard.

---

[78] Streicher, *Kurze Bemerkungen,* 4.   [79] *Ibid.,* 6.

Hence it will depend on *him* whether he wants to apply carefully everything that has been said above about touch, so that he can let his instrument speak *in the very manner* it wants to speak.[80]

So, in contrast to Beethoven, Streicher believes that the responsibility of the player is not to make his own tone, but rather to react to how the piano "wants to speak." He subtly but clearly puts the instrument in first place and wants the pianist to react sympathetically to it. Inadequate instruments, to Streicher, are those that through their inflexible tone or their heavy action inhibit the pianist from playing expressively in this manner.

Beethoven shared neither this belief nor a piano manufacturer's worries about the durability of an action. From his first Viennese piano works, his writing is clearly orchestral throughout, and his required palette of tone variations must have been large. It is doubtful whether he was looking for an instrument that only reproduced the effect of "the best wind instruments." An action that supports stronger playing, as found in Walter's pianos (and in instruments from many other Viennese makers), may have seemed less subtle to Streicher. However, the sound palette of a good specimen of a more powerful Viennese instrument apparently suited Beethoven better.

Any explanation of why Beethoven nevertheless borrowed a Geschwister Stein instrument for the Pressburg concert must necessarily remain speculative. The most reasonable explanation is that, for some reason, he was not fully aware of the difference between the instruments, or not fully prepared for the sound of this particular piano, despite his earlier familiarity with Stein's pianos. So his dissatisfaction with the piano he played in Pressburg might have been as much a surprise to him as it probably was to Streicher when he received the letter.

The instrument arrived in Pressburg on Thursday, November 17; the *Akademie* was on the following Wednesday. Beethoven wrote his letter after having access to the piano for about one day and a half – at the moment of writing, he may not even have had the opportunity to try out the piano in the acoustics of the concert hall. Perhaps the instrument was very new and not well played-in. It is also possible (though unlikely) that the piano the Streichers delivered to Pressburg simply was not a good instrument.

In view of the many conjectures about Beethoven's piano ideals that have accumulated over time, it would not be new to identify Beethoven's criticism as an early step in his quest for an essentially louder, more orchestral piano. I believe that Beethoven's opinion of a single piano on one occasion does not qualify for such an interpretation. It certainly cannot be seen as a fundamental criticism of early Viennese fortepianos in general. We know of at least thirty public or semi-public performances by Beethoven between 1795 and 1800; the number of unrecorded performances of various sorts must have been much higher. Even in the unlikely case that

---

[80] *Ibid.*, 12–13.

he used only one preferred piano at each public Viennese performance (as Mozart did), he still performed on a total of at least twelve different pianos at the various residences of the nobility and in other cities during his concert tours.

Apart from improvisation, the repertoire he chose for most of his concerts was restricted to rather few effective pieces, many of which (like the first two piano concertos, the first two cello sonatas, the Wind Quintet and the Horn Sonata) were written – or adapted – to suit specific upcoming concert events. It appears that Beethoven, at that time, played *with* the given conditions rather than *against* them, and that he tailored his active repertoire according to the situation. An interpretation of Beethoven's criticism as specifically addressing the pianos built by the Stein/Streicher firm at that time stretches the evidence as far as it possibly can.

BEETHOVEN'S PIANOS AROUND 1800

The information about Beethoven's pianos until 1803 is scattered and inconsistent. According to one of Wegeler's famous anecdotes, Beethoven transposed the piano part of his Piano Concerto in C major Op. 15 up a semitone during a rehearsal at his home.[81] This rehearsal could have been a preparation for one of the concerts that took place on December 18, 1795 and January 8, 1796 (a third alternative would be the concert on March 29, 1795).[82] Wegeler's account allows us to assume that Beethoven's piano at that time had the extended standard keyboard range up to g''', although he generally observed the high f in his printed keyboard music before 1803 (with the exception of one f#''' in the first movement of the the Sonata Op. 14/1).[83] True, we have no information about the nature of the solo part that Beethoven played on that occasion. He might even have improvised most of it, and it will have been a different version from the the first edition published in 1800.[84] In the published solo part, the top note f''' occurs very frequently in any case, fifty times throughout the concerto, and in two short trills and three whole bars of trills.[85] For many of these notes the figuration could have been changed, but hardly for all of them. To play the piece a semitone higher on a standard five-octave range would have presented many problems, at least if Beethoven were to avoid a complete loss of brilliancy by transposing whatever he played or improvised down a whole octave. If this interpretation is correct, the awkward f''' in the solo bar 172 of

[81] Wegeler and Ries, *Biographische Notizen über Beethoven*, 36.
[82] See the discussion in Plantinga, *Beethoven's Concertos*, 62–5.
[83] The significance of this anecdote for determining that the keyboard range of Beethoven's piano must have exceeded five octaves was, to my knowledge, first observed by Richard Maunder. See Maunder, *Keyboard Instruments in Eighteenth-Century Vienna*, 116.
[84] Plantinga, *Beethoven's Concertos*, 65–6.
[85] I have used the 1990 *Urtext* edition by Hans-Werner Küthen (Henle).

the first movement, which appears in the autograph and the first edition, must be a restriction for the publication of the piece: the f#''', which was necessary to play a major third as in the parallel bar 387, was available on Beethoven's piano.

In May 1799, Therese von Brunsvik paid her first visit to Beethoven. She remembers that she played the piano part of one of the trios for Beethoven on his piano, which was out of tune.[86] This recollection is the first report that describes the condition of one of Beethoven's personal fortepianos.

The almost ten-year-old Carl Czerny was introduced to Beethoven in the winter of 1799/1800. He remembers that Beethoven had a "Waltersches fortepiano" in his otherwise very untidy room, and adds that these instruments were "then the best."[87]

Theodor Frimmel's information about Beethoven's grand piano by the Hungarian instrument maker Sebestyén Antal Vogel is incorrect: Beethoven probably received this instrument in 1812, and not in 1800.[88] We know nothing about Beethoven's musical relationship to this piano.

Another piano builder who appears twice in Beethoven's correspondence just after the turn of the century is the Viennese instrument maker Johann Bohak (or Pohak). On June 23, 1802, Kaspar Karl von Beethoven recommends Bohak's products in a letter to the editor of the *Allgemeine Musikalische Zeitung* of Leipzig.[89] On November 23, 1803, Beethoven added a postscript to another letter by Kaspar Karl, in which he recommends Bohak to Breitkopf & Härtel, adds a price list of Bohak's instruments, and even recommends another maker, Anton Moser.[90] In November 1802, Beethoven owned or had access to a piano by Johann Jakesch, but was searching for yet another kind of instrument.[91]

The circumstances and consequences of this search will be the subject of the following chapter. To summarize, we can state that during Beethoven's first years in Vienna there was a great deal of interest among music lovers, players, and piano builders in the musical qualities of various pianos. It is obvious that Beethoven had his opinions and preferences in this matter. But the view that he could not find a medium to express himself adequately cannot be supported by the surviving historical documents, which, however limited, provide an insight into some of his key concerns about playing the piano.

---

[86] Robbins Landon, ed., *Ludwig van Beethoven. Leben und Werk in Zeugnissen der Zeit*, 115.
[87] Czerny, "Erinnerungen aus meinem Leben," 10. Unfortunately, this instrument has not been identified.
[88] See Fontana, "Ein Geschenk für Beethoven," and Frimmel, *Beethoven-Handbuch*, vol. 1, 267.
[89] Beethoven, *Briefwechsel*, vol. I, 114.   [90] *Ibid.*, 197–8.
[91] Letter to Nikolaus Zmeskall, November 1802, in *ibid.*, 137.

CHAPTER 4

The 1803 Érard grand piano

HISTORY OF THE INSTRUMENT

The first decade of the nineteenth century was a period of substantial change for Beethoven: he fundamentally re-formulated his goals in composition. At the same time his health, particularly his hearing, was causing him more and more problems. The consequences of this development on his pianism and piano writing are complex and difficult to understand. Luckily, one of his private pianos from this period is preserved, and Beethoven scholars and organologists have been able to piece some of its history together. This is the grand piano by Érard, which he received in 1803.[1]

The Érard piano has a keyboard compass of five-and-a-half octaves and an English-style hammer action. Around the time of its arrival, Beethoven extended the compass of some of his keyboard works, so a direct link between his compositions and this piano would seem self-evident. However, this instrument has received less attention in the literature than could be expected, mainly because the Érard, modern at the time of its arrival, quickly became outdated. Consequently, Beethoven expressed his disappointment with it in unequivocal terms only a few years after its arrival. William Newman writes of the Érard piano: "Beethoven was unhappy with this instrument from the start," partly because he found its English action to be "incurably heavy."[2]

There are various reasons for reconsidering the significance of Beethoven's Érard. First, Beethoven's interest in other styles – and especially English pianism – would by 1803 have been a more than sufficient reason to welcome and explore an English-style instrument like the Érard.[3] Some important compositions for piano written soon after the arrival of the instrument (starting with the "Waldstein" Sonata Op. 53) show the influence of the Érard during a short period of time. Additionally, the

---

[1] Oberösterreichisches Landesmuseum Linz, Inv. No. Mu61. The instrument has the serial no. 133. See also Tilman Skowroneck, "Beethoven's Erard piano: its influence on his compositions and on Viennese fortepiano building," *Early Music* 30/4 (2002): 522–38.

[2] Newman, "Beethoven's pianos versus his piano ideals," 484–504, reprinted with revisions in Newman, *Beethoven on Beethoven*. The citations are from *Beethoven on Beethoven*, 51 and 55.

[3] See also Alexander Ringer, "Beethoven and the London Fortepiano School," *The Musical Quarterly* 56/4 (1970): 742–58.

instrument plays an important role in Streicher's efforts to modernize the
production of his firm.[4] However, the common notion that it was
Beethoven who in the wake of his disappointment with his French piano
single-handedly conducted a "piano reform" over an extended period, and
that this resulted in actual change or even radical development in piano
building, finds very little support in the documents.

On August 6, 1803, the piano builder Sébastien Érard sent Beethoven a
grand piano. According to a recent discovery, this instrument was not
intended as a present from the Érard firm, although Beethoven apparently
never paid for it.[5] As early as in December 1803, Haydn biographer Georg
August Griesinger mistakenly stated in a letter that Beethoven had received
the piano as a gift.[6] As Maria Rose explains, the "gift" story was accepted by
Thayer's editor Riemann on the basis of information from Charles
Bannelier of the magazine *Revue et Gazette musicale de Paris*, who had
written a review of the 1873 Viennese world exhibition. At this exhibition,
the Érard piano was shown, accompanied by a description which apparently
originated from Beethoven's brother Johann (who owned the piano before
he donated it to the *Landesmuseum* in Linz, where it is today). This
description stated that the city of Paris had given the piano to Beethoven.
To verify the content of this notice, Bannelier contacted the Érard firm's
manager Schaeffer, who confirmed the gift myth by writing: "We see in our
books that on 18 thermidor, year XI of the French Republic, i.e. 8 August
1803 [*sic*], Sebastien Érard gave as gift a grand piano to L. v. Beethoven, then
living in Vienna."[7] This information is incorrect. The rediscovered notice
from the Érard archives reads as follows:

18 thermidor year II: M. Beethowen, *claveciniste* in Vienna, owes 1500 Francs for
the sale of a piano in the shape of a harpsichord, no. 133.[8]

Quite clearly, the piano was *sold* for 1500 francs directly to Beethoven. The
gift myth thus appears to have two origins.

First, Beethoven himself must have told Griesinger shortly after its arrival
that it was a present. An alternative could be that Griesinger only *thought*
that the piano was a gift because the Érard firm had sent a similar

---

[4] As discussed earlier, Andreas Streicher was responsible for the Streicher firm's correspondence. It was,
however, his wife Nannette who led the production, and we can assume that on many occasions
Andreas was expressing Nannette's convictions, even when writing in the first person.

[5] See Maria Rose, "Beethoven and his French piano: proof of purchase," *Musique, Images, Instruments* 7,
(2005): 110–22.

[6] Otto Biba, ed., *"Eben komme ich von Haydn." Georg August Griesingers Korrespondenz mit Joseph
Haydns Verleger Breitkopf & Härtel 1799–1819*, Zürich: Atlantis, 1987, 216.

[7] Rose, "Beethoven and his French piano: proof of purchase," 119, after Charles Bannelier, "Les
Instruments historiques à l'Exposition Universelle de Vienne (1873)," *Revue et Gazette musicale de
Paris*, September 5 (1875). The date should be August 6, 1803.

[8] "18 therm.^dor II/ Mr Beethowen Claveciniste à/Vienne D.^t L 1500 p Vte. Du piano/en forme de
Clavecin No. 133." Archives of the Érard firm, private collection. *Ibid.*, 110. Formatting after the
original.

instrument to Haydn in 1801. Whichever was the case, Beethoven seemed inclined to support the rumor. In a letter to Andreas Streicher from November 1810, he states that the instrument was a *"souvenir,"* adding, "Nobody here has honored me with anything similar."[9] The corresponding information from the 1873 exhibition naturally stems similarly in one way or another from Beethoven. Michael Latcham suggests that Beethoven perhaps even staged the whole story from the beginning, i.e. from the point he decided to order a piano in Paris.[10]

The second origin of the myth is misinformation from the Érard firm. Érard's manager Mr. Schaeffer was *unquestionably* able to read the abbreviations in the original archive notice that stand for "owes" (D.ᵗ for "doit") and "sale" (Vᵗᵉ. for "vente") respectively.

The Érard fortepiano was, as far as we know, Beethoven's first piano not to have been built in the German–Viennese tradition. On the other hand, Beethoven was acquainted with Haydn's Érard from 1801. This piano, lost today, most likely provided the inspiration for Beethoven to try to obtain a similar instrument from the Viennese maker Anton Walter. In a letter to Nikolaus Zmeskall (November 1802), who appears to have acted as a contact between Beethoven and Walter, Beethoven wrote:

You may give him to understand that I will pay him 30 ducats, though I can have it for free from all the others, but I will only give 30 ducats on condition that it is of mahogany, and I also want to have the *una corda* stop – if he does not agree, make him understand that I will choose one of the other [builders], whom I will tell all this, and whom I will also take to Haydn to have him see this [i.e. Haydn's Érard].[11]

Although none of Walter's surviving instruments from that time has an *una corda*, Beethoven's order does in fact describe one of Walter's available models. In the spring of 1802, the Swedish diplomat Fredrik Samuel Silverstolpe obtained a Walter piano for his superior, the Swedish envoy Jacob Graf de la Gardie. In a letter from June 5, 1802, he enthusiastically describes one of its new features, the *una corda*. This invention, he writes, "has been made in England for a long time, but is only now being imitated here."[12]

As far as we know, the negotiations between Beethoven and Walter amounted to nothing. Clearly Beethoven regarded Haydn's French piano

---

[9] Beethoven, *Briefwechsel*, vol. II, 168.

[10] Latcham, "The development of the Streicher firm of piano builders," copy provided by the author, 27–30, section "Beethoven."

[11] This is the same letter in which he mentions the visit of an unknown Frenchman (see below). Beethoven, *Briefwechsel*, vol. I, 137. This passage is difficult to interpret, since the word "this" ("dieses") is used three times, referring first to Beethoven's request, then the situation as a whole *or* Walter's possible refusal, and finally to Haydn's piano.

[12] Quoted in Silke Berdux and Susanne Wittmayer, "Biographische Notizen zu Anton Walter," in *Mitteilungen der Internationalen Stiftung Mozarteum*, ed. Rudolph Angermüller, Salzburg: Internationale Stiftung Mozarteum, 2000, 50.

as a model worth showing to the local builders, and the fact that he
eventually ordered an Érard for himself seems only logical.[13]

No particulars about the relationship between Érard and Beethoven,
or about the delivery of Beethoven's piano, are documented.[14] August 6,
1803 (a Saturday) may have been the date of dispatch of the instrument.
Although its exact arrival date in Vienna is unknown, it must have been
before October 22.[15] Beethoven now owned a new French fortepiano with a
larger keyboard range and a better resonance than most Viennese instruments. Testimony by Griesinger from December 1803 in a letter to Härtel
(discussed below) shows that, initially, Beethoven was very positive about the
instrument.[16]

An unidentified piano builder made modifications to the Érard's action
on two separate occasions before 1805.[17] In 1810 Beethoven called the
instrument "simply not of any use any more, of none whatsoever" and,
later, "now really unusable," admitting the only reason he did not sell it
was because it was a "*souvenir.*"[18] In the spring of 1813 Matthäus Andreas
Stein put it in order and in 1824 Beethoven gave it to his brother Johann.
From him, the piano came to the *Oberösterreichisches Landesmuseum* in
Linz in 1845. After this, the instrument was apparently never restored or
altered.[19]

---

[13] Michael Latcham was the first to interpret Beethoven's request as having been specifically
influenced by his experience with Haydn's Érard. See Latcham, *The Stringing, Scaling and
Pitch of Hammerflügel*, vol. I, 76, for a discussion of the *una corda* in the Viennese and
English traditions. In England the *una corda* was already being used generally in the 1780s.
The oldest surviving Viennese piano built by the Streicher firm with the *una corda* is dated 1807
(Germanisches National Museum, inv. no. MINe 135), and the oldest by Walter with this stop is
dated about 1810 (Collection Scala, Imola). My thanks to Michael Latcham for supplying this
information. However, Latcham's conclusion that Walter did not build an *una corda* at all in
1802 appears to be incorrect.

[14] Beethoven initially planned to dedicate the "Kreutzer" Sonata Op. 47 to Kreutzer and the pianist Jean
Louis Adam, since "he owed Adam something because of the *Klavier* from Paris." The nature of
Adam's service to Beethoven is unknown (Letter from Ries to Simrock, October 22, 1803. Beethoven,
Briefwechsel, vol. I, 190).

[15] See the discussions in Douglas P. Johnson, Alan Tyson, and Robert Winter, *The Beethoven
Sketchbooks: History, Reconstruction, Inventory*, Berkeley: University of California Press, 1985, 141–2,
and Barry Cooper, "The evolution of the first movement of the 'Waldstein' sonata," *Music and Letters*
58 (1977): 184–5. Ferdinand Ries' letter of October 22, 1803 suggests that the "*Klavier* from Paris" had
arrived before that date.

[16] Biba, ed., *"Eben komme ich von Haydn,"* 216.

[17] Perhaps Matthäus Andreas Stein. Beethoven very likely borrowed a Stein piano for his stay in
Oberdöbling in 1803 or 1804 (see Beethoven's undated letter to Ries, Beethoven, *Briefwechsel*,
vol. I, 172). The date of the changes can be concluded from a letter from Andreas Streicher
written January 2, 1805 (Lütge, "Andreas und Nanette Streicher," 65), which is discussed below.
The substantial character of these alterations suggests that the instrument was brought to a
builder's workshop.

[18] Two letters to Andreas Streicher, September 18 and November 1810. Beethoven, *Briefwechsel*, vol. II,
153 and 168.

[19] See Alfons Huber, "Beethovens Erard-Flügel, Überlegungen zu seiner Restaurierung," *Restauro* 3
(1990): 183.

BEETHOVEN'S ÉRARD AND THE ENGLISH AND
FRENCH BUILDING TRADITION

In 1803, the Érard's compass of five-and-a-half octaves FF – c'''' would have only been normal for the newest pianos made in Vienna.[20] The instrument has four pedals, one for the *una corda*, one for the dampers, and two other pedals for a lute stop and a moderator. To judge from Beethoven's notation and from his correspondence, the *una corda* and the damper mechanism were both of special interest to Beethoven.[21] Regarding the basic shape, compass and action principle, this instrument is quite similar to the pianos by the Broadwood firm around 1800, apart from its two extra stops. However, there are differences as well: Érard's scaling was slightly longer than Broadwood's except for the low bass, although the London and Paris pitches were more or less identical. The strings in the treble and middle were slightly thinner in Érard's instruments.[22] There are significant differences in interior construction and soundboard ribbing between the pianos of both builders that do have an influence on the tone of the instruments. Broadwood began to make his five-and-a-half-octave instruments sturdier from the turn of the century,[23] whereas Érard in 1805 still used a lighter but very effective inner construction.[24] In spite of these differences, English and French pianos of that era were seen as part of one tradition even in the historical literature, so I will refer to both as part of the same tradition.

The appearance of the names Érard and Broadwood can lead to incorrect associations in connection with the 1803 piano. Érard invented the repetition action, which made the English action faster and easier to control, but this was in 1821 (an earlier patent dates from 1808).[25] This invention has nothing to do with Beethoven's piano. Broadwood sent Beethoven a grand piano as well, but this was in 1817. This piano had a range of six octaves and was probably a more powerful instrument than any piano around 1800.

Several writers have discussed the differences between English-style pianos and those from Vienna.[26] The discussion as a whole has remained

---

[20] Latcham, *The Stringing, Scaling and Pitch of Hammerflügel*, vol. II, tables 1, 4.

[21] According to David Rowland, Beethoven probably used the moderator and other registers rarely. Rowland, "Beethoven's pianoforte pedalling," 68.

[22] The scaling from Beethoven's Érard and an 1802 Broadwood (No. 2343), measured by the author, compares as follows (Érard/Broadwood, millimeters): Iron c'''': 74/70. c''': 138/132. c'': 277/270. c': 558/543. c: 1114/1103. A: 1320/1305. Brass G#: 1104/1080. C: 1563/1590. FF: 1711/1723. My thanks to Alfons Huber for the scaling of Beethoven's Érard.

See also Alain Moysan, "L'Erard de 1790," in *Sébastien Erard 1752–1831 ou la rencontre avec le pianoforte*, Luxeuil-Les-Bains: Publi-Lux, 1993, 32. The pitch was around 435–40 Hz; see Bruce Haynes, *Pitch Standards in the Baroque and Classical Periods*, Ann Arbor, 1996, 139, 349.

[23] Koster, *Keyboard Musical Instruments in the Museum of Fine Arts, Boston*, 199.

[24] Moysan, "L'Erard de 1790," 41.   [25] Harding, *The Piano-Forte*, 158 and 173, Fig. 11.

[26] See Richard Burnett, "English pianos at Finchcocks," *Early Music* 13/1 (1985): 45–51; Christopher Kite, "Playing the early piano," *Early Music* 13/1 (1985): 54–6; Komlós, *Fortepianos and their Music*; and Bart van Oort, "The English Classical piano style and its influence on Haydn and Beethoven" and "Haydn and the English classical piano style," *Early Music* 28/1 (2000): 73–89.

somewhat inconclusive. The tone character especially, and the effect of the less efficient English dampers (in comparison to Viennese instruments), varies in different surviving instruments, and it changed as English and French pianos developed during the late eighteenth and early nineteenth centuries. On the other hand, many historical descriptions from the period praise the thick and singing treble of the English instruments. Sources from, say, 1805 and 1820 contain judgments that make use of very similar language. In practice, however, there is a world of difference between the pianos of these years. For the modern observer it requires a keen sense of chronology to understand exactly which constructions a writer is comparing.

Another problem is the discrepancy between historical descriptions and the properties of some of the surviving instruments. The poorly sustained treble of many English-style fortepianos is often caused by problems that can be identified and sometimes easily eliminated. Flattened hammer leathers, an escapement set up in the wrong way, inadequate stringing, loose bridge pins, or an excess of rust or dirt at the contact points, can be repaired or readjusted. Another problem of many of these instruments that is less easy to fix is their cheek twist, which can be very noticeable especially in English pianos. Sometimes the distortion can be so great that the downward string pressure on the treble bridge and the treble nut is substantially reduced. As a consequence, the massive bridge and the very thick soundboard in this area (around 8 mm at the treble end of the bridge)[27] do not resonate properly, and the tone becomes short and weak. This problem, however, is irrelevant in our discussion: Beethoven's Érard has little or no visible cheek twist and it surely had none when new. The Érard's soundboards were also less than half as thick as the Broadwood's in the treble.[28] This difference, together with Érard's longer and thinner strings, would have meant that the sound characteristics of these instruments differed when new in spite of certain similarities in their construction. Their aging patterns can certainly not be directly compared.

There is some disagreement in the literature about the typical level of imprecision of the damping in English-style fortepianos. In contrast to the Viennese ideal, English-style dampers often allow for a substantial afterring, especially in late Classical or early Romantic pianos. In an 1805 Broadwood, I measured an after-ring of the fundamentals of three to four seconds in bass chords; some overtones lingered substantially longer. These dampers have been in use for twenty-eight years. Bart van Oort writes that the worn-out dampers that were found in the double-strung *c.* 1827

---

[27] Broadwood grand piano No. 3228, built in 1805.
[28] No. 143 from 1803, which belonged to prince Lichnowsky, has a soundboard thickness of 3.5 mm at the treble front edge (Michael Latcham, personal communication). The soundboard of no. 176 from 1808 in the Brussels museum is only 3.3 mm thick at the treble front edge (John Koster, personal communication).

Broadwood grand in the Cornell University collection allowed for an after-ring of eight seconds in bass chords. After the replacement of the damper material this was still four to five seconds.[29] Clearly, the heavy strings of later instruments further enhance the after-ring.

There also seems to be a slight difference between English and French dampers from the period in question: the curator of the *Gemeentemuseum*, Michael Latcham, has confirmed that the damping of the 1808 Érard in that collection is very effective, suggesting that the difference between *new* French or English and Viennese dampers might be smaller than is sometimes believed.

My own observations of some replacements confirm that the after-ring of English-style dampers can be noticeably reduced by using new materials; however, the basic difference between English and Viennese dampers always remains clear. In English instruments, new damper cloth settles to a longer after-ring after two to three years, while well-made Viennese dampers keep their precision much longer.

WHY WAS THE ÉRARD'S ACTION ALTERED?

In an article about Beethoven's Érard, Alfons Huber summarizes the changes that were made to this instrument as follows.[30]

The balance rail was widened, the balance pins were moved, and new holes were made in the keys at the corresponding points. Thus the balance point of the keyboard was shifted 45 mm toward the player. This reduced the key dip from 8.5–9 mm to 6–6.5 mm.

The two lead weights on each key were taken from the rear end of each key lever and inserted at the front. As much wood as possible was removed from the underside of the key-ends.

The key levers were lengthened by 12 mm at the front and the original keyplates were shifted accordingly. The hammers were re-leathered and cut somewhat narrower.

In a letter dated January 2, 1805, Andreas Streicher states that two alterations of the action were made before that date in order to cope with what he elsewhere calls "drawbacks" of the English action (quoted further below).[31] The traces in the instrument indeed point to two separate interventions. It is not known by whom and in which order these changes were made. One is tempted to suppose that a first modification did not yield the desired result, or was made without proper consideration, so that soon a revision became necessary.

---

[29] Van Oort, "The English Classical piano style and its influence on Haydn and Beethoven," 30, n. 75. This instrument can be heard on a CD with music by Ignaz Moscheles, played by Tom Begin (Eufoda 1267, issued in 2000).
[30] Huber, "Beethovens Erard-Flügel," 183–5. Presented here in a different order.
[31] Lütge, "Andreas und Nanette Streicher," 65–6.

It is obvious that whoever made these changes did so in an attempt to give the Érard the equivalent of a Viennese key dip. After the balance points had been moved toward the front, the lead weights also had to be moved to restore the key balance. Possibly, this operation did restore the key balance to such a degree that the action was functional. Apparently, however, some circumstance initiated further changes nevertheless.

One such a circumstance could be a heavy touch because of the change in the relationship between key depression and hammer lift. A piano action is difficult to control if the acceleration given to the hammer on depressing the key is too high. After a reduction of the key dip from ~8 mm to ~6 mm, while maintaining its hammer lift,[32] the touch of Beethoven's piano must have become discernibly heavier, and dynamic control must have gotten noticeably more difficult. This was probably one of the reasons for under-cutting the key tails. At the same time, this undercutting would have reduced the overall key mass. This aspect of the revision was clearly a method to regain dynamic control and an attempt to reduce the inertia of the action.

The lengthening of the key fronts, however, is a clear indicator of a rescue action. I assume that the combined efforts of the previous steps did not sufficiently solve the leverage problems caused by the relocated balance point. It would in fact have been technically possible to relocate the balance points once again at some point between the original ones and the changed ones. But instead of undoing part of the initial work, the front key levers were now lengthened and the keyplates relocated. Apart from being work-intensive, this operation resulted in an unattractive gap between the rear ends of the keyplates and the nameboard.[33] The latter suggests that we are looking at the result of an uncomfortable compromise. From a technical viewpoint it makes no sense at all: lengthening one *end* of the key by 12 mm does little to correct leverage issues caused by the previous relocation of the balance point in the *middle* by 45 mm.

The last change, the re-leathering and narrowing of the hammers, might date from any moment in the early history of the instrument. Re-leathering is a standard procedure in fortepiano maintenance. Alfons Huber supposes that, during this process, the hammers were voiced to Viennese standards.[34] It would indeed seem natural that a Viennese builder, using Viennese hammer leather, would automatically tend to influence the tone according to Viennese ideals during such an operation. The re-shaping of the hammers would have reduced their mass somewhat. However, apparently only a very small amount of wood was taken away. It could simply be that, during

---

[32] The hammer lift in the 1803 Érard that belonged to Prince Lichnowsky is 53 mm at FF and 51 mm at f according to Michael Latcham's annotations.
[33] See Huber, "Beethovens Erard-Flügel," 185, Fig. 12.   [34] *Ibid.*, 183.

re-leathering, the hammers were trimmed down at the sides together with the leathers, in a fashion that is often observed.

Despite Streicher's description of Beethoven as a "strong player," the technical circumstances give evidence of the fact that these alterations did *not* have the objective of making the Érard action heavier: the contrary is evident.[35] If the initial modification had the objective of reducing the key dip according to the Viennese ideal, all the subsequent changes can be interpreted as efforts to *regain* a controllable touch, which had become heavier as a result of the first operation. This conclusion is vital for understanding Beethoven's technical approach. The notion that he, at this time, was longing for instruments with a heavier touch cannot be maintained.[36]

HÄRTEL'S AND BEETHOVEN'S INFLUENCE ON STREICHER'S CHANGE OF PIANO DESIGN

During the first years of the nineteenth century, the presence of French and English pianos in Vienna and Leipzig strongly influenced the Streichers' piano design. A well-known passage from Johann Friedrich Reichardt's "Vertraute Briefe," in which he describes a house concert at Nikolaus Zmeskall's on Sunday, February 5, 1809, illustrates what had happened in the Streicher firm in the preceding years. In this concert Dorothea von Ertmann played a Beethoven fantasy on Zmeskall's piano:

It was a beautiful instrument by Streicher, brought to life today as if it were a whole orchestra. Streicher has abandoned the soft, overly responsive, bouncing, and rolling [character] of the other Viennese instruments, and – upon Beethoven's advice and request – has given his instruments more resistance and elasticity in order to enable the virtuoso who performs with strength and meaning to have more control over the instrument's sustaining and carrying [power], and for the subtle emphases and diminuendos.[37]

We are reminded of Beethoven's letter to Andreas Streicher in 1796 in which he called a Streicher piano "too good" for him because it deprived him of the "freedom to create his own tone." The creation of a tone formed in the mind rather than dictated by the piano is an important aspect of modern piano playing and, in this light, Beethoven's criticism seems to be nothing less than a prophecy, since the 1796 letter describes a piano of exactly the "bouncing and rolling kind" that Streicher had now abandoned.

---

[35] At first sight, Streicher's description would even suggest that Beethoven found the action at the beginning too heavy.

[36] See my discussion of the Érard's touch and of the formulation "kräftiger Spieler" on page 100, which could, in this context, mean that Beethoven was *skilful* enough to deal with a problematic touch. It probably ought not to serve as proof that, around 1804, he already "preferred instruments with fewer partials and a heavier touch," as Eszter Fontana has suggested (Fontana, "Ein Geschenk für Beethoven," 272, n. 51).

[37] Reichardt, *Briefe, die Musik betreffend*, 287.

Reichardt's testimony to Beethoven's influence on Streicher and the resulting piano, which could be "brought to life as if it were a whole orchestra," has always been accepted as consistent with what could be expected of a man like Beethoven. Thayer assigns Beethoven "a new but characteristic role, that of an improver of the pianoforte."[38] In 1995, important publications still echo Paul Bekker, who in 1912 elaborated on Reichardt by presenting Beethoven as a "reformer of the piano" and by claiming that it was his goal to "enhance the tonal dimensions," to "increase the sustain" and to create "a tone that offered a richer palette of registers. In this way, the instrument must gain expression, soul, and color."[39]

One major source, apart from the surviving instruments, that illustrates the development that led to the "orchestral" piano is a collection of excerpts from 65 letters written by Andreas Streicher to Gottfried Christoph Härtel in Leipzig between 1800 and 1807. The letters are lost and only a list of their dates is preserved.[40] Fifteen fragments from Andreas Streicher's letters, six fragments from letters by Härtel, and the content of a contract, survive as literal transcriptions or indirect quotations in an article by Wilhelm Lütge from 1927. Apart from being music editors, Breitkopf & Härtel had started an instrument trade in 1802 in which Streicher pianos played a central role.[41] "Almost every single one" of Streicher's letters contained information about his main concern of that time, i.e. "the improvement of his instruments."

The letters from Georg Griesinger, Haydn's first biographer,[42] to Härtel are another important source of information about Streicher's pianos. The original letters are also lost. In 1987, the transcriptions of 126 of these letters by Carl Ferdinand Pohl (another Haydn biographer) became accessible to the public in Otto Biba's critical edition. Griesinger, who like Andreas Streicher was born in Stuttgart, had been in Leipzig from 1797 and in Vienna from 1799, where he acted as Breitkopf & Härtel's "unofficial" agent.[43] After 1801 he participated actively in the negotiations between Härtel and Streicher, and he had a keen interest in new tendencies in piano building. Griesinger also had contact with Beethoven: Breitkopf & Härtel were the publishers of some of Beethoven's works. Griesinger's success in settling their disagreement over Artaria's pirate edition of the

---

[38] Thayer, *Life of Beethoven*, 461.

[39] Paul Bekker's original term is "Klavierreformator" (Bekker, *Beethoven*, 110). Bekker was clearly only superficially informed about Beethoven's fortepianos and their characteristics. The term resurfaces in Chapter 8 of DeNora, *Beethoven and the Construction of Genius*, in a discussion of "Beethoven's impact on piano technology."

[40] I am grateful to Dr. Andreas Sopart from Breitkopf & Härtel for informing me about the circumstances and for providing this list.

[41] Lütge, "Andreas und Nanette Streicher," 61.

[42] Georg August Griesinger, *Biographische Notizen über Josph Haydn*, Leipzig, 1810, first appeared in a serialized form in the AMZ.

[43] Biba, ed., *"Eben komme ich von Haydn,"* 14.

Quintet Op. 29 in late 1802 shows that he was trusted by both sides.[44] In their correspondence with Härtel, both Streicher and Griesinger mention Beethoven's Érard piano at some point, and his opinion about fortepianos was used in their discussions.

Why Streicher's letters to Härtel contained so much information about piano building can be explained by the circumstance that, at the beginning of their business relationship in the autumn of 1802, there were several reasons to be critical of Streicher's instruments. When Nannette's brother Matthäus Andreas Stein left the Geschwister Stein firm in the midst of a scandal in the middle of 1802, the consensus was that he had delayed some necessary technical developments. The Streichers now re-arranged their business contacts and began to pay attention to the demands of the customers. Griesinger writes on October 23, 1802, to Härtel:

Hofmeister, Bernhard, music director Müller, and Köhler want to approach Streicher so he will send [them] his fortepianos, but he is disposed to do business only with you; he is an honest man whom you can trust. In order to establish your connection, it would be advantageous if you could anticipate him by placing a few orders. Now that he has separated from his unreliable and lazy brother-in-law, everything that was wanting in the instruments by the Stein firm shall be remedied. He was very glad to hear the opinions from Leipzig about [the instruments]. He says that the Stein instruments, as far as their keyboard and touch characteristics are concerned, have advantages that have not been surpassed by any other master; their more brilliant tone can easily be modified by making the case walls somewhat higher.[45]

Härtel placed an order with Streicher for twenty-five fortepianos with keyboard ranges of five, five-and-a-half, and six octaves.[46] Two of Griesinger's letters address the same event. On November 10, 1802, he writes, "[Streicher] has just told me that you placed an order for instruments with him," and on November 27, "Streicher is extremely happy with your splendid order."

The only preserved discussion from the first year of Streicher's and Härtel's association is about the addition of *Veränderungen* to the pianos, which Streicher (defending J.A. Stein's building tradition) considered "toys," whereas Härtel, according to Lütge, pointed out "over and over again" that the public "simply demanded" them.[47] On May 21, 1803,[48] Streicher gave up: "I am tired of wanting to improve [people's] taste, and it is less effort for me to make a lute stop than to convince an ignorant person in advance that he will have ceased to use it within four weeks."[49]

---

[44] See letters 110, 112 and 118–22 in Beethoven, *Briefwechsel*, vol. i, 128–44.

[45] Biba, ed., *"Eben komme ich von Haydn,"* 170.

[46] Lütge, "Andreas und Nanette Streicher," 63.   [47] *Ibid.*, 63–4.

[48] Not 1804, as Lütge says. The only letter in the Streicher–Härtel correspondence from May 21 was written in 1803.

[49] Lütge, "Andreas und Nanette Streicher," 64.

In the same year, 1803, at the time when Beethoven received Érard's piano, the piano actions made by the Streicher firm were still conservative. Other instruments, such as those by Anton Walter, were perhaps somewhat heavier to play, but they still had a shallower touch than French or English ones, and their touch made a lighter impression.[50] But if the advantage of the Viennese pianos was their light touch, the advantage of the English and French pianos lay in their superior, fuller tone. Griesinger refers to this tone in a letter to Härtel of December 14, 1803:

Presumably the instrument makers here will try to study and acquire the advantage of the brothers Érard. I therefore want to try to impress this on Streicher, even though he was not content with the one Haydn owns.[51]

Like Griesinger, but unlike Streicher, who disliked Haydn's Érard from 1801, Härtel had become interested in the English instruments. In 1803 he apparently ordered some pianos directly from Broadwood in London. However, he had difficulties in selling them,[52] perhaps because Broadwood's instruments were significantly more expensive than Viennese pianos.[53] It is unknown if or when Griesinger spoke to Streicher about the French "advantage," but we do know that Härtel now began to encourage Streicher to make pianos with an English action. Streicher's response from January 21, 1804, was essentially positive and he promised to collect information:

This is easy for me, since I have permission to make an exact drawing of a fortepiano by Érard of Paris that was once built in London.[54]

It seems possible that Streicher is referring to Beethoven's new piano. True, Prince Lichnowsky had also obtained a grand piano by Érard in 1803 (serial no. 143; it is the tenth instrument after Beethoven's), but this instrument

---

[50] Kenneth Mobbs writes: "English instruments are seen to be heavier than Viennese, but from 1790 to 1820 by not such a margin as might be imagined from a good many writings on piano history." Kenneth Mobbs, "A performer's comparative study of touchweight, key-dip, keyboard design and repetition in early grand pianos, *c*. 1770 to 1850," *The Galpin Society Journal* 54 (2001): 16. The practical value of a comparison of "touchweight for minimum sound" is, however, small: a player is confronted with the keyboard's resilience at *all* dynamic shades and at various playing speeds. In performance, heaviness, mass inertia, hammer acceleration, the possibility of control, key dip, and the sound contribute to a highly complex, partly psychological sensation of touch heaviness. In this sense, many writings about touch heaviness have been able to capture essential characteristics, where touchweight measuring has not.

[51] Biba, ed., *"Eben komme ich von Haydn,"* 216. Latcham, *The Stringing, Scaling and Pitch of Hammerflügel*, vol. I, 75.

[52] Lütge, "Andreas und Nanette Streicher," 66.

[53] See Maunder, *Keyboard Instruments in Eighteenth-Century Vienna*, 128–9, and David Wainwright, *Broadwood by Appointment. A History*, London: Quiller Press, 1982, 99.

[54] Lütge, "Andreas und Nanette Streicher," 66. The words "once built in London" perhaps mean a piano built by the London branch of the Érard firm, founded by Sébastien Érard in 1792 before returning to Paris in 1796.

was in Hradec Castle.[55] Haydn's Érard was not as new, and we already know that Streicher did not like it. Apparently, there were very few or indeed no other instruments by Érard in Vienna at that time, except for Haydn's and Beethoven's.

Härtel's continuing effort to influence the piano construction of the Streicher firm is documented again at the end of 1804. On December 7 of that year, he wrote to Streicher that those amateurs who want to play to a bigger accompaniment often prefer English, French, other German, or "Schanz-Müller'sche" instruments because they "insist on a stronger tone than that of your [Streicher's] instruments." He continues that Clementi had been his private guest for two months and had chosen the "strongest instrument with the most difficult [i.e. heaviest] touch." In his critical answer Streicher used Beethoven as an authority (January 2, 1805, mentioned above):

There is one single remark of which I cannot approve in your letter, namely the heavier and deeper keyboards as Clementi wants them ... Certainly the English pianos gain an advantage over ours if we make our keyboards [i.e. action] according to their principle, and this appears to be Clementi's intention. But it is also certain that the fortepiano will then cease to be the universal instrument, since nine out of ten Clavier amateurs will have to give up playing.

Beethoven is certainly a strong player, yet he can still not adequately treat his Fp., which he got from Érard in Paris, and he has already had it changed twice without the least improvement, because its construction does not allow for any other action.[56]

Despite the encouragement from Härtel, the Streicher firm did not build pianos with the English action for many years to come.[57] Instead, in 1805, the firm finally accepted the Viennese action and began to use hammer checks and brass Kapsels in their pianos. At the same time, they started to alter other construction details as well. Triple stringing in the treble of the instruments, larger hammers, and heavier bridges all show that the Streicher firm was now resolved to increase the volume of tone available on its instruments.[58] The development finally culminated in a fresh look at case construction.[59] It must have been the result of a prolonged phase of designing, discussing, testing, and rejecting or accepting various solutions.

---

[55] This instrument is already mentioned in Bekker, *Beethoven*, 110. Its location in Hradec (Gräz, near Troppau) connects it to the "Apassionata" Sonata Op. 57 and to Beethoven's spectacular flight from Gräz at the end of October 1806.

[56] Lütge, "Andreas und Nanette Streicher," 65.

[57] In 1823 Johann Baptist Streicher, the son of Nannette and Andreas, entered the firm as a partner. In 1831 he took out a patent for his own form of the English action.

[58] Much of this information comes from Latcham, *The Stringing, Scaling and Pitch of Hammerflügel.*

[59] See William Jurgenson, "The structure of the classical piano," paper presented at the Antwerpiano conference, Antwerp, 1989, 5, for a description of the changes in the case construction of Streicher pianos around 1807.

Some of the surviving letters relate specifically to this development. We learn that, by the summer of 1804, Streicher had built some new instruments whose action, however, had turned out to be too heavy for his taste. In 1805 he was able to report that his instruments were no longer softer than those of other builders. He could have made them louder still, but then the tone would become inflexible. On March 1, 1806, he again wrote to Härtel about English and French pianos:

You ask me about my opinion about the English and French Pf., and I may assure you in advance that I have always preferred the tone of these instruments to all others; I still do – I agree with Clementi and Dussek in finding this tone most suited for a grand and especially a public performance; on the other hand, the construction of the keyboard [i.e. the action] is so completely at odds with the structure of the hand that one can hardly think of anything less suitable, and also the whole action is so little durable as to be unfit for a true performance. The future will convince you that I am certainly not biased but that my judgment about these instruments is more justified than anybody else's. I have done even more: I sought to combine this tone with our usual action, and if I may trust the judgment of the best Clavier players and amateurs here, I have been quite successful.[60]

On April 3, 1807, the Streicher firm sent the first instrument of the new kind to Breitkopf & Härtel. This piano had a keyboard range of six octaves and the section of iron strings was triple-strung throughout. In a letter to the editor of the *Allgemeine Musikalische Zeitung* of Leipzig, Streicher gives the particulars of this instrument and precise instructions for a comparison of this piano with other English, French, or local instruments. In this letter, Streicher chooses not to mention the judgment of the Viennese pianists in order to encourage an impartial judgment. However, he cannot refrain from relating the history of improvements in the workshop:

[I want to] add that, after this instrument, five others have been made here, all of which turned out much more perfectly and even louder, and have the advantage of being easier to handle than this one. Anyway, this one, like all the first experiments, still has some imperfections which have been avoided in its successors.[61]

Specimens of these new Streicher pianos, with a compass of six-and-a-half octaves (CC–f′′′′) survive from 1807 and 1808.[62] Judging by Reichardt's description, Zmeskall's Streicher was very likely a similar instrument. We can conclude that these instruments were the result of at least four years of intense work in the Streicher workshop, headed by Nannette Streicher, and

---

[60] Lütge, "Andreas und Nanette Streicher," 66–7. Contrary to Streicher's opinion, time has shown that the English grand action is as sturdy as anyone could wish.

[61] Letter draft, dated April 4, 1807. Goebl-Streicher, Streicher, and Ladenburger, *"Diesem Menschen hätte ich mein ganzes Leben widmen mögen,"* 119–20.

[62] *Germanisches Nationalmuseum*, Nuremberg, inv. nos. MINe 135 (prod. no. 733) and MIR 1117 (prod. no. 764), listed in Latcham, *The Stringing, Scaling and Pitch of Hammerflügel*, vol. I, xiii, and vol. II, Table 3. In a corrected version of these pages, Latcham lists another instrument from 1808 (prod. no. 763). Between 1807 and 1830, the firm made six-octave and six-and-a-half-octave instruments alongside each other.

of Andreas Streicher's discussions with Härtel and Griesinger, and perhaps Beethoven. In any case, Beethoven was certainly one of the "best Clavier players" who approved of these new instruments: as late as 1817, he remembers: "Although I did not always have one of your pianos, I always preferred them to others after 1809."[63] However, Reichardt's assertion that Beethoven had a major influence on the development in Streicher's firm seems at least exaggerated, given the involvement of Härtel and Griesinger, and the fact that Beethoven is only sporadically mentioned in their correspondence in this connection.

DEAFNESS, IMPATIENCE AND THE MISUSE OF INSTRUMENTS

As a consequence of the development of Streicher's pianos, the Érard must have become unattractive for Beethoven at the latest in 1809. One need not interpret this as a fault of the instrument; it simply became outdated as regards its tone as well its keyboard range. This was so even in the eyes of French observers. In 1809, Louis Girod (later Baron de Trémont), who had just arrived in Vienna in the service of Napoleon, visited Beethoven, and his vivid description of Beethoven's untidy room includes "a rather old grand piano."[64] The French music lover Girod knew how to judge the pianos he was familiar with: this "rather old" piano was therefore probably the French Érard.

What Beethoven thought of the piano when he first received it is a different question, which must be separated from his ideas about pianos in about 1809. It is for this reason that we have to look again at Griesinger's letter from December 14, 1803, quoted above. Why would the Viennese instrument makers want to "try to study and acquire the advantage of the brothers Érard"? The reason was in fact Beethoven's brand-new piano:

The brothers Érard of Paris have made a present of a mahogany piano to Beethoven (as they did earlier to Haydn). He is so enchanted with it that he regards all the pianos made here as rubbish [*Quark*] by comparison. Because you are heavily involved in instrument dealing it will [not] be uninteresting for you to hear that Beethoven had already criticized the local instruments before. He said that they were wooden and that they get one into the habit of a small, weak touch. Beethoven being Beethoven might be right, but how many players are there like him? The keyboard of the Parisian piano is, even by Beethoven's admission, not as supple and elastic as on the Viennese pianos. But that is a trifle to a master like Beethoven.[65]

[63] Letter from July 18, 1817. Beethoven, *Briefwechsel*, vol. IV, 77. The date 1809 in this letter is clearly directly related to that specific stage of piano development in the Streicher firm.

[64] Kerst, *Die Erinnerungen an Beethoven*, vol. I, 135. The original French description is "un assez vieux piano à queue."

[65] Biba, ed., *"Eben komme ich von Haydn,"* 216. Translation from Latcham, *The Stringing, Scaling and Pitch of Hammerflügel*, vol. I, 75.

This passage, coming from a reliable source like Griesinger, is of singular significance because all other sources suggest that Beethoven did not like the Érard right from the beginning. But not only does Griesinger give us a unique picture of Beethoven's first opinion about the Érard, he also makes it clear that the nature of Beethoven's later problems with the instrument did not necessarily include its "incurable heaviness," as Newman suggested on the basis of Streicher's statement of 1805.

Streicher stated that Beethoven was a "strong" ("kräftiger") player and yet could still not "adequately treat" ("gehörig zu behandeln") his Érard. As we shall see, Beethoven was becoming such a "strong player" during this period as to frighten any piano builder; mere heaviness of action would certainly not have caused him problems. But Streicher's words may in fact suggest something different: the term "kräftiger Spieler" could mean both "forceful" and "dexterous," and to be "unable to treat his fortepiano adequately" may indicate that he could not *express* himself adequately on the piano. This appears in any case to be Griesinger's opinion when he calls the Érard action "not as supple and elastic as on the Viennese pianos." The comment "But that is a trifle to a master like Beethoven" makes it vividly clear that *initially* Beethoven was highly motivated to overcome the difficulties of the instrument, obviously because it also offered some welcome new possibilities. His statement that the Viennese pianos "get one into the habit of a small, weak touch" could even indicate that Beethoven initially saw the Érard's action as a welcome challenge.[66]

So it is surprising that he suddenly decided to have the action changed, an operation that was carried out some time between December 1803 and January 1805. This is not so much a practical issue: the piano could very well have been moved to a piano workshop during Beethoven's illness in May 1804[67] or during the summer, without interfering with his work. Beethoven's only letter about his piano from around this time, to his student Ferdinand Ries, was written in Oberdöbling near Heiligenstadt, where Beethoven might have stayed during the summer of 1803.[68] This date has not been confirmed, however, whereas it is certain that he was in Oberdöbling in August and September 1804.[69]

That the letter was written in 1804 rather than 1803 seems to be corroborated by the piano-related content: Beethoven asks Ries to go to the piano

---

[66] This convincing notion was put forward in Rose, "Beethoven and his French piano: proof of purchase," 116.

[67] See Wegeler and Ries, *Biographische Notizen über Beethoven*, Nachtrag 10–11, and Cooper, ed., *Das Beethoven Kompendium*, 164.

[68] See, however, van der Zanden, "Ferdinand Ries in Wien," 207–8. Circumstantial evidence suggests that Beethoven was in Heiligenstadt in 1803, as in the previous year. Van der Zanden doubts that Ries's letter was written in 1803. In an anecdote about the composition of the Sonata Op. 31/2, even Czerny combines Heiligenstadt and the summer of 1803 (Czerny, "Anekdoten und Notizen," 18). This is, however, incorrect. This sonata was completed earlier and appeared in print in August 1803.

[69] Beethoven, *Briefwechsel*, vol. 1, 172–3.

builder Matthäus Andreas Stein to rent an instrument "for money," since he was "afraid" to have his own piano brought to Oberdöbling. Beethoven hardly had such qualms about whichever piano he owned a month or so *before* he got the Érard in August 1803. More probably he was afraid to move his new Érard in *1804*. If he indeed borrowed a piano by Stein instead, Stein had the whole late summer and early fall to work on the French piano which was left in Vienna. This supposition that Stein and not Streicher re-worked the action would offer yet another, personal explanation for Streicher's reservation about the success of that operation: after Stein had broken up with his sister and left the firm, Streicher was certainly not well disposed toward his work.

In any event, the discrepancy between Griesinger's letter in 1803 and Beethoven's decision to alter the action very shortly thereafter is difficult to explain. From a musical standpoint, the theory that he suddenly became utterly tired of the instrument makes little sense. More attractive is perhaps the notion that a visiting piano builder made deprecatory remarks about the Érard and influenced Beethoven to change his mind about its qualities. If we can believe Streicher's later judgment that the changes in the action were unsuccessful, one of the consequences would inevitably have been Beethoven's disappointment with the instrument.

Another circumstantial explanation suits the timing of the changes to the Érard surprisingly well, and helps explain why Beethoven's change of mind came so suddenly: possibly, Beethoven's initial "enchantment" with the Érard was partly a consequence of his general interest in matters French.[70] Famously, this interest was abruptly terminated in the wake of his indignation at Napoleon's coronation in May 1804.[71] Given the scale of his outrage, the idea that Beethoven initiated immediate measures to make his piano "less French" is an attractive hypothesis.

In 1805 at the latest, Beethoven's positive attitude toward the piano was gone. At best, the Érard went from being a new inspiration to a medium of mere daily routine, and was apparently treated in that spirit.

In May 1810, Beethoven wrote to Andreas Streicher in order to complain about a Streicher piano he had borrowed: his opinion was that the instrument wore out too quickly.[72] He had had the Streicher for some time by then, and had obviously used it very intensively instead of the Érard. Twice during the fall of that same year, Beethoven wrote to Streicher about his Érard: first to borrow another piano after the summer because the Érard was in a bad state, and later about the possibility of repairing the Érard yet again.[73]

---

[70] See Rose, "Beethoven and his French piano: proof of purchase," 112.
[71] Wegeler and Ries, *Biographische Notizen über Beethoven*, 77–9; Thayer, *Life of Beethoven*, 348–9.
[72] Letter from May 6, 1810. Beethoven, *Briefwechsel*, vol. II, 120.
[73] Letters to Streicher, September 18 and November 1810. *Ibid.*, 153 and 168.

In 1816, Peter Josef Simrock heard Beethoven play on the Érard at home in Vienna. Apparently it was, at that time, the only piano Beethoven had in Vienna, whereas he was using a good piano in Baden. By now, the Érard was in complete disorder: "Completely worn out, out of tune; several strings were in fact missing. Beethoven mentioned, too, that the instrument was not in perfect tune; but he was unable to hear just how false it sounded; at times the two visitors could barely conceal their unease."[74]

An analysis of the strings preserved in the instrument gives an impression of the scope of the problem.[75] While the overall average diameter is not too thick – unlike with many other historical pianos maintained or restored by later makers – the stringing is irregular and inconsistent. The piano is triple-strung throughout; twenty-six strings of the lowest ten notes are original; only nineteen strings out of a remaining total of 174 (fifty-eight notes) have a diameter appropriate to their pitch, as compared with the 1802 Érard in the *Musée instrumental* in Paris.[76] The distribution of all the strings other than those in the bass shows no regularity; sometimes differences of a tenth of a millimeter occur between strings of the same note. Normally such a difference would occur between two notes spaced apart at an interval of about two octaves. All this suggests that many strings are replacements. A standard practice observed on many old pianos seems to have been to save broken strings from lower down the instrument and use them to replace broken strings in the treble. Thus, the middle of the instrument has relatively thin strings (on average, 0.03 mm thinner than on the Paris 1802 Érard) whereas those in the treble are generally too thick (0.07 mm thicker than on the Paris instrument).

It may even be that Beethoven himself replaced strings in this way, or was responsible for replacing broken strings in the piano with ones provided locally, which would account for the variation in the loops with which the strings are attached to the hitch pins. No builder ever appears to have made an effort to re-string the instrument in its entirety; no regular pattern in the strings can be identified, apart from the few strings left in their original places. The overall picture is one of neglect and casual repair.

This, and the fact that the average of the strings is not too thick, indicates that the instrument's condition deteriorated early on in its history. Clearly, too, the instrument was left alone relatively early on. It appears, therefore, that Beethoven broke up to seventy-eight percent of the strings in his Érard during the period he was actually using it; replacements were made to a very unequal standard. An instrument in this state, with strings in

---

[74] Kerst, *Die Erinnerungen an Beethoven*, vol. 1, 204.

[75] My thanks to Alfons Huber for sending me his notes about all individual string diameters, and the various types of string loops found in the instrument.

[76] The Paris Érard is sometimes referred to as a twin of Beethoven's piano. Moysan, "L'Erard de 1790," 31, provides a stringing list. A comparison with Huber's material shows that Moysan's assertion that the strings in Beethoven's Érard are "almost identical" with those in Paris is not correct.

ever-increasing disarray, can only continue to deteriorate in sound. An instrument played in such a way as to break most of the strings is also likely to have been mistreated generally, detracting from its working order as a whole.

So my initial statement that the Érard became uninteresting for Beethoven simply because it was outdated does not tell the entire story. It is possible, even likely, that the Érard was a good and powerful piano when new, and that Beethoven's initial "enchantment" was genuine. It is just as likely that the quality deteriorated noticeably and steadily due to the way he began to treat this piano. This decline in quality would in its turn explain his later dismissal of the instrument.

THE FIRST PIECE FOR THE ÉRARD: THE "WALDSTEIN" SONATA

The "Waldstein" Sonata Op. 53 was written shortly after Beethoven had composed the Eroica Symphony in 1803. Other important works of that year are the "Kreuzer" Sonata Op. 47, the Third Piano Concerto and the Oratorio *Christus am Ölberge*, all written before the arrival of the Érard. The "Waldstein" Sonata is the first major work that Beethoven wrote after receiving the Érard. The sketches for this sonata and for the Andante WoO 57, which was initially planned as the slow movement, all date from between November 2, 1803 (well after the piano arrived) and January 4, 1804 (just less than three weeks after Griesinger's report about Beethoven's enthusiasm).[77] This sonata was certainly directly inspired by the new, yet unchanged, Érard. It is probably one of a very few of Beethoven's works that draw on the resources of this particular type of piano in a positive and direct way.

However, many of today's fortepianists seem to be convinced that, while the sonata was perhaps written with the Érard piano in *place*, it was not written with the piano in *mind*. Bart van Oort writes:

Beethoven would never demand techniques that his instrument could not handle, nor a sound that it could not produce. The clear attack of the leather-covered hammers, the rapid decay of the tone and quick damping, all so crucial to any good piano of around 1800, gave Beethoven the tools to conceive an opening theme which consists almost solely of motor rhythm in the lower registers of the instrument.[78]

There is no reason to criticize van Oort's choice of a six-octave Viennese-style fortepiano from about 1815 for his performance. In 1815, Beethoven or his pupils would have played this sonata on similar instruments and would have been content with them. But in a search for the inspiration of that first

---

[77] Cooper, "The evolution of the first movement of the 'Waldstein' sonata," 184–5.
[78] *Beethoven, the Complete Piano Sonatas on Period Instruments*. Claves CD 50–9707/10, 1997, booklet, 52.

moment, when Beethoven would have used an instrument's characteristics as tools to conceive a theme, the presence of the Érard points in another direction. His criticism of the Viennese pianos as wooden – "rubbish" compared to the Érard – refutes the notion that, in his eyes, "the clear attack of the leather-covered hammers, the rapid decay of the tone and quick damping" were "crucial to any good piano." Indeed, quite the contrary is evident. The tools to conceive the "Waldstein" theme were obviously different from the average Viennese ideal of 1803. At least initially, the leathers of the Érard would have been thicker (and their attack relatively less clear) and its damping less distinct. Moreover, a "singing tone" as opposed to a "rapid decay of the tone" had already been Beethoven's stated ideal at least six years before he openly criticized the Viennese pianos.

Beethoven had been interested in the music of the London fortepiano school for a long time; from early on, many of his own works were inspired by, or even modeled on, pieces by Clementi, Dussek, and other composers associated with the English manner of playing.[79] One could expect a new sonata for the Érard to be another "Anglophile" sonata in the spirit of Op. 7, Op. 22, or the finale of Op. 26, to name but the most obvious. Indeed, even if the following summary of characteristics encountered in this sonata and in the Andante WoO 57 does not reveal entirely new techniques, the coincidence of various textures that suit an English-style instrument particularly well, and the absence of others that would work better on Viennese instruments (or poorly on English ones), seem to show ways in which Beethoven was influenced by the Érard. The importance of this direct insight into Beethoven's workshop at the outset of his middle period, just before deafness became a noticeable hindrance, cannot be emphasized enough.

EXTENDING THE KEYBOARD RANGE

Before examining the English or French textures in the "Waldstein" Sonata, it is appropriate to discuss the keyboard range of the Érard, which does not in fact completely match the "Waldstein" Sonata (it does match several slightly later works, such as the "Appassionata" Op. 57).[80] In a recent book section, Siegbert Rampe addresses this issue as follows:

Truly, one could conclude from the extension of the Waldstein Sonata Op. 53, while still being sketched, from f''' to a''', that Beethoven suddenly had access to a

---

[79] See the music examples in Ringer, "Beethoven and the London Fortepiano School."

[80] The keyboard compass of Beethoven's piano works has often received casual attention in the literature. John Henry van der Meer provided a thorough discussion of keyboard compass and historical instruments in John Henry van der Meer, "Beethoven et le pianoforte," in *L'interprétation de la musique classique de Haydn à Schubert. Colloque International, Evry, 13–15 octobre 1977*, 67–85, Paris: Minkoff, 1980; and, in German, John Henry van der Meer, "Beethoven und das Fortepiano," *Musica Instrumentalis* 2(1999): 56–82. Even if I do not share some of van der Meer's views on the issue, his presentation of keyboard compasses is helpful and complete.

new fortepiano with the keyboard range FF-a′′′. But he would not have used this [instrument] again until 1809, that is, a good five years later, for the Sonatine Op. 79, which does not seem understandable, since, in the meantime, compositions came into being for the ranges FF-f′′′ (Op. 54), FF-c′′′′ (Op. 56, 57, WoO 80, Op. 78), and FF-f′′′′ (Op. 58, 61, 73, 80). The Sonata Op. 53 can in any case not have been destined for the Érard grand piano, because the avoidance of the tones b′′′ and c′′′′ in a brilliant C major sonata is completely unfounded. Even if one can observe certain influences from the French sound, it remains for the time being undecided which instrument Beethoven had in view when he worked on Op. 53.[81]

I need to point out that Rampe divides his material into a presentation of data, titled "Klaviaturumfänge," and an evaluation of those data, titled "Interpretation." My excerpt is taken from the first of these sections. In his "Interpretation," Rampe does in fact give various convincing reasons for the varying keyboard ranges, along lines similar to my argumentation below about commercial decisions in published music. But the statement I have quoted is nevertheless written in the spirit of a tradition in Beethoven studies that presupposes a direct and tight connection between Beethoven's instruments and the specific keyboard ranges that appear in his music. My following discussion of the timetable of Beethoven's extensions of the keyboard range shows that such a connection cannot be shown in some important and often-discussed cases.

It is well established that Beethoven's earlier adherence to the five-octave compass resulted in many compromised textures and omitted notes in the treble and in the bass.[82] We can, therefore, interpret the five-octave compass in Beethoven's oeuvre as a *restriction*. When Beethoven began to go beyond this compass in 1803, it was the first time in his career as a keyboard composer he had done so (disregarding the already discussed notes in earlier works that suited the FF–g′′′ compass, such as the (avoided) f#′′′ in his Concerto Op. 15 and in the Sonata Op. 14/1). No written documents about Beethoven's decisions during this process are preserved, so we must try to understand the situation through an interpretation of the traces left in his music.

For Beethoven, expanding the compass may have been attractive, but pushing the limits was clearly not equally essential, so he did not immediately fully exploit the compass extension to c′′′′ on his Érard – welcome as it undoubtedly was. The keyboard ranges of his later works show in fact that as a rule he was hesitant in fully exploiting new keyboard compasses.

This observation is entirely unsurprising. At a time when the keyboard compass of pianos was rapidly changing, the publication of keyboard music for the various levels of an amateur and semi-professional market was a hazardous enterprise. Naturally, composers and editors alike were keen to

---

[81] Rampe, "Beethovens Klavier – Klangwelt und Aufführungspraxis," copy provided by the author, 34. A reference to my article is added in the middle of the last sentence.

[82] See, for example, van der Meer, "Beethoven und das Fortepiano," 59–63.

observe a keyboard range that was accessible to the average public.[83] There were several ways to anticipate and meet the conditions under which the music was going to be played, but whether one opted for an overall safe keyboard range, prepared different versions for different markets (as Clementi did, for example, in his Sonata Op. 33/1),[84] or provided *ossia* readings in one and the same score, all such amendments were necessarily conservative. My first observation, therefore, is that it is the appearance of an *extended* keyboard range that should draw our attention. It is substantially less conclusive when a keyboard work happens to fit a *narrower* range. This seemingly trivial statement seems necessary since several writers have expressed their astonishment about, for example, the five-octave range of Beethoven's Sonata Op. 54.

The idea that the tessitura of a piece of music guides us to the instrument that Beethoven was using when he wrote the work is only one of several possible assumptions in this discussion. It applies, conveniently, to the first piece in which Beethoven used the five-and-a-half octave compass to c'''': the Third Piano Concerto Op. 37. Although Beethoven announced this concerto to Härtel for later publication while he was still writing it,[85] no commercial considerations seem to have played a role in his choice of compass, since he decided to enhance it in the middle of the sketching process. The sketches with the extended compass pre-date the concerto's first performance on April 5, 1803.[86] This performance took place around five months before the Érard arrived. Thus a major work suddenly exceeded the keyboard compass before any of Beethoven's known pianos did. At some moment Beethoven was clearly informed that he could perform the concerto on a (now unknown) piano with the extended compass – which, of course, is what eventually happened. One may suppose that he subsequently began making sketches that reflected this situation. As I have mentioned, the compass FF–c'''' was relatively new but not unknown in Vienna at the time.[87] The *publication* of the concerto was another worry, but that was easily solved: the first edition from 1804 provides *ossia* readings suited for a five-octave range.[88]

---

[83] Most explicit about this topic is Barry Cooper, "The evolution of the first movement of the 'Waldstein' sonata," 185. Siegbert Rampe also discusses the commercial aspect of the choice of keyboard range in published music. Rampe, "Beethovens Klavier – Klangwelt und Aufführungspraxis," copy provided by the author, 36–8, beginning of the section "Interpretation."

[84] My thanks to Geoffrey Govier for pointing this out.

[85] Letter from Kaspar Karl van Beethoven to Breitkopf & Härtel, January 22, 1803. This letter is the first one that resumes a business-like spirit after a prolonged row about a double publication of the Quintet Op. 29. Beethoven, *Briefwechsel*, vol. 1, 149.

[86] Plantinga, *Beethoven's Concertos*, 128–30.

[87] This does not exclusively apply to the Streicher firm. A list of pianos made by the Viennese maker Bohak from 1803 contains models in four different finishes with alternative keyboard ranges to g''' or c''''. Beethoven, *Briefwechsel*, vol. 1, 198.

[88] Plantinga, *Beethoven's Concertos*, 293.

In Beethoven's other works from around that time, however, he exploits the new keyboard range hesitantly and inconsistently. The Violin Sonata Op. 47, performed on May 24, 1803, stays within the old five-octave compass. The "Waldstein" Sonata Op. 53 has a‴ as the highest note. The Sonata Op. 54, written in 1804, returns to the well-known five-octave range FF–f‴. The full range of the Érard, FF–c″″, appears, again in 1804, in the Triple Concerto Op. 56 and the "Appassionata" Sonata Op. 57. We can observe a similar hesitation when Beethoven extends the compass of his works again, first to six and then to six-and-a-half octaves.[89] In the light of this cautious approach, neither the presence of the larger compass (as in the Third Concerto), nor its absence (as in the Sonata Op. 54) need be seen as significant statements for or against any specific piano. On the other hand, considering the developments in piano building (especially in Streicher's pianos), it seems only natural that around 1807 Beethoven occasionally wrote for the six-octave range of the latest Viennese instruments.

It was clearly not the arrival of the Érard in Vienna that caused the sudden extension of the five-octave range to g‴ and a♭‴ eleven pages into the sketches.[90] The piano was available during the whole compositional process. Apparently Beethoven took some time to decide whether a larger range was acceptable in a publication. Perhaps he even waited to receive permission by his publisher before he extended the range.

The question of why Beethoven terminated the "Waldstein" compass at a‴ can, on the other hand, not be answered by discussing pianos or marketing. The majority of the surviving pianos from the time in question had keyboard compasses to f‴, g‴, c″″, or f″″. In his study, Michael Latcham lists only six pianos from two makers with the range FF–a‴. These all date from between 1795 and 1805. Only three of these come from a well-known master (Johann Schanz). This has to be contrasted with forty-four pianos from the same period from thirteen makers, including Stein/Streicher and Walter, with one of the other compasses.[91]

[89] In Op. 81a the compass extends to six octaves, albeit only in the finale. Op. 90 stays within the earlier compass. The beginning of Op. 101 suits smaller instruments but in the finale, the treble and bass ranges extend above c″″ and below FF. In Op. 110 and 111, too, the keyboard range differs between the movements. Beethoven accepted that single movements were played instead of the whole sonata. This is evident from his 1798 performances of the last movement from Op. 2/2 (Kerst, *Die Erinnerungen an Beethoven*, vol. I, 31–3). So the compass differences between movements could be another marketing strategy. Some movements were playable on older pianos, but not others. I agree with Siegbert Rampe that Beethoven used the largest compass because the players who could play some of the late sonatas probably also had modern instruments. Whether this was truly a way to "extricate these works from the masses" cannot be answered (Rampe, "Beethovens Klavier – Klangwelt und Aufführungspraxis," copy provided by the author, 38).

[90] Cooper, "The evolution of the first movement of the 'Waldstein' sonata," 185. See also Johnson, Tyson, and Winter, *The Beethoven Sketchbooks: History, Reconstruction, Inventory*, 141–2.

[91] In Latcham's survey, only six pianos from around 1800 have the a‴ as the top note. See Latcham, *The Stringing, Scaling and Pitch of Hammerflügel*, vol. I, xviii, and vol. II, Tables 1–7.

Example 4.1. Sonata in C major Op. 53, mvt. 1, Allegro con brio, bars 71– downbeat 74
(Bureau des Arts et d'Industrie, 1805)[92]

Example 4.2. Sonata in C major Op. 53, mvt. 1, Allegro con brio, bars 232– downbeat 235

An analysis of the high passages in the "Waldstein" Sonata in its final form leads to another explanation for its keyboard range: the a''' could in fact not be exceeded without substantially re-writing parts of the piece. Admittedly, the formulation "re-writing" is retrospective and hypothetical whereas, during the act of creation, completely different compositional solutions might have presented themselves. On the other hand, the apparent pattern of Beethoven's decisions is fairly consistent and worth considering.

Two kinds of passages are of special interest. To the first category belong subjects or motifs in the recapitulation of a sonata movement that were changed or compromised in comparison with the exposition in order to stay within a defined upper range. To the second category belong passages in which a predictable continuation or a sequence is altered in order to stay within that range.

In the "Waldstein" Sonata, the only example of the first category can be found by comparing bar 73 in the exposition of the first movement (Example 4.1) with bar 234 of the recapitulation (Example 4.2):

The solution in bar 234 that avoids the top note and changes the rhythm bears the typical stamp of a compromise for reasons of keyboard compass. A literal transposition of bar 73 a sixth up would have gone to d'''', i.e. beyond the top c'''' of the five-and-a-half octave range that is relevant in this discussion.

If Beethoven had wanted to preserve the original sixteenth-note move-ment in his transposition of this bar, he could have written b''' instead of

[92] All examples from Beethoven's first editions are reproduced with the kind permission of Tecla Editions.

Example 4.3. Sonata in C major Op. 53, mvt. 1, Allegro con brio, bars 235–6

Example 4.4. Sonata in C major Op. 53, mvt. 1, Allegro con brio, bars 270–2

the d''''. In that case, the codetta that follows in bars 235–6 (shown in Example 4.3) could also have stayed in the same high octave, beginning with a chord similar to the downbeat of bar 74 (see the last bar in Example 4.1) of the exposition.

But this is the key problem with the whole passage: the right hand of the codetta of the exposition (in A minor, beginning with its dominant E major) begins with e''' and reaches f''' in its second bar. If the codetta of the recapitulation had been transposed up a sixth, i.e. written in the higher octave, an unavailable d♭'''' would have been reached in the middle of bar 236 unless the passage had been completely re-written. The preceding bar 234 had to be conceived to match the available compass in itself, *and* it had to provide a suitable lead-in so that the codetta (from bar 235) could be reproduced in its original form, but transposed down a third or, in other words, one octave lower relative to the exposition.

The second passage where we encounter a clear compromise is the fourth in a sequence of right-hand phrases: in bar 272 of the coda of the first movement (Example 4.4), the line suddenly continues an octave lower than the preceding passage.

The whole cadenza-like sequence starts with four-bar phrases in bar 259, switches to two-bar phrases in bar 267, and then to one one-bar phrase in bar 271. In order to maintain a connection between the upward chain of half-bar sequences (beginning in bar 272) and the previous phrases, a continuation at the same pitch would perhaps be preferable. This would, however, create compass-related problems in bar 273, where d'''' would be reached. And even for a full six-octave range (which is, of course, not an option in this case), the climax in bar 275 (Example 4.5) would necessarily

Example 4.5. Sonata in C major Op. 53, mvt. 1, Allegro con brio, bars 274–5

Example 4.6. Sonata in C major Op. 53, mvt. 3, Rondo Allegretto moderato, bars 258–72

have to be transposed downward. The result in either case would be a break at a very unsuitable point. Instead, Beethoven breaks the phrase at an inconspicuous point relatively early on. Again, this solution was clearly chosen for rather complex reasons of texture as well as compass, and not specifically in order to avoid the notes b♭''' to c''''.

A similar problem occurs in bar 263 of the third movement, the sixth bar in the following example (Example 4.6). From bar 263, Beethoven changes the tessitura in an established pattern of six-bar sequences. Again, it would seem that he tried to avoid going past the a''' with his solution. But even in this case, the decision to change the pattern was taken early on in order to avoid breaking up the middle of the six-bar phrase in bar 267, when the unavailable d'''' would have been reached. For a piano with a range up to c'''', this definitely seems the better solution.

One single instance that could in fact have been transposed up one octave on the Érard's compass is bars 227–8 of the recapitulation of the first movement (Example 4.7).

In the corresponding bars 66–7 of the exposition, the first note of the top line is b'' and the highest note is e'''. In the recapitulation, these two bars are transposed down a third instead of up a sixth. Transposed up, the top note c'''' would still have been available on the Érard. Needless to say, the passage would have had a less massive character in the high octave.

Example 4.7. Sonata in C major Op. 53, mvt. 1, Allegro con brio, bars 227–8

All these examples except the last one show that Beethoven kept the "Waldstein" Sonata within the range of FF–a''' for a variety of reasons, and that his avoidance of b''' and c'''' in a sonata in C major is perfectly understandable but coincidental.

THE "WALDSTEIN" SONATA AND THE FRENCH ACTION

The remaining question is whether characteristics of the French piano other than its compass may have influenced Beethoven's playing and his compositions: are its specific touch, damping, and sonority reflected in his compositional style of that period?

In the "Waldstein" Sonata and in the Andante WoO 57, quick repetitions in passages, broken chords, or melodic material are avoided almost consistently throughout.[93] This is uncharacteristic in comparison to the piano works of the seven previous years.[94] With two exceptions (mvt. 1, bar 267, and mvt. 3, bar 415) the fastest repetitions in the "Waldstein" Sonata are found in the first subject. Some repetitions in the Andante would probably be executed at about the same speed. It is quite possible that this peculiarity reflects Beethoven's unfamiliarity with the action of the new Érard piano.

Kenneth Mobbs has shown that the repetition speed on many English-style piano actions is about as fast as on a modern piano: two Broadwood grand pianos from 1801 and 1808 achieved repetition rates of 8.8 and 8.2 per second; the corresponding values for two Steinways from the 1980s were 8.1 and 8.7.[95] To put the execution of quick repeats on English pianos into a musical perspective, the quickest possible repetition in such pianos would be reached around the speed that is required for bars 185–8 of the Allegro molto of the second Cello Sonata Op. 5/2 (in Czerny's MM ♩. = 84).[96] To

---

[93] There are very few quick tone repetitions in the Sonatas Op. 2, but sometimes whole movements are dominated by this effect, as in Op. 31/1. The Cello Sonatas Op. 5 and the early variations show that Beethoven wrote tone repetitions sparingly but consistently.

[94] That is, the Sonatas Op. 31, the Variations Op. 34 and 35, the variations on "God save the King" WoO 78, and, to a lesser degree, the variations on "Rule Britannia" WoO 79.

[95] Broadwood pianos No. 2204 at the Finchcocks Collection and No. 4099. Mobbs, "A performer's comparative study of touchweight," 38.

[96] Carl Czerny, "Die Kunst des Vortrags der älteren und neueren Klavierkompositionen, zweites und drittes Kapitel," in *Über den richtigen Vortrag der sämtlichen Beethoven'schen Klavierwerke*, ed. Paul Badura-Skoda, Vienna: Universal, 1963, 80. I use this figure only as an example. There is no indication as to whether it has anything to do with Beethoven's practice.

Example 4.8. Sonata in G major Op. 31/1, mvt. 2, Adagio grazioso, bars 67–8
(Simrock, 1803)

achieve this speed, not only must the action be sufficiently fast, but the pianist must be well acquainted with the instrument.

The problem of performing on an English-style instrument lies not in the repetition speed but rather in the clarity and control. For instance, the first subject of the "Tempest" Sonata Op. 31/2 sounds imprecise on an English piano.[97] Other examples are the alternating chords of bars 65ff. of the Adagio grazioso of Op. 31/1 (Example 4.8), bars 50–5 of the Scherzo of Op. 31/3, and the "a quattro" of the "Eroica" Variations Op. 35. On an English action, such repeated notes are difficult to play *piano* and would not sound staccato as indicated.

Clear articulation seems to be a basic requirement for all figures that involve pairs of slurred quick notes, or short slurred groups alternating with notes marked staccato such as in the standard classical figure given by a slur and two staccato dots. Detailed articulation indications of this sort can be found in many of Beethoven's piano works. Even in the "Tempest" Sonata Op. 31/2, which in many ways anticipates Beethoven's later style, short slurs are an essential part of the first subject. On an English piano a clear rendering of such figures is not easy – in the lower register they remain blurred in any case. The Andante WoO 57 does have a few examples of short slurs and staccato dots, although at moderate speed. Short slurs do not appear anywhere in the "Waldstein" Sonata. Here the shortest slurred figure is three notes followed by a rest; otherwise only larger groups of notes are slurred,[98] while dots are used to accentuate or articulate the beginnings and endings of phrases, and to indicate staccato in a few diatonic progressions.

A technique well established in Beethoven's late work, and occasionally encountered in his earlier works, is to move the voices far apart and leave the middle register of the piano empty. In the "Waldstein" Sonata this technique is used freely and at important structural points such as the last few bars before the recapitulation of the first movement. Here, the two voices move several octaves apart, creating a somewhat hollow sound that recalls similar

---

[97] Observations like this one remain subjective. What I call imprecise here is the result of various factors: an action which has almost reached the end of its possibilities and may respond irregularly at this speed, and the characteristic tone and after-ring, all contribute to this effect.

[98] Except for a few two-note *portato* indications in the slow movement.

effects in the "Apassionata" Sonata Op. 57, many passages of the Cello
Sonata Op. 69, the opening of the Trio Op. 70/1, and most of the late piano
pieces. In the "Waldstein" Sonata, instead of writing chords or reinforcing
octaves, Beethoven often relies on only two single lines to create *f* and *ff*
(for instance, in mvt. 1, bars 152–5 and 299). One would perhaps expect this
texture to appear in places where the old range limit of five octaves is
exceeded but this is not the case. Bars 152–5 of the first movement, for
instance, fit a five-octave early Viennese piano perfectly. Yet the passage
sounds rather dry on such an instrument and it is difficult to create the
required *fortissimo* impression. It seems likely that this notation was
Beethoven's reaction to the different sonority, and especially the stronger
bass register, of his Érard.

About half of Beethoven's sonata movements up to the Sonatas Op. 31
contain left-hand textures that in some way present problems of balance or
clarity when played on an English piano or on modern pianos. In particular,
full chords or melodic material in the lower octave easily become unclear.
Beethoven certainly often intended the bass to sound massive. Many early
German or Viennese pianos did not meet this requirement well, so his
characteristic left-hand scoring can partly be seen as a compensation for
their light tone. But in the "Waldstein" Sonata, the stable left-hand tremolos and broken chords at *pp* or *p* are relatively easy to control even on later
pianos, and most of the remaining sixteenth-note activity in the left hand is
written in single-voice passages. Dense chords and demanding arpeggios in
the left hand appear only when a really forceful or excited impression is
clearly intended (as in bars 352–85 of the Rondo).

One of the new features of the Érard was a pedal to raise the dampers.
Late eighteenth-century Viennese pianos usually had knee levers for this
purpose. Many pianists of our time have demonstrated that a modern pedal
technique with quick and frequent changes is possible using knee levers
(whether historically appropriate or not), but for Beethoven the new pedal
would undoubtedly have been an invitation to try out new effects. In
contrast to the earlier notation *con/senza sordino*, the "Waldstein" markings
are indicated as *ped* and O.[99] Also, the finale of the "Waldstein" Sonata is
the first of his sonata movements with extensive pedal markings.[100]

Parallel with the acceptance and later dismissal of the Érard itself,
Beethoven later retained some of the characteristics and techniques that
have been discussed, whereas he soon abandoned others. Obviously, his
interest in sonorous instruments persisted, initially not necessarily only
because of his increasing deafness, which became noticeable around the

---

[99] Beethoven had already used this notation in the first movement of the "Tempest" Sonata Op. 31/2,
   although sparingly.
[100] See David Breitman, "The damper pedal and the Beethoven piano sonatas: a historical perspective,"
   DMA thesis, Cornell University, 1993, and Rowland, "Beethoven's pianoforte pedaling."

same time. Examples of the style formulated in the "Waldstein" Sonata can, for instance, be found in the "Apassionata" Op. 57, the Fourth Piano Concerto Op. 58,[101] and the Cello Sonata Op. 69. Many of the elements are evident even in the Sonata Op. 54, although it is written for five octaves and lacks pedal indications. This sonata was perhaps written during Beethoven's stay in Oberdöbling in August–September, 1804, using an M.A. Stein piano, as discussed above.

It is likely that the damping characteristics of the Érard would have inspired important subjects and figurations in the works from the Érard's heyday – for instance, the first subject of Op. 53, the repeated chords in the first movement of Op. 54, the organ points and tremolos in Op. 57, and the first subject of the Fourth Piano Concerto. These passages gain a special soft-edged, non-aggressive quality when played on such an instrument. Similar figures in earlier works (like the opening and the chord repetitions in Op. 7) do not seem to require this gentle, wash-like quality. However, this effect can be simulated on any piano using the damper pedal and it persisted in Beethoven's notation after the Érard was dismissed (as can be seen in the Sonata Op. 90 from 1814). On the other hand, indications of a detailed articulation, which would have been less effective on the Érard, re-appear gradually in Beethoven's later piano works.

An element definitely not maintained in later compositions is the avoidance of quickly repeated notes. In the "Appassionata" Op. 57 such repetitions are still relatively rare; in the passage with repeated sixteenth notes in the development of the first movement (bars 125–9), the pedal is held down throughout and the level is *ff*, which would guarantee a massive sound, even if the repetition were not perfect (the eighth note organ points in the first movement present no repetition problems). Perhaps the changes made to the Érard's action in 1804 did make its touch crisper after all. Perhaps Beethoven also became less and less content with the sacrifices he apparently had to make to his usual brilliant playing technique on account of the Érard. In any case, in the Fourth Piano Concerto, quickly repeated notes in an exposed context occur in the first subject of the Rondo. The first few variations in WoO 80 (from October 1806) have quick note repetition as one of the two main features and can alternatively be understood as "études for the Érard" or, more likely, as a manifestation of Beethoven's lost interest in, or even frustration with, his piano. Certainly, after Beethoven started to write for six-octave Viennese pianos, repeated notes re-appeared in his scores: the first movement of the Sonata "Les Adieux" (composed in 1809) contains two notoriously difficult passages based on quickly repeated

---

[101] Sketches from February 1804. An early version was for five-and-a-half octaves. In his 1808 performance, Beethoven used a six-octave instrument. See Barry Cooper, "Beethoven's revisions to his Fourth Piano Concerto," in Robin Stowell, ed., *Performing Beethoven*, Cambridge University Press, 1994, 23–48.

chords (bars 32–3 and 124–5), and throughout the Allegro vivace of Op. 78 (also from 1809, ironically written for the English market), repetition is used almost obsessively.

It will remain impossible to solve all the riddles presented by the Érard piano. Our information about Beethoven's attitude, his exact reasons for altering the action, and the degree of his growing disapproval of the instrument, is too fragmentary to lead to final conclusions. It is, however, evident that this instrument influenced Beethoven's ideas during a short but important period. When Beethoven dismissed the Érard, Viennese builders like Streicher, partly influenced by the Érard and other similar instruments, had undergone a major development in the design of their pianos. Beethoven's return to Viennese pianos might therefore have felt like another step forward. However, his complaints about a Streicher piano that wore out too quickly, as well as the alarming number of broken and badly replaced strings in his Érard, suggest that, toward 1810, deafness and impatience had seriously begun to undermine Beethoven's professionalism as a pianist. The decline in the quality of Beethoven's Érard is most certainly a result of a vicious circle of disappointment and bad treatment.

For most piano works written between Op. 37 and Op. 79, a performance on a good French or English piano of the period would doubtless offer a rewarding alternative to using Viennese pianos, without necessarily implying a better or more correct solution. There is little doubt that especially the earliest works of this period, and notably the "Waldstein" Sonata, were much inspired by the Érard. A performance of these works on an instrument similar to the Érard is likely to reveal aspects of Beethoven's composition which would otherwise remain hidden.

PART II

Sound ideal and performance

Introduction

Beethoven's opinions about piano playing and the piano, as outlined in the previous chapters, concentrate on three elements: tone *length* (or, as he expressed it, a "singing" manner of playing and a singing piano tone), tone *character* (evident in his wish to create a "personal tone" and in his disapproval of a "wooden" tone), and tone *volume* (evident in his middle-period interest in the French piano and eventually also due to his deafness). For a full understanding of these concepts in our time, practical experience with early instruments is indispensable. There are, however, obstacles to gaining that experience.

One difficulty when discussing the merits of historically informed approaches to music is the modern concept of a successful performance and an audience's adherence to comparison with earlier experiences. Whether this is a problem or not depends greatly on the circumstances. Early pianos of all kinds have become a fact of contemporary concert life. The audience's increasing experience of listening to these instruments, as well as the performers' ability to handle them with authority, has relieved them of their aura of imperfect exoticism. There should be no reason to be partial other than for reasons of admitted personal taste, except perhaps in the case of a direct comparison between several similar instruments. Nevertheless, the unavoidable confrontation of the early piano with its modern successor in the experience of the modern listener makes a discussion of the potential and the merits of the former a complicated task. Often, the pianist is forced to assume the unintended role of a categorical defender of one or the other concept, as if early pianos and modern ones were *meant* to be opponents that rule out each other.

Now one could point out that fortepianists also make use of their awareness of that confrontation in order to demonstrate something special to the audience, and that the juxtaposition between old and modern pianos in everyone's experience is the very element that makes the idea of the "new old" sound in fortepiano concerts "work." In his influential 1983 article on the performance practice movement, Laurence Dreyfus draws a picture of the effect of "defamiliarization" associated with the Early Music culture.[1]

---

[1] Laurence Dreyfus, "Early Music defended against its devotees: a theory of historical performance in the twentieth century," *The Musical Quarterly* 69/3 (1983): 306–8.

For many musicians and listeners at that time, the thrill of "old" instruments played in the "old" way was primarily caused by the "otherness" of the sound. From the perspective of the audience, something of this spirit lingered, even after performances on historical instruments became more generally accepted and after the original impact, preserved in Dreyfus' description of the Early Music movement as "able to rock the foundations of mainstream musical culture," had somewhat worn off.

For a listening audience, then, an element of comparison cannot be avoided. For the performer, on the other hand, investigating the various expressive possibilities of historical pianos is often enough of a challenge in itself. The practical experience gained while exploiting the potential of an instrument, and the growing awareness of the properties of the different kinds of instruments, become much more relevant than any comparison with the modern piano. Far from strategically calculating the unfamiliar effect an early piano might have on modern listeners, the early keyboard specialist usually comes on the stage largely unaware of how accustomed the audience is to his or her instrument. Clearly, for such a performer, the sound of the instrument is only of any consequence in itself insofar as its regularity, degree of mellowness or sharpness, and tone sustain are part of that particular piano's expressive potential. These elements, and the performer's notion of pleasantness or beauty, influence his or her psychological reactions. In contrast, the element of "otherness" compared to the modern piano is largely unimportant in this situation.

This is admittedly a personal standpoint which is motivated by a lifetime of working exclusively with period keyboard instruments. Many fortepiano specialists have in fact discussed the differences between early pianos and the modern piano, and keep doing so.[2] I am not arguing against a preoccupation with the comparison between old and modern pianos, but I claim that, for the performer at the moment of a performance, the awareness of such a difference is necessarily replaced by an awareness of the individual characteristics of the instrument at hand. If I prepare a program on an early instrument, my only chance of approaching my expectations of a successful performance is to fully focus on the properties of that instrument alone for the time being.

A performer will thus exploit the properties of the piano in relation to the expressive content of a piece (representing the composer's intentions, or at least the requirements of stylistic convention). She or he might ask, for example, what effect the music produces on the chosen piano. Conversely,

---

[2] See Eva Badura-Skoda and Paul Badura-Skoda, *Interpreting Mozart on the Keyboard*, New York: St. Martin's Press, 1962, Chapter 1; Malcolm Bilson, "Beethoven and the piano," *Clavier* 12/8 (1983): 18–21; Paul Badura-Skoda, "Playing the early piano," *Early Music* 12/4 (1984): 477–80; Melvyn Tan, "The technique of playing music authentically does not mean simply using the appropriate instruments," *Early Music* 12/1 (1985): 57–8; and Malcolm Bilson, "The myth of the authentic pianoforte," *International Piano Quarterly* (July 2003): 47–53.

the question could be whether the piano at hand accommodates the expressiveness that she or he expected the music to have. The subtle difference between these two approaches is that in one case the piano is expected to tell us something new about the music, while in the other case the music helps us to formulate what to expect from the instrument.

Baroque players of our time have traditionally favored the first of these approaches. As soon as musicians were technically able to master their old instruments, playing the repertoire resulted in an abundance of "aha" experiences. In their writings, and in interviews with Early Music pioneers, their enthusiasm about this effect is always overwhelmingly present.

Against this backdrop, Beethoven's piano music calls for special attention. On an instrument that, for example, is perfectly suited for expressing Haydn's many articulations convincingly, a pianist faced with Beethoven's whole-phrase legato slurs might not necessarily find a good solution at all. Here the second view seems to prevail: we assume that the indications in Beethoven's scores require certain instrumental properties; we expect the instruments to be a certain way in order to do justice to the music. The "aha" experience is replaced by a rather more complicated balancing of expectations and experiences.

Katalin Komlós, like many other pianist/scholars, interprets the difficulties of performing Beethoven on early pianos as an essential experience:

From the very beginning of his Viennese career, Beethoven stretched the limits of the fortepiano. Disregard of the capabilities of the instrument is a crucial feature of Beethoven's artistic approach which is not evident when the music is played on a modern piano. Op. 27 certainly does not outstrip the resources of a Steinway or a Yamaha concert grand, and thus an essential aspect of the music is lost. In Beethoven's case, the use of an eighteenth-century fortepiano (or copy) may be even more relevant than in Haydn's or Mozart's.[3]

Similar standpoints are widely accepted among present-day fortepianists. The experience hidden behind these words is that the pianist's struggle is necessary to express the music properly. A piano that is suitable to convey true Beethovenian impact is one that, during this process, comes to the brink of its resources.

But the idea of an inevitable Beethovenian struggle is just another version of the image we already possess. The traditional picture of a frowning titan who fights against the impossibility of his material surroundings remains untouched. True, our awareness of both the composer and his reception history forces us to live with the risk of associations that ultimately tend to confirm what we already thought about Beethoven. On the other hand, such associations stand in the way of experiencing early pianos in the first of

---

[3] Komlós, *Fortepianos and their Music*, 61.

my two ways, while our struggle is really a struggle for a phantom: the demands of the score.

Obviously, the assumption that textures or expressive indications in the score unequivocally lead to a catalog of preferred instrumental properties is false. Legato indications, *sforzato* accents, extreme dynamics, and seemingly massive textures, can all be interpreted in various ways. Modern Western musical common sense is a bad guide to this interpretation because it is inseparable from traditional beliefs about Beethoven performance. The effort to side-step such beliefs leaves our hands emptier than one might expect: scrutinizing a score alone reveals little of how its indications translate into appropriate piano characteristics. Without the image of an impatient and impulsive Beethoven, without the tradition that asks for the most massive sound to express *these* characteristics (and not necessarily those of the music), any fortepianist would be free to translate Beethoven's indications into sounds that (a skeptic would say, merely) suit the properties of his fortepiano, just as a clavichordist makes Müthel's music fit his instrument, and just as pianists also play Haydn or Clementi on early pianos.

But to use a historical piano to prove a practical point of performance is also problematic. One old piano may be perfectly suited to a realistic interpretation of a certain expressive notation which would appear "visionary" on another piano of the same time. Even without the complicating factor of a strong tradition (as in Beethoven's case), choice and preference quickly become additional tools for the performer. Both perspectives, whether the meaning of a historical score is to be confirmed in the properties of an instrument (which happens whenever we already possess an idea about a piece of music before we begin to work on it), or a historical keyboard instrument gets tested on a historical score (which happens whenever we try out an unfamiliar piece on our familiar fortepiano), result in methodological complication, mainly caused by their circularity. Paraphrasing Komlós' statement above, one could say that, when interpreting Beethoven's piano music, the thought that any of these approaches leads to final answers must be abandoned, perhaps even sooner than with most other composers. Thus, in a modern situation, even for the informed fortepianist, the confrontation between various early pianos and Beethoven's piano works of the same period offers no inevitable revelations.

While we must accept that the answers provided by such a confrontation are not final, playing Beethoven's music on instruments of his time remains fully acceptable in various ways. Most important of all, this approach opens up a path toward a *dialogue with the past*. This idea, originally based on Gadamer, is borrowed from a 1988 article by Gary Tomlinson. Tomlinson quotes cultural anthropologist Clifford Geertz, who explains the basic principle of such a dialogue as a "colloquy in which the historian examines, ponders, and questions his subjects and then, through an act of historical imagination … supplies responses for them." For an anthropologist,

Tomlinson writes, this conversation is a real one. In studies of performance practices, it becomes a metaphor. Tomlinson contrasts the idea of discourse as a metaphor (that is, to talk to "the work's creators shining through" the work in order "to broaden our world of discourse") with viewing the work in "easy but all-too-familiar meanings," where "we talk mainly among ourselves, reflected in the work."[4] Viewing the work as an aesthetic object outside its original context is thus depicted here as counterproductive. But what is original context?

In *any* case in principle, and very clearly in the case of Beethoven, a creator or his close surroundings immediately re-formulate contexts for his works, and hence the dialogue becomes extremely difficult. This is why, for instance, a book title *Beethoven on Beethoven. Playing His Piano Music His Way* does not in any way guarantee consistent revelations.[5] First of all, as I will discuss further below, "his piano music" is essentially more than we possibly can perceive today. Most importantly, however, Beethoven – metaphorically speaking – answers differently every time we ask him. Without a discussion of contexts, the documents often suggest inconsistency and confusion. Rather, the discussion of contexts becomes the *only* truly rewarding preoccupation in Beethoven performance practice studies.

Various historical pianos can provide one such context – or rather, a discussion of the context of some of the pianos can provide answers that help to answer some questions about Beethoven. In spite of the complications mentioned above, we can still try to get better at exploiting the characteristics of the various early pianos, and of the music, in an attempt to bring the contextual implications of both as close together as possible. We can discuss the parameters for an informed judgment against the background of the abundance of fortepianos that are, for one reason or another, deemed suitable for a rendering of Beethoven's works. Historical judgment about Beethoven's playing can serve as a counterpoint to this discussion. Relating back to Beethoven's interests, one can view the aspects tone length, flexibility, and volume, on one hand as a result of fortepiano construction, and on the other as factors that influenced Beethoven's practice and that, finally, are reflected in Beethoven's notation. This will be the topic of the following chapters.

---

[4] Gary Tomlinson, "The historian, the performer, and authentic meaning in music," in Nicholas Kenyon, ed., *Authenticity and Early Music*, Oxford University Press, 1988, 119–21.

[5] Newman, *Beethoven on Beethoven*. I am addressing only the choice of title here.

CHAPTER 5

The builder's influence

FORTEPIANOS GOOD AND BAD

Organologists have invested much energy in studies of the various piano action types of the late eighteenth and early nineteenth centuries. From a player's point of view, this research obviously needs no justification: the touch of a keyboard defines the player's contact with the instrument and directly triggers his psychological and artistic response. But the focus on action design distracts from the fact that it has significantly less influence on the tone than all the combined elements of an instrument's construction and the instrument's state of repair.

In 1985, the fortepianist Linda Nicholson wrote about an "alarming variation in quality between different [fortepianos] both old and new," adding,

> There exist even now only a handful of early pianos that may be considered fully satisfactory. Indeed some of those made available in museums and academies and at international festivals and competitions are distressing to the serious player and might be expected to prejudice even the most open-minded listener against the revival of the instrument.[1]

In spite of such inconsistency in fortepiano quality, one occasionally meets a curious lack of concern for an instrument's condition in the literature on early piano performance practices. For example, Sandra Rosenblum includes descriptions of fifteen new and old pianos played for her study, but mentions only in passing that their various tonal properties could be a consequence not only of differences in style but also of their age or state of repair. She certainly does express her astonishment about the following observation: "The replica of a Walter built around 1785, which I know well, is an instrument of dulcet quality; one of the surprises for me at the Kunsthistorisches Museum [in Vienna] was how much quieter and gentler was the tone of an original Walter built in 1795." An analysis of the causes of this difference, however, or a comparative discussion of various fortepiano properties, has not found its way into her text: "These

---

[1] Linda Nicholson, "Playing the early piano," *Early Music* 13/1 (1985): 52–4.

differences become insignificant in contrast to those between fortepianos and modern pianos."[2]

A discussion about fortepiano properties and fortepiano quality can only be conclusive if it is not separated from individual technical issues, which could range from case construction to the escapement point of individual tones. It is exactly this necessity of *not* disregarding the specific state of instruments that makes the whole discussion about fortepiano aesthetics unwieldy and extremely difficult to systematize.

The practical situation for fortepianists described by Nicholson has certainly changed since her article appeared in 1985. Eighteen years later, Malcolm Bilson was able to approach the issue of fortepiano quality with much more optimism when he wrote in 2003: "We now have beautiful pianos from all periods, both replicas and originals, pre-Steinway pianos that are in quality and reliability on a level comparable to what we expect of our modern instruments, and access to them has become ever easier."[3]

This change happened not only in fortepiano building and restoring. It was also a result of the players' increasing trust in their capabilities of discrimination and, as a consequence, their increasingly authoritative demands for specific qualities. Such growing confidence, positive in itself, nevertheless risks falling prey to an idealizing simplification of fortepiano construction, fortepiano properties, and fortepiano history. Accepting Bilson's description as accurate, one would be tempted to believe that the many "beautiful" variations of the early piano reflect the successful result of an interaction between musical taste and good craftsmanship in historical times. Ideally, all those who played a part in this interaction – the criticizing observer, the composer who encouraged a builder to make alterations, and the piano builder, who either initiated innovation himself or agreed (or hesitated) to innovate upon customers' requests – would have checked each other against precipitate leaps in development. At any stage in the development of the piano (after the initial problems of devising the hammer action had been overcome), the very best specimens of the fortepiano would represent a faithful translation of the sound ideals and mechanical preferences of their time. But is this an accurate picture?

As I will discuss further below, the idea of the flawless fortepiano that represents the very essence of the ideals of its time is contradicted in many historical sources and often, too, by the reality encountered in the instruments. Various pianos of the same date can sound so dissimilar that the assumption of single regional sound ideals during specific periods is difficult to maintain. But if, as a result, we accept the unique sound properties of each early piano as a historical micro-reality, the possibility of assessing quality vanishes unless there are very clearly discernible signs that

---

[2] Rosenblum, *Performance Practices in Classic Piano Music*, 54.
[3] Bilson, "The myth of the authentic pianoforte," 53.

something is seriously amiss with the instrument in question. This is why, for instance, Bart van Oort's dissertation focuses mainly on the contemporary sources about fortepiano properties, instead of on the restored instruments available. "We cannot be certain whether these [instruments] are restored well enough to approach the quality of the original new pianos or whether they have been restored according to the same aesthetics under which they were built," he explains.[4] Expanding on this thought, we cannot, in fact, be certain whether a builder wanted to make his piano sound in a specific way, or whether it merely turned out in that way; whether time took its toll on the instrument, whereupon it became unrepresentative of the builder's work, or whether the instrument sounded bad from the beginning.

There are no hard-and-fast rules to help solve the problem of the aesthetic judgment of early pianos. For a modern performer it might indeed be compelling to expect a level of "quality and reliability" from historical models that is comparable to modern instruments. For the historian, such a connection is not automatically apparent.

ACCLAIM AND CRITICISM OF FORTEPIANOS
AROUND 1800

Not surprisingly, a concern for an instrument's quality and its suitability for certain music is just as true of historical times as it is of ours. A review of Beethoven's Sonatas Op. 26, 27/1, and 27/2 in the *Allgemeine Musikalische Zeitung*, for example, contains an explicit request:

> But one must possess a truly very good instrument if one wants some satisfaction in the execution of some of his movements – for instance, the whole first movement of No. 3.[5]

The movement in question is the Adagio sostenuto of the "Moonlight" Sonata. The fact that the reviewer chose a slow piece with a regular movement marked *pianissimo* as an example, rather than the virtuosic finale of the same sonata, suggests that "truly very good" means that such a piano should have a good sound and a reliable action, and be easy to control. This in turn means that such instruments were in fact available, albeit perhaps rarely.

Elsewhere in the documents we find every possible shade of praise or disapproval of pianos. Such judgments were made for the most various reasons, and they were inspired by widely divergent knowledge, experience, and preferences.[6] In the case of Elisabeth Bernhard, who in 1800

---

[4] Van Oort, "The English Classical piano style and its influence on Haydn and Beethoven," 7.
[5] AMZ June 1802, 652.
[6] The new piano was typically contrasted with the harpsichord and the clavichord. See Carl Parrish, "Criticisms of the piano when it was new," *The Musical Quarterly* 30/4 (1944): 428–40. This article is

wrote to her former teacher Andreas Streicher about various pianos in Germany, her friendship with the Streichers leaves little doubt about what inspired her criticism. One piano made in the city of Worms was "passable."[7] Two others by Louis Dülken and an unknown builder fare less well in her judgment:

The Clavier or fortepiano was so heavy to play that, during the sonata, I thought for a moment that I had to stop playing. Because it is not only heavy to play, but also so irregular that some keys play at the slightest touch, while one must press fairly hard on others before they give a tone. The tone is rather good in the bass, but in the treble it is too sharp. Finally it sounds so weak that, even with a very cautious *accompagnement*, I nevertheless had to play very strongly to be heard.[8]

About a fortepiano from Göttingen of a kind "which in all of Elberfeld are known as excellent instruments," Elisabeth Bernhard writes:

[They] are veneered in I don't remember which wood and look outwardly rough and massive, the wood is common. The tone is weak and the keyboard makes just as much noise as the hammers when striking the strings, so that no pure tone can be produced.[9]

Joseph Haydn's famous criticism of Anton Walter's instruments also rests on a comparison of sound and playability. In a letter to Marianne von Genzinger from 1790, Haydn explains that "his friend" Anton Walter's production was, despite his fame, so uneven "that sometimes only one out of ten instruments can truly be called good." Besides, his instruments were "rather expensive," and their action heavy and difficult to control. Instead of Walter's instruments, Haydn favored the fortepianos by (Wenzel) Schanz.[10]

Johann Ferdinand von Schönfeld's criticism of the varying quality of Walter's instruments has already been mentioned in Chapter 3. Von Schönfeld's advice to the future customer is to select his instrument carefully; a clear indication that there were also instruments in Walter's production that justified his good reputation.[11]

Carl Maria von Weber, who in 1813 traveled to Vienna to find musicians for the Prague *Ständetheater*, and to buy some pianos for "rich families in Prague" and for himself, took up the challenge of comparing many instruments quite seriously, although he was not happy with this task.[12] On April 16, 1813, von Weber wrote to a friend:

partly outdated, but the picture given of the introduction of hammered keyboard instruments in Germany appears to be faithful. In Vienna around 1800, comparisons were made between various fortepianos.

[7] Goebl-Streicher, Streicher, and Ladenburger, *"Diesem Menschen hätte ich mein ganzes Leben widmen mögen,"* 89.

[8] Letter from Elisabeth Bernhard to Andreas Streicher, Frankfurt, October 6, 1800. *Ibid.*, 85–6.

[9] Letter from Elisabeth Bernhard to Andreas Streicher, Düsseldorf, November 6, 1800. *Ibid.*, 89.

[10] Letter to Marianne von Genzinger. Quoted, for example, in Lelie, *Van piano tot forte*, 118.

[11] Schönfeld, *Jahrbuch der Tonkunst von Wien und Prag*, 87–90.

[12] Dagmar Droysen-Reber, "Carl Maria von Weber und sein Brodmann-Hammerflügel," in Monika Lustig, ed., *Zur Geschichte des Hammerklaviers*, Institut für Aufführungspraxis Michaelstein, 1993, 58.

I bought two marvelous instruments, one by Streicher and one by Brodmann. One day, I certainly saw fifty by Schanz, Walter, Wachtel, etc., none of which were worth a shot of gunpowder compared with these.[13]

Von Weber selected one of these instruments for himself. The six-octave grand piano by Josef Brodmann, housed today in the Berlin collection, still shows something of the nature of his preference.[14] When I examined it, the instrument was very even with regard to both the light and easily controlled touch and its transparent, almost brilliant sound. The lightness of the action, the shallow depth of touch, and the sound struck me as akin to much earlier Viennese fortepianos, unlike the more full-sounding ideal that became fashionable in Vienna after 1810.[15] The six-and-a-half-octave Streicher from 1814 in Stockholm's *Musikmuseet* has, by comparison, a rounder, fuller tone and its touch feels heavier.[16]

The examples I have chosen suggest that the quality expected of the instruments by professional musicians was high. The Viennese pianist at the turn of the eighteenth century seems to have used the definition "fully satisfactory" even more sparingly than fortepianists would today. On the other hand, the average standard of the pianos clearly left much to be desired. One only has to imagine one of our fortepiano specialists rejecting nine out of ten original Walter fortepianos, as Haydn would have done in 1790, or 96 percent of the fifty original Viennese instruments that von Weber tried out in 1813. By comparison, Malcolm Bilson's statement quoted above suggests that the accessibility of high-quality fortepianos today exceeds a typical Viennese situation of around 1800.

FORTEPIANO CRITICISM AND MARKETING

The implications of such historical opinions are not always easy to understand. Neutral observers like von Schönfeld, for instance, balanced criticism and positive acknowledgment rather too carefully to please the modern reader, who would have preferred more information and less tip-toeing. Von Weber's gruff comment about the instruments he dismissed is hardly surprising, given that he had spent a whole day comparing about fifty instruments in at least five workshops; perhaps the instruments were not really all that bad. His choice of a brilliant and bright sound, and a responsive and equal action, as found in his Brodmann piano, reflects a strong personal preference that was perhaps even slightly old-fashioned.

[13] Letter to Johann Baptist Gänsbacher, April 16, 1813. Ludwig Nohl, ed., *Musiker=Briefe*, Leipzig: Duncker und Humblot, 1873, 224. See also Droysen-Reber, "Carl Maria von Weber und sein Brodmann-Hammerflügel," 59.
[14] The instrument is in the Berlin collection of musical instruments. Examined in 1982.
[15] Dagmar Droysen-Reber describes a similar impression in Droysen-Reber, "Carl Maria von Weber und sein Brodmann-Hammerflügel," 60.
[16] No. 1011. Stockholm Musikmuseet Inv. No. F332. Examined in August 2006.

Elisabeth Bernhard's clear musical – even technical – preference for Streicher's instruments was certainly in part a result of her lifelong friendship with the Streichers.

Many of the historical statements about pianos served several goals at once, including marketing. In the hard reality of Viennese keyboard instrument making, only the very best firms had the resources to spend time on fundamental changes and improvements, or on extensive experimenting with tone. Like similar statements today, many of the historical opinions about fortepianos were nevertheless based upon discussions of tone quality in order to meet or create competition.

One famous, possibly market-oriented, judgment about fortepianos is arguably not even related to the selling of the instruments. In his fortepiano tutor from 1797, Philipp Jacob Milchmeyer recommends the use of square pianos. He explains that the larger instruments are unwieldy and have fewer *Veränderungen* than the squares, and concludes with the following remark:

Additionally, I have observed in large pianofortes that the two highest octaves comparatively seldom possessed a beautiful, bright, and penetrating tone. Their bass was often extremely loud and the upper tones weak.[17]

Milchmeyer's *Die wahre Art das Pianoforte zu spielen* was specifically conceived as a self-instruction manual for the growing number of amateurs who wished to play the fashionable piano. Selling more than 530 copies, the book was an immediate and striking success.[18] It is quite possible that Milchmeyer voiced his sincere opinion in the quoted passage. However, his criticism of the treble of grand pianos might just as well have been intended to please those readers who could not afford a larger instrument, and may not represent an informed judgment on fortepiano quality at all.

A rather low form of marketing was the spreading of rumors. On May 31, 1792, only three months after J. A. Stein's death, Nannette Stein wrote in a letter: "A certain Frosch and Louis have claimed that our instruments now cannot possibly be made as well as before."[19] A year later Nannette alluded to "printed lies" by some instrument builder in another letter.[20] Even as late as 1800, Elisabeth Bernhard writes to Streicher about similar rumors from Frankfurt.[21]

A builder's self-promotion that influences the opinions of the musicians can be encountered at all times. The most famous example is Mozart's praise of J. A. Stein's pianos in a letter to his father (October 17, 1777).

---

[17] Johann Peter Milchmeyer, *Die wahre Art das Pianoforte zu spielen*, Dresden: Meinhold, 1797, 57, quoted after Komlós, *Fortepianos and their Music*, 14.

[18] Silke Berdux, "Johann Peter oder Philipp Jacob Milchmeyer? Biographische und bibliographische Notizen zum Autor der Hammerklavierschule 'Die wahre Art das Pianoforte zu spielen'," *Musica Instrumentalis* 2 (1999): 112.

[19] Goebl-Streicher, Streicher, and Ladenburger, *"Diesem Menschen hätte ich mein ganzes Leben widmen mögen,"* 62.

[20] *Ibid.*, 69.   [21] Letter from Elisabeth Bernhard to Andreas Streicher, November 6, 1800. *Ibid.*, 89.

Mozart's detailed description raises the suspicion that he was trying to impress his father using the same technique that had earlier impressed him, that is, Stein's own presentation of his production.[22]

From a modern standpoint it remains difficult to judge whether early fortepiano acclaim or criticism had such promotional or commercial motivations. What can we make, for example, of Haydn's advice, later in his letter to Marianne von Genzinger, to buy a fortepiano by Schanz, who was "the best master in this profession"?[23] Only rarely do the documents disclose the percentage earned through such promotion, as in the case of Beethoven's friend Carl Amenda, who, after having left Vienna, ordered several instruments from Streicher and Walter between 1800 and 1806; his commission was 10 percent of the price.[24]

Especially hard to interpret is technical information from documents that explicitly promote the production of a piano maker. A good example is Jakob Bleyer's description of inner construction distortion in relatively new fortepianos, written in 1811. The key passage is the following:

> If one makes a [fortepiano] case in the usual manner, that is, with massive sides, and if one braces the walls ever so much, one finds after half a year, if one rips out the soundboard, that as a result of the string pressure, which can be up to 90 *Centner*, all the braces have been pressed one line[25] deep into the walls and now become completely loose.[26]

Technical information is by its very nature more acceptable in a modern discussion. However, if one is to believe Bleyer, pianos "made in the usual manner" were inevitably a structural disaster and fortepiano makers had a routine of "ripping out" soundboards after only half a year. Understandably, modern restorers do occasionally find such a description confirmed,[27] but it is important to note that some well-built and well-treated historical pianos have none of these structural problems at all even after more than 200 years.

Bleyer's text was written to promote a "newly invented system" by Bleyer and Wachtel, piano makers of Vienna, which was supposed to provide not a "strong" structure but rather a "firm" one. His description is written in a particularly competitive spirit, as it is a claim of priority in a dispute with another Viennese instrument maker Martin Seuffert who, according to Bleyer, imitated this new system and claimed it as his own invention.[28]

---

[22] Mozart, *Briefe und Aufzeichnungen*, vol. II, 69.   [23] Lelie, *Van piano tot forte*, 119.

[24] See Goebl-Streicher, Streicher, and Ladenburger, *"Diesem Menschen hätte ich mein ganzes Leben widmen mögen,"* 76, 80.

[25] One twelfth of a *Zoll* (inch).

[26] Jakob Bleyer, "Historische Beschreibung der aufrechtstehenden Forte-Pianos, von der Erfindung Wachtl und Bleyers in Wien," *Intelligenz-Blatt zur allgemeinen Musikalischen Zeitung* 17 (November 1811): 75.

[27] See Michael Latcham, "Soundboards old & new," *The Galpin Society Journal* 45 (1992): 52.

[28] Bleyer, "Historische Beschreibung der aufrechtstehenden Forte-Pianos, von der Erfindung Wachtl und Bleyers in Wien," 74–5.

Given this background, Bleyer obviously depended on generalization and exaggeration to get his point across. Neither was there a "usual manner" in which everyone else built pianos, nor is there any reason to believe that the internal mess in the instruments he describes was the inevitable consequence of not using Bleyer's new system.

One conclusion from an analysis of such historical fortepiano texts is that the more outspoken and vivid ones may not always be the ones that should be taken most literally. In a modern discourse, where historical texts are used to justify choices and preferences, this is an important point to bear in mind.

TRANSITION AND WEAK DESIGN

This last observation is especially pertinent in the case of early criticism that compares "newer" pianos with "older" ones, of which there are many well-known examples. In 1806, Clementi criticized previous stages in the development of the English fortepianos, "whose faulty construction had previously almost totally precluded a more cantabile, legato style of playing."[29] In a similar vein, Carl Czerny wrote in 1842 about the "extremely weak and imperfect" earlier forms of the Viennese fortepiano.[30] In April 1820, in a conversation about the trio of the *Menuett* of Beethoven's Piano Sonata Op. 2/1 from the mid-1790s, the pianist Joseph Czerny wrote in Beethoven's conversation book: "Also, in those days the pianos were worse." Historical opinions such as these provide the arguments for modern commentators such as Martin Hughes who dismiss the early piano as an option for concert use:

Sadly, a solo fortepiano is rather less attractive to the ear than a piano; not even the possibility of modern fabrication can significantly improve on what was a transient instrument of weak design. Its feeble and often uneven tone, its lack of colour and its mechanical unreliability make it unsuitable for concert use, and indeed it owes its revival largely to commercial recording where these issues can be overcome.[31]

If, unlike Hughes, one accepts historical piano models as useful and aesthetically adequate concert instruments, one needs to explain why pianists such as Clementi, and Carl and Joseph Czerny, were so negative about the earlier types of this instrument. The key to distinguishing between negative historical judgment and negative modern opinions about various fortepianos lies in the fact that the term "transient" (in the sense of "not of lasting value") describes the story of the piano's development accurately only in the light of individual historical experience.

---

[29] From Leon Plantinga, *Clementi, His Life and Music*, London: Oxford University Press, 1977, 290–1, quoted in Lelie, *Van piano tot forte*, 157.
[30] Czerny, "Erinnerungen aus meinem Leben," 22.
[31] Martin Hughes, "Beethoven's piano music: contemporary performance issues," in Robin Stowell, ed., *Performing Beethoven*, Cambridge University Press, 1994, 231.

This is not a matter of taste at all. The crucial flaw in representations such as Hughes' of fortepiano development as a large-scale phenomenon of transience is their failure to appreciate the characteristic of transience as a positive force in the experience of the individual. Most people look down on the "transient" earlier stages of their personal development. The desire to overcome one's present state is a major motivation to keep on working, to accumulate skills, and to gain recognition.

The various meanings of the term "improvement" for the individual historical builder all bear the stamp of such a motivation. The improvement of the output of a piano workshop can, for example, relate to expansion and economic success. This can be seen in the developments of all the note-worthy piano manufacturers around 1800. Improvement might apply to changes in technical design and aesthetic standards. This could be a single master's effort to improve an existing model, action, or structure, or the introduction of a completely new design. The latter could be motivated by the need to keep production up to date with current demands, or by the desire to realize a new idea. All these improvements mirror the master's (or workshop owner's) personal striving for progress.

The problem of a retrospective description arises as soon as a new piano with an altered construction stands in the workshop. Even if this is still an experimental instrument – even if the new version perhaps still needs adjust-ment – the builder's relationship to the usual product instantly becomes a historical one: the traditional model is all of a sudden "old" and the exper-imental instrument "new." For example, around 1805, the Streicher firm made instruments with double and triple treble stringing side by side because some of the Clavier players still preferred the older, more delicate sound.[32] Soon, however, the earlier design was abandoned. All of a sudden, the earlier "Stein" type pianos seemed weak, inadequate, and outdated, along with many piano models by their competitors. Even Streicher himself would now have called obsolete what in 1801 he defended in many well-chosen words.

The personal development of any composer of piano music, pianist, or piano pedagogue of the early nineteenth century was linked to the rapid development of the piano. In looking back, the individual would naturally experience the earlier stages of both developments as "now overcome." For a performance practice study that wants to capture specific moments or relatively short periods, a global view on the phenomenon of transience is unhelpful because it puts itself in the place of original historical experience.

STRUCTURAL STABILITY AND CHRONOLOGY

The reproach that some fortepianos had a weak design, however, remains valid. Achieving a safe structure is a concern shared by many historical and

---

[32] Lütge, "Andreas und Nanette Streicher," 64.

most modern fortepiano builders. Structural problems in historical pianos are mentioned in some early descriptions. Such problems often attract attention: the sound of an early piano can be infinitely excused for being unfamiliar today but historically ideal; a twisted case, a cocked cheek, or a cracked soundboard leave considerably less space for such optimistic interpretations.

However, many organologists believe that an analysis of the technical state of an instrument is scarcely less complicated than its aesthetic evaluation. Although structural stability was also a historical concern, the approach of historical builders might have differed from modern attitudes. Some specialists suggest that the idea of over-dimensioning and safety margins in the modern sense was not applied by some of these builders.[33] Time has revealed all sorts of risk-taking, and structural failure has occurred even in instruments by important builders. Michael Latcham, for instance, has discussed the nature of, and the possible reasons for, soundboard replacements that he found in various historical pianos by makers as famous as Anton Walter, Nannette Streicher, and Ferdinand Hoffmann.[34] Interestingly, some of the replacements seem to have taken place early in the history of the respective instruments. Latcham's list of reasons for the soundboard replacements includes "case failure" (discussed with the help of two Walter pianos from 1796 and around 1800, where the soundboards were probably removed to get access to the inner construction in order to deal with a twisted case), "a loose bridge" (with reference to Gall's *Clavier–Stimmbuch* from 1805[35]), "a damaged soundboard," and "a sunken soundboard."[36]

An example of a consistent design flaw is presented in Sabine Matzenauer's description of the restoration of one of J. A. Stein's fortepianos from 1790. Stein attached the oak wrestplanks to the case by means of two tenons on each end, which are too small for the string tension. In nine out of ten pianos compared, they broke off so that the wrestplanks loosened and were displaced backwards.[37] Considering Stein's concern for quality, as well as the sturdiness of other aspects of his casework, this rather fundamental misjudgment remains a mystery.

Contrary to what one might expect, a later piano was not necessarily sturdier or less prone to structural failure than an earlier one. Case stability must always be viewed in relationship to string load. Case failure can often be shown to be the consequence of a change of various production factors

[33] William Jurgenson, "The case of the weak case," paper presented at the Antwerpiano conference, Antwerp, 1993. Opinions about this point vary among modern organologists.
[34] Latcham, "Soundboards old & new."   [35] Gall, ed., *Clavier–Stimmbuch*, 98.
[36] Latcham, "Soundboards old & new," 56.
[37] Sabine Matzenauer, "Zur Restaurierung eines Piano-Fortes von J. A. Stein – erhaltene Instrumente im Vergleich," in Monika Lustig, ed., *Zur Geschichte des Hammerklaviers*, Institut für Aufführungspraxis Michaelstein, 1993, 52.

at the same time during the course of an overly rapid development. All surviving instruments that display some sort of structural failure point to the same central problem: the high production rate of many important piano builders, which guaranteed the establishment of a strong tradition in very short time (between, roughly, 1780 and 1800), could not fully compensate for the lack of long-term experience that was, for instance, known from harpsichord building. But such long-term knowledge would have been welcome to meet the specific challenges of the hammer principle. Beginning with the first known fortepianos by Cristofori, fortepiano stringing was heavier than that of comparable harpsichords.[38] This was a necessary response to the different manner in which a hammer excites a string, and to compensate for its damping effect after the attack.[39] Heavier stringing was adapted by Gottfried Silbermann[40] and later by Johann Andreas Stein,[41] and accepted as indispensable in fortepiano building even before the piano was designed to be actually louder than the harpsichord. The move away from the harpsichord and clavichord building tradition appears to have been dictated mainly by the need to match the increasing string tension (and, with regard to soundboards, string pressure) with appropriately sturdy constructions. Consequently, pianos from 1813 can be found in which a tail twist of around 3 degrees competes with a cheek cocked by at least the same amount in the opposite direction (Carl Maria von Weber's Brodmann),[42] whereas an early piano from 1783 can have a straight tail and an almost straight cheek (the Trondheim Stein).

Another important factor that influenced the quality in unpredictable ways was the changing organization of piano workshops. The move toward bigger shops and a higher production rate necessarily resulted in rationalization. Not all the design changes were necessarily structural improvements or adaptations to better match tone ideals (neither does every unchanged design necessarily represent a statement about the preferability of a certain tone character). It is not always possible to understand the exact reasons for some of these changes. For example, the early models of the Walter firm, including Mozart's piano from 1782, have a rather elaborate outline with an s-shaped bentside and a separate tailpiece (Figure 5.1, left).[43] The bridge of this type of piano is jointed in the foreshortened bass section rather than having an s-shape. The s-shape of the side nevertheless ensures

[38] Heavier stringing for Cristofori is described in Scipione Maffei's report from 1711. Facsimile in Lelie, *Van piano tot forte*, 300–8.

[39] See Gätjen, "Das Hammerklavier – akustisches Bindeglied zwischen Clavichord, Cembalo und modernem Flügel?" 150–1. The hammer stays between a half and (in the treble) "up to several vibration periods" at the string. See also Anders Askenfeld, ed., *The Acoustics of the Piano*, Uppsala: Almqvist & Wiksell, 1991, 45–50.

[40] Stewart Pollens, "Gottfried Silbermann's pianos," *The Organ Yearbook* 17 (1986): 103–21.

[41] Latcham, "Mozart and the pianos of Johann Andreas Stein," 145–6.

[42] See the photograph in Droysen-Reber, "Carl Maria von Weber und sein Brodmann-Hammerflügel," 59.

[43] See also Latcham, "Mozart and the pianos of Gabriel Anton Walter," 395.

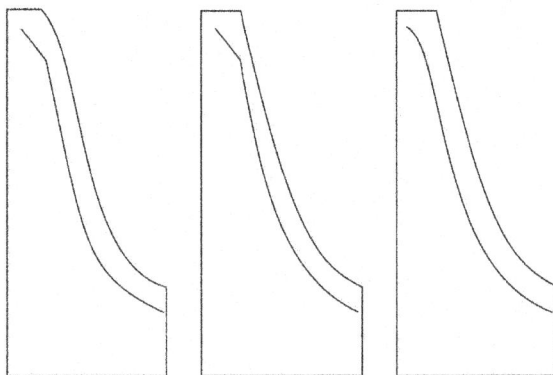

Figure 5.1. Schematic representation of bridge and bentside shape in three Walter models

that its distance from the bridge remains fairly constant up to the joint. Some slightly later Walter pianos (*c.* 1790) have similar bridges, but a single bentside with a separate tailpiece (Figure 5.1, middle).[44] In the area of the bridge joint (around F), the straight section of the bentside comes closer to the bridge than in the previous model. In even later instruments, the bass end of the bridge is shaped in a curve instead of being jointed at an angle (Figure 5.1, right).[45] Here, the distance from the side is, again, kept more even.

In some of the instruments of the second kind with a single bentside and a jointed bridge, a tonal imbalance in the critical area can be observed, which is clearly audible in direct comparison with the earliest model.[46] Such an observation does not prove perhaps that Walter improved the efficiency of his production by simplifying the bentside shape at the expense of tonal quality, or that he later fixed the problem in the cheapest way by adjusting the shape of the bridge. Generally speaking, however, a connection between production economy and design is a factor to keep in mind when analyzing specific fortepiano features. Whatever the causes, this example certainly shows that an earlier model can possess qualities that were not necessarily surpassed by later ones.

A side effect of larger workshops is evident in examples of indisputably faulty craftsmanship. It may be so that "most of the downright nasty instruments from the shallow end of the pool have quite rightly ended up as calories," as fortepiano maker and restorer Christopher Clarke suggested. Nevertheless, one occasionally still encounters them:

---

[44] A Walter piano of this type is mentioned in Latcham, "The development of the Streicher firm of piano builders, 1792 to 1823," copy provided by the author, 19 n. 37.

[45] These are instruments that belong to "group II" or later, from *c.* 1785 as presented in Latcham, "Mozart and the pianos of Gabriel Anton Walter," 395–7.

[46] Personal observation and communication with Michael Latcham.

How about the 1806 Broadwood grand where the workman cracked the kerfed bentside liner as he was gluing it (reducing its strength to zero at that point) and patched the crack with a shaving before the foreman arrived? The cheek twisted a good quarter inch after stringing, in the Broadwood shop, and the top was planed flat and veneered … Or the Johann Fritz six-and-a-half-octave grand, once owned by one of Rossini's prima donne [*sic*], where the action maker screwed up on the bearing angle of the escapement pawl, making it impossible to play louder than *mezzoforte* before the escapement occurred prematurely? … The original strings of this instrument … [had] never been stressed higher than their tuning tension – and so the instrument had never been played at all hard.[47]

We can conclude that flaws in fortepiano construction do belong to the reality of historical pianos. Such flaws can be caused by factors as diverse as misjudgment, chutzpah, or deliberate risk-taking, unsatisfactory craftsmanship, and high production levels. A connection between the type and period of a piano and its susceptibility to structural failure can, however, only be established when specific features are closely analyzed. We have to face the possibility that a builder simply tried to achieve a certain result and failed. But this observation is largely independent of the actual phase of development of the piano. A direct chronological connection between pianos of various stages and their stability is a myth.

BEETHOVEN'S SOUND IDEAL AND MODERN FORTEPIANO COPIES

For the fortepiano customer, less has changed between Beethoven's time and today than might be expected, apart from the possibility of being able to choose models from various periods. Now, as then, one has the option of choosing instruments according to one's taste and financial means. For the maker of fortepianos the differences are greater. The success or failure of various constructions has, after more than two centuries, become plain, which enables a modern builder to make choices, to add corrections to a chosen model, and even to develop new designs of a would-be historical kind. At the same time, the demand for copies of fortepianos is limited and today's workshops are far smaller than most workshops of Beethoven's time. As a consequence, quality control is usually shared between few people. Most new fortepianos today are handmade quality articles. Such a definition applies only to very few of the historical instruments. Many of the playable surviving antiques, on the other hand, are probably only preserved because they were especially good. If carefully restored, they may still represent the very best of historical fortepiano making in spite of their age.

---

[47] Christopher Clarke on the fortepiano mailing list at: launch.groups.yahoo.com/group/fortepiano/message/4755 (last accessed March 2, 2009).

In 1810, Beethoven wrote to Streicher: "It is my motto to play on a good instrument, or not at all."[48] For Beethoven's music, the high standards and expectations of modern fortepiano specialists seem entirely appropriate. But this says little about the properties that make a fortepiano especially suited for his music. In the quest for such properties, the modern fortepiano maker faces two fundamental problems.

The first of these is the loss of the original sound. The sound of preserved historical pianos, whether pleasant or disappointing, always differs from their original sound. Besides possible problems with the case structure and bad repair, there are many reasons for this phenomenon, such as changes in the original wood, leather, and cloth, and the unpredictable influences of various replacements of ephemeral materials. Choosing the "best" tone on the basis of comparative fortepiano criticism is an impossible task: a modern maker of pianos after historical models imitates a historical building process in order to achieve a tone which, in the original instruments, is irretrievably gone.

On the other hand, it is technically possible to come close to what we *think* was the new sound of old pianos. This introduces a second problem for the modern maker, who will, unlike the historical piano firms, have to strive for improvement *within* a chosen model. If a customer in 2005 orders a copy of an 1805 Streicher which is to be delivered in 2007, he expects an optimal representation of the 1805 instrument and not an improved Streicher model from 1807. This peculiar situation in our time has led to two main approaches in historical instrument making. One is to produce very close copies of selected models. The other approach is based on trying to understand the mindset of a historical maker in order to create instruments that combine historical ideas and properties with the modern maker's individual touch and personal stamp.[49]

Here is not the place to elaborate on the virtues of either of these approaches. The problems associated with strict copies have been discussed elsewhere.[50] The possibilities and hazards of the second approach are obvious. By re-creating instead of copying, the maker is able to correct obvious flaws and can avoid adding new inaccuracies to the possible imprecision of the original. A maker can also respond to specific customer requests within certain limits. On the other hand, with every step away from the original, an instrument loses some of its information value on which performance practices are based.

---

[48] Letter to Andreas Streicher, November 1810. Beethoven, *Briefwechsel*, vol. II, 168.

[49] See Markus Fischinger, "Historische Tasteninstrumente im 20. Jahrhundert am Beispiel der Restaurierung eines Hammerflügels von J. H. E. Fessel, Dresden (um 1800)," Magisterarbeit, Humboldt Universität, 2005, Part I.

[50] See, for example, Martin Skowroneck, "Cembalobauer als Kopisten," paper presented at the Colloquium of the Ruckers Genootschap, Antwerp, 1977.

Two features come to mind when we consider the possibilities a fortepiano maker may have for realizing Beethoven's piano preferences – a singing tone, a flexible tone character, and more volume – within a given historical model. These are the construction and quality of the soundboard, and the appropriate stringing. I will discuss both features briefly as an example. I want to stress that the soundboard is by no means the only part of the instrument that can influence the tone in a substantial way.

Historical sources are often vague about soundboard construction, although the importance of a good soundboard is universally acknowledged. Modern research has introduced the terms "impedance" and "impedance mismatch," which aim to describe soundboard properties, string properties, and the relationship between them.[51] This terminology inspires analogies to electricity that are unappealing to physicists, and encourages a false hope that tonal properties are predictable. I will therefore explain the principle of the soundboard–string relationship using everyday language instead.

Simply put, soundboards need to be thin enough to reproduce the vibration of the strings appropriately. "Appropriately" means that the soundboard properties have to be balanced against the resistance of the strings in order to reproduce the sound in the manner desired by the builder. These properties include mass, springiness, and stiffness with and across the grain. A builder influences them through careful selection of appropriate softwood, planing the soundboard to an appropriate thickness (using appropriate tools that leave the fibers intact), and by choosing an appropriate soundboard ribbing. All these measures have the function of safeguarding the soundboard against cracking or sinking under the string load. However, natural variation in the properties of soundboard wood contributes to the phenomenon that similar soundboards can still have varying properties. Referring to clavichords, Jakob Adlung wrote that, inexplicably, the sound of one of two identical instruments was "twice as loud and more graceful by far."[52] Everyone accustomed to the puzzling difference of sound character that can occur in otherwise identical instruments will agree that the term "springiness" only clumsily conceals the abundance of possible characteristics possessed by pieces of soundboard wood of the same dimensions.

Producing a tone of desirable length and volume involves a trade-off. If a soundboard is stiff and has a high mass, the same strings will tend to produce a longer but softer tone. If a soundboard is made thinner, that is, lighter and more flexible, the same strings will produce a louder tone with less sustain. In very thin soundboards, this effect is usually enhanced by the tendency of the surface to subdivide into areas that beat in opposite directions, thus prematurely absorbing the sound.

---

[51] See Askenfeld, ed., *The Acoustics of the Piano*, 16 and 83–99.
[52] Adlung, *Musica Mechanica Organoedi*, part II, 152.

If one approaches the matter from the stringing side instead, a given soundboard will produce more volume with thicker strings, but the tone will probably decline faster. The same soundboard, re-strung with thinner strings, will give a softer tone with a longer sustain.

This model still neglects various important factors, above all the influence of hammer mass on the tone. Relatively heavy hammers could interact with very thin strings so as to reverse the prediction made above. Relatively light hammers could under-excite a stringing that in other respects was appropriate for a thick soundboard.[53]

Many historical builders apparently did not base their decisions about string diameter on soundboard thickness or vice versa.[54] I am using this explanation only because it shows that an instrument maker can indeed influence factors like tone length, character, and volume. However, applied within a given school of construction, the possibilities are restricted because of the trade-off between volume and sustain mentioned above. Also, the results are difficult to predict. The practical value of such background information for the player lies in any case not in prediction; the goal is to become confident about one's judgment of the properties of existing fortepianos in order to be able to compare various instruments and to make meaningful choices. There are even some historical examples of such a comparison. As mentioned earlier, on April 4, 1807, Andreas Streicher sent a piano of a newly developed kind to Härtel and asked him for his judgment. A day later, the *Allgemeine Musikalische Zeitung* received Streicher's detailed advice on how this instrument was to be compared with others:

I asked [Breitkopf & Härtel] to let the instrument stand for a few days so they could organize the test at leisure and at ease. Since I can expect from your kindness that you do not interpret my wish as an instruction, I am asking you

(1) to compare this instrument (which is made of slab-sawn ash, has the compass contra F–f'''', a white keyboard, and the section with iron strings is triple-strung throughout) if possible with some others from French, English, and local masters, in a larger room without wall coverings.

(2) to let this instrument be played alone for some time, so one truly remembers its tone, and only then to begin the comparison with the others.

(3) that all the Claviere are opened in the same fashion, and their outer lids are removed if possible. The *Tonboden* [i.e. an extra sound sheet above the strings] can remain in those instruments that have one.

(4) that besides the player, three to four persons are present, who test the instruments not only close by, but from various distances and especially from far away.

---

[53] The relationship between hammer mass and string mass has a direct influence on the duration of hammer contact with the string (Askenfeld, ed., *The Acoustics of the Piano*, 45) and hence on the partials and on tone length.

[54] Communication with Martin Skowroneck, Michael Latcham, Paul Poletti, and personal observation.

(5) that the same piece, the same chords are played on each of the instruments, in order to make the judgment easier and more precise. For this reason, the Clav. must be tuned in the same fashion as well.
(6) that the player tries to produce all shades from the softest *piano* to the utmost force in one single chord in both hands, on this and on the other instruments.[55]

No doubt, Streicher expected his instrument to excel under these controlled conditions of an almost clinical setting. Of course, true objectivity is not at all guaranteed in such comparisons, because the judgment of the sounds remains personal, however similar the conditions are under which the instruments are presented or recorded.

A completely different question is how the properties of a fortepiano are experienced during an extended period of time in various settings and in relationship to varying repertoire. Long-term experience is scarcely less subjective than direct comparisons in the manner of Streicher's test. Over a longer period of time, however, it is possible to accumulate a more acute sense of what "works" well on a certain instrument and what does not. My following observations are based on such experience.

I have compared the effect of a variety of Beethoven's musical textures on two Walter copies that possess different sound characters and react differently to gradations of touch.[56] The first of these combines a stronger attack with a shorter sustain, and its tone character is rather uniform throughout the dynamic range. The second piano has a rounder attack, more sustain, and a tone character that can to a larger degree be influenced by touch. On the first instrument it is easier to produce, in the words of Andreas Streicher, a *körnicht* ("pithy") tone;[57] on the second more dynamic nuance is available. One might think that the second instrument is the better candidate for Beethoven's music. In practice, however, it turns out that the variety of textures found in his music for five-octave pianos leads to different choices in different situations.

In *cantabile* lines at slow or moderate tempi, for example, the difference between the instruments was smaller than expected, but there was a slight preference for the second instrument, with more sustain and a less direct attack. The same applies to passages of a "floating" quality,[58] such as the opening Adagio sostenuto of the "Moonlight" Sonata Op. 27/2, which on the first piano were more difficult to control.

The more direct attack of the first piano, however, was clearly superior in all sorts of passages at various dynamic levels that require clarity or have a percussive element, such as fast runs, broken or repeated chords, or articulated themes of various sorts. Such passages abound in Beethoven's piano

---

[55] Goebl-Streicher, Streicher, and Ladenburger, *"Diesem Menschen hätte ich mein ganzes Leben widmen mögen,"* 119.
[56] These are two pianos by Martin Skowroneck after two different originals by Anton Walter.
[57] Streicher, *Kurze Bemerkungen,* 9 and 15.
[58] See also Küthen, "Ein verlorener Registerklang. Beethovens Imitation der Aeolsharfe."

music. Only at *fortissimo* levels, this piano acquired a forced and somewhat narrow tone, especially in the bass. For these passages there are advantages to both pianos and it is up to the player whether he prefers more clarity or a somewhat less restricted sound.

In movements with alternating melody lines and staccato, sforzato, and articulated textures at slow speed, both instruments had clear strengths and weaknesses. An example is the Largo e mesto from the D major Sonata Op. 10/3; in this piece, each phrase seems to call for a different sound and level of clarity.

This catalog of observations is only a very compressed version of my experiments. The most important result is that there seems to be no automatic connection between Beethoven's criticism of contemporary fortepianos and his style of composing. Although his *cantabile* writing calls for a piano that does not frustrate legato playing, much of his music fares better with a responsive, direct, and perhaps more rustic tone. A fortepiano with too sustained a tone seems definitely less suitable in these cases. The example of the Largo e mesto of Op. 10/3 suggests that Beethoven was not interested in some selected properties, but hoped to find a greater variety of possibilities combined in one instrument. Pieces like this one ask for a truly singing tone but – in order to realize the outbursts and contrasts – ask at the same time for directness of a kind that usually occurs in fortepianos with a shorter tone. This universal concept may well be the only truly Beethovenian piano ideal of that time.

On the other hand, finding a piano that is unsuited for this music requires no experiments: this would be any instrument that thwarts the creation of a legato line, that resists producing controlled dynamic shades, that is irregular, or that refuses to reproduce clean accents or articulations. But this is, simply, a bad piano. It is important to realize that a rendering of Beethoven's ideas does not principally lie beyond the properties of pianos of a historical model. Usually the player will be able to work out a solution that brings the piano's properties and the music close to each other. This responsibility of the pianist is the subject of the following chapter.

CHAPTER 6

The player's influence

REPORTS ABOUT BEETHOVEN'S PLAYING

The preceding excursion into practical issues has shown how the fortepiano can be used in modern Beethoven performance. This provides an opening for understanding the character of Beethoven's dealings with his instruments as a matter of musical practice instead of a mere struggle. On a personal level, however, this question needs further investigation. Most of the time, Beethoven was struggling with various aspects of his life. One might think that piano playing was a part of this pattern, even if his fame among his contemporaries was undeniably based on his exceptional musicianship and not, for instance, on his endless quibbles with friends, servants, and editors, on his imagined or real financial worries, or on his complex relationship with women. Piano playing was absolutely central for Beethoven during his early life. Even in one of the famous letters in which he announced his upcoming deafness, he defiantly stated that he had "substantially perfected" his piano playing.[1] In the spring of 1802 (a year later), crisis apparently subdued his ambitions for a while; Griesinger wrote: "In the future, Beethoven wants to write only a little for the Klavier, but more polyphonic [music]."[2] But on 18 October of the same year 1802, a week after writing the final version of the "Heiligenstadt Testament," Beethoven proudly announced the variations Op. 34 and 35 to Breitkopf & Härtel, which were written in a "truly completely new manner." So here piano playing and piano composition actually played a crucial role in overcoming his crisis.[3]

In order to find out more about the character of Beethoven's playing, and to determine when and how it became a struggle, we can analyze the

---

[1] Letter from July 1, 1801, Beethoven, *Briefwechsel*, vol. 1, 85, in which Beethoven asks Amenda to join him on a concert tour "if after half a year my ailment has proved incurable."
[2] Letter from April 7, 1802. Biba, ed., *"Eben komme ich von Haydn,"* 159.
[3] Letter from October 18, 1802. Beethoven, *Briefwechsel*, vol. I, 126. Solomon argues that the Heiligenstadt Testament is a fair copy and that the crisis was at its end at the moment of writing (Solomon, *Beethoven*, 118–19). The self-confident letter to Breitkopf & Härtel supports this notion. See also Peter Schleuning's analysis in Peter Schleuning and Martin Geck, *"Geschrieben auf Bonaparte" Beethovens "Eroica": Revolution, Reaktion, Rezeption*, Reinbeck: Rowohlt, 1989, 78–108.

historical reports that mention his playing. Several have already been mentioned; they will reappear here in chronological order.

The list begins with Reicha's anecdote from around 1790 about Beethoven's performance of a Mozart concerto, during which he broke several strings but insisted on playing the piece to the end.[4] One is bound to think that the musical enjoyment of the listeners was hampered by Beethoven's problems, but Reicha gives us no particulars. Various other witnesses from the Bonn period acknowledge Beethoven's skills as an improviser but, as we have seen, before the 1791 trip to Mergentheim, his playing remained clearly unsophisticated in some manner, so that some observers in retrospect called it "rough and hard."

In Junker's description from 1791, and in the newspaper article from the *Berlinische Musikalische Zeitung* October 26, 1793 that also contains Beethoven's grateful letter to Neefe, we find descriptions of Beethoven as one of the foremost players of that time.[5]

Reports about Beethoven's playing from the first period in Vienna are scarce. Probably before the summer of 1793, Beethoven competed with Gelinek. According to Czerny, Gelinek described Beethoven's playing in the following words:

I have never heard anyone play like that! He improvised on a subject that I had given him in a manner that I have not heard even from Mozart. Then he played his own compositions, which are in the highest degree amazing and sublime, and he produces difficulties and effects on the Clavier of which we never dreamt.[6]

Johann Schenk's description of Beethoven's improvisation probably refers to the late summer of 1793.[7] The tone of his account is enthusiastic and its content is entirely positive.

In November 1793, Beethoven wrote about the jealousy of the Vienna *Klaviermeister*, which indicates that his playing had made a strong impact.

On March 29, 1795, Beethoven played a piano concerto in an Akademie at the Burgtheater, and the *Wiener Zeitung* reported "undivided acclaim."

On April 29, 1796, Beethoven, was in Dresden on his way to Berlin. Hofrat von Schall, who knew Beethoven from Bonn, wrote to Elector Max Franz that Beethoven was "said to have improved infinitely and to compose well." Among other things, one evening he was granted a solo performance of one-and-a-half hours for the Elector of Saxony, who was a music connoisseur. Von Schall later stated, "Everybody who heard him play the Klavier was enchanted." The Elector was "extremely content."[8]

In Berlin, Beethoven had great success according to various reports. He played several times at the Singakademie, moved the audience to tears, and

---

[4] Prod'homme, "From the unpublished autobiography of Antoine Reicha," 351. See my discussion in Chapter 2.
[5] Beethoven, *Briefwechsel*, vol. I, II.   [6] Czerny, "Erinnerungen aus meinem Leben," 10.
[7] Kerst, *Die Erinnerungen an Beethoven*, vol. I, 25–7.   [8] Schiedermair, *Der junge Beethoven*, 320–1.

was asked by the King of Prussia to become Kapellmeister, which he declined.[9]

On April 4, 1795 or 1797, either before or after the Berlin trip, Beethoven improvised privately on a Walter fortepiano for half an hour, which he "mastered enchantingly," as Kübeck von Kübau reports.[10]

On April 6, 1797, Beethoven played in Schuppanzigh's concert with his own works, including the Woodwind Quintet Op. 16. According to an entry from a meeting of the *Tonkünstlergesellschaft* on May 10, Beethoven "distinguished" himself in this concert and also added an improvisation.[11]

In 1798, Tomášek heard Beethoven in two concerts and a private performance in Prague. Tomášek accumulated some criticism about the inorganic development of ideas in Beethoven's music. Nevertheless, the performances as such clearly impressed him. After the first concert, he called Beethoven's playing "magnificent," and after the third concert "strong" and "brilliant." Only Beethoven's performance at the second concert (with the Second Piano Concerto) did not make "such an enormous impact" on Tomášek.[12] The *Patriotisches Journal für die k.k. Staaten* in 1798 wrote of the same performances that in spite of all acclaim some connoisseurs had seen the "great faults of this budding master." They praised "his dexterity, his difficult jumps and figurations [Griffe]" but criticized the fact that he "neglected all the singing, all equality in his playing, all subtlety and comprehensibility, that he was only in search of originality without actually having it and that he exaggerated everything both in playing and composing."[13]

Around 1798–99, Karl Amenda reported that one evening Beethoven played a "wonderful" improvisation, which he then repeated.[14] At that time Beethoven noticed the first signs of his approaching deafness, as he later admitted in a letter.[15]

The confrontation between Beethoven and Josef Wölffl in 1799, apparently arranged by Baron Raimund von Wetzlar and Prince Lichnowsky as an entertainment for the Viennese music-loving society, reached dimensions that clearly lay beyond the ambitions of either of the pianists. In his later account, Ignaz von Seyfried admits that the two contestants, who played their own compositions, improvised at will, gave each other subjects for improvisation, and even attempted "one or another four-hand capriccio" during several soirées in von Wetzlar's villa, in fact respected each other, and paid little attention to the fuss made by their patrons. Wölffl was, in the ears of the Viennese, the first true challenge to Beethoven. In a comparison between the two from April 22, 1799, the reviewer of the AMZ tries to remain impartial

[9] Wegeler and Ries, *Biographische Notizen über Beethoven*, 109–11, and Thayer, *Life of Beethoven*, 184–7.
[10] Kerst, *Die Erinnerungen an Beethoven*, vol. 1, 68–71.   [11] Thayer, *Life of Beethoven*, 191, 197.
[12] *Ibid.*, 207–8.   [13] Quoted in Molsen, *Die Geschichte des Klavierspiels in historischen Zitaten*, 67–8.
[14] Kerst, *Die Erinnerungen an Beethoven*, vol. 1, 34.
[15] Letter from July 1, 1801. Beethoven, *Briefwechsel*, vol. 1, 85.

but nevertheless mentions that Beethoven's playing, "extremely brilliant" as it might be, was less subtle than Wölffl's and became, at times, indistinct. However, in the free fantasy, Beethoven was "truly completely extraordinary." Possibly inspired by this review, and very likely influenced by his later experience with Beethoven, Seyfried describes Beethoven's playing as completely enraptured. Occasionally he "compelled the instrument to such an utterance of force that the strongest structure was hardly able to obey."[16]

In a review of the variations WoO 73 from June 19, 1799, the AMZ acknowledged Beethoven's playing in a curious manner: "Hr. van Beethoven may be able to improvise, but he does not know how to write variations."[17] This is one of several examples of reviews where Beethoven's works are criticized, but his status as "one of the most foremost pianists" is never questioned.[18]

Johann Baptist Cramer visited Vienna between September 1799 and spring 1800. Visiting Beethoven one day, he heard him play from the anteroom and was "completely entranced" by what he heard.[19] Cramer was less enthusiastic when Beethoven played one of his own compositions: "One day, he would play it with great spirit and expression, but the next day he would sound moody and often muddled to the point of becoming indistinct."[20] This account is confirmed by Czerny, who says that in the period "up to 1810," Beethoven's improvisation was exceptional but his performance of his published works was "less successful." "Since he never had the patience or took the time to practice them again, his success usually depended on coincidence and his mood."[21]

The Akademie of April 2, 1800, where Beethoven played, among other pieces, the First Piano Concerto and improvised, got a mixed review in the AMZ, mainly due to the unequal and uninspired orchestra. Beethoven, on the other hand, "extemporized masterfully." On April 18, he played again in the *Burgtheater* with the horn virtuoso Punto (Wenzel Stich). In spite of the new theater decree which prohibited the giving of encores and loud applause in the theater, the audience applauded "very loudly" and the complete Horn Sonata (Op. 17) had to be repeated.[22]

On May 7, 1800, Beethoven and Punto played in Pest. The review mentions especially Beethoven's "artistic" playing that "drew much attention from those present."[23]

---

[16] Kerst, *Die Erinnerungen an Beethoven*, vol. 1, 36–9.

[17] Translation from Thayer, *Life of Beethoven*, 278.

[18] See, for instance, the reviews quoted in Schindler, *Beethoven as I Knew Him*, 76–7.

[19] Thayer, *Life of Beethoven*, 209.   [20] Schindler, *Beethoven as I Knew Him*, 413.

[21] Czerny, "Anekdoten und Notizen," 22.

[22] AMZ July 2, 1800, quoted in Robbins Landon, ed., *Ludwig van Beethoven. Leben und Werk in Zeugnissen der Zeit*, 78.

[23] *Ungarischer Kurier*, 1800, quoted in *ibid.*, 77.

On December 9, 1800, Josephine von Deym's guest Duchess Julia von Giovane was "enchanted" when Beethoven played a cello sonata and the Violin Sonatas Op. 12 at von Deym's residence.[24] On January 30, 1801, another concert with Punto was reviewed favorably in the *Wiener Zeitung*, although a member of the audience found that Punto's horn could not be heard far back in the hall.[25]

On December 5, 1802, Beethoven played his new variations Op. 34 and 35 "with his well-known talent" privately for Griesinger.[26]

In 1803, Abbé Vogler was in Vienna. Johann Baptist Gänsbacher, who heard Vogler and Beethoven, writes:

Beethoven's excellent Klavier playing, combined with an abundance of most beautiful thoughts, surprised me immensely; however, my feelings could not rise to the same enthusiasm that Vogler's learned playing, unequaled in harmony and counterpoint, inspired in me.[27]

Gänsbacher, who was Vogler's pupil, does not say that Beethoven and Vogler actually played on the same occasion; he only compares their style of playing.

On April 4, 1803, Beethoven performed the Third Piano Concerto Op. 37 for the first time, together with the oratorio *Christus am Ölberge* and the Second Symphony. According to various reports, this concert was not a success, due to the insufficiently rehearsed orchestra and because the oratorio was too long and elaborate. The *Zeitung für die elegante Welt* wrote, "Hr. v. Beethoven, who is otherwise known as an excellent pianist, performed [the concerto] also not completely to the audience's satisfaction."[28]

Beethoven and the violinist George Polgreen Bridgetower played the first performance of the "Kreuzer" Sonata Op. 47 on May 24, 1803 in the Augarten. Beethoven was apparently back in shape by then. In his copy of the music, Bridgetower noted down his impressions from the first performance: "Beethoven's expression in the Andante was so chaste, which always characterized the performance of all his *slow movements*, that it was unanimously hailed to be repeated twice."[29]

Ignaz Pleyel and his son Camille heard Beethoven improvise and play a cello sonata with the cellist Lamarre in 1805. While Ignaz Pleyel, according to Czerny, was so astounded by Beethoven's improvisation that he "kissed his hands,"[30] Camille analyzed Beethoven's pianism critically in a letter:

He has unlimited technical skills but no schooling, and his execution is not polished, that is, his playing is not clean. He has much fire, but he pounds slightly too much; he realizes diabolical difficulties, but not entirely neatly. All the same he gave me much pleasure when improvising. He does not improvise coldly like

[24] *Ibid.*, 74–5.   [25] *Ibid.*, 78.   [26] Biba, ed., *"Eben komme ich von Haydn,"* 177.
[27] Frimmel, *Beethoven-Handbuch*, vol. 1, 158.   [28] Translation from Thayer, *Life of Beethoven*, 330.
[29] Original English. *Ibid.*, 333.   [30] Czerny, "Anekdoten und Notizen," 21.

Woelfl. He realizes whatever enters his head and he is extremely daring. Sometimes he does astonishing things.[31]

According to Schindler, Cherubini around 1805 found Beethoven's playing simply "rough." Clementi, too, who heard Beethoven play "various works" in 1807, called his playing, "Not polished … frequently impetuous, like himself, yet … always full of spirit."[32] Johann Friedrich Nisle was enthusiastic about Beethoven's improvisation but his remarks about his playing technique were consistent with Cherubini's and Clementi's: "True, as a pianist, he was inferior to some others regarding elegance and technical advantages. He also played rather loudly because of his bad hearing."[33] Probably addressing the same period, Czerny describes how Hummel's followers accused Beethoven of "mistreating the piano, of lacking all cleanness and clarity, of creating nothing but confused noise in the way he used the pedal."[34]

Still, some time between 1804 and 1808, Therese v. Hauer remembers Beethoven's performance in the summer resort of Baden positively:

He came, let himself be entreated for a while, finally he approached the Klavier, made a sour face but nevertheless played on subjects given by some ladies, improvised fantasies with an overwhelming sensitivity and outstanding skill, so at the end everyone left the hall fully satisfied with this enjoyment.[35]

On December 22, 1808, Beethoven gave the famous Akademie in which the Fourth Piano Concerto Op. 58 and the Choral Fantasy Op. 80 were inaugurated together with the Fifth and Sixth Symphony (Op. 67 and 68), and two movements of the C major Mass Op. 86. The program was too long, the hall was too cold, and in the Choral Fantasy an embarrassing re-start was necessary. The many ambivalent reports of this event should not detract from the fact that Beethoven (as his ambitious programming indeed shows) expected this concert to be extremely important for his career. One is tempted to conjecture that he prepared himself especially painstakingly at the piano for this program. This would provide an explanation for Johann Friedrich Reichardt's enthusiastic reports from December 1808. Perhaps Reichardt was inclined to be extra generous with Beethoven, but he would surely have noticed any serious problem in Beethoven's performances. Nothing of the sort transpires: at the beginning of December, at Countess Erdödy's, Beethoven played for an hour and Reichardt was "completely enchanted." A second time, still before December 10 and also at Erdödy's, Beethoven played one of the Trios Op. 70 "extremely well and determinedly." The Akademie left Reichardt unsatisfied in many respects, but not with how Beethoven

---

[31] French original in Komlós, *Fortepianos and their Music*, 143.
[32] Schindler, *Beethoven as I Knew Him*, 413. [33] Kerst, *Die Erinnerungen an Beethoven*, vol. 1, 128.
[34] Carl Czerny, "Recollections from my life," *The Musical Quarterly* 42 (1956): 309, quoted after Komlós, *Fortepianos and their Music*, 142. This passage is missing from the German edition, Czerny, "Erinnerungen aus meinem Leben."
[35] Frimmel, *Beethoven-Handbuch*, vol. 1, 200.

performed: in the Fourth Concerto he played "astonishingly well, and in the absolute fastest tempi." In the second movement, he "genuinely sang on his instrument with a deep, melancholic feeling." In a long free fantasy, he "showed all his mastery."[36]

Some time before December 31, Beethoven again played trios at Erdödy's "completely masterfully and enthusiastically."[37]

Louis Girod, for whom Beethoven improvised in 1809, was impressed by Beethoven's wealth of ideas, but "his fingering was often wrong, which affected the beauty of the tone."[38]

Bettina von Arnim's letters to Goethe from July 1810 provide a variety of curious details but are musically not very informative. Bettina heard Beethoven play a fantasy "wholly excellently," and another time he "played for a long time on his own initiative ... thus excited, his spirit produces the incomprehensible and his fingers accomplish the impossible." Another time von Arnim heard him play a sonata "superhumanly." Von Arnim's description of Beethoven's living quarters has attracted attention because it seems to show that Beethoven neglected his various pianos at that time: "His apartment is very curious. In the first room [there are] two or three grand pianos, all lying without legs on the floor, suitcases with his things, a chair with three legs, in the second room his bed."[39] Even for Beethoven's frequently documented disorder, this description is extreme. It might be assumed that he just had moved into this particular apartment; the "two or three" pianos had not yet been set up, and his things were not yet unpacked. This would also explain why "nobody knew where he lived."

In 1811, the writer Varnhagen von Ense heard Beethoven's improvisation and wrote, "The man appealed to me even more than the artist." Goethe, however, wrote in his diary on July 21, 1812: "In the evening at Beethoven's. He played exquisitely."[40] It would seem that, in Goethe's view (mirrored in Bettina von Arnim's descriptions), spirit was always more "exquisite" than matters of playing technique. Other accounts from 1812 surely suggest that Beethoven's performances had become highly unpredictable. Occasionally, he still played amazingly. The pianist Friedrich Starke describes one of these occasions:

[He improvised] in three distinct styles, first in polyphonic style [*gebundener Stil*], second in a fugue where a subject in sixteenth notes was developed divinely and in an amazing manner, and third in chamber music style, where Beethoven succeeded in combining the greatest difficulties with his special temper.[41]

I will conclude this presentation with two recollections from around 1812. The first is Franz Glöggl's report of an improvisation in Linz in 1812. Glöggl

---

[36] Reichardt, *Briefe, die Musik betreffend*, 266–9. Reichardt uses the term "brav" for Beethoven's playing, which in modern usage would mean "well-behaved."

[37] *Ibid.*, 278.

[38] Kerst, *Die Erinnerungen an Beethoven*, vol. I, 137–8. Girod later became Baron de Trémont.

[39] *Ibid.*, 142, 146.   [40] *Ibid.*, 167, 169.   [41] Frimmel, *Beethoven-Handbuch*, vol. I, 135.

was the son of the *Kapellmeister* of Linz cathedral. He later reported to Thayer:

Count von Dönhoff, a great admirer of Beethoven … gave several soirées in his honor during the composer's sojourn. I was present at one of these. Pieces were played and some of Beethoven's songs were sung and he was requested to improvise on the pianoforte, which he did not wish to do. A table had been spread with food in the adjoining room and finally the company gathered about it. I was a young lad and Beethoven interested me so greatly that I remained always near him. Search was made for him in vain and finally the company sat down without him. He was in the next room and now began to improvise; all grew quiet and listened to him. I remained standing beside him at the pianoforte. He played for about an hour and one by one all gathered around him. Then it occurred to him that he had been called to the table long before – he hurried from his chair to the dining room. At the door stood a table holding porcelain dishes. He stumbled against it and the dishes fell to the floor. Count Dönhoff, a wealthy cavalier, laughed at the mishap and the company again sat down to the table with Beethoven. There was no more thought of playing music, for after Beethoven's fantasia half of the pianoforte strings were broken. I recall this fantasia with pleasure because I was so fortunate as to have heard it so near him.[42]

The violinist Louis Spohr was in Vienna between 1812 and 1816. He heard Beethoven only once, in a rehearsal of a new piano trio. Spohr indicates that the piece was in D major, three-four time, which suggests the third movement, Andante cantabile, of the Trio Op. 97. Ignaz Schuppanzigh, Joseph Linke, and Beethoven performed this trio in a benefit concert on April 11, 1814. Perhaps Spohr witnessed the preparations for this concert. He writes:

A pleasure it was not; for first of all the pianoforte was much out of tune, which concerned Beethoven little because he heard nothing of it in any case, and second, because of his deafness, almost nothing was left of the virtuosity once so admired. At *forte* the poor deaf man pounded so strongly that the strings jangled, and at *piano* he played so softly that whole groups of notes were left out.[43]

POSITIVE REPORTS, NEGATIVE REPORTS: AN ANNOTATED CHRONOLOGY

Listing these reports chronologically reveals a crucial fact about Beethoven's career: between late summer of 1791 and 1798 no single negative report about Beethoven's performances exists. Even Tomášek who, after his initial shocked amazement, found fault with Beethoven's *music*, did not include Beethoven's *playing* in his disapproval, apart from the remark that the performance of the Second Concerto did not make "such an enormous impact" as the others.

---

[42] Translation from Thayer, *Life of Beethoven*, 541.
[43] Kerst, *Die Erinnerungen an Beethoven*, vol. 1, 176.

However, the *Patriotisches Journal für die k.k. Staaten* in 1798 did address his playing in the same concerts: "He neglected all the singing, all equality in his playing, all subtlety and comprehensibility." The review ends, "He stimulated only our ears but did not touch our hearts; therefore he will never be a Mozart for us."[44] This is the first time that Beethoven's playing did not please. What puzzles most are the statements that he neglected all the singing [*Gesang*] in his playing and that he stimulated the ears of the audience, not their hearts. A singing manner of playing was Beethoven's professed explicit ideal; that he in fact *did* move most of his listeners is documented abundantly elsewhere. Perhaps the reviewer had an axe to grind. Were the musical elite of Prague still faithful to Mozart? Were they jealous of Vienna? Had the reviewer talked to Tomášek and been influenced by his apparent *jalousie de métier*? While these questions remain unanswerable, some elements of this review certainly seem dishonest. This review terminates, in any case, the series of positive reports from the preceding years.

Traditionally, these reports have been taken at surface value without worrying too much about their chronology. William Newman, for example, combines Wegeler's 1791 description of Beethoven's rough playing, Cramer's 1800 criticism that Beethoven played his own compositions in an inconsistent manner, and Cherubini's, Clementi's, and Pleyel's judgments from around 1805, treating Junker's positive report as an exception.[45] This arrangement allows him to conclude that Beethoven persisted in "requesting a sturdier instrument … capable to withstand his animal energies," suggesting that this request represented Beethoven's lifelong disposition.[46] Also Katalin Komlós combines Wegeler's, Cherubini's, Pleyel's, and Clementi's opinions and adds: "Another recurrent criticism is that Beethoven's performance was 'unclear' or 'indistinct.'"[47] Siegbert Rampe, finally, claims that the reports of Beethoven's rough technique that "regularly led to breaking strings … run like a thread through the descriptions of his playing from his time in Bonn onward."[48] The prevailing opinion is that Beethoven's playing was always more vigorous than customary, and consistently stronger than was really good for his instruments.

This picture is unfaithful. The absence of any negative reports about Beethoven's playing over a period of at least seven years is significant, even if the number of reports from this time is rather small. We are here contemplating the time of his most intensive public activity as a keyboard virtuoso. To anticipate part of my reasoning, I believe that the reports show Beethoven's development from a young, talented keyboard player, who in

[44] Quoted after Molsen, *Die Geschichte des Klavierspiels in historischen Zitaten*, 68.
[45] Newman, *Beethoven on Beethoven*, 80–1.   [46] *Ibid.*, 63.
[47] Komlós, *Fortepianos and their Music*, 142–3.
[48] Rampe, "Beethovens Klavier – Klangwelt und Aufführungspraxis," copy provided by the author, 22.

spite of his virtuosity and ambition still lacked refinement, to one of the foremost virtuosos of his time, who combined individuality, technical skills, and considerable performing experience. The story of the decline of this capacity through his deafness, contradictory and non-linear in itself, seems to be unrelated to the early reports. I will present three kinds of support for my view. First, its general likelihood can be tested. Second, the significance of the surviving positive reports can be established in comparison with what, at the time, was regarded as a good or bad presentation of keyboard virtuosity. Third, the first negative reports can be analyzed individually in order to establish whether Beethoven was criticized for one or several aspects of his playing and, in case of the latter, whether these aspects were related to each other or not.

The assumption that Beethoven started out as a rough and unruly pianist and remained such throughout his life, however true to the canonical Beethoven picture, disregards the typical learning patterns that could be expected of any talented young keyboard player at any time. One such pattern would be a period of learning that displays an inconsistent mix of promise and immaturity including occasional failure, followed by a consolidation of skills where the performances become more reliable and predictable.

Both eighteenth-century keyboard tutors and modern books on learning and practicing techniques often contain the advice not to rush the learning process, in an attempt to counteract the student's natural tendency toward impatience and too high a level of ambition.[49] The young Beethoven's rough playing represents just such an impetuous stage in his development. Talented and headstrong, he was striving to become an excellent keyboard player but he had not yet achieved his goal. The cluster of anecdotes from 1791, then, is consistent with a consolidation of his skills, whereas the notion that Beethoven's playing stayed rough and harsh would not be representative of anything except failure.

Instead of failing, Beethoven advanced to "one of the foremost players" within a few years. In this light, the story of his consistently coarse technique is unlikely. In a musical amateur a mix of ambition and inconsistency might indeed live on: Andreas Streicher's previously discussed "piano strangler" is such a figure. But in a performer of Beethoven's status, this would certainly have left its mark in history. Late eighteenth-century Vienna was not looking for a romantic hero who transgressed material and conventional boundaries for the sake of pure personal expression. In his booklet from 1801, Andreas Streicher is delightfully clear about the kind of virtuoso attitude that an audience in 1801 would not have accepted, and writes:

---

[49] See Renate Klöppel, *Mentales Training für Musiker*, Kassel: Gustav Bosse, 1996, 101–6, and Madeline Bruser, *The Art of Practicing*, New York: Bell Tower, 1997, 10–25.

All musical instruments, *even the human voice*, have their own range of expression, which cannot be transgressed without making a bad impression on the listeners, or provoking reproach from the *connoisseur* … [the fortepianist] shall neither tyrannize his instrument, nor shall he be its slave. Bravely he surrenders to all the fire of his passion; but pure taste holds the reins and prevents him from producing ugly tones … *Everybody flies from rough expression.*[50]

It seems altogether unlikely that a society that cherished such values would have hailed Beethoven as Mozart's successor in keyboard improvisation, had his playing contained too many instances of "rough expression" or other peculiarities that would have repelled the connoisseur. Any sort of wild demeanor at the keyboard would not have passed uncommented: during the 1790s, Beethoven's friends recorded many of his everyday eccentricities and peculiar social conduct, but they remained silent about his playing.

One characteristic of writing down a positive experience is that it is difficult to create a detailed narrative; by contrast, negative criticism provides more occasions for verbal and argumentative differentiation, while anecdotes of various kinds offer opportunities for excursion into gossip. The impression that most of the reports of the 1790s are less specific than the later ones is, therefore, partly deceptive. If, for example, von Schall states that everybody who heard Beethoven play in Dresden was enchanted and that the Saxon Elector was extremely content, this information is in fact as outspoken as one could wish, although it leaves matters of musical detail unmentioned. When witnesses write again and again that everyone was "enchanted" by Beethoven's improvisation, this seeming lack of inventiveness of vocabulary does not mean that these were merely casual remarks; the terms "bezaubert" or "entzückt" communicate all that is necessary. Only a negative reaction would have called for a detailed explanation.

An analysis of the earliest critical reports makes it possible to stretch the period of Beethoven's public success as a pianist until a few years after 1799. The criticism in these reports is always based on some special circumstance. This applies, for example, to the comparison between Beethoven and Wölffl. The presentation of the Beethoven–Wölffl encounters as a semi-public confrontation of virtuosos made it necessary for the impartial reviewer to analyze the advantages and disadvantages of both players – so naturally there was some criticism in the AMZ report of the encounter.

Ignaz von Seyfried's report about Wölffl and Beethoven is probably the one most frequently quoted in the literature. Writing in 1832, Seyfried remembers how Beethoven's improvisation contrasted with Wölffl's, who was educated in Mozart's spirit and (hence, one understands) was "more accessible to the majority." Whatever the real differences between the two pianists were, Seyfried presents them as representatives of controlled yet

[50] Streicher, *Kurze Bemerkungen*, 3, 18–9.

brilliant classicism and unrestrained romantic genius respectively. He describes Beethoven as follows:

When improvising, Beethoven even then did not deny a tendency in his character rather towards the eerie and gloomy; as soon as he had begun to revel in the immeasurable realm of tones, he was also carried away beyond the earthly realm; the spirit had burst all restricting shackles and shaken off the yoke of servitude, and rose, triumphantly rejoicing, up into light, ethereal spaces, whereupon his playing surged along like a wildly foaming cataract, and the conjurer [i.e., Beethoven] sometimes compelled the instrument to such an utterance of force that the strongest structure was hardly able to obey, now he sank back, exhausted, exhaling gentle plaints, dissolving in melancholy.[51]

Such descriptions of Beethoven's improvisation are relative. We do not know how Wölffl played; hence the vital criterion for weighing these accounts is lost. A secure interpretation of Seyfried's report is further complicated because of its date. Romantic Beethoven lore would have it that Beethoven's *spirit* was the only ruling force, while material factors played a subordinate role or stood in the way of his creativity. It is, however, very much a question of whether these ideas applied to the actual situation in 1799. Later testimonies of Beethoven's failing powers as a virtuoso provide the background against which Seyfried had to try to remember how Beethoven was playing in 1799; the main problem is that he writes thirty-three years after the event (five years after Beethoven's death), and it is unlikely that his memory at that point was *not* afflicted by events and tendencies from Beethoven's later life.

In another comparison from 1803, Gänsbacher preferred Vogler's style in spite of the fact that he found Beethoven's approach "excellent." The special circumstance in this case is that Gänsbacher was Vogler's student. The playwright and former *Burgtheater* director August von Kotzebue had a different opinion about Vogler: "[He] plays fugues in particular with great precision, although his rather heavy touch betrays the organist."[52]

With one last exception, all remaining accounts of Beethoven's perform-ances between 1800 and 1803 are just as positive as the earlier ones. This exception is J. B. Cramer's critical remark from 1800. According to Schindler, Cramer criticized Beethoven's performances of his own compositions as being inconsistent. Czerny confirms this information; Ries adds that Beethoven did not like to play his own compositions at all.[53] So Cramer's complaint was very likely genuine, but as such uncontroversial: most pianists play badly when they perform works without being motivated or well prepared. The special circumstance here is that the criticism addresses the performance of printed compositions instead of improvisation or the inau-guration of new works. These accounts might, as Czerny says, illustrate

---

[51] Kerst, *Die Erinnerungen an Beethoven*, vol. 1, 37. My translation differs from Thayer's.
[52] Thayer, *Life of Beethoven*, 325.   [53] Wegeler and Ries, *Biographische Notizen über Beethoven*, 100.

Beethoven's impatience with having to practice older works or, just as likely, his lack of time; they do not lend themselves to speculations about the state of his pianism. Cramer's unrestricted enthusiasm about Beethoven's improvisation supports this view.

Poor preparation clearly also accounts for the critical reception of Beethoven's first performance of the Third Piano Concerto in April 1803, which was "not completely to the audience's satisfaction." The reason for this is not hard to guess: Seyfried, who turned the pages for Beethoven, later wrote that the solo part was almost completely void and that Beethoven played mostly from memory.[54] This was a first performance of a new work. The special circumstance is that the solo part was incomplete – perhaps symptomatic for Beethoven, distressing for the page turner, and unsatisfactory for the audience but, again, not necessarily typical for Beethoven's playing as a whole. Bridgetower's account from the Augarten performance of Op. 47, one-and-a-half months after the Third Concerto, is again entirely positive.[55]

But the situation was soon to change. On November 12, 1804, Stephan von Breuning informed Wegeler how deafness had influenced Beethoven in recent time. "You would not believe, dear Wegeler, what an indescribable, I would like to say horrible, impact the decline of his hearing has made on him."[56] Unhappiness, reservation, mistrust, and indecision had joined his usual vehemence, and most of the time his company was "truly strenuous." The next critical report by Camille Pleyel from 1805 contains all the elements of Beethoven's later playing that have entered the literature as "typical": Beethoven still possessed an abundance of technical skills, but his playing was not polished, not always neat, and he played too loudly.

Beethoven's health and state of mind were clearly especially unstable at the time. In June 1805, probably shortly before the event that Camille Pleyel recorded, he wrote to von Zmeskall that he could not see the Pleyels because he had felt ill for eight days and was getting more sullen by the day.[57] Based on an account of Ernest Legouvé, Theodor Frimmel reports that, at that time, Beethoven once "failed" in a concert when he had to improvise, and another time, he stood up after playing, "pale, trembling, and exhausted."[58] Cherubini's, Clementi's, and Nisle's descriptions suggest that a true change had in fact taken place.

The few scattered remaining positive accounts can be viewed in two ways. On the one hand, surely Beethoven's playing technique had not collapsed all of a sudden. The most convincing evidence for this suggestion can be found in Reichardt's accounts from the time around the concerto performance at the end of 1808. Beethoven had apparently prepared himself

[54] Thayer, *Life of Beethoven*, 329, after a report in *Cäcilia*, IX, 219–20.
[55] However, even Op. 47 was written at the last minute. Wegeler and Ries, *Biographische Notizen über Beethoven*, 82–3.
[56] *Ibid.*, Nachtrag 10–11.   [57] Beethoven, *Briefwechsel*, vol. I, 261.
[58] Frimmel, *Beethoven-Handbuch*, vol. II, 24.

diligently for this occasion and, consequently, played brilliantly during the whole period, even in other performances.

On the other hand, many of his devotees were plainly no longer bothered by details. Reports like Bettina von Arnim's, for instance, are designed to convey the experience of meeting a great man but are completely unconcerned with fingering and missing notes. In many of the favorable late reports of Beethoven's playing, certain features clearly remained unmentioned out of tolerance. It is important to emphasize that this circumstance does not apply to *early* acclaim, when Beethoven was still less famous. The public's tolerance for his bad playing would have been lower, and his jealous colleagues would have seized every opportunity to comment on his failures.

Thus, the only explanation for the change of the tenor in the reports about Beethoven's playing is the decline of his health: his increasing deafness and the change in his psychological condition.

This discussion leads to several conclusions. Most importantly, it provides a tool for distinguishing desirable and less ideal performance situations that otherwise all fit Beethoven's character, energy, creativity, and spirit. From the viewpoint of Beethoven's own "ideal" practice, exceeding the limits of the fortepiano appears not to have been an essential part of expressive playing. The accounts from the peak of his performing career mention no peculiarities such as the breaking of strings or excessive pounding, whereas his brilliant musicianship is mentioned at all times. The idea of essential Beethovenian "animal energies"[59] is a retrospective construct, understandable in view of some late accounts, but unsupported by most early documents and, for several reasons, implausible. Finally, the curve of Beethoven's fortepiano criticism, although less well documented, matches the observations about his success as a virtuoso. In 1796, he played a concert on a Geschwister Stein piano with a light touch and wrote with reservations but otherwise encouragingly about its qualities – a flexible professional player. Some time after 1800, he found that the Viennese pianos sounded "wooden" and encouraged a "small and weak touch" – a search for alternatives began. When he attempted to "greatly improve his playing" during a crisis, some mixed reports document a varying standard in his performances. In 1804, after an initial period of enthusiasm, he began to treat his new Érard in such a manner that today it serves as proof of his ever rougher playing – a change of approach that also becomes evident from many other documents from exactly the same time.

A LOST ELEMENT: BEETHOVEN'S IMPROVISATION

Before we turn to Beethoven's notation, in which tone length, volume, and character reappear as central characteristics, another detour is necessary. For

---

[59] Newman, *Beethoven on Beethoven*, 63.

Beethoven, playing the piano was not primarily about the interpretation of a musical score by using an appropriate instrument, as it is for us when we play his music. It was playing music, writing music, and performing or teaching written music – often using any instrument that happened to be available, and sometimes, perhaps, playing a specially chosen instrument. At the same time, the most important part of Beethoven's piano playing, his improvisation, can only be discussed sketchily.[60] We must realize that the very essence of Beethoven's personal performance practice – the mastery of, and trust in, spontaneous inspiration – is lost. What is lost as well is a clear picture of how Beethoven (before his deafness) would have reacted to pianos of varying quality when improvising.

In a famous passage from his "Anekdoten und Notizen über Beethoven" from 1852, Carl Czerny divides Beethoven's improvisations into three categories:

1st. In the form of the first movement or the final rondo of a sonata, where he concluded the first part in a regular manner and also introduced a middle melody etc. in the related key in that part; in the second half, however, he surrendered to his enthusiasm, completely freely, but still using the motive in all possible ways. In an allegro the whole was enlivened with bravura passages, which most of the time were more difficult than one can find in his composed works.

2nd. In the free-variation form, such as his Choral Fantasy Op. 80 or the choral finale of the Ninth Symphony, which both give a faithful picture of this variety of his improvisation.

3rd. In a mixed style, where one thought followed another in potpourri fashion, as in the solo Fantasy Op. 77.[61]

Considering the fundamental difference between Beethoven's thorough composing process and the concept of spontaneous improvisation, Czerny's reference to composed works is at first somewhat confusing. Czerny apparently wished to illustrate the matter clearly for a readership that was perhaps familiar with Beethoven's works but, in 1852, altogether unfamiliar with his performances. But perhaps he also wanted to show that for Beethoven the connection between composing and improvising was closer than one might think. I will return to this point later.

After hearing Beethoven improvise in the early 1790s (obviously in the "potpourri" style), Johann Schenk described the musical events as follows. The improvisation began with some "quasi tossed-in" figures, "casually gliding along." Then Beethoven gradually departed from the "magic of

---

[60] When most of this chapter was already finished, Siegbert Rampe kindly sent me a draft of his essay: Siegbert Rampe, "'*Figurieren*' und '*Fantasieren*': Improvisationen bei Beethoven," in Wolfram Steinbeck and Hartmut Hein, eds., *Beethovens Klaviermusik. Das Handbuch*, Laaber, in preparation. Rampe's encyclopedic approach includes a presentation of the eighteenth-century background of musical improvisation and its terminology. In contrast, I am presenting selected sources and their interpretation as a part of a larger argument, rather than providing an annotated documentation.

[61] Czerny, "Anekdoten und Notizen," 21. Czerny wrote his "Notizen" on behalf of the musicologist and biographer Otto Jahn.

his sounds [sonorities]." He made a bold modulation to remote keys[62] in order to express "strong passion." Afterwards, he introduced a rising "agreeable modulation" using "varying motives (or 'turns')"; soon he arrived at a "heavenly melody." After all this "virtuosity," he transformed the "sweet sounds" into "sad and melancholic sounds," "delicate and moving affects," or "glad or joking" moods.

The first five stages described here might well reflect the actual order of events, whereas the remainder clearly sums up impressions that came along during Beethoven's playing. In this improvisation, there were no repetitions, no accumulations of unrelated musical thoughts, and no extended *arpeggiandi*. The whole performance, which lasted somewhat longer than half an hour, radiated "the utmost rightness."[63]

Czerny describes another improvisation in 1805:

As usual, he let himself be asked endlessly, and finally he was pulled by the ladies, almost with force, to the Clavier. Indignantly, he rips the still open second violin part of the Pleyel quartet from the violin desk, tosses it onto the desk of the fortepiano, and begins to improvise. Never has one heard him improvise more brilliantly, originally, and magnificently than on this evening. However, through the whole improvisation, the notes, in themselves completely unimportant, that stood on the page of the quartet that happened to be open could be heard in the middle voices like a thread or a *cantus firmus*, while on top of it he built the most daring melodies and harmonies in the most brilliant concerto style.[64]

Both Czerny's and Schenck's accounts focus on the musical events. Ignaz von Seyfried, in his abovementioned account referring to 1799, describes the *act* of improvising instead. As a result, his description seems to give a better impression of Beethoven's relationship with the instrument than any of the musical descriptions. But is this impression likely? Seyfried's narrative suggests that Beethoven would not have worried about tone length, volume, or character, or whether a piano's "structure" obeyed his "constraining" efforts by granting an "utterance of force" or not. After he had finished, he would in fact not even have noticed any of the piano's qualities at all, since he had been so enraptured by the "immeasurable realm of tones" as to forget everything around him. This image fits the textbook picture of the genius Beethoven, but it is incompatible with other evidence. Especially the degree to which Beethoven was "carried away" seems to mirror processes within the listener rather than the act of improvising itself.

How "carried away" was Beethoven? Sometimes, he prepared public improvisations ahead of time. His harmonizations of the *Lamentations of Jeremiah*, performed in Bonn some time in the early 1790s, have been

[62] Various readings of this word occur in the literature. "Tonleitern" ("Scales") from Kerst appears as "Tonarten" ("Keys") elsewhere. "Scales" or "runs" would make no sense in the context.
[63] Kerst, *Die Erinnerungen an Beethoven*, vol. 1, 26. As discussed on page 65, the date suggested by Schenk (summer 1792) is wrong.
[64] Czerny, "Anekdoten und Notizen," 21.

mentioned earlier. Franz Gerhard Wegeler explains how the singer's melody of four notes was usually accompanied freely by a Clavier player, since the organ was not played during Holy Week.[65] The court singer Heller, known for his imperturbable command of pitch, allowed Beethoven, upon request, to try making him get lost during the performance. Beethoven succeeded in this by means of some bold modulations, even though he kept on playing the melody together with the singer.

Mistaking the date by at least five years, Thayer elaborates: "While the singer delivered the long passages of Latin text to the reciting note, the accompanist might indulge in his fancy, restricted only by the solemnity fitted to the service."[66] We are to believe that the fifteen-year-old Beethoven freely improvised those chords that threw the experienced singer Heller off balance.

But in the Kafka collection of early Beethoven sketches, on a densely filled sheet, we find seven complete and many more fragmentary elaborations of accompanying harmonies that seem to date from two distinct occasions.[67] Most of these are notated as written-out bass lines and continuo figures, others as full chord adaptations; the names of two other singers (not Heller) appear at two cadences. Beethoven's homework looks so thorough that it seems beside the point whether he actually took the sketch into the performance or memorized it. What seems clear is that in this situation he did not risk losing *his* harmonies; the stunt was prepared and rehearsed.[68]

Another example, this time from the end of Beethoven's performing career, confirms his practice of devising an improvisation safety net whenever he felt it inappropriate to take any risks. Together with his sketches for the song "Sehnsucht" (WoO 134, from 1807/8) and other works, some musings about improvisation are preserved. Beethoven writes, "In the true sense, one improvises only if one pays no attention to what one plays[.] In the same manner one would improvise best and most truly in public [by] abandoning oneself unrestrainedly [to] whatever comes into one's mind."[69] But on another sheet, he comments: "[The] lied varied, concluding with a fugue, and ended pianissimo. Every fantasy to be devised in this fashion and performed afterwards in the theater."[70] Doubtless the ideal formulated in the first quotation was risky even for Beethoven, at least in the case of an

---

[65] Wegeler and Ries, *Biographische Notizen über Beethoven*, 14f.

[66] Thayer, *Life of Beethoven*, 81–2. The approximate date is established in Kerman, ed., *Ludwig van Beethoven Autograph Miscellany from ca. 1786 to 1799 (The "Kafka" Sketchbook)*, vol. II, 287.

[67] *Ibid.*, vol. I, f. 96r. See also Cooper, "The ink in Beethoven's 'Kafka' sketch miscellany," 322.

[68] Beethoven's various comments and the indication of the names of the singers Simonetti and Delombre at two points in the *Jeremiah* sketches suggest that their function was directly associated with a performance.

[69] Beethoven-Haus Bonn, Sammlung H. C. Bodmer, HCB Mh 75, leaf 3r.

[70] *Ibid.*, 3v. This might refer to the concert on December 22, 1808, at the Theater an der Wien. "Every" fantasy (i.e. improvisation) most likely refers to various private (and, as we learn, preparatory) improvisations.

exposed public performance. So he devised a concept to guide him along and he based several preparatory improvisations on this plan.

Very detailed preparations of improvisations must, however, have been the exception for Beethoven. In a conversation book from December 1823, the following collection of statements by Beethoven's nephew Karl is recorded:

> If you were to improvise in your Academie as you have done today, the success would be wonderful. For this, it takes more than a good Clavier player. I am already looking forward to hearing Moscheles improvise – in fact I do not believe at all that Moscheles' fantasies, if one may call them such, are the work of one moment. I believe that he prepares himself. The general ideas.[71]

Beethoven's nephew was thoroughly familiar with Beethoven's practice; he would not have given any attention to Moscheles' prepared improvisations had such a preparation of "the general ideas" been Beethoven's normal routine. However, the two previous examples do show that, at two very different points in his career, Beethoven knew how to choose a safe road toward improvisation.

The terms improvising, sketching, and composing do not in any case automatically reveal how spontaneously Beethoven's creation of music occurred. As we learn from Czerny, Beethoven's improvisations were at times closely related to a composed fantasy style, perhaps especially in the more organized forms from his list. The abundance of sketches that contain various keyboard patterns and fragmentary solutions for cadenza-like structures perhaps had a function beyond that of a "keyboard exercise." Such patterns could be seen as a precaution against "drying up" during a public improvisation.

However, Schenk's description of "quasi tossed-in figures" at the beginning of an improvisation does show a spontaneous aspect of Beethoven's improvising. Several observers confirm Beethoven's habit of beginning an improvisation with some unrelated chords and sounds, and only gradually developing "the most wonderful melodies."[72] Apparently Beethoven's method for overcoming his reluctance to play upon request was to force himself to react to a more or less random, self-created musical environment. Another, more controlled way of creating such an environment was to make use of chosen subjects (or subjects given by the audience), as in Czerny's anecdote that involves the violin part of a Pleyel trio.

---

[71] Beck, Köhler, and Herre, eds., *Ludwig van Beethovens Konversationshefte*, vol. IV, 308. Beethoven's Akademie took place on May 7, 1824 (*ibid.*, 359, n. 311), but he did not improvise on that occasion.

[72] Wegeler and Ries, *Biographische Notizen über Beethoven*, 19. According to Seyfried (Kerst, *Die Erinnerungen an Beethoven*, vol. I, 79) he sometimes even slapped the keys with a flat hand or made other kinds of jokes, laughing heartily. This idiosyncrasy is confirmed in many other reports. Czerny writes, for example: "Often only a few single unimportant notes were enough to improvise a whole tone-work, in the manner of the finale of the Third D major Sonata from Op. 10." Czerny, "Anekdoten und Notizen," 21.

We see here a "stimulus and response" principle at work, which is one of the standard formulas for explaining the improvisatory process, sometimes also defined as "the creation of music in the course of performance."[73] But in contrast to the picture evoked by Seyfried, and in agreement with Beethoven's occasional preparations beforehand, it also shows that, as a rule, the initial stimulus for Beethoven was not the wealth of his own ideas. His *ideal* of an improvisation might well have been to get completely lost in the activity of improvising, but in *practice* he first needed to touch the keyboard, to produce some (planned or unplanned) fortepiano sounds, in order to be able to forget his surroundings and settle into music-making. Such a series of sounds only gradually led to a musically coherent response.

It is at this point that we come to consider the function of the piano at hand. By producing these sounds at the beginning of an improvisation, it acted as a catalyst for getting the creative process underway. But this does not automatically tell us what to expect from the individual instrument. True, musical common sense implies that a better instrument, or a better regulated and tuned one, would lead to a more successful improvisation. But improvising on a less successful instrument can still initiate musically brilliant reactions appropriate to the circumstances, and the improviser can still experience an agreement between artistic ambition and the material world. Hence the success of an improvisation, the creation of truly musical effects, is not dependent on the quality of the instrument as such. More probably, any *distinctive* instrument can be expected to stimulate the creative process, whereas a neutral one perhaps does less so. If, on the other hand, an improviser merely overrides the characteristics of his instrument, the result for the listeners would certainly not be an impression of "the utmost rightness," as Schenk called it. Consequently, any report of a Beethoven improvisation – even one that does not mention the instrument at all – gives us at least some basic understanding of how he handled the instrument on that occasion.

COMPOSING FOR THE EARLY PIANO

The discussion of Beethoven's relationship to the pianos of his time, whether seen in the mirror of contemporary accounts or deduced from what we know of his improvisation practice, remains, of course, inconclusive. It guides us to a possible catalog and to a convincing chronology of Beethoven's attitudes, but the most careful interpretation of the witnesses' accounts cannot recreate any of the situations for us.

---

[73] See "Improvisation, Extemporization" in the New Harvard Dictionary of Music (1986) and the entries on "Improvisation," for instance, in MGG (1957), vol. vi, 1094. For an elaboration on "stimulus" and "response," see Malcolm Bilson, "The emergence of the fantasy-style in the Beethoven piano sonatas of the early and middle periods," DMA thesis, University of Illinois, 1968, Chapter 1.

In contrast, composed music provides *proof* of an effort; an effort to create moods and structures, and to reconcile a mental concept with physical circumstances. As in improvisation, such reconciliation might be unproblematic and straightforward. Special effects drawn from the instrument's best sides are naturally to be preferred, especially when a composer is concerned about selling his published scores. However, one can just as easily imagine how a piano that failed to transform a mental concept into convincing sounds (at a given moment, to a given individual) could cause heartfelt frustration, especially to an impatient and headstrong composer like Beethoven. Finally, a composer has the choice of altogether disregarding his instrument and responding solely to his inspiration.

Thus Beethoven's early expressive piano notation could be expected to include any of the following. In the case of a piece that is in concordance with at least some of the existing pianos, the notation is realistic. A notation that introduces new forms of pianism or expression may be innovative or pedagogical. A notation that goes beyond the possibilities of the average player or the average instrument would be idealistic, and one that describes effects that are not yet, or simply not, possible is a visionary notation.

Beethoven's ambition in his double role as pianist and composer at the beginning of his career was certainly mostly realistic. He knew, simply, how to use the piano and used it accordingly. His early keyboard technique, no longer rough and too practiced to be called merely intuitive, was deliberately tailored to compete with other virtuosos. Whether he thought he had not "found in the playing of the most famous Klavier players what he supposed he had a right to expect," intended to embarrass other Viennese "Klawiermeister" by publishing difficult music, or complained about the "uncultivated manner" with which his contemporaries treated the Klavier, this challenging attitude is rooted in plain professionalism. His many sketches from the 1790s of figurations and technical exercises, accompanied by recurring written comments on the "effect" of a certain texture, show his concern for practicability and his industry in the matter of playing technique.

But some of his formulations suggest that Beethoven's competitive attitude had much to do with being in contrast to the common manner of playing. For many keyboard virtuosos, the ability to deal with various instruments in a competent manner may very well have been sufficient for public success or even a special trademark. Beethoven, on the other hand, was clearly resolved from early on to *enhance* the potential of the piano through a different way of playing. We might speak about a different level of inspiration through the instrument, compared to his contemporaries. For him, the "chopping," "harping," and "scale grinding" of his opponents were clearly synonymous with uncharacteristic playing and a preoccupation with gadgetry and surface effects. We can see his wish to "sing" at the piano as an effort to go beyond the surface of the most obvious tonal characteristics of the Viennese piano and to explore its hidden potential. An example is his reported legato technique in chords and the *gebundener Stil* applied to coax a *cantabile* out of the instrument in all the voices.[74]

The idea of enhancing the potential of an instrument was not universally known. Instead, historical opinions about how musicians were inspired by their instruments fall into two categories. One school of thought saw a particular style as a consequence of the instrument's properties, and believed that exposure to a single type of instrument inevitably influenced the player in a predictable way, be it positive or negative: composers write for the way their instrument sounds. If an instrument has ineffective dampers and a long sustain, the composer writes melodic music with many legato effects. The other school of thought interpreted a particular style of composing as a compensation for the shortcomings of the instrument or, ideally, trusted the capability of the player to make his instrument sound especially well. Some of the sources combine elements of both sides.

A citation from Kalkbrenner's keyboard tutor illustrates the first of the two ways of thinking:

The English pianos ... have caused the professional musicians of that country to adopt a grander style and that beautiful way of singing, which distinguishes them.[75]

Bart van Oort explains the principle expressed here as follows:

Ever since the beginning of piano building, there have been reciprocal influences between piano builders on the one hand and performers and composers on the other. Builders have always been aware of the taste of their customers; at the same time, performers and composers have been influenced in their playing and composing by the instruments they had available ... A particular style of building led to a certain performance and composing style, which in its turn made the builders search for ways to reinforce those features of their pianos which suited that style best.[76]

Similarly, Katalin Komlós writes: "Legato playing suited English fortepianos more than Viennese instruments; consequently, it was heard more in London than on the Continent."[77] The player's wish to compensate for any of the instrument's characteristics does not belong to this philosophy, and indeed, Kalkbrenner was unfamiliar with this concept when he had to play on a Graf piano in Vienna in 1824:

In spite of all my efforts, I did not succeed in playing any singing phrase the way I liked it and I was at the point of canceling my public appearance when the idea occurred to me to put a piece of cork under the damper rail in the treble, so the

---

[74] Czerny, "Anekdoten und Notizen," 22.

[75] Frédéric Kalkbrenner, *Méthode pour apprendre le piano-forte à l'aide du guide-mains. Op. 108*, Paris: 1831, 10, quoted and translated in van Oort, "The English Classical piano style and its influence on Haydn and Beethoven," 3.

[76] Van Oort, "The English Classical piano style and its influence on Haydn and Beethoven," 7–8.

[77] Komlós, *Fortepianos and their Music*, 139.

upper two octaves were almost not damped; thus I succeeded in avoiding that dryness and separateness that existed between the notes and in realizing the effects I wanted.[78]

Kalkbrenner seems biased and single-minded about his preferred style. Instead of adapting his expectations to the Viennese Graf piano, adjusting his playing style, or experimenting with its damper pedal, he found it just as effective to block the damper rail in the treble permanently and to forget about the whole problem.

However, the idea of enhancing the obvious characteristics of the pianos was certainly known in English and Continental piano playing. One example of such compensation in English piano music is the subject of van Oort's chapter "Counter-resonance notation." English pianists had to make a special effort if they wanted their instruments to sound "un-English," that is, articulated. So the English notation for detached textures often contains short note values with meticulously inserted rests.[79] Another example is J.B. Cramer's advice to practice the legato touch. For Cramer, the famous legato of the English pianists was less a result of their being inspired by the singing tone of their pianos than of a specific playing technique:

No one will excel as a Performer on the Piano Forte without a good touch, to acquire which students must cultivate a legato style of performance, whereby the inability of sustaining sound on the Piano Forte is materially obviated.[80]

So even if, in the sense of Komlós' summary, the English pianos inspired a preference for legato among pianists, the players still had to learn how to counteract the natural tendency of any piano to lose its sustain by cultivating their legato touch.

In the German tradition, the idea of compensation for the drawbacks and enhancement of the obvious potential of an instrument is deeply rooted in eighteenth-century keyboard pedagogy. In a letter reflecting on C. P. E. Bach's style, J. F. Reichardt expresses this philosophy as follows:

Bach's manner of playing could not have been invented without the clavichord [orig.: Klavier] and he has in fact invented it for the clavichord; but anyone who has learned it plays the harpsichord completely differently than one who has never touched a clavichord, and hence for this person one can write harpsichord music of a kind that would sound dull, often incomprehensible, and incoherent under the hands of a mere harpsichord player.[81]

---

[78] Kalkbrenner, *Méthode*, 10, quoted in van Oort, "The English Classical piano style and its influence on Haydn and Beethoven," 36–7. Translation slightly changed.

[79] Van Oort, "The English Classical piano style and its influence on Haydn and Beethoven," 86–7.

[80] From Cramer's preface of the 1835 edition of his *Studio per il Piano Forte*, quoted in Komlós, *Fortepianos and their Music*, 138–9.

[81] *Briefe eines aufmerksamen Reisenden, die Musik betreffend 1776*, erster Brief, in Reichardt, *Briefe, die Musik betreffend*, 87.

This description illustrates the virtues of searching for the hidden capacities of the instrument (in this case the harpsichord).[82] According to this philosophy, the expressive potential of the clavichord enables it to inspire techniques and a taste that exceeds anything that an exposure to the harpsichord alone would have inspired in a player. This player will excel not only on the more expressive clavichord. When returning to the harpsichord, he will be able to treat this instrument differently as well.

But to play the expressive clavichord is a difficult task in itself as well. C. P. E. Bach writes about the challenge of playing an adagio on this instrument:

Because of the lack of a long sustain and of the complete decrescendo and crescendo of the tone, which is rightly called shadow and light, it is no mean task to play an adagio in a singing fashion on our instrument without showing too much empty time and naivety through too few embellishments, or becoming indistinct and ridiculous through too many fancy notes.[83]

According to Reichardt, Bach was well up to this challenge. Earlier in the letter quoted above, he writes:

You would be not a little surprised by how much he can do on his own clavichord. Not only would H[err] B[ach] play a quite slow, singing adagio for you with the most moving expression, to the shame of many instrumentalists who on their instruments could come close to the singing voice with far less effort; he will also, in this slow movement, sustain a tone of the duration of six eighth notes for you in any gradation of softness or loudness, and this in the bass as well as in the treble.

On the other hand, this is perhaps only possible on his very beautiful Klavier by Silbermann, for which he has specially written some sonatas with long, sustained single notes.

The same applies to the extreme loudness which H. B. at times gives to a place; it is the utmost fortissimo; another Klavier would go to pieces; and the same is true for the softest pianissimo which would not even sound on another Klavier.[84]

Here, the two ways of thinking about the interaction between player and instrument are combined without conflict: Bach was able to play *cantabile* in the way he describes in his tutor by counteracting the instrument's decrease of tone through a singing and expressive touch. The special excellence of his performance, however, was based on his especially outstanding instrument.

Beethoven's understanding of compensation as a vital element of his keyboard approach was, as these examples show, not completely innovative. Among contemporary fortepiano virtuosos he was perhaps, as he himself claimed, unique in this respect. However, his idea of the virtuoso as someone who should "sing" and not "harp" or, in other words, his intention to give the piano everything that it did not already possess, shows that his idea

---

[82] For another example, see the introduction to Bach, *Versuch über die wahre Art, das Clavier zu spielen*, 11.
[83] *Ibid.*, 119.   [84] Reichardt, *Briefe, die Musik betreffend*, 85–6.

of the player's influence on the musical effect was essentially close to the values of the North German Clavier tradition.[85] In this respect, his idiosyncratic approach was firmly grounded in eighteenth-century aesthetics.

THE VISIONARY COMPOSER AND THE EARLY PIANO

Around 1803, when Beethoven complained about the Viennese pianos that sounded "wooden" and induced "the habit of a small, weak touch," he had more than a decade of experience of performing professionally on such instruments. As his change of ambition toward the turn of the century makes clear, he became more and more possessed by a vision of producing musical *works*. The step from the wish to compensate for the surface characteristics or even the weaknesses of a piano to *requiring* from the instrument that it allow for the reproduction of certain expressive effects might, at that stage, have been smaller than the difference in principle suggests.

Not surprisingly, idealistic elements form an important stock of notational idiosyncrasies in Beethoven's piano music. It is common to interpret such idiosyncrasies as oddly connected yet incongruent with the characteristics of the early fortepiano. For more than a century, Beethoven interpreters have experienced the light sound and the relative lack of dynamic variation on early pianos as a problem. All the same, the identification of musical passages said to be easier to perform – or to produce special effects – on the early piano has always been a popular pastime. An early representative of this tradition is Adolf Bernhard Marx, who writes in 1863:

Some difficulties of Beethoven['s style] are caused by the difference between the instruments for which Beethoven wrote and those that are preferred today. Our better instruments have wider keys with more depth of touch; the advantages of this are well known and need no further discussion here. Beethoven had to depend on the Viennese grand pianos of the past, which had a light, agreeable touch and sound, but little depth and power.[86]

Marx has had innumerable followers, and even today a publication on playing Beethoven's piano music is hardly imaginable that does not mention, for instance, the problems of playing the octave glissandi in the "Waldstein" Sonata on a modern piano. However, this approach bears the risk of inspiring an anecdotal trivialization of the fortepiano's influence on Beethoven's compositional decisions. It exaggerates the instrument's importance for certain spots in the music and fails to let us understand

---

[85] I am here referring exclusively to the player's influence on the musical effect that comes forth from his instrument. I am not suggesting that Beethoven was cherishing every aspect of the ideals of the North German Clavier school.

[86] Marx, *Anleitung zum Vortrag Beethovenscher Klavierwerke*, 47.

the implication of its non-dramatic, ubiquitous presence in Beethoven's everyday life.

The step from here to the myth of Beethoven as a composer of piano music of a visionary kind is small. The supposed existence of such visionary qualities is a main reason why, in many discussions, Beethoven's pianos and Beethoven's music are presented as irreconcilable by definition. Not unexpectedly, most examples of visionary textures are said to be found in his late works. Alfred Brendel writes, for example: "Beethoven's piano works pointed far into the future of piano building. Decades had to pass after his death before there were pianos – and pianists – equal to the demands of his 'Hammerklavier' Sonata Op. 106."[87] Even this view has a long tradition, as Carl Czerny's remark from 1852 shows:

Since Beethoven was used to composing everything with the help of the piano and to try out certain places innumerable times, one can imagine how much influence it had when his loss of hearing made this practice impossible. Hence the awkward pianistic writing in his last sonatas, hence the harshness of the harmony and, as Beethoven himself confided, hence the lack of fluent coherence and the departure from the traditional form.[88]

This is one of several of Czerny's attempts to connect Beethoven's deafness with the peculiarities of his late style. While the passage expresses an eye-witness's empathy, it also conveys Czerny's opinion that Beethoven's late style posed a true problem. However, the jumble of issues, where "departure from the traditional form" is apparently seen as just as problematic as a "lack of fluent coherence" or "awkward pianistic writing," shows that Czerny's unease has little to do with any deeper understanding. His criticism demonstrates just how far Beethoven's work pointed into the future – in any case beyond Czerny's perception. Such a combination of criticism and lack of full understanding was certainly not atypical for Beethoven reception in the early nineteenth century.[89]

Czerny's lack of appreciation for truly visionary tendencies in style, such as Beethoven's departure from tradition in the formal, harmonic, and textural, seems to be unrelated to his comment on pianism. Czerny privately performed the Diabelli Variations Op. 120 and the late sonatas Op. 106, 110, and 111 in early 1824, according to (authentic) entries by Anton Schindler in the conversation books. The most technically challenging Sonata Op. 106 "gave Czerny much trouble," in the words of Schindler.[90] Apparently,

[87] Alfred Brendel, *Musical Thoughts and Afterthoughts*, London: Robson, 1976, 1998, 15.
[88] Czerny, "Anekdoten und Notizen," 19.
[89] The *Beethoven Kompendium* summarizes the opinions among the musicians and reviewers of the time as follows: "Some truly rejected his music because they did not understand it, while others expressed deep admiration." (Cooper, ed., *Das Beethoven Kompendium*, 356) See also K.M. Knittel, "Wagner, deafness, and the reception of Beethoven's late style," *Journal of the American Musicological Society* 51/1 (1998): 49–82.
[90] Beck, Köhler, and Herre, eds., *Ludwig van Beethovens Konversationshefte*, vol. v, 133.

Czerny's pupil Franz Liszt, then ten years old, played the Sonata Op. 106 (published in 1819) as early as 1821/22.[91] The pianist Joseph Czerny (not related to Carl) played at least some parts of the same sonata privately in 1819.[92] We understand that – in contradiction to Brendel's view – the more accomplished pianists of the time were at least eager to attempt performances of Beethoven's most difficult works, while some Viennese pianos were clearly well up to the test of enduring performances of Op. 106 by around the date of its publication.

Brendel's opinion may represent innumerable similar ones that question the early piano's validity for Beethovenian musical expression and argue that his music was visionary, the music of a genius. The modern pianist has learned to associate that vision with the modern piano's versatility of sound, and the structural profoundness of Beethoven's compositions with the piano's neutral patience to reproduce all required shadings and phrasings, as he has accepted a connection between its dynamics and the harshness of Beethoven's character. Some results of this association have been highly successful. An excellent musician like Brendel would probably not even accept a *good* fortepiano from the time of the "Hammerklavier" Sonata, or the information that some musicians were actually able to play the piece around the time it was composed, as arguments that disproved his assertion. Some modern observers understand names such as the "Hammerklavier" Sonata as being synonymous with both a score and its realization, and a realization that sounds different is simply not the same sonata any more. Wherever reception history has generated and assigned meaning to a musical work in this way, a full appreciation of the performance circumstances at the time of the work's origin can no longer be expected. It is only natural that the findings of performance practice research in Beethoven prove to be at odds with certain demands that have accumulated during almost two centuries of listening to Beethoven's music. In this sense, an original, undisputable fact about an instrument, a performance, or the manner of playing a certain figuration can very well be called "not Beethovenian." But then the latter term describes those demands and not Beethoven's own ones.

Yet the reconciliation of the idea of Beethoven the visionary pianist with the comparatively prosaic straightforwardness of a performance practice study is impossible for another reason. It is the elusiveness of the term "visionary" in practice that leaves this discussion without a possible solution. One can always find elements in music that seem to be "pointing into the future." With luck and skill, the existence of such elements can be

---

[91] Albrecht Riethmüller, ed., *Beethoven. Interpretationen seiner Werke*, Laaber, 1996, vol. II, 136, quoting Fr. Liszt, *Briefe an die Fürstin Sayn-Wittgenstein*, Part IV, 164. See also Beck, Köhler, and Herre, eds., *Ludwig van Beethovens Konversationshefte*, vol. V, 117, 133.

[92] See Beck, Köhler, and Herre, eds., *Ludwig van Beethovens Konversationshefte*, vol. I, 92, where Joseph Czerny writes: "Zmeskall now listens to no other music than your Sonata Op. 106, which I have already played for him several times."

revealed by analysis, by stylistic comparison, or by a discussion of a work's reception history. However, Beethoven's vision of an ideal piano cannot be demonstrated by musical analysis. We cannot, at any point, provide unequivocal proof that a composition was ahead of the development of instrument building, with one obvious exception: the case where it is simply not playable on the instrument. And even here, the ground is unstable. We need only think of the extensive dynamic markings in some of the clavichord literature from the second half of the eighteenth century. Nobody, whether in the eighteenth century or today, disputes that the clavichord is a soft instrument by nature and that its strength lies in the possibility to reproduce a wide range of dynamic shadings within that limitation. This implies that a fortissimo in a clavichord piece is *relative* by general consensus. Nonetheless, modern writers on performance practice occasionally fail to appreciate this connection and rule out the clavichord for certain pieces by arguing for *absolute* dynamics.[93]

To tie this discussion back to the end of the previous section, an acceptable rendering of the Largo e mesto from Op. 10/3 requires an instrument not only with a singing tone but with a percussive directness as well. The fact that Beethoven asks for both elements in this piece is not a sign that he had given up on his pianos. If, in practice, the tone of a fortepiano happened to be too percussive for the *cantabile* lines in this piece, a performer would be required to counteract this shortcoming and to try and apply a touch that helped his dry instrument along in these melodies, and perhaps to adjust the dynamics so that his instrument would "sing." The idea of simply accepting the most obvious properties of a fortepiano as mandatory for the style of playing is alien to Beethoven. This has consequences for the playing of his music on any kind of piano, no matter whether it prompts legato playing because it sounds best when played legato (as is the case on the modern piano), or inspires a detached style of playing because of its direct and dry sound. The greatest challenge for the player of Beethoven's music is at most times not dexterity or virtuosity, but the underlying demand of making the music speak or sing at the appropriate places. His scores may seem demanding for the maker of fortepianos, but first and foremost they are a challenge to the player.

---

[93] See, for instance, Rosenblum, *Performance Practices in Classic Piano Music*, 27.

PART III

Sound ideal, notation, and stylistic change

Introduction

This part is devoted to two topics that have played a major role in the discussion of the development of style in the early nineteenth century. Both topics have also been seen as important ingredients of Beethoven's pianism. In Chapter 7, I will discuss Beethoven's alleged preference for legato and present a history of the development of his legato notation. Chapter 8 discusses the interpretation of Beethoven's trills.

The task of managing the triangle of performance conventions, Beethoven's notation, and execution is complex. Whenever we try to pinpoint one of these elements in order to view its relationship to the others, we bypass some unanswered question. For example, it is difficult to demonstrate Beethoven's role as a stylistic innovator in a narrative that makes use of musical examples if we neglect to analyze what the intent of his notation was. Would he also notate his ideas in a novel manner, or would he rely on conventional methods to express a novel thought? In the case of Beethoven's trills, an uncertainty here could produce directly opposed conclusions. In the discussion about Beethoven's legato style, the question is whether he learned it by interpreting Clementi's or Dussek's notation,[1] by experimenting for himself and only adapting that notation, or by listening to other performers who played legato. In passages that lack a specifically marked articulation, we must know whether the intended "background level" of articulation for Beethoven was modern (assuming that "modern" means legato) or traditional (meaning that any variation of a late eighteenth-century common touch could apply). Beethoven's status as a pivotal figure in the development of style essentially contributes to the fact that similar questions of Beethoven performance practices remain the source of disagreement.

To smooth the way into these issues, I will in both chapters demonstrate the development of Beethoven's notation in his earliest works and sketches, and illustrate the path and pace of his learning. This provides important information about the intent of his mature notation. Additionally, instead of concentrating exclusively on the rules formulated by the theorists, as some of my predecessors have done, I will highlight those discussions in the sources that demonstrate the historical vastness of available expressive options, and describe changes in taste.

---

[1] See Ringer, "Beethoven and the London Fortepiano School," for examples.

CHAPTER 7

Common touch and legato

CONFLICTING OPINIONS ABOUT THE DETACHED STYLE

In Beethoven's legato style, the quest for a singing fortepiano tone and the manifestation of a singing manner of playing are combined. One source that depicts Beethoven's legato practice is Carl Czerny's recollection of his first fortepiano lessons with Beethoven in the winter of 1799–1800. Czerny was introduced to Beethoven and played a few pieces for him; Beethoven agreed to teach him. Czerny relates:

> After I had finished, Beethoven turned to my father and said: "The boy has talent, I want to teach him myself and I will take him as a pupil. Send him to me a few times every week. Above all, get him Emanuel Bach's tutor on the true manner of playing the Clavier, which he must bring along the very next time."
>
> During the first lessons, Beethoven kept me exclusively busy with scales in all the keys, showed me the only right position of the hands, the fingers, and especially the use of the thumb (at that time still unknown to most players) – only much later did I learn to understand the full extent of the usefulness of these rules.
>
> Then he went with me through the exercise pieces that belong to this tutor and especially drew my attention to the legato, which he himself mastered in an unsurpassed fashion and which all other pianists at that time judged to be unattainable on the fortepiano, since (still from Mozart's time) the chopped and shortly articulated way of playing was in fashion.[1]

At the end of the eighteenth century, taste in keyboard articulation was certainly changing. One early use of the word "chopped," used to denounce an excess of articulation, appears in Daniel Gottlob Türk's famous criticism of C. P. E. Bach. In a footnote to his paragraph about the "common manner" of touch, "that is, neither detached nor slurred," Türk finds fault with Bach's instruction to sustain these notes for half of their value. He writes that their execution would become rather "short (chopped)" if one were to play according to Bach's advice.[2] Türk's formulation, of course, reminds us of Czerny's characterization of the articulated piano touch "from

---

[1] Czerny, "Erinnerungen aus meinem Leben," 11.
[2] Türk, *Klavierschule*, 356. The original terms are "kurz" and "hackend." See also Barth, *The Pianist as Orator*, Ithaca and London: Cornell University Press, 1992, 41–5.

Mozart's time." The general consensus about the large-scale characteristics of the late eighteenth-century "common" keyboard touch and the shift towards legato, as said to be represented in Beethoven's style, certainly invites us to view Türk's and Czerny's formulation "chopped" as the expression of one and the same phenomenon.

Only a few writers have remarked upon the incongruence between Czerny's description of Beethoven's request for legato and the general thrust of C. P. E. Bach's *Versuch* in favor of an articulated, expressive touch. A few explanations for this incongruence suggest themselves. For example, George Barth has shown in meticulous detail that Czerny's representation of Beethoven's slurs in his *Über den richtigen Vortrag der sämtlichen Beethoven'schen Klavierwerke* was a modernization in search of a long melody line, mostly at the cost of Beethoven's original articulation.[3] From this perspective, Czerny's recollection of Beethoven's pedagogical application of the *Versuch* could be explained as having been tailored in order to appear consistent with his own world (but not necessarily with Beethoven's and certainly not with Bach's).

Another possibility is to take Czerny at his word and to assume that Beethoven indeed only used the *Übungsstücke* as raw material, while he otherwise instructed his pupil according to his own ideas. In that case, Czerny would not have been exposed to the whole content of Bach's book, and so the incompatibility of a strict legato with Bach's own articulated style perhaps did not even occur to him. Furthermore, Czerny does not explicitly say that Beethoven wanted him to play legato all the time, so there is some room for interpretation in his description.

A final possibility could be that the possible range of interpretations of Bach's text was greater than is evident at first glance, and that the distance between the practices described by Bach and Beethoven's style is smaller than is usually suggested.

Mainly because of Czerny's descriptions, Beethoven's favorite keyboard touch is, in any case, generally interpreted as being predominantly legato in concurrence with the newest style from Clementi's or Milchmeyer's piano methods. William Newman thus characterizes Beethoven as "the unique, consummate master of legato on the fortepiano," and as a "leader in the performance practices of the time" that were characterized by the "transition from non-legato to legato as the 'usual touch'."[4] (It should be noted that Czerny in fact provided more details than that in his accounts of Beethoven's legato. He especially mentioned his "strict legato in the chords," which he also calls a "full-voiced legato," his legato in the

---

[3] George Barth, *The Pianist as Orator*, Chapter 3. Barth refers to Czerny, "Die Kunst des Vortrags."
[4] See also William Newman's discussion, using Schindler's report of Beethoven's disdain of the brilliant staccato style, or "finger dance." Newman, *Beethoven on Beethoven*, 229–30.

"gebundener Stil,"[5] and his enchanting performance of adagios and slurred *cantabile* passages.)[6]

Interestingly, even Barth, who otherwise devotes the largest part of his book to a careful and multi-faceted discussion of Beethoven's "speaking style," and who shows with many examples how Czerny's taste in legato was different from Beethoven's, talks about Beethoven's "cultivation of a legato common touch."[7]

The question here is not at all whether Beethoven played a lot of legato or not. It is the suggestion of a legato default touch that is problematic. The joint use of "legato" and "common touch" obscures the difference between notational convention and personal practice. The various German terms that have been translated into "common touch" by definition describe the usual way of playing all those notes in a score that bear no other indication for articulation or legato (for most eighteenth-century authors this was some degree of non-legato).[8] Understanding common touch has to do with understanding the meaning of the score; this is a matter of convention and communication through notation. Beethoven could very well have excelled in legato *playing* without having ideas about the common touch in musical scores that differed in any way from other pianists or composers. His documented mastery of legato tells us nothing about how he wanted his unmarked notation to be interpreted. This would only have been different had he simultaneously been the author of a didactic work that tells us otherwise. Clementi, for example, explicitly asks for a legato basic touch in his piano school, which naturally helps us to understand the meaning of most of Clementi's unmarked passages (and admittedly might have influenced the practice of his followers).[9]

The apparent mismatch between the principles put forth in C. P. E. Bach's *Versuch* and Beethoven's legato tuition for Carl Czerny is but one example of the contradictory signals that stand along the path toward legato playing. Others have to do with the choice of instruments and with national style. Czerny's reminiscence of Beethoven's teaching continues with the following parenthesis, partly quoted earlier:

[5] Traditionally, this means the strict polyphonic style. "Gebunden" was not automatically synonymous with legato. This usage began to change toward the end of the eighteenth century. See, for example, Türk, *Klavierschule*, 405, and Ludger Lohmann, *Studien zu Artikulationsproblemen bei den Tasteninstrumenten des 16.–18. Jahrhunderts*, Regensburg: Bosse, 1986, 196. It is, however, not entirely clear whether Czerny uses the term in this specific meaning, or just "in pieces that require legato."

[6] Compiled from Carl Czerny, *Vollständige theoretisch-praktische Pianoforte-Schule in drei Theilen op. 500* (*1839*), Wolfenbüttel: Holle, without date, Part III, 497, § 3 and 6; Czerny, "Anekdoten und Notizen," 22.

[7] Barth, *The Pianist as Orator*, 114.

[8] Bach, *Versuch über die wahre Art, das Clavier zu spielen*, part 1, 127; Friedrich Wilhelm Marpurg, *Anleitung zum Clavierspielen 1765*, New York: Broude, 1969, 29; and Türk, *Klavierschule*, 356. For a modern discussion, see Lohmann, *Studien zu Artikulationsproblemen*, 244–9.

[9] Muzio Clementi, *Méthode pour le Piano Forte c. 1803*, Rotterdam: Giuseppe Accardi, 1989, 8.

Beethoven told me in later years that he had heard Mozart play several times and that, since in his time the invention of the fortepiano still was in its infancy, he had, on the harpsichords that were common at that time, gotten accustomed to playing in a fashion that was not in the least suited for fortepianos. Later I became acquainted with several persons who had taken lessons with Mozart and I found this remark confirmed in their playing.[10]

The explanation that Mozart's style was influenced by harpsichord playing suggests a connection with the Italian style, as described in 1776 by J. F. Reichardt in the following passage:

The Italians have never gotten accustomed to the Klavier and only make use of the harpsichord; hence their manner of playing must be viewed in connection with the harpsichord and there, I think, it cannot be different … So those who have not learned on the Klavier to join the notes, whether by means of fingering or through embellishments, can only [resort to] fast notes and broken chords – in a word, the pieces that are made to suit them can only have the purpose of exciting admiration through technical skills. And this is, I believe, the character of all pieces that are not written in [C. P. E.] Bach's style matching Bach's manner of playing.[11]

As Reichardt puts it, the Italian brilliancy is a direct result of exclusive exposure to the harpsichord and its possibilities. As a result, players do not learn to connect the notes, so they develop a detached style.

The tendency of writers such as Reichardt to combine observations with some more or less successful attempts at their explanation leaves us with the difficult task of disentangling the various levels of information. The allusions to typical ways of treating one or the other instrument, and the claims about how this influenced the way musicians played in general, often seem to be too constructed to be true. In another description Czerny, for example, links Beethoven's legato style to organ playing:

Beethoven said … that he had heard Mozart play; [Mozart] had a delicate but chopped touch, with no legato, which Beethoven at first found very strange, since he was accustomed to treat the fortepiano like an organ.[12]

In her comment on this passage, Sandra Rosenblum quotes a letter in which Leopold Mozart describes how the cellist and Clavier player Josef Reicha had played on Leopold's harpsichord in a "quite bound and organ-like manner."[13] Referring to Rosenblum, George Barth elaborates on both passages and writes: "By the century's end, Beethoven was creating a sensation with his general application of a legato touch at the fortepiano, something that had formerly been associated mainly with organ playing."[14]

[10] Czerny, "Erinnerungen aus meinem Leben," 11.   [11] Reichardt, *Briefe, die Musik betreffend*, 87.
[12] Carl Czerny to Otto Jahn in 1852. Quoted after Rosenblum, *Performance Practices in Classic Piano Music*, 24 and 411, n. 132.
[13] Letter from January 26, 1778. Mozart, *Briefe und Aufzeichnungen*, vol. II, 241.
[14] Barth, *The Pianist as Orator*, 42.

From this, it would seem that Beethoven was at all times opposed to Italianate or otherwise non-pianistic eighteenth-century keyboard styles, and that his particular manner of treating the piano was a direct conse-quence of organ playing in his youth. Problematic for this conclusion is that, in eighteenth-century German keyboard practice, the clavichord and the organ were very closely related.[15] An accomplished keyboard player had – within certain limits – access to any style of execution, no matter which instrument he played. If Josef Reicha – in the example above – was able to treat a harpsichord in an organ-like manner, this means that he was able to choose between performance styles at will. Even Mozart was equally familiar with the clavichord and the organ, and not at all an example of a narrow-minded player who played everything else in the same fashion as he would play the harpsichord.

Also in Beethoven's case, the assumption that his playing style was not simply founded on the would-be standardized manner of playing one particular instrument (such as the organ), but that he was able to choose between various styles of playing, is the most convincing one. Also the tutors that were very likely relevant for Beethoven's time are explicit in requiring a large variety of styles of touch. As I will show, this variety was central to most discussions, unlike the phenomenon described by the formulation "common touch." This helps to explain how Beethoven's characteristic keyboard approach developed out of the background of an eighteenth-century keyboard education.

TÜRK'S PRINCIPLE OF A VARYING KEYBOARD TOUCH

Beethoven was probably acquainted with C. P. E. Bach's *Versuch* from his youth. The usual assumption is that Neefe used it for Beethoven's lessons, because Neefe tells in his autobiography how he himself had learned key-board playing according to Marpurg's and Bach's methods.[16] Even if, as I have suggested, Neefe's lessons were about composition rather than about keyboard performance, Bach's book, which at the time was still the most influential German keyboard method, must have been around at some stage during Beethoven's tuition. Neefe's own keyboard compositions were directly inspired by Bach. Beethoven himself started giving keyboard les-sons in his mid-teens, so we can assume that he also became familiar with the *Versuch* early on from a teacher's perspective.[17]

However, Beethoven lived in a musical culture that was more modern than Bach's. Beethoven may have played on the Bonn court organ in the

[15] See Joel Speerstra, *Bach and the Pedal Clavichord: An Organist's Guide*, The University of Rochester Press, 2004, Part I, Chapter I, for descriptions of pedal clavichords as home practice instruments for organists.

[16] Neefe, "Christian Gottlob Neefens Lebenslauf," 2a.

[17] See Wegeler and Ries, *Biographische Notizen über Beethoven*, 9, 18–9.

gebundener Stil, and on the clavichord, harpsichord, or fortepiano in any of the fashionable manners, including the North German clavichord style, but perhaps also the detached manner suitable for Italianate keyboard style. When Beethoven played continuo in one of the many operas at the court theater, or rehearsed the singers, he would definitely have played in the Italian style, together with musicians that had been trained by the Italians Lucchesi and Mattioli.[18] Simultaneously he developed his personal, virtuosic way of playing based on his own hard work and growing experience.

A well-informed late eighteenth-century musical tutor that reflects the musical culture of Beethoven's youth is Türk's *Klavierschule* from 1789. Türk was strongly inspired by Bach, and one of his objectives was to reformulate and systematize Bach's topics. Occasionally he includes discussions of other theoretical works on music as well.[19] Most important in the present discussion is Türk's sixth chapter, which treats the clarity of musical delivery and the subtleties of style. At the beginning of this chapter, Türk announces that his advice is aimed at people who can actually perform his instructions well.[20] In this sense, he is just as much an observer of current style and fashion as he is a teacher. Although Bach, too, often speaks from a professional perspective, he seems to express his personal practice more often than Türk.

Such a personal element in Bach's text may be the reason for Türk's abovementioned criticism of Bach's passage about "the notes which are neither detached nor bound nor held [for their full value]," but that are to be held "for half of their value; unless the word Ten.: (held) is printed above." Türk reads Bach's description as applying to unmarked notes *in general*. As mentioned, he finds this halving of the note value too short and "chopped" for these notes. More importantly, he finds that "the character of the piece leads to various reservations [about Bach's rule]," and that the difference between these articulated notes and the ones to be played staccato would vanish in a strict application of the rule.[21] But Bach is actually very specific in his example: "These notes are usually eighth notes and quarter notes in moderate or slow tempo, and they must be played not weakly, but with a fire and with a very slight impulse."[22] So Bach actually *is* considering character and *does* provide some reservations by pointing out the tempo and note values, but he fails to make himself sufficiently clear for Türk to see his point. Türk's analysis might be a simple misunderstanding.[23]

---

[18] Thayer lists Gassmann, Guglielmi, Schuster, d'Antoine, Grétry, Benda, Neefe, Michl, and Holzbauer as composers for the season 1781–2 (Thayer, *Life of Beethoven*, 31). Most of these represented the galant Italian style.

[19] See Türk, *Klavierschule*, 356–7.   [20] *Ibid.*, 333, § 4 and 6.   [21] *Ibid.*, 356.

[22] Bach, *Versuch über die wahre Art, das Clavier zu spielen*, part I, 127, § 22.

[23] To my knowledge, only Ludger Lohmann has previously interpreted this passage in this way. See Lohmann, *Studien zu Artikulationsproblemen*, 244.

Türk's emphasis on the character of the music in question and on various reservations regarding the common touch (as he understands it) highlights his special interest in classifying and describing rather sophisticated aspects of musical expression. In this respect he provides a more refined picture than any of the earlier keyboard tutors.[24] Türk's reference, in his criticism of Bach, to the character of the piece additionally shows that his predominant concern in the presentation of his material is not at all an explanation of a detached common touch *per se*. Nevertheless, in modern discussions, his sixth chapter about musical execution is normally mined for articulation rules and used especially as a demonstration of how eighteenth-century taste in keyboard touch evolved. But this seeming development in taste, apparent in his criticism of the degree of detachment in Bach's execution of the common touch, is a red herring. The true development masked by Türk's words is an increasing sophistication in expressive notation and in the ways to describe the appropriate touch for the various styles and affects.

Modern analyses of Türk's book do usually not reflect this development. In an article devoted to Türk's sixth chapter with a compact and largely accurate summary of Türk's advice, Daniel M. Raessler, for example, calls Türk's approach to unmarked notes "inflexible," thus fundamentally misinterpreting his intentions.[25] George Barth claims that Türk "continued to recommend a syllabic common touch" but was "soon radically outdone."[26] There is in fact no indication that Türk "recommends" the common touch at all. Bart van Oort cites Türk's request for "mechanical clarity" but claims that Türk's "most important requirement to achieve" this clarity is "the non-legato touch, described by Türk as the 'normal' touch."[27] This analysis over-emphasizes Türk's few remarks on articulation in the long section about clarity. At the beginning of her chapter on "Articulation and touch," Sandra Rosenblum uses Bach, Türk, and Kochs' *Musikalisches Lexikon* to work out a detailed table that shows the proper articulation in various expressive contexts. She goes on, however, to suggest, based on the term "usual (gewöhnlich)" touch, that during the eighteenth century non-legato was not only the basic touch but also the most important one.[28] This is certainly correct for many sources from the middle of the century. But even an analysis of Bach's *Versuch* shows that flexibility was becoming more important than simple rules and formulas, and that the true problem for the theorists was the formulation of the subtleties in writing. Already for Bach, and certainly for Türk, in view of his highly differentiated application of gradations of touch throughout his chapter, the word "common" had

[24] See *ibid.* especially 243–51 for a discussion of Bach, Türk, and various other German tutors.
[25] Daniel M. Raessler, "Türk, touch and slurring: finding a rationale," *Early Music* 17/1 (1989): 57.
[26] Barth, *The Pianist as Orator*, 42.
[27] Van Oort, "The English Classical piano style and its influence on Haydn and Beethoven," 34.
[28] Rosenblum, *Performance Practices in Classic Piano Music*, 149.

evidently lost much of its importance. William Newman, finally, makes practically no use of either Türk, Bach, or any other eighteenth-century tutor in his chapter on articulation, although this could have solved some of the riddles of what he calls inconsistencies in Beethoven's notation.[29]

Türk's main topic, of course, is not articulation at all, but musical execution or delivery, which he regards as "the most important thing for the musician."[30] The specific requirements for a good execution are general playing skills, secure timekeeping, and knowledge of thoroughbass and the piece itself (this is his first point), but especially:

(2) clarity of execution, (3) expression of the prevailing character, (4) a practical use of embellishments and of certain other means etc., (5) a correct feeling for all the emotions and passions to be expressed in the music.[31]

Türk devotes his entire sixth chapter to a discussion of these five points. Most of the space is reserved for the "expression of the prevailing character." In this third section, Türk presents some basic expressive techniques and gives musical guidelines for their correct application. The techniques he discusses are dynamics, touch length and character, and the tempo.

Türk's discussion of touch length and character, also called "heavy and light execution," is in turn divided into two sections. The first of these deals with articulation as indicated in notation. This includes, in close imitation of Bach,[32] explanations of the execution of the basic touches: staccato, the clavichord-specific *Tragen der Töne*, legato (including superlegato in broken chords), and the "common" touch. The second section elaborates on the terms "heavy and light execution." Türk says that heavy and light execution are mainly related to touch and only indirectly to dynamics. The execution called "heavy" is achieved by "playing every note firmly (resolutely) and by holding it until the end of its entire duration." The light execution is achieved with a less resolute touch and by "lifting the fingers somewhat earlier than the value of the notes requires."[33] Introducing yet another sub-level in this discussion, Türk lists criteria that help to determine whether execution in a piece should be light or heavy, which are:

(1) The character and indications of a piece, (2) the indicated tempo, (3) the meter, (4) the note values, (5) the progression of the notes etc. Additionally even national taste, the manner of the composer, and the instrument for which the piece is meant can be considered.[34]

Türk spends the next five pages on examples that illustrate these points in detail. Not only on these pages, but throughout his entire discussion, Türk misses no opportunity to exemplify the connection between touch and

---

[29] Newman, *Beethoven on Beethoven*, Chapter 5, "Articulation," 121–62.
[30] Türk, *Klavierschule*, 333, § 4. [31] *Ibid.*, 333, § 5.
[32] Bach, *Versuch über die wahre Art, das Clavier zu spielen*, part I, 125–7, § 17–22.
[33] Türk, *Klavierschule*, 358–9, § 43. [34] *Ibid.*, 359, § 43.

character, style, harmony, musical texture, tempo, and rhythm, and to mention the necessity of varying the expression within a piece. Although he, like other eighteenth-century theorists before him, admits in his introduction that no amount of explanations and rules can substitute for a "soul full of feeling,"[35] he seems in fact almost ruthless in trying to eliminate uncertainties about the appropriate application of keyboard touch in specific, carefully graded, musical situations. Thus, he fits most notes, whether or not they bear an indication for dynamics or articulation, into a framework of meaning and musical contexts. Although in a short paragraph he still presents the "gewöhnliche Art," that is, the common kind of unmarked notes that are played neither staccato nor legato, the thrust of the entire text practically extinguishes the importance of that concept for keyboard performance practice.

In place of a generalized "common" manner of articulation, Türk employs the "light" execution. The light execution is by definition non-legato to varying degrees according to the musical context. The crucial point is that Türk asks the player to judge unmarked notes according to their content, and to decide whether they are to be executed with a heavy or a light touch, or any differentiation in between. In other words, an unmarked note can receive *any* kind of touch, *including* legato and legatissimo, if other indications in the music clearly suggest the intended character. Türk thus asks the player to choose between styles of touch and expression according to the character of each passage, the character of a piece, or the style of writing.

Türk's treatment of articulation can be used as a model for describing the variations within the most sophisticated German public taste at the time Beethoven's career was beginning. It supplies all the tools that are necessary to interpret Beethoven's notation of accentuation, articulation, and legato, and it additionally provides an apparatus for approaching the unmarked and seemingly (or actually) inconsistent instances in his music. The interesting questions are how Beethoven learned to use expressive notation effectively and which style, or change of style, it conveys; how his notation can be interpreted in specific cases using our knowledge about eighteenth-century notation; and at which points and to what effect he began to develop a personal style of notation. The following sections will discuss these questions.

THE DEVELOPMENT OF BEETHOVEN'S NOTATED ARTICULATION IN HIS EARLY WORKS

In an article about Beethoven's personal copy of the "Kurfürsten" sonatas WoO 47, Michael Ladenburger characterizes Beethoven's early notation as

---

[35] *Ibid.*, 347, § 26.

different from the usual practice: "It is striking that Beethoven, at such an early moment, so richly indicates the dynamics and articulation of his piano parts, in contrast to his contemporaries and even to his teacher Christian Gottlob Neefe."[36] A glance at Neefe's *Klaviersonaten* from 1773 confirms that, seen as a whole, he indeed used expressive indications more sparingly. In some movements, however, the concentration of signs is in fact rather high. Neefe's sonatas were dedicated to Bach and, fittingly, his notation is painstakingly true to the principles in Bach's *Versuch*. He consistently indicates the proper tempo with, sometimes suggestive, "Italian art-words" that match the fastest note values in a predictable manner.[37] His embellishments are varied and correspond to the different affects. He indicates dynamics in every shade from *pp* to *ff*, as well as *crescendo* and *decrescendo*. His indications for touch include slurs, dots, strokes, the combined dots and slurs that stand for the *Tragen der Töne*, and the occasional abbreviation *ten.* that indicates that a note must be held for its complete value. The instances where an affect indicated earlier is temporarily changed are marked with special care. This happens, for example, in the first movement of the seventh sonata.[38] This is an allegro in four-time which, according to the usual practice as described by Bach, should be played with detached notes.[39] Neefe uses four notations to change this prevailing standard to legato locally: short slurs to indicate groups of two, three, and four sixteenth notes; two instances of the indication *dolce*, which is both times canceled by *f*; the abbreviation *ten.*, which in two instances is used even though a tie already indicates that the note is to be held; and finally an unusually long slur in bars 9–10, which joins four groups of four sixteenth notes across the bar line. Seen as a whole, Neefe's sonatas convey an eagerness to write well in the style of his time; they represent an excellent example of the consistency of theory, notation, and intended expression.

In contrast, Beethoven's earliest pieces show a rather less consistent approach to the various categories of expressive notation. Beethoven's first known work, the "Dressler" variations WoO 63 (1782), certainly does not reach the standard of his early sonatas as described by Ladenburger. It contains very few embellishments, no dynamics, and the articulation marks (wedges and slurs) are used rather sparingly, except for the passage-work in the second variation. In the three sonatas WoO 47 (1783), Beethoven's use of the embellishments has indeed become noticeably richer, but remains inconsistent. In these pieces, he fully indicates the dynamics, possibly reflecting his experience with newer fortepiano

---

[36] Michael Ladenburger, "Der junge Beethoven – Komponist und Pianist. Beethovens Handexemplar der Originalausgabe seiner Drei Klaviersonaten WoO 47," *Bonner Beethoven Studien* (2003): 109.

[37] See Bach, *Versuch über die wahre Art, das Clavier zu spielen*, part I, 121, § 10.

[38] Christian Gottlob Neefe, *Zwölf Klaviersonaten 1773*, ed. Jean Saint-Arroman, Bressuire: J.M. Fuzeau, 2004, 36–9.

[39] Bach, *Versuch über die wahre Art, das Clavier zu spielen*, part I, 118, § 5.

music.[40] His indications are usually predictable. Sometimes, however, he uses dynamics to shift an accent away from a good beat, and in a few cases (such as in the Andante of the first sonata) he prescribes an especially forceful effect that seems to be unrelated to the general mood of a piece.

Beethoven, like Neefe, indicates left-hand articulation much more sparingly than right-hand articulation in these pieces. As is typical for the period, his left-hand notation includes a mixture of continuo bass lines and standard fill-outs such as Alberti basses. In view of the conventional character of his left-hand writing in these pieces, using the tutors of the time to interpret its accentuation and articulation is also unproblematic. Their various descriptions of a slightly detached common touch clearly do apply in this case.

At first sight, Beethoven's treatment of the movement headings seems conventional as well. The marking "cantabile" for the Allegro of the first sonata, which begins with a rather pompous horn-like motif, perhaps betrays a lack of routine, like the indication "sostenuto" for the Menuetto of the third sonata that is subsequently developed in a series of highly articulated variations. For a thirteen-year-old composer, such a lack of experience is scarcely surprising. More difficult to understand is the contrast between the movement headings and his use of articulation for fast note values. Beethoven meticulously prescribes small-scale articulation in most of his passagework in sixteenth notes or thirty-second notes throughout the early sonatas. He does this in the form of alternating two-note slurs, often but not always at the beginning of a group, and detached notes, indicated by strokes. Groups of four sixteenth notes are usually articulated with two slurred and two detached notes, and much more rarely in groups of three plus one, or two or four notes slurred. Groups of six notes are articulated in various ways, sometimes differently in successive groups, and most usually with two slurred notes at the beginning. Groups of eight notes are again generally broken down to slur–stroke–stroke patterns.

Example 7.1 shows a few bars from an Allegro where Beethoven applies an identical articulation to four distinct sixteenth-note patterns that include one-plus-three groups, broken chords, compound melodies, and stepwise motion. In the left hand sixteenth notes, one can also see the same articulation inverted and one slur over a whole group.

Beethoven uses the same meticulous and inflexible articulation in most of the movements of the sonatas, and indeed throughout all his earliest pieces that contain passagework: the second variation of the "Dressler" variations, the sonatas WoO 47, the rondos WoO 48 and 49, and the song "An einen Säugling" WoO 108.

---

[40] This does not necessarily imply any experience with the fortepiano, as Michael Ladenburger has suggested (Ladenburger, "Der junge Beethoven – Komponist und Pianist," 109).

Example 7.1 Sonata in D major WoO 47/3, mvt. 1, Allegro, bars 28–35 (Bossler 1783)[41]

The prescription of an articulation of two slurred and two detached notes is not characteristic for Beethoven but ubiquitous in classical music.[42] However, Beethoven's almost obsessive continuous chains of such groups in a fast tempo, disregarding texture and musical context, are, as far as I can see, poorly grounded in the performance practices of his day. His uniform approach might indeed have been brilliant for his own taste, but it should be noted that it is not the kind of clarity usually recommended for fast passagework. Türk, for one, is unambiguous about the proper performance of such passages: one should be able to hear the tones "fully and distinctly." The player may not skip or "swallow" any of the tones, but must produce them "fully and distinct from each other." Also playing too strongly, too softly, too staccato, or conversely letting the fingers lie too long on the keys, would result in a lack of clarity.[43] Apart from not being "clear" in the described manner, Beethoven's articulation in these examples shows none of the necessary "insight into the true affect of a piece," as Bach expresses it,[44] or the requirement to "express the prevailing character," as Türk puts it.[45] That Beethoven notates the same kind of articulation in movements called Andante, Larghetto, Vivace, Scherzando, Allegro, and Presto, and in four-four time, two-two time, *alla breve*, three-four, three-eight, and six-eight time, suggests that he still had to learn how to handle the relationship between affect, texture, and touch.[46]

[41] © British Library Board. All Rights Reserved. Shelfmark h.388.b (1).
[42] See, for example, the "vierte Veränderung" of violin bowing in Leopold Mozart, *Versuch einer gründlichen Violinschule 1756* (Frankfurt: Grahl, 1976), 124.
[43] Türk, *Klavierschule*, 335, § 11.
[44] Bach, *Versuch über die wahre Art, das Clavier zu spielen*, part 1, 119, § 8.
[45] Türk, *Klavierschule*, 347 and 359–61.
[46] This list refers again to WoO 4, WoO 47, 48 and 49, WoO 63, and WoO 108.

Example 7.2. Sonata in E flat major WoO 47/1, mvt. 1, Allegro cantabile, bars 19–21[47]

In the eighteenth-century tradition, such a detailed articulation would often not even be necessary. The character indication and the meter of a piece would in most cases have guided the player to an appropriate articulation of the passages. For Beethoven, however, the marks were important: in his personal copy of the printed version of the sonatas, he even completed several instances where the articulation was missing, and sometimes changed the existing articulation.[48] Example 7.2, bar 21, shows an instance where he changed a printed long slur in the bass into his standard articulation.

Possibly, Beethoven's excessive use of strokes and small slurs was meant to override the default way of approaching these passages, and in this sense, they reveal his special playing skills at that time. This seems even more likely after analyzing the few sets of fingerings that he added to his personal copy of WoO 47 (Example 7.3).

It should be observed that Beethoven wrote a dot above the figure "1" at that time. The fingering reads 2 (corrected from 1)–1–4–1–5–4, 2–5–2–4–1. In his analysis of this example, Michael Ladenburger points out that these fingerings are "on the one hand only possible, but on the other hand probably necessary from his perspective if one wants to properly observe the articulation indications and especially the staccatos."[49]

Beethoven's added articulations and fingerings in the "Kurfürsten" sonatas indeed raise the question of how they were to be performed. If the texture he gave to his passages is unlike the recommendations for clarity in the tutors, and also does not consistently match the meter and character indications of the pieces, what was their intended effect? To answer this question, we have to turn to one interesting feature in the hand-written addition shown in bar 21 of Example 7.2. In contrast to the printed version (and in contrast to similar articulations in the other pieces of the time), here (and in his other additions) Beethoven notates not only a slur to connect the first two notes but also a stroke above the last of these two notes. So the end of the group should be played shorter than the indicated note value.

[47] © British Library Board. All Rights Reserved. Shelfmark h.388.b (1).
[48] See Ladenburger, "Der junge Beethoven – Komponist und Pianist," for a complete description of these additions.
[49] Ladenburger, "Der junge Beethoven – Komponist und Pianist," 111–12.

Example 7.3. Sonata in E flat major WoO 47/1, mvt. 3, Rondo vivace, bars 24–7[50]

According to contemporary systematic descriptions of the interpretation of slurs, strokes, and dots, this notation serves three purposes. First of all, it indicates that these notes must be connected, which in keyboard terms means, of course, that one "leaves the finger on the key until the duration of the indicated notes is completely over, so that not the slightest separation occurs."[51] Second, the length of notes with wedges or dots is usually "somewhat less than half their value."[52] According to Türk, dots and strokes had the same meaning, but some people wanted to articulate the strokes even more than the dots. In his example of a combination of slurs ending with a stroke, as in Beethoven's articulation, Türk indicates half the value for the second note.[53] Türk's other remark about staccato performance describes the third purpose of these strokes, which is the proper accentuation:

I should not need to point out that soft notes can also be played detached; however, from some players one hears all detached notes played *strongly* [emphasis original] without any variation, completely contrary to the correct expression.[54]

This observation corresponds with Türk's warning elsewhere in his book not to accentuate the end of a period.[55] In contrast, the *beginning* of a slur always receives an almost imperceptible emphasis, a practice clearly not only reserved for violin players,[56] since both Bach and Türk explicitly mention it.[57]

Interpreting Beethoven's hand-written notation of his "typical" early articulation according to these remarks suggests a characteristic touch with a somewhat accentuated beginning and a steady lightening toward the end of each group. The fingering shown in Example 7.3 confirms this analysis. The transition between the two groups of sixteenth notes by fingers 4–2 would be less of a problem if it was not followed by finger 5. It is, however, no problem at all if the last stroke of the first group is interpreted

[50] © British Library Board. All Rights Reserved. Shelfmark h.388.b (1).
[51] Türk, *Klavierschule*, 355.
[52] Bach, *Versuch, über die wahre Art, das Clavier zu spielen*, part 1, 125, § 17; Türk, *Klavierschule*, 353, § 36.
[53] Türk, *Klavierschule*, 356, § 39.   [54] *Ibid.*, 353–4, § 36.   [55] *Ibid.*, 342, § 22.
[56] Compare with Mozart, *Versuch einer gründlichen Violinschule*, 122–7.
[57] Bach, *Versuch, über die wahre Art, das Clavier zu spielen*, part 1, 126, § 18; Türk, *Klavierschule*, 354, § 38.

as *lightest* of all, and after that the hand is relocated to play the whole second group with an accented second finger at the beginning. Beethoven's thoroughness in completing and fingering these articulations shows that his notation was not merely a gimmick. Instead it indicated his actual performance practice around 1783 and was perhaps even something of a trademark of his early virtuosity.

Legato, on the other hand, was not a specialty of Beethoven at that stage. In the sonatas WoO 47, long slurs are still the exception. In the Andante of the first sonata, one complete group of eight thirty-second notes is slurred (bar 22), contrary to the meticulous articulation of most of the other groups of thirty-second notes in the piece. In the Andante of the second sonata, one flourish of sixteen sixty-fourth notes, which is the fastest occurring note value, is slurred (bar 57). Otherwise, groups of three or four (occasionally also eight) slurred sixteenth notes occur sporadically throughout the sonatas; however, these are few in number compared to the ubiquitous short slurs and dots.

In the group of works following the published pieces from 1783, Beethoven began to employ a more varied expressive notation. At the same time, longer legato slurs appeared in his scores. The works in question are the concerto WoO 4 from 1784, the Klavier quartets WoO 36 from 1785, and the trio for flute, bassoon, and Klavier WoO 37 from 1786,[58] along with a manuscript fragment of a Romance for the same solo instruments and orchestra (Hess 13) from *c.* 1786 that survives in the "Kafka" sketch collection.[59]

These works form a group for various reasons to do with their expressive notation. First of all, they all reflect the increasing expressive breadth that is revealed in the changes to Beethoven's notation. Second, they were all written before the period of low compositional productivity from 1785 to 1789 that Maynard Solomon has proposed (his hypothesis has found additional support in Douglas Johnson's analysis of Beethoven's early handwriting).[60] Third, they are all either preserved in a corrected copy or in fully marked autographs – even the romance fragment contains expressive markings at the beginning – so they can be easily compared. These works are of crucial importance in helping us to understand the progress of Beethoven's expressive notation.

Beethoven's new approach to expressive notation is immediately present in the concerto WoO 4. Leon Plantinga characterizes the virtuosity of this

---

[58] Kinsky and Halm, *Das Werk Beethovens: Thematisch-Bibliographisches Verzeichnis,* 433, 477, 479; Johnson, *Beethoven's Early Sketches in the "Fischhof Miscellany,"* vol. 1, 220–1.

[59] Kerman, ed., *Ludwig van Beethoven Autograph Miscellany from ca. 1786 to 1799 (The "Kafka" Sketchbook),* vol. 1, 74v.–80v. Date discussed in Johnson, *Beethoven's Early Sketches in the "Fischhof Miscellany,"* Berlin Autograph 28, vol. 1, 221–3.

[60] Solomon, *Beethoven,* 27–9; Johnson, *Beethoven's Early Sketches in the "Fischhof Miscellany,"* vol. 1, 219–25.

Example 7.4. Concerto in E flat major WoO 4, mvt. 2, Larghetto, second half of bar 63–65[61]

concerto as "an appealing display of keyboard agility and ingenuity, a celebration of the incipient virtuosity of Beethoven at thirteen. We have here something of an anthology of keyboard figurations."[62] The same could be said about the articulation markings: The "old" articulation – two slurred, two detached, and its derivations – does still appear, especially in the first and second movements. But Beethoven additionally uses a large variety of longer legato indications. Now, for example, the majority of figurations in thirty-second notes and sixty-fourth notes (in the second movement, Larghetto) are slurred to be played legato. Another novelty is the occasional detachment of the *first* note of a group of eighth or sixteenth notes, after which the following three or seven notes are slurred.

Example 7.4 shows an excerpt from the second movement of the concerto that includes all these kinds of articulation. In contrast to these legato groups, in the Rondo Beethoven does not indicate any articulation at all for the majority of the virtuosic sixteenth-note triplets and thirty-second notes, highlighting the few occasions where such notes are slurred.

This apparently sudden change to longer legato indications raises the question of where Beethoven got the inspiration for this notation. Leopold Mozart's systematic variations of violin bowing come to mind,[63] but no connection is known to exist between Beethoven's notation and Mozart's violin school. Extending Plantinga's interpretation of the concerto's figurations as an "anthology," it seems more likely that, by the time he composed the concerto, Beethoven had gained experience with the music of other composers. This would have been music of the newest kind; the harpsichord concerti from composers of the older generation, such as C. P. E. Bach or J.C. Bach, typically contain very few articulation marks.

A possible source of inspiration for Beethoven's legato notation is Clementi. But, as Sandra Rosenblum writes, the question of "whether Beethoven might also have been influenced by Clementi's broad lines and long slurs is … hardly answerable." Rosenblum mentions that the music

---

[61] Reproduced with the kind permission of the Staatsbibliothek zu Berlin – Preussischer Kulturbesitz. Musikabteilung mit Mendelssohn-Archiv. Mus.ms.autogr. Beethoven Artaria 125.

[62] Plantinga, *Beethoven's Concertos*, 33.

[63] See Mozart, *Versuch einer gründlichen Violinschule*, 122–35.

dealer Simrock advertised three of Clementi's sonatas with violin Op. 13 in
1786.[64] The year 1786 is in any case too late to be relevant for this discussion.
In the search for other appropriate sources for notational inspiration, it is
worth looking at Beethoven's remaining works of the period because here
some of the sources for *compositional* inspiration are in fact known.
However, the chronological order of these works, their classification according to notational styles, and the dates of Beethoven's possible sources of
inspiration align badly.

For instance, a comparison between the expressive notation of the *c.* 1786
Romance and the 1785 Klavier quartets suggests the reverse of their actual
chronology. The slurring and articulation at the beginning of the romance
fragment represents a rather inconspicuous notation in the Classical style.
Beethoven writes half- or whole-bar slurs, slurred triplets, a few staccato
runs, and whole-bar slurs over groups with dotted eighth notes and sixteenth notes. Conveniently, the same style of slurring appears in Mozart's
violin sonatas Op. 2. Three of these sonatas (KV 296, 379, and 380) served
Beethoven as a model for the Klavier quartets.[65] However, in the Adagio
assai introduction to the E flat major quartet and in the Adagio con
espressione of the D major quartet, Beethoven also writes long legato
slurs over large groups of fast notes. Slurs of this kind are not found in
these particular sonatas by Mozart. One is tempted to look for other
influences to explain their presence.

Ludwig Schiedermair states that some passages in the quartets are rem-
iniscent of Mozart's piano concerti KV 413, 414, and 415, "with which the
young Beethoven had surely become acquainted at the time."[66] These
concerti had been published by Artaria around 1784/5. Schiedermair sensed
likenesses between the second subjects of Mozart's concerti and
Beethoven's quartets, but interestingly, there are similarities in the expressive notation as well. Especially in the slow movements of KV 413 and 415,
Mozart notates his articulation meticulously and he, too, uses legato slurs
over longer cantilenas and passages quite frequently. On the other hand,
extended passages in small note values to be played legato are also found in
Beethoven's earlier concerto WoO 4 (as shown in Example 7.4). When
Beethoven wrote WoO 4, Mozart's new concerti were probably not yet
available,[67] so Schiedermair's reference is of no help with regard to
Beethoven's expressive notation.

[64] Rosenblum, *Performance Practices in Classic Piano Music*, 152.
[65] Schiedermair, *Der junge Beethoven*, 290.   [66] *Ibid.*
[67] The composition of the concerto WoO 4, of which the piano part and orchestral reduction survive in
     a copy with Beethoven's corrections, is usually dated 1784 because of the age given on the title page.
     The dates when the copy was written and when Beethoven corrected it are unknown. According to
     Johnson, the handwriting of Beethoven's corrections is similar to his manuscripts from 1784–86.
     Some of these corrections involve the lengthening of previously shorter slurs. Perhaps the expressive
     notation was adapted after Beethoven's newest experience with Mozart's scores. However, this
     assumption is hypothetical.

As regards determining how Beethoven wanted his articulation to be performed and how he wanted the unmarked notes to sound, the influence of other composers on his expressive notation is in any case a secondary issue. If, for instance, he indeed had the opportunity to study Clementi's notation early on, the question of how he translated those slurs into his personal practice remains open. It makes no sense to imitate notational patterns if they do not simultaneously convey some practical meaning. Beethoven's "new" notation shows a steady increase in his experience of handling affect, meter, and the musical idiom. This can be seen in, among other things, his treatment of the string instruments in the quartets, which are spared most of the figurative and expressive acrobatics that distinguish his keyboard writing. Their slurs, wedges, dynamics, and even occasional pizzicato indications suggest that Beethoven had not only seen such indications in other scores, but also possessed some rehearsal experience; they are in general practical and to the point. To mention two examples, legato slurs in the string parts usually do not exceed the length of a bow, and jumps are usually not slurred.

Another example of Beethoven's increased knowledge and experience is the closer match between time indications, movement headings, and musical texture in most of the works discussed. In the four-four time allegros (WoO 4, mvt. 1; WoO 36/3, mvt. 1; WoO 36/2, mvt. 1) and the two-four time rondos (WoO 4, mvt. 3; WoO 36/3, mvt. 3), for example, the intended character can be quickly understood by the players because the meters, indications, and musical textures match well. On the other hand, a slow movement in two-four time is now called Adagio assai (WoO 36/1, mvt. 1) instead of Andante, as earlier ("Kurfürsten" sonata WoO 47/1, mvt. 2), but the note values are doubled and the effect of right-hand cantilenas and passages against the left-hand accompaniment in broken chords is virtually the same. It is difficult to know whether the term Adagio in this case shows Beethoven's increasing understanding of the difference in mood, even though the performance tempo of the fastest note values is nearly identical, or if he was still experimenting with terminology.

At the same time, Beethoven became more economical with his expressive notation. In the earliest of the discussed pieces, the concerto, Beethoven displayed his new expressive notation more thoroughly than in any of the remaining ones. The number of expressively marked bars decreases throughout the following works, taken in chronological order, with the exception of the woodwind trio WoO 37. Whereas in the concerto, 65 percent of the bars are marked, the first quartet (according to the autograph numbering)[68] has 50 percent of the bars marked, the second quartet 46 percent, and the third

---

[68] 1: C major; 2: E flat major; 3: D major, as opposed to the numbering after the 1828 edition that has been adapted by Kinsky. See Kinsky and Halm, *Das Werk Beethovens: Thematisch-Bibliographisches Verzeichnis*, 477–8.

quartet 38 percent.[69] WoO 37 has a special position here. It was written for the father, a son, and a daughter of the Westerholt-Gysenberg family, and it appears that the score had an instructive function. The daughter, Maria Anna Wilhelmine, was a good pianist and a pupil of Beethoven.[70] In this piece, only a few isolated bars lack articulation marks. Otherwise, even between the beginning and the end of the concerto, the decrease in expressive markings is clearly visible. In the first movement, the vast majority of the passages (sixteenth notes, in the four-four time Allegro moderato) are fully and uniformly marked, but in the Rondo, most passages in varying note values are unmarked, except for certain moments of special importance. Also, the marked passages show a greater variety of articulation patterns. At the same time, we can see a decrease in intensity but no lack of consistency. Many of the unmarked bars fall on cadences and on keyboard passagework of a certain kind; other passages are fully marked out. Often, unmarked and marked bars alternate regularly, leaving no doubt that they form part of a coherent notational concept. No true gaps, neglected pages, or obvious mistakes in the notation of dynamics or articulation can be found in any of these works.

The decreasing frequency of Beethoven's expressive marks can be seen as an economization and an avoidance of redundant notation. The Thema cantabile of the E flat major quartet (WoO 36/1, mvt. 3), for example, is presented *piano* without any slurs or other expressive indications, clearly because the word "cantabile" calls for a singing expression in any case. Conversely, the beginning of the D major quartet (WoO 36/2, mvt. 1), an Allegro moderato alternating between dotted eighth notes and a sixteenth-note rhythm, needs no staccato indication because the execution of such rhythms in an allegro would have been detached in any case, or played with a "somewhat lighter" touch as Türk puts it.[71] The articulation of other note values needs to be indicated at their first appearance, so in bar 11 the regular sixteenth notes are slurred and the repeated eighth notes have staccato dots.

The keyboard passages in sixteenth notes that follow, however, remain generally unmarked, like the fast passagework in sixteenth-note triplets in the last movement of WoO 4 and many similar textures throughout all of these works. We need not even turn to Türk's request for clarity to find an explanation here. This particular feature, too, is likely the result of practical experience: anybody who has performed chamber music or concerti on early keyboard instruments has been in situations where he had to change the basic articulation of passagework substantially in response to the acoustics of the hall. An intricately differentiated articulation is often superfluous in fast concerto passages, and the notation of any articulation is often unnecessary.

---

[69] This applies to the markings for any of the instruments. So a fully marked violin part with an unmarked piano part counts as one.

[70] Kinsky and Halm, *Das Werk Beethovens: Thematisch-Bibliographisches Verzeichnis*, 479.

[71] Türk, *Klavierschule*, 361–2.

Example 7.5. Concerto in E flat major, WoO 4, mvt. 3, Rondo, second half of bar 44–48[72]

On the other hand, unexpected character changes do need to be indicated. Example 7.5 shows a two-bar passage and its elaboration from the concerto.

The passage in its first form, bars 45–6, is marked *piano* and lacks articulation marks (the four bars following this example are also unmarked). The varied repetition, bars 47–8, begins *forte* and at first is still unmarked, then turns unexpectedly into a chromatic upward scale and a varied ending figure, to be played *piano*. Here, the change in character is expressed by the texture (a chromatic scale) and the *piano* indication, but in order to further distinguish the effect from the preceding passagework, Beethoven also calls for a legato and portato touch.

Another example of a particular touch being indicated to underline a specific affect occurs in the E flat minor episode later in the same movement (bars 160–96).[73] The variation on the main motif is written in sixteenth notes in groups of four. Of the twenty-one bars during this episode that contain sixteenth notes, only the penultimate bar before the cadence is not marked; the other groups are fully marked in varying ways. Thus all kinds of slurs of eight, four, three, and two sixteenth notes occur, either on their own or in combination with one detached note at the front, or two at the end of a group. This locally increased attention to notational detail in an otherwise sparingly marked movement would help a player to understand that a specific affect, more intense and detailed than the usual passagework for virtuosic display, was intended in this episode. All these are examples of notational economy on the basis of pre-understood conventions such as, for example, Türk describes.

However, none of the pieces in this group was published until much later. Although the level of clarity and consistency in the sources for these pieces is high, we do not know whether their notation is representative of

---

[72] Reproduced with the kind permission of the Staatsbibliothek zu Berlin – Preussischer Kulturbesitz. Musikabteilung mit Mendelssohn-Archiv. Mus.ms.autogr. Beethoven Artaria 125.
[73] Calculated using the longer of two earlier solo endings added by Beethoven, this would be bars 161–97.

what Beethoven thought published music should look like during that period. These scores show only that, in the mid-1780s, Beethoven was learning to notate more facets of musical expression, that he was incorporating new trends in his notation, and that he was gradually becoming more aware of the implications of meter, character indications, and texture for touch, and hence becoming clearer and at the same time more sparing in the notation of slurs, dots, and wedges. As is evident in the Woodwind Trio WoO 37, where nearly every bar bears expressive markings, Beethoven's early notation was occasionally extremely thorough. In the following section I will discuss how Beethoven revised his notation in his first published works after 1792.

PUBLISHING FOR THE VIENNESE: EXPRESSIVE NOTATION VERSUS PRE-UNDERSTOOD KEYBOARD TOUCH

Before addressing Beethoven's first published Viennese works, I want to mention some notation that is incomplete by nature: in Beethoven's sketches from his last year in Bonn, we find almost no expressive notation such as dynamic indications, slurs, strokes, and dots. This absence places emphasis on the very few indications that do exist in these sketches. Some of these probably had the function of reminders; others demonstrated unusual solutions and highlighted points of special interest.

The two-note slurs with strokes on the second note, written over the first two pairs of notes in a downward scale in Lombardic (sixteenth-note–dotted eighth-note) rhythm in an otherwise entirely unmarked symphony fragment were most likely a reminder.[74] Such notes were usually played legato in any case.[75] Examples of unusual solutions include slurs that cross the bar line or connect groups in disregard of the metric hierarchy. Such slurs appear, for instance, on f. 154r. of the "Kafka" miscellany: in a right-hand sequence of groups of one quarter note and two eighth notes in four-four meter, the eighth notes are slurred to the following quarter note, even if the slur crosses the bar line. In addition, the quarter notes are marked *ten.*, which effectively indicates a legato touch throughout the fragment.[76] Finally, Beethoven would express a point of special interest by a notation that is either strikingly unconventional or accompanied by words that further explain the intended effect. This category includes some examples of very long slurs across several

[74] Hess 298. Kerman, ed., *Ludwig van Beethoven Autograph Miscellany from ca. 1786 to 1799 (The "Kafka" Sketchbook)*, vol. 1, f. 70r. 13/5. Dated *c.* 1788–90 (Cooper, "The ink in Beethoven's 'Kafka' sketch miscellany," 327).

[75] Türk, *Klavierschule*, 363, § 48.

[76] Kerman, ed., *Ludwig van Beethoven Autograph Miscellany from ca. 1786 to 1799 (The "Kafka" Sketchbook)*, vol. 1, f. 154r. 10/5; 11/5. Dated *c.* 1790–91 (Cooper, "The ink in Beethoven's 'Kafka' sketch miscellany," 327).

bars, as well as the strikingly irregular slurs in a fragment of a duo for violin and cello, on Kafka 130r.[77] Kafka 88v. is interesting because it contains a fragment with extreme dynamics, a fragment with *legato prestissimo* upward scales marked with long legato slurs, and a few bars of an Allegro con brio that contain sixteenth notes with strokes (or vigorously written dots) and the written indication "completely staccato."[78]

Of the last group of sketches that convey some special interest in expressive notation, a fragment from around 1790 with a written explanation of the legato touch deserves particular attention. On two lines of a bifolio with sketches, Beethoven writes an ascending A major scale in sixteenth notes across the entire keyboard. The scale is marked "adagio molto" and the touch is indicated legato by means of a long slur that is only interrupted at the transition to the second line. In the accompanying explanation, Beethoven writes: "The difficulty here is to bind the whole passage so that one cannot hear the touch of the fingers; instead it must sound as if it were played with a bow."[79] This short description explains the direct link between Beethoven's early legato notation and his personal practice of playing legato. Even if Beethoven perhaps used the notation of other composers as a model, he had a personal concept of how legato could be achieved and his own idea of how it should sound. He found this ideal "difficult" to realize, but apparently not impossible on the instruments he knew and with the playing skills he possessed. Beethoven's legato was a product of musical imagination. It had to be achieved by discipline, could be thwarted by instruments that did not produce the intended "bowed" effect and, most importantly, was expressed in notation by long slurs.

By 1791, musical expressivity had become one of the specialties of Beethoven's playing. After hearing him, Junker wrote about his "sheer inexhaustible wealth of ideas," the "completely personal kind of expressivity in his playing," and his unusual dexterity.[80] When Beethoven prepared new works for publication in the early 1790s, rather than merely "embarrassing" the Viennese *Klaviermeister* with single passages, he evidently wanted to display the whole universe of his abilities, both as a composer and as a pianist. One means of showing off these special abilities was his expressive notation. It is reasonable to suppose that Beethoven, at that time,

[77] Kerman, ed., *Ludwig van Beethoven Autograph Miscellany from ca. 1786 to 1799 (The "Kafka" Sketchbook)* vol. I, f. 130r. 1–10. Dated *c.* 1792 (Cooper, "The ink in Beethoven's 'Kafka' sketch miscellany," 328).

[78] Kerman, ed., *Ludwig van Beethoven Autograph Miscellany from ca. 1786 to 1799 (The "Kafka" Sketchbook)* vol. I, f. 88v. 7/9, 8/9 and 11/5. Most of the slurs are left out in the transcription vol. II, 229. Dated October 1790 (Cooper, "The ink in Beethoven's 'Kafka' sketch miscellany," 327).

[79] Koblenz, Wegeler Collection, SV 329 f. 1r. See Johnson, *Beethoven's Early Sketches in the "Fischhof Miscellany,"* vol. I, 271. Dated *c.* 1790 according to the description at the digital archive of the Beethoven-Haus. This sketch is briefly discussed in Rosenblum, *Performance Practices in Classic Piano Music*, 152.

[80] See my earlier discussion on page 57.

reconsidered his notational style and level of notational intensity. We can examine this assumption by comparing the subjects and figuration from the C major Klavier quartet (WoO 36/3; No. I in the autograph) with their revised form in the piano sonatas Op. 2/1 and Op. 2/3. These passages and subjects fall into three groups.

First, there are two predominantly unmarked passages where the difference in expressive notation is small. The passage with scales in sixteenth notes against an eighth-note accompaniment in WoO 36/3, mvt. I, bars 43–7 and 86–90, is similar to Op. 2/3, mvt. I, bars 39–44 and 173–8. The touch is in both cases entirely unmarked. Beethoven indicates *forte*, but in the sonata, he additionally highlights accents on changing harmonies or dissonant chords with *sf* (however, in the first edition this *sf* was omitted in bars 40 and 42 of the exposition; an autograph of the sonata does not exist). Another, less conclusive example is the left-hand tremolo figuration in sixteenth notes, WoO 36/3, mvt. I, bars 79ff., which corresponds to a similar texture in Op. 2/3, mvt. 4, bars 28–34, 40–4, 217–22, and 228–34. The touch in this figure is unmarked in both works, whereas the articulation of the (dissimilar) right-hand motifs is fully indicated in both cases. In both examples, the musical structure in and of itself conveys an appropriate touch. In sixteenth-note passages in a consonant harmonic environment in an allegro, this touch would *not* have been legato, or a heavy touch, unless such a touch was explicitly called for by expressive indications.[81] Beethoven chose not to write slurs, so he did not intend these passages to sound legato.

Second, we have one example where in the quartet there are actually more expressive indications than in the later sonata. This is the left-hand figuration in sixteenth notes in WoO 36/3, mvt. I, bars 18–21, which corresponds with Op. 2/3, mvt. I, bars 21–4 and 155–8. In the quartet, half-bar slurs are indicated in bar 18, obviously to be continued throughout the passage. In the sonata, the left hand is unmarked in both cases. The question is whether Beethoven intended this accompaniment to sound less legato in the sonata, or whether he wanted it to sound legato but found the slurs superfluous. Continuing my reasoning about the first two examples, the answer must be that, in the sonata, Beethoven wanted a different effect. Fast sixteenth notes would not automatically be played legato. A possible explanation for taking the slurs away is that Beethoven achieved more contrast between the melody and the accompaniment by playing the left hand with a lighter touch.

Third, there are two instances where the subjects in the quartet have fewer expressive indications than the corresponding subjects of the sonatas. The first example is the second subject of WoO 36/3, mvt. I, bars 37–41 and 122–7 (Example 7.6).

---

[81] See Türk, *Klavierschule*, §. 10, 43, 46, and 49.

Example 7.6. Klavier Quartet in C major WoO 36/3, mvt. 1, Allegro vivace, keyboard part, bars 37–41 (autograph)[82]

Example 7.7. Sonata in C major Op. 2/3, mvt. 1, Allegro con brio, bars 27–32. (Artaria, 1796)

In the second bar of this subject, only the melody has a slur and two strokes to indicate the articulation. This passage corresponds with the beginning of the second subject group of the sonata Op. 2/3, mvt. 1, bars 27–38 and 161–72 (Example 7.7).

In the sonata, the first four bars of the left hand are slurred, to be continued in a similar fashion, and the melody is completely marked with slurs, dots, and accents. The fact that this passage has the same function as the second subject in both works, is written in the same key, and that the melody is identical for four bars, very strongly suggests that its intended expression in both works is similar (although the subject in the quartet, being part of a single statement in a shorter phrase, is played *crescendo*, whereas the dynamic level stays *piano* throughout the whole of the second subject group in the sonata). Although a lyrical second subject might be expected to require more legato, or a "heavier" touch, Beethoven apparently wanted to make sure that his intentions were properly understood in the published version. This is an example of how, in a published work, he chose a notation that left no room for interpretation, instead of relying on the stylistic intuition of his public.

The second example in this group is the beginning of the Adagio con espressione in WoO 36/3, mvt. 2, bars 1–5 (Example 7.8).

---

[82] Reproduced with the kind permission of the Staatsbibliothek zu Berlin – Preussischer Kulturbesitz. Musikabteilung mit Mendelssohn-Archiv. Mus.ms.autogr. Beethoven Artaria 126.

Example 7.8. Klavier Quartet in C major WoO 36/3, mvt. 2, Adagio con espressione,
keyboard part, bars 1–5[83]

Example 7.9. Sonata in F minor Op. 2/1, mvt. 2, Adagio, bars 1–5 (Artaria, 1796)

This corresponds to the beginning of the Adagio of the sonata Op. 2/1,
mvt. 2, bars 1–5 (Example 7.9) and the beginning of its variation bars 32–5.
The Adagio con espressione of the quartet is marked "sotto voce," and
the touch in bars 2–4 is indicated with slurs. An expressive difference
between the versions appears in the Mozartean dynamic indication *pfpf*
in bar 4 of the quartet.[84] Bar 4 of the sonata is simply marked legato without
a new dynamic indication, whereas in bar 35 of the quartet, the variation of
the same connecting run as a chromatic scale in sixteenth-note triplets is
marked portato with dots and slurs. Otherwise, the intended affect appears
to be identical in both versions. However, in the sonata, the expressive
indications are distributed in a new way. The movement is called Adagio,
and Beethoven transfers the content of the "espressione" to the specific
indication *dol*[ce] and replaces the "sotto voce" by *p*. The melody is now
also fully slurred, and later in the movement all passages in thirty-second
notes are slurred without exception, which is not the case in the quartet. So
it seems obvious that, in the Adagio of the sonata, Beethoven had the
ambition of meticulously indicating the legato, even though its character
indications, as well as the melodic character, would in any case have guided
the player to a *cantabile* touch.
  As these examples make clear, Beethoven in some cases reconsidered the
expression of motifs when he re-used them in the published sonatas. In

---

[83] Reproduced with the kind permission of the Staatsbibliothek zu Berlin – Preussischer Kulturbesitz.
   Musikabteilung mit Mendelssohn-Archiv. Mus.ms.autogr. Beethoven Artaria 126.
[84] A scale with similar dynamics appears in Neefe's Sonata 7, mvt. 2, bar 37 (1773).

those cases where he retained the original expression, he completed his notation in a manner that restated the obvious in unequivocal terms. For instance, unexpected or dissonant chords are additionally marked *sf*, and an Adagio receives legato slurs in addition to the indication *dolce*.

Even in all the other cases where no comparison with earlier material is possible, it is clear that Beethoven's newly published scores were very richly annotated or, as William Newman writes, "Beethoven was exceptional among his contemporaries in tending to complete more if not all of his markings in a section, or even a whole piece."[85] In the variations for piano and violin WoO 40, published in 1793 (the very work that contained passages meant to "embarrass" the Viennese pianists), the notation is completed with fingerings, and occasionally almost borders on the pedantic. Regarding slurs, strokes, and dynamics, the Trios Op. 1 are even more richly marked. This tendency to rigorous completeness is to some degree a return to the notation practice in Beethoven's very first published works, with the important exception that the range of variety is now greater and that the notation conveys true musical expression rather than, as often in the "Kurfürsten" Sonatas, finger acrobatics.

Beethoven's habit of stating musical expression in various layers, with meter, tempo indications, additional words, and a meticulous application of expressive indications, draws our attention to those moments where the touch is not indicated. A typical instance is the third bar in both of the last two examples, where an eighteenth-century player would very likely have been influenced in his left-hand touch by the sixteenth-note rests in the melody. The left-hand touch would have become lighter than at the beginning of the piece. This bar is the first one where slurs in the left hand would in fact have been indispensable if Beethoven wanted to make sure that the player played legato all the time. But slurs do not appear either in this bar or (in the sonata) in the corresponding bar 34. Against a background of late eighteenth-century keyboard touch, there is no doubt that Beethoven wanted the left hand in these bars to be performed in accordance with the right-hand articulation, that is, slightly detached.

This observation provides an opening for my review of other unmarked passages in Beethoven's keyboard works. It is, however, important to remember that this area has long been acknowledged as a minefield of misinterpretations. The most obvious issues that create difficulties in interpretation in Beethoven's work are inconsistencies, errors at one or several stages during the drafting, copying, or engraving of a score,[86] and the influence of a *simile* notation practice on the appearance of the music.[87] In any discussion of unmarked passages in Beethoven's work, especially irregular ones, the possibility of an error cannot be completely excluded.

[85] Newman, *Beethoven on Beethoven*, 122.   [86] See *ibid.*, Chapter 5.
[87] See my discussion on page 200, and Barth, *The Pianist as Orator*, 110, on this point.

Example 7.10. Sonata in D major Op. 10/3, mvt. 1, Presto, bars 105–13 (Eder, 1798)

Example 7.11. Sonata in D major Op. 10/3, mvt. 1, Presto, bars 286–98

Often, however, notational irregularities have their structural counter-part. An example is the differing treatment of the codetta in the exposition of the opening Presto of the D major Sonata Op. 10/3 and its extension in the recapitulation. In the exposition this section begins with two four-bar phrases in half notes that each conclude with a perfect cadence in A major (Example 7.10).

The final cadence in this example is not marked legato. Especially in a concluding formula, this indicates that the last four chords (disregarding the tie) are to be played slightly detached to underline the concluding character of the cadence. Seen by itself, this notation is scarcely remarkable. In the corresponding passage in the recapitulation, however, the second, conclud-ing full cadence (this time back to D major) is replaced by an extension of four bars that leads to G major (Example 7.11).

The extension begins unaccented and continues with a *crescendo* under a long legato slur that extends to the final accented chord.[88] In this example, the psychology of confirmation through a repeated perfect cadence is inverted: the listener is deprived of this confirmation. Instead, floating insecurity ensues, to be resolved in the *f*/*sf* G major chord. The extended legato slur makes this effect possible. Viewed in this way, the omitted slur in Example 7.10 is by no means an error; rather, the extended slur in Example 7.11 is an addition, essential to that particular moment alone.

Throughout Beethoven's oeuvre, instances can be found where slurs have been "taken away" to indicate a lightening of touch. This typically occurs at

---

[88] A *crescendo* toward, and an accent at, the end of a phrase was an irregularity in comparison to common practice, and therefore needed to be precisely indicated.

Example 7.12. Sonata in F major Op. 10/2, mvt. 2, Allegretto, bars 1–8

Example 7.13. Sonata in D major Op. 10/3, mvt. 4, Rondo allegro, bars 105–13

the end of a phrase or a piece. One example is the beginning of the Allegretto in Op. 10/2 (Example 7.12). If one plays the beginning so that it sounds "as if it were played with a bow" without an audible touch of the fingers, as Beethoven would have done, the basic meter remains unclear until bar 7. In order to provide metric clarity at the end of the phrase, the left-hand conclusion and the last right-hand chord are unslurred and are not meant to sound legato.

In passagework, too, a lightening of touch toward the end of a phrase or a piece could be expressed by discontinuing preceding legato slurs (Example 7.13).

In this example, the lightening at the end of the piece is brought about by the right-hand passagework. Here, the broken chord texture and the absence of a specific legato notation work together to indicate an almost leggiero ending.

Taken together, these examples not only show that sometimes Beethoven probably wanted the touch of an unmarked passage to be light, but they also demonstrate that for Beethoven the convention of determining the proper touch from the musical context alone, even without additional indications, was still useful.

EIGHTEENTH-CENTURY TOUCH AND SEPARATED AND MEETING SLURS

Unmarked passages, to be interpreted according to traditional conventions, can be found even in Beethoven's latest works for piano. For example, the

left hand of the half and full cadences (bars 8 and 16) in the opening Allegro
of the "Hammerklavier" Sonata Op. 106 are notated exactly as in bar 7 of
Example 7.12. However, Beethoven often omits legato or staccato indications for notational economy. Especially in his late work, the reason for
these omissions becomes more difficult to judge. For instance, the subject in
regular dotted quarter notes of the final Fuga in Op. 110 is slurred, as is the
countersubject in eighth notes. But these slurs appear only at the beginning
of the movement and recur in very few phrases later on. The solution in this
case may lie in the fact that this is a movement in moderate speed with
predominantly stepwise motion that begins softly, and is written in a
serious, polyphonic style. Any of these features would in traditional practice
indicate a heavy touch.[89]

However, in the finale of the A major Sonata Op. 101, the eighth notes of
the *fugato* subject that marks the beginning of the development section have
staccato dots only in bars 127 and 128, and later on, as a reminder, only in a
very few other instances. This is, of course, a livelier piece, but it is also
serious and polyphonic – the motion of the eighth notes is often stepwise. In
this case the player is clearly expected to read the dots as to be continued
simile. The choice of an appropriate touch for the sixteenth notes (mostly
scale fragments) in the same movement is also left to the player, except for
very few specific legato indications. The decision of how the sixteenth notes
are to be played depends entirely on whether one believes that in 1816, when
Beethoven composed the sonata, he expected the "usual" touch to be
traditional or legato.

Assuming a change in basic touch during Beethoven's lifetime and in his
personal practice not only affects our understanding of his unmarked music,
but also our interpretation of his slurs. William Newman has shown that it
is often difficult to determine where Beethoven actually meant slurs to be
separated or continued.[90] On the basis of an extensive analysis of various
slurs, Newman arrived at "seven tentative explanations for Beethoven's
slurring." In Newman's order, these are: (1) psychological slurs, in
Newman's examples often spontaneously "illogical" ones (such as the slur
across a rest in Op. 101, mvt. 1, bars 19–20); (2) legato slurs; (3) slurs that
enclose a harmonic function such as a chord or an organ point; (4) slurs that
define local rhythmic groupings in the manner of Bach, Haydn, and
Mozart; (5) "infraphrasal" slurs that divide subphrases into a "musically
intelligible portion"; (6) slurs that coincide with complete phrases; (7) illogical slurs that extend "beyond one's typical mind-set for slur limits."[91] At the
basis of these distinctions lies the question of the extent to which Beethoven
actually associated the slur with "the span of a musical idea," that is, with
attack and release. Newman states, "The answer may be that he did so more
than his predecessors Haydn and Mozart did, more where his ideas are

[89] Türk, *Klavierschule*, 360, § 45.   [90] Newman, *Beethoven on Beethoven*, 123–33.   [91] *Ibid.*, 134–7.

Example 7.14. Sonata in C minor Op. 13, mvt. 2, Adagio cantabile, bars 1–8 (Hoffmeister, 1799)

motivic or fragmentary rather than complete and more when his tempo is fast rather than slow."[92]

How we shape the attack and release of any kind of slur, whether a legato slur, a slur to indicate small groups, subphrases, or whole phrases, or an "illogical" slur, depends directly on how we choose to interpret the basic touch. Ludger Lohmann points out, "Curiously, the question of what meaning a legato slur has in music in which a legato touch is the rule anyway is never asked."[93] Like Grundmann and Mies in their study on Beethoven's legato, Lohmann quotes Milchmeyer's passage from 1801 about the three kinds of touch ("Spielarten"): natural, slurred ("gebundene"), and detached. According to Milchmeyer's definition, the natural manner of playing is what today would be called legato.[94] However, a concentration on "usual" or even "natural" ways of playing does not help to solve the problem mentioned by Lohmann. As I have outlined in the beginning of this chapter, the choice of touch depends on the character of the piece or passage, which was indicated in more ways than through expressive notation alone. This further suggests that questions about the attack and release of slurs, and the degree of detachment between successive slurs, cannot be answered in a general way. I will illustrate this point by discussing an example that appears in the article by Grundmann and Mies, and that Newman refers to as an example of illogical slurs. This is the slurring of the opening theme of the Adagio cantabile of the "Pathetique" Sonata Op. 13 (Example 7.14).

This example is instructive because the same irregular slurring appears at every restatement of the theme, so the possibility of a mistake is excluded. Grundmann and Mies write: "This theme shows clearly how [Beethoven]

---

[92] *Ibid.*, 124.   [93] Lohmann, *Studien zu Artikulationsproblemen*, 259.

[94] Milchmeyer, *Die wahre Art das Pianoforte zu spielen*, 5, quoted in Herbert Grundmann and Paul Mies, *Studien zum Klavierspiel Beethovens und seiner Zeitgenossen* (Bonn: Bouvier, 1966), 84 and Lohmann, *Studien zu Artikulationsproblemen*, 260.

makes an effort to bridge bar-line articulations and the regular order of the structure and of the emphases. The bar lines at the end of bars 4 and 6 are bridged even in the treble. Thus, the eight-bar melody becomes asymmetric and can hardly be analyzed in terms of its parts any more."[95] Newman acknowledges this interpretation as an "ingenious rationale."[96] The problem, however, is that the interpretation of these slurs in performance is not at all unequivocal. But it is necessary to hear what they sound like in order to develop any opinion about their irregularity or their illogical character. Newman also quotes Franz Kullak, who in 1881 reacted against the opinion that the slurs need to be regulated. Since the Op. 13 slurring is clearly not an engraver's mistake, Kullak wanted to retain the original slurs. However, he adds: "We have not asserted that the hand ought to be lifted at the end of every slur."[97] The question raised here brings us closer to understanding the original meaning of these irregular slurs.

One key to that understanding is, again, that an Adagio cantabile with clear melodic lines would be indication enough to justify a heavy touch. Even C. P. E. Bach states that an Adagio should normally be played with *getragene* and slurred notes.[98] Türk seconds this opinion in his discussion of heavy execution (which nevertheless does not need to be loud).[99] Bach adds that one has to consider the character of the piece even when playing staccato.[100]

Türk is more explicit: "Occasional short tones in an Adagio may not be played as detached as in an Allegro."[101] So even if one interprets the end of a longer legato slur as the end of a period and hence plays it somewhat shorter than notated, the degree of detachment in an Adagio would be less than in an Allegro. All the same, Türk explicitly warns against making gaps between consecutive groups of four slurred eighth notes. The musical phrase in his accompanying example would otherwise be chopped up in sections of four notes each.[102] This warning evidently also applies to bar-line articulations generally, which weakens Grundmann and Mies' interpretation that Beethoven used the slurs to bridge such articulations.

Türk's warning might have been especially addressed to music that, on the basis of notational convention or engravers' customs, was slurred in groups of only a few notes at a time, although a continuous legato was the true intention.[103] However, it would also apply to the manner of joining

[95] Grundmann and Mies, *Studien zum Klavierspiel Beethovens*, 77.
[96] Newman, *Beethoven on Beethoven*, 130. See also Rosenblum, *Performance Practices in Classic Piano Music*, 182–3.
[97] Franz Kullak, "Allgemeine Bestimmungen über den Vortrag der Beethoven'schen Klavierkonzerte," in *Beethovens Klavierkonzerte*, Leipzig: Steingräber, 1881, xii, discussed in Newman, *Beethoven on Beethoven*, 130.
[98] Bach, *Versuch über die wahre Art, das Clavier zu spielen*, part 1, 118, § 5.
[99] Türk, *Klavierschule*, 359, § 43.
[100] Bach, *Versuch über die wahre Art, das Clavier zu spielen*, part 1, 125, § 17.
[101] Türk, *Klavierschule*, 354, § 36.   [102] Ibid., 340–2, § 19–22.
[103] See Rosenblum, *Performance Practices in Classic Piano Music*, 177–9.

Example 7.15. Sonata in D major Op. 10/3, mvt. 2, Largo e mesto, bars 8–12

legato slurs that do not demarcate phrases, like the ones in Op. 13, and it would certainly apply to pieces such as an Adagio cantabile. So unless one maintains that the slurs in Op. 13 are meant to demarcate phrases and sub-phrases, albeit in an "illogical" manner, there is every reason to suppose that their transition was played almost or completely legato.

What, then, do these irregular slurs convey? A possible explanation can be found in the dynamic shape of a slur. Generally, the beginning of a slur was to be accentuated "very slightly (almost imperceptibly)" with a *diminuendo* toward the end.[104] Accepting the definition of a slur as indicating an almost imperceptible beginning emphasis, in the general legato environment the irregular slurring of this example would help to subtly shape the melody as if it were sung with words that contain various consonants. The slurs would convey specific but subtle meaning. If indeed the intended musical effect of these slurs is a thin layer of irregularity above the prevailing *cantabile* character in regular phrases, this is only possible if they are not understood as indications of a perceptible attack and release.

Newman's fourth category remains to be discussed: the slurs that define local rhythmic groupings in a traditional manner. For example, the second movement of the Sonata Op. 10/3 is called Largo e mesto, suggesting a truly heavy touch. What does this mean for the shaping of the cantilena that begins in bar 9 (Example 7.15)?

In this case, even the early Romantic tutors supply an explanation, because by the 1820s, when legato had become the accepted touch, small-scale articulation slurs were still seen as different from the longer ones. Thus Carl Czerny writes in his *Klavierschule* that in shorter slurs across two or three notes, the last note gets shortened, whereas successive legato slurs across several notes are to be played legato throughout.[105] In other words, small slurs were understood as extended articulation marks even in the nineteenth century. However, as demonstrated earlier, such articulation, whether indicated with small slurs or staccato dots, should be performed in a manner that suits the general character of the piece. So in this case, all the

---

[104] Türk, *Klavierschule*, 355, §38. Bach, *Versuch, über die wahre Art, das Clavier zu spielen*, part 1, 126, § 18. Mozart, *Versuch einer gründlichen Violinschule*, 135, § 20. Grundmann and Mies, *Studien zum Klavierspiel Beethovens*, 98, quote a passage from Friedrich Starke's *Klavierschule* from 1819 that is a literal transcription of Türk.

[105] Czerny, *Vollständige theoretisch-praktische Pianoforte-Schule*, vol. 1, 95, Chapter 18, § 22 and 24.

reservations for serious, slow, and sad music discussed above apply: a staccato dot would mean that the note is *somewhat* articulated, but it does not mean that it is accented. A short slur receives an almost imperceptible accent at the beginning, is played *diminuendo* and is shortened at the end, but not so much as to disturb the general affect of the passage. The end of a phrase is dynamically tapered and shortened. The left hand, however, should probably sound "as if it were played with a bow."

One question that cannot be answered by analyzing Beethoven's scores is when, or even if, his concept of a normal touch for regular passagework in quick movements shifted from eighteenth-century clarity to a true legato. After he ceased notating small-scale slurs and dots in his *allegro* sixteenth notes, he marked only very few of his passages meticulously with slurs. A good example is the opening Allegro con brio of Op. 22, where in the exposition and recapitulation we find only few slurs, associated with certain motifs, whereas the large-phrase writing of the development section is indicated with whole-bar slurs. Beethoven's passagework slurring becomes rather scarcer through time; one could explain this by suggesting that Beethoven wanted it to be played legato in any case. This is, however, impossible to verify in his scores. Even in the Diabelli Variations Op. 120, *allegro* sixteenth notes are largely unmarked, but in the sixteenth variation all the sixteenth notes are suddenly slurred although the character given is "piacevole" anyway. Both halves of the eighteenth variation, a Vivace, begin with unmarked sixteenth-note triplets and end with several bars of slurred ones. So even in the latest works for piano, the intention of these slurs still seems to be to indicate a touch distinct from the unmarked manner of playing passages, which, logically, would have been less legato.

Beethoven's opinion about legato in passages in 1816 is documented in some advice to Carl Czerny, who was the teacher of Beethoven's nephew at the time. Referring to passages of descending and ascending broken thirds, he writes:

At certain passages such as [example of descending broken thirds] etc., I occasionally also like to use all the fingers … so one can bind them, such [passages] certainly do sound, as they say, 'pearly (if played with few fingers) or like a pearl,' however, sometimes one likes to have a different kind of jewelry.[106]

Here Beethoven advises Czerny to instruct his nephew in a legato touch, because "sometimes" it is preferable to the "pearly" touch. The undertone of this message might well be that Beethoven wanted to safeguard his nephew from subscribing to the techniques of the fashionable brilliant style. In this case he was fending off a novelty rather than preaching legato as a contrast to the old eighteenth-century "chopped" style. However, his additions "occasionally" and "sometimes" ("zuweilen"; "auch einmal") clearly convey that

---

[106] Beethoven, *Briefwechsel*, vol. III, 237–8.

he is talking about alternatives. I cannot see any "annoyance with Czerny's interest in pearly effects" in this particular passage, as George Barth did,[107] but rather find it a confirmation of the supposition that Beethoven used a variety of touches throughout his life, according to the musical context, without preferring any one in particular.

SUPERLEGATO

One marking that seems relatively easy to interpret is Beethoven's indication for superlegato.[108] In French harpsichord music, and in pieces inspired by that style, hidden two-part writing was a means of indicating a prolonged touch for reasons of sonority.[109] However, the first inspiration for Beethoven's prolonged touch notation was apparently polyphonic music; for example, the two organ/fortepiano preludes Op. 93 from 1789 contain many examples of polyphonic writing. This notation, especially in left-hand textures, was a novelty for Beethoven at that moment. The left hand in his earlier works usually has little to do apart from occasional virtuosic display in passages. It is likely that Beethoven began considering the use of this notation in fortepiano music sometime in 1791 when he decided to work out the Righini Variations WoO 65 as a piano composition. The sketches for WoO 65 on Kafka 123v./123r. still bear the inscription "orgelVariationen."[110] In fact, these sketches contain only few polyphonic passages compared to the final variations that were written for "Clavier ou Pianoforte."[111] In this work the writing is, however, not only strictly polyphonic. Sometimes it also serves to indicate superlegato as, for instance, in the thirteenth variation, bars 13–14, left hand.

Although he was aware of this notational technique so early on, Beethoven first exploited it at length in the sonatas Op. 2. The first instance where he clearly uses part writing for reasons of sound is in the Prestissimo finale of Op. 2/1 (Example 7.16).

In the right hand in bars 131–4 of this example, the top line of the triplets is suddenly indicated as a melody line in quarter notes. Because the melody line of the triplets is prominent throughout the movement without being especially pointed out, the notation in this instance is unexpected. Of course, the ninth chord on a dominant organ point a few bars before the recapitulation is special and exposed, so there are harmonic and structural

[107] Barth, *The Pianist as Orator*, 131, n. 159.
[108] Sandra Rosenblum introduced the term "prolonged touch" for superlegato, legatissimo, or "finger pedal," following Czerny. Rosenblum, *Performance Practices in Classic Piano Music*, 155, n. 31.
[109] *Ibid.*, 155.
[110] Kerman, ed., *Ludwig van Beethoven Autograph Miscellany from ca. 1786 to 1799 (The "Kafka" Sketchbook)*, vol. 1, 123v., 123r., early 1791. See Cooper, "The ink in Beethoven's 'Kafka' sketch miscellany," 327.
[111] Kinsky and Halm, *Das Werk Beethovens: Thematisch-Bibliographisches Verzeichnis*, 513. See also my discussion on page 50.

Example 7.16. Sonata in F minor Op. 2/1, mvt. 3, Prestissimo, bars 126–37

Example 7.17. Sonata in D major Op. 10/3, mvt. 2, Largo e mesto, bars 13–17

reasons for emphasizing this particular part of the melody. Nevertheless, it is pointed out by means of a superlegato notation, unique for the piece. This type of notation can be found throughout Beethoven's works for piano, including the latest ones – for example, the second Bagatelle of Op. 126, upbeat bar 66–79.

Several other movements of Op. 2 contain various forms of superlegato notation as well. In bars 222–7 of the cadenza at the end of the first movement of Op. 2/3, for instance, broken chords are notated to be held throughout each bar. For C. P. E. Bach and Türk, written-out superlegato in chords meant the same as legato chords expressed with a simple slur. Both writers give examples of legato broken chords and explain that the "fingers are to be left on the keys until a new harmony occurs."[112] For Beethoven, however, this notation clearly meant something different than the usual legato notation. In Example 7.17, which is the continuation of Example 7.15, we can see an example of a transition from regular legato to written-out superlegato.

In this particular example, the two-part notation first appears after four-and-a-half bars of simple slurred sixteenth notes, so the plain slurred sixteenth notes are not meant as a simplified continuation of an initially

[112] Bach, *Versuch über die wahre Art, das Clavier zu spielen*, part 1, 126, § 18. Türk, *Klavierschule*, 355, § 38. For Türk the superlegato notation, since it was more explicit, was preferable.

Example 7.18. Sonata in Op. 53, mvt. 1, Allegro con Brio, bars 116–19

Example 7.19. Sonata in A major Op. 2/2, mvt. 2, Largo apassionato, bars 4 and 61

more explicit indication. Because Beethoven uses both notations alongside one another in a clearly deliberate fashion, one can assume that he does not mean them to be treated in the same way. The most logical way to interpret his superlegato notation is to understand it as an intensification of the usual legato. In Example 7.18, a phrase from the development section of the "Waldstein" Sonata, this is very clearly visible.

This phrase is restated three times in transposition, using the same notation. Of course, the notation of this passage has to be read as a gradual intensification of the legato, ending in explicit *legatissimo*.

A last example of superlegato notation is Beethoven's fairly frequent stepwise movement with held notes. The Largo apassionato of Op. 2/2, for example, has four instances of this notation in bars 4, 35, 61, and 62 (Example 7.19).

Of all of Beethoven's legato indications, his superlegato notation is the one that gives us the most concrete understanding of how his technique was different from the "harping" of his competitors, because it comes closest to conveying the actual action of the fingers. Even so, the technique of "leaving the fingers on the key" is not unanimously accepted in modern practice. Some modern pianists do accept or even prefer the practice of superlegato, especially for broken harmonies. For example, Hans Kann argues that, even on the modern piano, a legatissimo touch leads to more clarity, especially when the other voice has trills or runs.[113] However, many performers see a

---

[113] Hans Kann, ed., *Johann Baptist Cramer, 21 Etüden für Klavier: Nach dem Handexemplar Beethovens aus dem Besitz Anton Schindlers*, Vienna: Universal, 1974, iii.

superlegato touch as a problem, especially in stepwise motion as in the last example. A common verdict is that this technique perhaps suits the harpsichord but sounds muddy on pianos, including early ones.

Ambivalence about the application of superlegato is, of course, not an issue in those instances where Beethoven clearly notated this effect. But when we want to take his notation from one example as an instruction for other moments in his music, the appropriate techniques do need to be discussed. Regarding *cantabile* or legato melody lines, it often seems that Beethoven's notation does not quite give us enough information about what he would have done. On the one hand, a notation such as the transition from unmarked notes via legato to superlegato as in Example 7.18 makes it clear that three distinct techniques are indicated. Since Beethoven was otherwise so explicit and complete in his notation, it might seem inappropriate to borrow a superlegato technique for giving a melody more tone when playing on a dry-sounding instrument, for instance. Nevertheless, this is precisely what one suspects Beethoven himself would have done with melodies such as those in examples 7.6, 7.15, 7.18, and perhaps even 7.9, when playing on a piano that had a tricky treble.

Czerny's various characterizations of Beethoven's legato, his "strict legato in the chords" or "full-voiced legato," his legato in the "gebundener Stil," and his "enchanting" performance of adagios and slurred cantabile passages, do not help to solve this particular problem in terms of touch and finger technique, although in another more explicit elaboration on the legato chords he makes it clear that the term *finger* technique is correct: "[Beethoven] understood remarkably well how to connect full chords to each other without the use of the pedal."[114]

Beethoven's notation in the majority of his compositions provides examples of his specialties, but sometimes specific performance indications seem to be lacking. I am convinced that a fair portion of experimentation is in fact necessary to work out the effects indicated in his music. I believe that, since superlegato, or "finger pedal," was grounded in a polyphonic tradition known to Beethoven, this technique is an important addition to the fortepianist's toolbox.[115]

LEGATO IN MELODIES AND THE SPLIT DAMPER PEDAL

Czerny's statement about Beethoven's technique of binding chords with the fingers alone can be used in many instances where legato lines are balanced

---

[114] Quoted in Rowland, "Beethoven's pianoforte pedalling," 61, after Gustav Nottebohm, *Zweite Beethoveniana*, Leipzig: Peters, 1887, 356.
[115] See also Breitman, "The Damper Pedal and the Beethoven Piano Sonatas: A Historical Perspective," 91 for a discussion of Beethoven's "finger pedal."

against a detached accompaniment, as, for example, in the Largo apassionato of Op. 2/2. This is, however, not a general statement against the use of
the pedal.[116] There is no question that the player also has to experiment with
the use of the damper pedal in Beethoven's music. Czerny explicitly says:
"He used the pedals very often, far more frequently than indicated in his
works."[117] Beethoven began indicating the lifting of the dampers in his
published works in 1801. So if we assume, on the basis of his indication for
the use of knee levers in the "Jeremiah" lamentations from around 1792,[118]
that he also used the pedal in his earlier works, Czerny's words are hardly
surprising. The question is not whether a player should use the damper
pedal, but rather when she or he would use it.[119]

Beethoven's use of the damper pedal has inspired a steady stream of
publications, each of which has added important new knowledge to this
issue.[120] The literature is, to various degrees, based on: analyses of the
instances where Beethoven indicated the use of the damper pedal; presen-
tations of Beethoven's pedaling against the backdrop of organological
information and the practice of other composers; and performers' analyses
that add insights from personal practical experience. Statements made in the
latter category, especially by fortepianists, often add a practical perspective
that is perhaps lacking in other cases, but there is also an admitted risk of
subjectivity in these discussions. A typical example is David Breitman's
suggested pedaling for the opening of Op. 2/3: "The first twelve bars are
marked *p*, and are followed by a subito *ff*. Although we can never know for
certain, it seems very likely that Beethoven intended the first bars – carefully
articulated with Mozartean slurs and dots – to be played without pedal, and
for the following passage to be pedaled. I would go further, and suggest that
the *essence* of the music at bar 13 is the pedal … In this case, depending on
the particular piano, it should be possible to keep the dampers up throughout the entire passage, until the repetition at m. 17."[121]

Breitman's view builds on the historical information that many players
used the damper pedal for whole phrases rather than changing it

---

[116] Whenever I mean the device that lifts the dampers, I will use the word "pedal" for better readability, disregarding its mechanism.
[117] Czerny, "Anekdoten und Notizen," 22.
[118] Kerman, ed., *Ludwig van Beethoven Autograph Miscellany from ca. 1786 to 1799 (The "Kafka" Sketchbook)*, vol. 1, 96r. See also my discussion on page 51f.
[119] I agree with David Breitman that Grundmann and Mies' interpretation of Beethoven's pedal as "a kind of register" is often convincing, whereas their recommendation to use the pedal in the later works only when indicated is too rigid. Grundmann and Mies, *Studien zum Klavierspiel Beethovens*, 32–4, and Breitman, "The damper pedal and the Beethoven piano sonatas," 3–4 and 75–6.
[120] See Grundmann and Mies, *Studien zum Klavierspiel Beethovens*, 11–59; Rosenblum, *Performance Practices in Classic Piano Music*, Chapter 4; Newman, *Beethoven on Beethoven*, Chapter 8; Breitman, "The damper pedal and the Beethoven piano sonatas"; van Oort, "The English Classical piano style and its influence on Haydn and Beethoven," 174–82 and elsewhere; and Rowland, "Beethoven's pianoforte pedalling."
[121] Breitman, "The damper pedal and the Beethoven piano sonatas," 95–6.

frequently.[122] However, one could suggest an equally valuable interpretation that favors making the horn-like thirds and fourths of the middle voices audible in imitation of an orchestral effect. This would involve re-taking the pedal every half bar. Orchestral imitation is evident in the music's texture and could thus be called "historical" information as well.

I have mentioned this example to show how personal interpretations in performance practical studies, at low risk, add an inspiring element even though one might not agree in all cases (Breitman's analysis made me reconsider this particular passage). It is the more astonishing, then, that Beethoven's specific reference to a separated damper pedal for treble and bass has not received more attention.[123] True, it is hard to determine Beethoven's attitude to the split pedal, and any suggestion as to how he used it is necessarily a guess. David Rowland writes: "Nowhere in his music does Beethoven specify the separate use of treble or bass dampers."[124]

However, Beethoven specifies in one case that the split pedal is *not* to be used. In the right margin of the first page of the autograph of the "Waldstein" Sonata Op. 53, he writes: "Nb. Where *ped.* is indicated, the whole of the damping of the bass as well as of the treble is lifted. *O* means that it is to be dropped again."[125] It seems logical to interpret this instruction as another indication that Beethoven had conceived the sonata using the newly arrived Érard piano; the Érard has a single foot pedal for the damping. Several questions arise, however, in connection with this instruction, and this assertion is to some degree dependent on the answers to these questions.

First of all, it is unclear whether Beethoven initially intended his remark, which did not make its way into the first edition of the sonata, to be included in this publication. Was Beethoven reasoning based on his own, pre-Érard practice, or was he planning to instruct the public because he knew that the split pedal was used by other pianists? Second, does it seem likely that he used the split pedal until the Érard arrived, or do we understand this particular remark as a general dismissal? Third, if we believe that he actually did have practical experience with the split damper pedal, how could this device have been constructed? Finally, if we arrive at reasonable answers to these questions, does Beethoven's music contain examples where the split pedal can be used with advantage, or might even be indispensable?

To begin at the end, I believe that, in certain textures in Beethoven's earlier works, a split pedal not only seems to come in handy but actually

[122] The background to this approach is discussed in David Rowland, *A History of Pianoforte Pedalling*, Cambridge University Press, 1993.
[123] The split pedal is shortly mentioned in Newman, *Beethoven on Beethoven*, 66–7, 248; Rosenblum, *Performance Practices in Classic Piano Music*, 135; Breitman, "The damper pedal and the Beethoven piano sonatas," 48; Rowland, *A History of Pianoforte Pedalling*, 47–8; and Rowland, "Beethoven's pianoforte pedalling," 58.
[124] Rowland, "Beethoven's pianoforte pedalling," 58.
[125] The autograph of Op. 53 is available at the digital archive of the Beethoven-Haus at www.beethoven-haus-bonn.de/sixcms/detail.php//startseite_digitales_archiv_de (last accessed March 2, 2009).

helps to solve a particular problem strikingly well. This circumstance encourages me to elaborate on the other questions. I will return to musical examples further below.

It is reasonable to assume that this instruction was initially intended to be included in the printed version of the sonata, or at least meant as a reminder of some sort for the editor. The text is comparable in style to Beethoven's instruction at the beginning of the "Moonlight" Sonata Op. 27/2 to lift the dampers throughout the movement. In contrast, the pedal instruction from the "Waldstein" manuscript did not make it into the first edition, but this circumstance says little about the intended function of the note. Whichever was this intention, it is clear that Beethoven had an opinion about the practical aspect of the split pedal; that is, he must have tried, heard, and judged its effect.

The question is whether Beethoven dismissed the use of the split damper pedal only in this particular instance or in general. William Newman argues that Beethoven did not mention the split pedal anywhere else and thus his dismissal very likely expressed his general preference.[126] However, Beethoven was addressing this device no later than 1803 and at that time he had hardly mentioned the pedal at all. Apart from manuscript indications in the "Jeremiah" sketch and one other instance, and in versions of the concertos Op. 15 and 19 from 1795,[127] Beethoven's first pedal indications appear in the sonata Op. 26 from 1800–01 and, from then until 1803, only sporadically and in very few works. Beethoven's original pedal indications before the "Waldstein" sonata are too few to enable any conclusions to be drawn about his preferences.

In order to proceed, it is important to know what kind of device we are discussing. Newman's formulation that Beethoven "at least fifteen years before his Broadwood with the split damper pedal arrived (1818) ... knew about that type of pedal"[128] suggests somehow that the split pedal would have been particularly modern. This is not the case. Split damper rails of a variety of constructions are known from square pianos much earlier than that, even from instruments where hand stops are the only means of operating the dampers. Beethoven's own Broadwood grand piano has no place in this discussion either. We are looking here at an instruction that reflects the completely different situation of 1803.

Viennese pianos from before 1803 that are relevant for Beethoven were in fact still made with knee levers for lifting the damping. For instance, in some fairly early fortepianos by Anton Walter from the late 1780s, the damping is operated with knee levers that emerge from both sides and meet in the middle. Typically, such an instrument would have a moderator

---

[126] Newman, *Beethoven on Beethoven*, 67.
[127] *Ibid.*, 233. See also the indication "dämpf[u]ng" in a sketch for Op. 15 (Kafka 138v. 3).
[128] *Ibid.*, 66.

that is hand-operated by means of a stop button in the middle of the nameboard, just above the nameplate.[129] In Stein's pianos, we find a similar construction with symmetrical knee lever arms, but the meeting ends of the levers were originally linked together.[130] Beethoven was probably using a piano with knee levers until the Érard arrived, but in any case at least until 1796. One of the sketches with a pedal indication is from that year, where, under a *pianissimo* restatement of a motive, he wrote the words: "With the knee-pusher."[131]

In Walter's pianos with this construction, the arms are not connected as in Stein's instruments. Instead, they overlap in the middle where they meet. When the left arm of the lever is pushed up, it engages the right arm and hence operates the entire damper rail. But the right arm – the treble arm, so to speak – can be operated alone.[132] In this case, the damper rail is only lifted at one end: the treble is completely freed of the dampers, a "half-pedal" effect is achieved somewhere in the middle register, and the bass is completely damped. It is technically impossible to reverse the split damper effect in this particular construction: one cannot lift the bass dampers separately in order to sustain a bass note while maintaining a clear treble.[133]

The overall number of surviving instruments compared to the production level of the time is insufficient to make any judgment about how common this or similar constructions were. However, this is a matter of no consequence in our discussion. Since Beethoven, judging from his written instruction in Op. 53, was evidently familiar with the split pedal, it must have been some sort of divided knee lever such as the one described above. This assumption is supported by the fact that, without exception, the pedal in the "Waldstein" Sonata is indicated to support notes or chords in the bass, or to join them with the following passages higher up. The pedal is in fact an integral part of the first theme of the piece and its transformations. Lifting the treble dampers alone would not help in realizing any of these indications. The "Waldstein" finale pedal indications are just as specific

---

[129] Some early pianos had only hand levers for the damping. See Latcham, "The development of the Streicher firm of piano builders," copy provided by the author, 19 n.37. Mozart's 1782 Walter originally had hand levers, but knee levers were later added (Latcham, "Mozart and the pianos of Gabriel Anton Walter," 388). My evaluation of the split damper is based on another Walter from *c.* 1790 and two copies.

[130] Latcham, "Mozart and the pianos of Johann Andreas Stein," 128.

[131] "Mit dem Knieschieber." Kafka 82r. 6/10. Date according to Cooper, "The ink in Beethoven's 'Kafka' sketch miscellany," 331.

[132] Some later Walter pianos have two knee levers, one for the moderator and one for the whole damper pedal. Latcham, "Mozart and the pianos of Gabriel Anton Walter," 393.

[133] In 1955, the (not original) knee levers of Mozart's Walter piano operated in the same manner: the right arm lifted only the treble, whereas the left arm lifted the whole damping. See Ulrich Rück, "Mozarts Hammerflügel erbaute Anton Walter, Wien," *Mozart Jahrbuch* (1955): 251. My thanks to Michael Latcham for mentioning this description. The knee levers presently in the instrument must be new. Their overlap is inverted, lifting either the bass alone or the whole damping.

regarding the intended effect as Beethoven's handwritten note is explicit about the effect he wanted to avoid.

On the other hand, the function of most – though not all – of Beethoven's earlier pedal indications includes bass support as well. These are the few instances in Op. 26, 27/2, and 31/2, and in the variations Op. 35. This is why I believe that neither Beethoven's remark accompanying the "Waldstein" nor his pedal indications in that sonata had anything to do with the undivided pedal of his new Érard. This instruction was more likely a reaction against a misjudgment of some sort that he might have observed when other pianists played his works. This increases the probability that he indeed intended this remark to be published at some point.

We can conclude that the use of a split pedal of the kind discussed is unsuitable for Beethoven's early pedal indications in general, and for the indications that appear in the "Waldstein" Sonata specifically. The key word here is "indications." This observation makes any speculation about whether Beethoven rejected the split pedal *in general* irrelevant. We simply do not know the answer, just as we do not know how much or where he used the pedal generally when applying it "far more frequently than indicated in his works." The only two conclusions to draw are that he knew of the split pedal and, given that he excludes it in cases where bass notes are supported, that it is likely that he specifically addresses split knee levers of a kind that would offer the option to lift the treble dampers alone.

From a practical point of view, however, the possibilities of the split pedal are interesting for Beethoven's music. The treble part of the knee lever is operated with the right knee. Half the damper rail is easier to lift than the whole rail, which makes the device easy to operate and responsive. Its use enhances the sound in the treble through sympathetic vibrations, whereas it leaves the middle register still relatively clear and the bass distinct. The use of the treble part of the damper pedal is, in terms of the technical principles involved, not in any way different from using the whole pedal. One is tempted to take the argument that Beethoven never explicitly indicated the use of the split damper pedal and turn it around. For neither is there any indication that Beethoven, if he indeed used the damper pedal more often than indicated, did *not* use the knee levers of his instrument in the manner they were intended, that is, by either fully or partially lifting the damper rail.

In almost all of Beethoven's earlier piano music, we encounter musical textures such as the one in Example 7.20. This is one of his characteristic textures: a legato cantilena in octaves for the right hand against an active left hand. We find examples of this texture throughout Beethoven's works for five-octave pianos from around 1797, beginning with Op. 7, continuing until Op. 22 and then somewhat less frequently until Op. 31/2. As soon as leaps in the melody are involved, such passages become difficult, sometimes impossible, to perform literally legato as notated. Such problems can be solved if one accepts a continuous legato

Example 7.20. Sonata in C minor Op. 10/1, mvt. 1, Allegro molto e con brio, bars 115–37

Example 7.21. Sonata F major Op. 10/2, mvt. 1, Allegro, bars 18–20

sound and uses a modern pedaling technique with many syncopated pedal changes. However, as far as we know, neither in the historical pedaling of that time, nor in Beethoven's playing (judged from the indications in his music) did frequent pedal changes belong to the usual technique.[134] If one resorts to phrase-long pedaling instead, the left hand in Example 7.20 becomes muddled and incomprehensible. This is clearly not the intended effect.

The problem in this passage is, however, easily solved if the damper rail is only lifted in the treble. Most importantly, there is no need to change the pedal until the first rest in bar 125. The left-hand notes might get something of a halo, but they will remain distinct. The melody will sound legato whereas, on typical Viennese pianos of the time, the single tones will not be sustained enough to create excessive blur in progressions such as in bars 120–1.

A practical test of the split pedal shows a surprising versatility. In the second subject of the Allegro of Op. 10/2, for example, the melody in octaves and chords begins rather low (Example 7.21).

Using a single pedal, one would have to change and re-take the pedal quite often. When played with a tenuto touch and with the treble part of the

---

[134] See Rowland, *A History of Pianoforte Pedalling*, Part II, especially Chapter 5.

pedal lifted, the melody sounds legato as indicated, because the damping loses its precision in the middle register while the left hand remains clear. Again, the whole phrase can be pedaled through until the first rest occurs.

If Beethoven's legato slurs in these instances are meant to represent the resulting sound at all, it seems very likely that he did use this pedaling technique, or at least approved of it. All of the legato passages with melodies in octaves in works of this period can be realized with little effort as they are notated, using the treble part of the damping in the manner described. The split damper effect is not only most compellingly helpful in these passages, it is also in agreement with our ideas about historical pedaling insofar as it allows the pedal to remain unchanged for longer stretches.

CONCLUSION: BEETHOVEN'S LEGATO NOTATION REVISITED

We have seen that the alleged contradiction between the old style, represented by a flexibility of touch, and the new one, where legato is understood as the basic touch, can in practice be small. A flexible response to the musical content is paramount in either of these styles. Thus a player might decide to play a passage strictly legato even if, according to the eighteenth-century fashion, a detached common touch might be appropriate in other, unspecified musical contexts.

Beethoven, on the other hand, was exceptionally explicit, albeit not always consistent, in his expressive notation. The development of his notational habits is clear enough to give us an impression of when and how he discovered legato for his playing style. In his first Viennese published works, legato is indicated far more often than in his previous compositions and more often than was usual at the time. Except for the use of the pedal, which he does not indicate in his published works until Op. 26, Beethoven's notation can be assumed to reflect his personal performance practice; it fits descriptions of his style such as those related by Czerny. The traditional conventions of reading notation were still largely valid for Beethoven. Instead of assuming that the reader knew about his legato preferences, Beethoven chose to indicate legato where he wanted it. Applying Clementi's new advice (to play all unmarked notes generally legato) to Beethoven's music would remove a whole layer of expressive possibilities and make a multitude of indications in the music incomprehensible. Instances where no legato is indicated need, therefore, to be interpreted *a discrezione*, as suits expression of the passage. This could include a legato touch, but legato is by no means mandatory.

If we accept that the character of the common touch in Beethoven's vision is *not* automatically given, we can take a fundamentally different approach to inconsistencies in the slurring of his scores. Additionally, it becomes easy to explain some curious, seemingly old-fashioned habits, such as his occasional use of *ten.*, or tenuto. This indication only makes sense if the usual way to play a certain note is non-tenuto.

One problematic point in many of Beethoven's early works is that certain legato indications – for instance, in melodies in octaves – cannot be performed as written. Resorting to Czerny's report that Beethoven used the pedal often, and accepting the possibility of his using the split damper mechanism, this problem can be solved. If one has access to instruments with such a mechanism, one can perform these passages legato as indicated without the necessity of many pedal changes or of modern syncopated pedaling.

CHAPTER 8

The performance of Beethoven's trills

BEETHOVEN'S TRILLS: TRADITIONAL VIEWS

The trills in Beethoven's music have been acknowledged as being important, not only because of their expressive function in the music, but also as indications of Beethoven's stylistic preferences and how they changed.[1] They often have an essential structural function (perhaps most of all in his later work). Their importance, it is usually argued, requires a precise performance, so their notation must be unambiguous; indeed, Beethoven himself *intended* it to be unambiguous, whatever problems of interpretation we might encounter today.

Annotations such as trill signs in Beethoven's scores are usually seen being just as obligatory as the notes themselves. Two historical performances of the quintet for wind instruments and piano Op. 16 show that Beethoven once altered a composed piece during his own performance, but was furious when somebody else made such an attempt. During his first performance in 1804, Beethoven added a lengthy cadenza before a theme entry in the Rondo, to the entertainment of the listeners (but to the irritation of the accompanying musicians).[2] In another performance in 1816, Carl Czerny was playing the piano. Czerny altered some passagework, using the high octave of the larger piano, and received a rebuke from Beethoven.[3] In contrast to the practice of adding notes to the keyboard music of the Baroque repertoire, there seems to be a general consensus among modern players to be restrictive when playing Beethoven. Apparently Beethoven's *quod licet jovi, non licet bovi* attitude made an impression far beyond Czerny.

The appropriate performance of his trills has, however, remained a matter of argument. Most importantly, the question of trill starting notes has caused disagreement and bewilderment. The discussion is inspired by

[1] William Newman writes: "The trill is used more [than in vocal music] in Beethoven's writing for wind instruments, and considerably more in that for strings. It is never exploited quite so extensively or resourcefully ... as in his most advanced piano writing." William S. Newman, "The Performance of Beethoven's Trills," *Journal of the American Musicological Society* 29/3 (1976): 440. I am here mainly discussing Beethoven's piano music.

[2] Wegeler and Ries, *Biographische Notizen über Beethoven*, 79–80.

[3] Anecdote from 1845 in Czerny, "Die Kunst des Vortrags," commentary, 1.

an awareness of the shift toward main note trills that began some time in the second half of the eighteenth century and was finally formulated as a rule by Hummel in 1828.[4]

Many of the discussions about Beethoven's trills seem, however, to depend on information that is influenced by later, Romantic notions. Some writers argued in the mid-nineteenth century that the current fashion in performance was a better vehicle for meaning than the practice of Beethoven's day, because it linked the masterpieces to the taste of the current public. In 1842, in a chapter called "On the correct performance of the complete works for piano solo by Beethoven," Carl Czerny wrote:

Through the changing spirit of the time, the spiritual perception [of Beethoven's work] receives a different meaning and it must on occasion be expressed with other means than [were] necessary in those [earlier] times.[5]

Clearly, the term "correct" in Czerny's chapter title does not describe an interest in the stylistic solutions relevant for Beethoven's time, but rather the task of keeping up to date in the musical communication of the meaning that Beethoven's work was accumulating through time. Nevertheless, Czerny's statements are – albeit sometimes reluctantly – admitted to the company of objective first-hand Beethoven sources, even though here he openly disqualifies himself as a bearer of indisputable information on performance practice.

When Adolf Bernhard Marx published his *Anleitung zum Vortrag Beethovenscher Klavierwerke* in 1863, the concept of meaning and understanding, as opposed to a "purely theoretical education," had become an important aspect of Beethoven reception and interpretation.[6] The performance practice of his works was, at best, seen as only one possible element of "understanding works of art by [understanding] the nature and the life of their creator."[7] Marx discusses the reconciliation of "understanding, technical mastery, the objective content of the work, and the subjective mood and disposition of the performer," under the general rule of the latter's "maturity."[8] In the end, Marx's book turns out to be less the promised *Vortragslehre* than a pianist's guide to depth as seen from a subjective mid-nineteenth-century standpoint.

On the other hand, Franz Kullak's essay from 1881 about the performance of Beethoven's trills could be described as an attempt to reconcile the "purely theoretical education" which Marx argued against with practical "mature" late nineteenth-century musicianship.[9] It is the first true study of

---

[4] Johann Nepomuk Hummel, *Anweisung zum Pianoforte-Spiele 1826*, Straubenhardt: Zimmermann, 1989, 394. A summary of the "Evolution of the trill start" can be found in Rosenblum, *Performance Practices in Classic Piano Music*, 241–4.

[5] Czerny, "Erinnerungen aus meinem Leben," 26.

[6] Marx, *Anleitung zum Vortrag Beethovenscher Klavierwerke*, 34.

[7] *Ibid.*, introduction to the first edition.   [8] *Ibid.*, 122.   [9] Kullak, "Über den Triller."

performance practice with regard to Beethoven's trills. Kullak concentrates on collecting and understanding historical information, and on finding contrasts and contradictions in the sources.

However, Kullak fails to address the question of how important the individual rules in eighteenth-century tutors were in their time, and he does not discuss the possibility that some of those rules might not be relevant for Beethoven. Perhaps in reaction to Kullak's apparent unawareness of these problems, many later writers about Beethoven's trills have been reluctant to use historical tutors for more than an occasional convenient reference. One exception is Shin Augustinus Kojima's article from 1977, which juxtaposes tutors' rules with musical examples from fifty-one of Beethoven's works for piano.[10] According to Kojima, Clementi's influence on Beethoven caused a change in his trills after 1802. In his analysis of Beethoven's trill practice before that date, Kojima generally refers to eighteenth-century practice.

To many other writers, Beethoven's work and the directly surrounding evidence remain central. This approach shapes, for example, William Newman's article about the performance of Beethoven's trills and the ensuing controversy with Robert Winter.[11] We find similar approaches in Kenneth Drake's chapter on ornamentation in his book about Beethoven's sonatas and in Sandra Rosenblum's chapter on Beethoven's trill starts (as a part of a rather larger body of collected source information on embellishment practice during the Classical period).[12]

The biggest problem for anyone dealing with this topic is the impossibility of explaining systems from within. Trill signs are shorthand and their proper execution is principally based on the ability to read that shorthand. If one suggests that the rules were just changing, while at the same time trying to interpret trill signs by analyzing consistency, analogy, and deviations in the shorthand of the scores, the likelihood of achieving verifiable results becomes very small, as Franz Kullak already regretted.[13] Rather, the chances are much greater that the outcome of the study merely reflects the values fed into the system at the beginning.

One factor that makes many scholars doubt the relevance of general contemporary evidence, such as the tutors invariably provide, is Beethoven's own character and his refusal to fit into categories, both as a person

---

[10] Shin Augustinus Kojima, "Über die Ausführung der Verzierungen in Beethovens Klaviermusik," in Rudolf Klein, ed., *Beethoven Kolloquium*, Kassel: Bärenreiter, 1977, 140–53.

[11] Newman, "The Performance of Beethoven's Trills"; Robert Winter, "Second thoughts on the performance of Beethoven's trills," *The Musical Quarterly* 63/4 (1977): 483–504; William S. Newman, "Second and one-half thoughts on the performance of Beethoven's trills," *The Musical Quarterly* 64/1 (1978): 98–103; Robert Winter, "And Even more Thoughts on the Beethoven Trill …," *The Musical Quarterly* 65/1 (1979): 111–16; and the relevant chapters in Newman, *Beethoven on Beethoven*.

[12] Kenneth Drake, *The Beethoven Sonatas and the Creative Experience*, Bloomington: Indiana University Press, 1994, 164–95; Rosenblum, *Performance Practices in Classic Piano Music*, 250–5.

[13] Kullak, "Über den Triller," xii.

and as a composer. Newman interprets Beethoven's reaction during a discussion with Ferdinand Ries about parallel fifths as proof that Beethoven was opposed to conventions in general. "In effect," Newman writes, "Beethoven … respond[ed] 'Who makes the rules!'" This phrase recurs several times in Newman's work as if it was actually a quotation.[14]

Winter, too, concludes his response to Newman, which explains a theory about Beethoven's "apparent conception of the trill" being based on the "principle of strong-beat dissonance," with a remark of a similar gist. He writes, "Nothing … suggests that the composer applied this guide with the zeal of a Baroque theorist, for such an interpretation would misconstrue Beethoven's understanding of ornamentation – we need no more antihistory." This statement is in fact unhelpful for *our* understanding of Beethoven's ornamentation. In order to justify the joint appearance of the writer *about* music (the "theorist"), the writer *of* music (the composer), and the modern historian's "guides" in an account of any verisimilitude, we first need to know how they should be characterized and how they should interact.

Most importantly, the status and the self-image of the theorist, and the appropriate manner of applying rules or "guides," are by no means automatically defined. The characterization of the "zealous theorist" is a reminder of the unease felt by nineteenth-century scholars in relation to the tutors of the eighteenth century, rather than a faithful description. In an article about ornamentation from 1979, Peter Schleuning has drawn our attention to Franz Kroll's preface to the 1866 edition of J. S. Bach's *Wohltemperiertes Klavier*, which, in Schleuning's words, was the "first comprehensive description of the ornamentation of a defined period of earlier music." Kroll's judgment of eighteenth-century tutors such as C. P. E. Bach was harsh. He attacked them for their dogmatism, for making "insufficient" or even "absurd" rules and "mystic principles," and for their "greatly twisted and no less than stringent" ideas.[15]

Most important in Schleuning's discussion is the fact that we learn about the long-lasting result of Kroll's bewilderment with eighteenth-century music theory. In apparent frustration with the "dogmatic" but "absurd" historical writers, Kroll took stringency into his own hands and formulated his own list of rules of exception for the eighteenth-century rule of the upper note trill.

The trill had to start from the main note 1) at a "leap to a distant interval or an interval in another key"; 2) if otherwise "a dissonant against another part arises"; 3)

---

[14] Newman, "The performance of Beethoven's trills," 445; Newman, *Beethoven on Beethoven*, 192, 302. See also Wegeler and Ries, *Biographische Notizen über Beethoven*, 87.

[15] Peter Schleuning, *Verzierungsforschung und Aufführungspraxis. Zum Verhältnis von Notation und Interpretation in der Musik des 18. Jahrhunderts*, Basler Jahrbuch für historische Aufführungspraxis, vol. III, Winterthur: Amadeus, 1979, 15–16.

if a "sudden occurrence in *medias res*" takes place; 4) in "chromatic progressions"; 5) at the "beginning of a piece"; and 6) at a "repetition of the same note."[16]

This list, Schleuning writes, "was quoted in embellishment scholarship for a long time – always without mentioning Kroll – and this is the reason why it solidified into the very thing that Kroll had intended to fight, namely an arsenal of unquestioned rules."[17] Remnants of these rules keep turning up in most contributions to the discussion about Beethoven's trills on all levels, and even today they still obscure the connection between the practices of Beethoven's time and Beethoven's own practice.

Most of the theorists of the eighteenth century openly stated the ambiguities of embellishment practice and often provided proof of their flexibility.[18] C. P. E. Bach writes:

As I am not aware of any predecessor in this difficult task [i.e. of describing the embellishments and indicating their appropriate placement], who would have prepared this slippery path for me, nobody will blame me for believing that in spite of some clearly defined cases there might also perhaps be a possibility for an exception.[19]

Friedrich Wilhelm Marpurg, whose keyboard method is often characterized as especially rigid, writes about the variability of an appropriate and tasteful practice in the following passage:

It is impossible to develop rules that can be applied to all possible cases, as long as music is an inexhaustible ocean of options, and one person has in part a different feeling from another. One can test this by giving a piece of music, without embellishments indicated, to ten different people, all of whom play according to the good taste of the time, and ask them to add their own embellishments. In certain cases, many might perhaps agree; in others, however, they will all disagree. Each person will add these different embellishments according to his own particular taste; one will have more, the other less; one will use a trill where another has a turn, one will use an appoggiatura where another asks for a mordent, or vice versa.[20]

---

[16] Franz Kroll, ed., *Joh. Seb. Bachs Clavierwerke, 3. Bd. Das Wohltemperierte Clavier*, Leipzig: C. F. Peters, 1866, xxx, quoted in Schleuning, *Verzierungsforschung und Aufführungspraxis*, 16.

[17] Schleuning, *Verzierungsforschung und Aufführungspraxis*, 16.

[18] I disagree with Frederik Neumann, who contrasts the cautioning attitude of the early Baroque French writers toward giving embellishment rules with what he calls an atmosphere of "ultimate hardening" created by the "Berlin disciplinarians," i.e. C. P. E. Bach, Agricola, and Marpurg (see, for instance, Frederik Neumann, *Ornamentation in Baroque and Post-Baroque Music*, Princeton University Press, 1978, 365).

[19] Bach, *Versuch über die wahre Art, das Clavier zu spielen*, part 1, 55, § 12. There were in fact predecessors of Bach's careful and flexible attitude: Johann Mattheson writes that not much can be said about the *Manieren*, since they do not depend on rules alone, but are rather a result of practice, exercise, and experience. In addition, Mattheson quotes a whole paragraph by Heinichen, who shares his view and writes, in accordance with Bach, "The *Manieren* and musical embellishments are countless, and they change according to the taste (of everyone) and (individual) experience." Johann Mattheson, *Der vollkommene Capellmeister 1739*, ed. Margarethe Reimann, Kassel: Bärenreiter, 1954, 112, § 18 and 19.

[20] Marpurg, *Anleitung zum Clavierspielen*, 44, § 3.

Apart from providing another example of the open-minded, practical attitude of an eighteenth-century theorist, Marpurg reveals here that a "rule" is something more, or even something different, than a teaching tool. It must, as we learn, first be "developed" – that is, it is the result of collecting facts and examples, of a sorting process, and of some kind of compression or simplification. Moreover, it must be designed to apply to as many "cases as possible." A rule is thus a compact, organized description of existing practice, shorthand and nameplate in one. Marpurg acknowledges that this act of collecting, sorting, and reducing remains inadequate because reality, or existing practice, is more diverse than its reflection in the rules. Existing practice is in fact "inexhaustible." So although the aim of methods such as Marpurg's *is* undeniably pedagogical, the authority of the rules that appear within such a method is often weakened by their character as a processed, reduced, and organized picture of real musical practice.

In view of the many similar careful introductions and reflections by eighteenth-century theorists, any quick judgments about any of these authors, no matter whether we find their information "insufficient," "absurd," or "mystic," or call them, in contrast to the creative composer, zealous "baroque theorists," are not merely unhelpful, they even help to obscure the very issues we seek to learn to understand. How much variation did the general praxis of musical embellishment permit in the German-speaking countries during the latter half of the eighteenth century? Which topics were seen as important, which details led to controversy, and what was at various times considered "modern"?

The trill start discussion of the nineteenth century cannot give any answers here, first of all because it resulted in controversy in its own time. Moreover, it is often unclear whether this discussion represents nineteenth-century practice, or reflects historical thinking and addresses older music. Even some rather late defenses of the upper-note trill (that is, late for those who claim that Hummel's main-note trill rule of 1828 was the *end* of a development) are not necessarily historically informed, but were meant to influence contemporary Romantic practice. Ernst David Wagner, for example, wrote in 1869 that the main-note trill "does not sound" and that Hummel's and Czerny's main-note practice was, among other things, a "backward step" and "superficial."[21] The lineage of an upper-note preference continues for an unexpectedly long time: the eighteen-volume-strong *Meyers Konversations=Lexikon* from 1897 gives the following explanation of the trill:

The trill is a prolonged alternation of the (notated) main note and its (major or minor) upper second, and it begins as a rule on the upper note and ends on the

---

[21] Ernst David Wagner, *Musikalische Ornamentik oder die wesentlichen Verzierungs-Manieren im Vortrage der Vokal- und Instrumental-Musik*, Berlin: Schlesinger, 1869, 167–8, 185, quoted in Schleuning, *Verzierungsforschung und Aufführungspraxis*, 18.

main note, usually after touching upon the lower auxiliary once (the so-called *Nachschlag*) … In his piano school Hummel has suggested starting the trill on the main note, which has often been accepted in piano music, but has no validity at all for the works of the Classical composers.[22]

However, the remainder of this entry describes separate practices for newer piano music and (general) classical music, and care is taken not to condemn the main note trill as such. One might assume that even Kullak had a similar opinion.

The flexibility of eighteenth-century embellishment practice seems difficult to grasp even today. When we challenge the few well-known French or the French-influenced German keyboard tutors of the eighteenth century by using other contemporary information, we cannot maintain that the upper-note trill was a generally accepted preference throughout the period.[23] A certain degree of inconsistency was apparently characteristic for that time. This is, for example, evident in two preserved musical clocks from 1792 and 1793 made by Haydn's friend and student Primitivus Niemecz, and in one undated clock attributed to Joseph Gurck, an apprentice of Niemecz. The trill starts in Haydn's pieces on these clocks are largely arbitrary. In some pieces, for example, longer trills would start on the main note and short ones with the auxiliary, suggesting that there was a system. However, in other pieces the long trills also begin with the auxiliary, while some short trills begin with the main note. Trills on I_4^6 sometimes begin with the auxiliary, suggesting a standard appoggiatura function, but sometimes even these trills begin with the main note. According to the literature, the trill solutions sometimes differ in identical pieces on different organ clocks.[24]

Such information has, in a somewhat belated reaction to the evidence produced by Frederik Neumann, recently inspired a new type of relativism in scholars' conclusions about late Baroque and Classical embellishment practice.[25] Clive Brown, for instance, presents various historical opinions and modern assertions about possible starting-note preferences and the degree of variation in late eighteenth-century practice. However, after quoting several recommendations or rules of thumb for practical trill solutions by nineteenth and twentieth-century writers, he ends with these words: "It may be legitimate to maintain a degree of skepticism about assuming too readily that what seems musical and tasteful to us in these matters would necessarily have done so to musicians of previous

[22] *Meyers Konversations=Lexikon*, Leipzig and Vienna: Bibliographisches Institut, 1896, vol. XVI, 1029, entry "Triller."
[23] See Clive Brown, *Classical & Romantic Performing Practice 1750–1900*, Oxford University Press, 1999, 493.
[24] See Rosenblum, *Performance Practices in Classic Piano Music*, 243, and Brown, *Classical & Romantic Performing Practice 1750–1900*, 494–5.
[25] Neumann, *Ornamentation in Baroque and Post-Baroque Music*.

generations."[26] In view of several efforts in the literature to solve ornamentation issues by force, this remains a valid reservation.[27]

When discussing Beethoven's use of embellishment symbols, we are again confronted with the problem that we know too little of his opinion about the information given in the keyboard methods. One solution to this puzzle would be to show that passages such as the following one would certainly have encouraged a young, determined, and unconventional Beethoven to find his own way. In this thoughtful paragraph, C. P. E. Bach discusses the possibility of new influences and gives his view on the dynamics of "taste":

Since the embellishments and the manner of using them form a major contribution to refined taste, one should neither be too fickle and accept any new *Manier* right away without further scrutiny, no matter who is proposing it, nor should one possess too many preconceptions about oneself and one's taste so that, out of stubbornness, one refuses to accept anything unknown. A critical examination is certainly necessary before accepting something unfamiliar, and it may well happen in time that good taste through the introduction of unnatural novelties becomes as rare as science.[28] But although one must not be the first, one should also not be the last in following certain new embellishments, in order to avoid going out of fashion. One must pay no attention if they do not always taste well at the beginning. As appealing as novelty sometimes may seem, it can be just as repelling at other times. The latter often proves the quality of something that afterwards lasts longer than other things that initially please all too much. Such things are usually exploited so much that they soon become unbearable.[29]

This statement and the one by Marpurg quoted above suggest that there was no contradiction between the recommendations in these books and Beethoven's ambition. But even if Beethoven was acquainted early on with parts of C. P. E. Bach's or Marpurg's methods, we do not know what he thought about the musings of these authors. Although, through

[26] Brown, *Classical & Romantic Performing Practice 1750–1900*, 497.

[27] Frederik Neumann (Frederik Neumann, *Improvisation and Ornamentation in Mozart*, Princeton University Press, 1986, 114, quoted in Brown, *Classical & Romantic Performing Practice 1750–1900*, 497) provides a general system for finding the proper trill by first leaving out the trill, asking which kind of appoggiatura shape might be a "desirable addition to the bare melody," and then adding the corresponding type of trill. Neumann concludes: "Where none of these ornaments fit, the main-note trill is indicated."

   Kenneth Drake writes: "A preference for beginning the trill on the main note seems stronger." Drake, *The Beethoven Sonatas and the Creative Experience*, 166.

   Siegbert Rampe, claims the opposite: "Right into the 19th century, the trill began generally with the upper note (including the music of Ludwig van Beethoven) in the German-speaking countries." Rampe, *Mozarts Claviermusik*, 195.

[28] Or "knowledge." It remains unclear what Bach had in mind with this side-thought.

[29] Bach, *Versuch über die wahre Art, das Clavier zu spielen*, part 1, 60–1, § 27. When the text was conceived, its fame had yet to be established. Like Couperin, Bach uses his keyboard method not only to teach contemporary practice, but also to introduce some "embellishments of his own," thus offering a single eighteenth-century view. He acknowledges that some readers might not approve of his embellishments and advises against being biased in matters of style (Bach, *Versuch über die wahre Art, das Clavier zu spielen*, part 1, 59–60, § 26).

analysis, we can understand the practical attitude of various writers, their involvement with their musical surroundings, and – as in Marpurg's example – their awareness of the limitations of theoretical writing, Beethoven's connection to their message can only in rare cases be shown in detail.[30]

On the other hand, the fact of his connection to *his* musical surroundings naturally needs no further discussion. That Beethoven was concerned with providing a complete expressive notation can clearly be seen in his first Viennese works. The usual idea is that he preferred one way of notating his ornaments, and that the inconsistencies within this practice represent imprecision and deviations that occasionally result in contradictions. Scholars have disagreed about what "rules," "exceptions," and "inconsistencies" in Beethoven's notation actually are, but the idea that he adhered to one specific practice and only occasionally deviated from it seems to be accepted by all.

In the following, the issue of consistency will get ample attention. In addition to assessing some common interpretations of Beethoven's trill notation, I will provide an alternative explanation for some of the trills in Beethoven's music that seem difficult to solve. In an "inexhaustible ocean of options," as Marpurg called music, choices of ornamentation and notation were very likely made at *all* levels of importance and focus, instead of being an abundance of options at one level. Even for a Classical composer who perhaps had a stricter idea of notation than Baroque musicians, the choice of an embellishment was probably in some cases less vital than in others. This would naturally have resulted in various, perhaps even intentional levels of notational imprecision. Before investigating that question, however, I will review how Beethoven's practice of notating embellishments developed.

BEETHOVEN'S EARLY NOTATION OF TRILLS

Not surprisingly, the development of Beethoven's embellishment practice appears most clearly in his few very early compositions. Like other aspects of his music writing, his practice of indicating embellishments soon stabilized despite some persistent idiosyncrasies, but the early works give at least a little insight into his learning process.

The young Beethoven's first basic concern would have been to apply the symbols for ornaments in the correct way and in the appropriate places. Most of the tutors, and certainly Bach's *Versuch*, show great concern for the correct application of the ornaments. The tasteful, or occasionally even "correct," placement of the embellishments in a composition was least as important as their appropriate execution. This emphasis on notation had its

---

[30] See Richard Kramer, "Notes to Beethoven's education," *Journal of the American Musicological Society* 28 (1975): 72–101.

origin in an inconsistent practice. There is great variation in both the style
and consistency of the notation of ornaments in eighteenth-century music.
Miklòs Spànyi writes:

In 18th century music two different methods of indicating the ornaments were
used. According to one the various ornaments were marked with different, specific
signs. In the other, less "precise" notation only a few general markings were used
which could mean – depending on the musical context and traditions – a number
of different ornaments.[31]

After an explanation of the precise notation with the help of examples
from Bach's *Versuch*, Spànyi explains the "less precise" one in which a
variety of signs is used to indicate various kinds of ornaments (a practice
apparent, for instance, in the early works of C. P. E. Bach and in many
contemporary transcriptions of J. S. Bach's works), and adds:

*It is very important to remember that a transitional, hybrid notation of ornaments is
also possible and was often adopted by C. P. E. Bach in many of his later works, too.
Precision of the notation of ornaments may thus vary from one composition to another*
[italics original].[32]

Spànyi's observation that even C. P. E. Bach's own later notation occasionally disagrees with the principles of his *Versuch* is accurate and can be
verified from many of Bach's manuscripts.[33] However, Spànyi's choice of
the word "method" and his idea of a precise/imprecise dichotomy create
the impression of deliberate, exchangeable practices. The imprecise notation of embellishments could in fact be caused by any number of things,
including an ill-trained composer's lack of practice, a faulty rendering by
an unconcerned or unobservant engraver, or a composer's simple lack of
concern with consistency. In other words, imprecise notation is characterized by the fact that a method does not actually exist. Sometimes a
hybrid notation also occurs within single pieces. This could result from
mere lack of concern or from the ill-informed use of single features
within an otherwise consistent notation, but perhaps also from a deliberate
differentiation of the indications depending on their importance to the
composer. The last possibility will be one of my concerns here.

In Beethoven's very early works, of which no autographs survive,
we do not know how much influence his teacher Neefe or the engraver
had on the final appearance of the piece. When discussing the trills in
Beethoven's first known work, the Variations on a March by Dressler
WoO 63 (originally published in 1782), this is hardly a point of great
consequence. The Dressler Variations contain relatively few trills. Apart
from various appoggiaturas in small notes, we find only eight trill signs

[31] Miklòs Spànyi, "Concerning the ornaments in Carl Philipp Emanuel Bach's keyboard music," in *Carl
Philipp Emanuel Bach: Sämtliche Klavierwerke*, I, Budapest: Könemann Music, 1999, 156.
[32] *Ibid.*, 158.   [33] My thanks to Ludger Rémy for his advice.

(indicated as *tr.*) and six turns (∾), all in uncontroversial contexts. The only interesting feature, an obviously misplaced turn in bar 7 of the theme, was corrected in a later edition and might have been a misprint in the first edition rather than a mistake made by Beethoven. Two other turns in bars 5 and 6 of the theme were slightly re-aligned in the later version (obviously for clarity).

In the sonatas WoO 47, Beethoven employs four signs to indicate an embellishment: the short trill sign ⤳, the ordinary trill *tr.*, one turn ∾, and one mordent ⤳. Of these, only the *tr.* sign is applied consistently in the relatively few longer trills (some of which are cadential trills with a written-out turn in small notes).[34] In these sonatas, Beethoven's preferred notation for a trill on the strong beat of a $^6_4 - ^5_3$ progression and on the weak-beat resolution to the dominant in I^6_4–V–I progressions (for example, in sonata 3, mvt. 2, theme, bar 7) is the ordinary trill sign *tr.* (instead of ⤳).[35] Another specific application of *tr.* appears on the weak beats in broken chord figures in quarter notes (sonata 2, mvt. 1, second subject, bars 17–18 and – slightly altered – in bars 69–70). The majority of these instances allow for an interpretation of the *tr.* sign as a full trill (i.e. started with the auxiliary note) with a turn. The shortest form of this trill is ♫♫♫. The position of these signs in the music and this interpretation are, given the German practice of the time, largely uncontroversial. However, it seems clear that, at this stage, Beethoven was not aware of C. P. E. Bach's distinction between a shorter trill symbol ⤳ and a longer one ⤳⤳, or that he was disregarding this distinction.[36]

However, in I^6_4–V half-cadences with a trill on the strong beat, both signs are used, apparently without any intended difference of execution. Otherwise, ⤳ is applied throughout these sonatas in a variety of contexts. The latter could mean that the single mordent ⤳ in sonata 3, mvt. 2, bar 4, which is somewhat awkwardly placed, is an engraver's misreading. However, the other sign to appear only once, a single turn ∾ in sonata 2, mvt. 1, bar 14, gives a specific character to the first phrase of a sequence and hence seems to be intentional in spite of its occurring only once.[37]

The ⤳ symbol appears on weak and strong beats at moderate tempos (Example 8.1); on off-beat beginnings of quicker groups (Example 8.2); in the context of slow tone repetition; and on harmonically stable downbeats. Its application in dotted, signal-like motives, such as at the beginning of the development of the opening movement of the first sonata, seems slightly unorthodox (Example 8.3):

---

[34] Sometimes these small notes are missing compared to parallel instances.

[35] In Beethoven's handwriting, the distinction between ⤳ and ⤳ is always clear, so the possibility that inconsistencies in editions of his music are based on misread handwritten signs is unlikely.

[36] Marpurg writes that this distinction is unnecessary. Marpurg, *Anleitung zum Clavierspielen*, 54, §4.

[37] One modern *Urtext* edition corrects this ∾ to ⤳ for no apparent reason but leaves the mordent ⤳ unaltered.

Example 8.1. Sonata in F minor WoO 47/2, mvt. 2, Andante, bar 26 (transcription after Bossler, 1783)

Example 8.2. Sonata in E flat major WoO 47/1, mvt. 2, Andante, bar 45, right hand (transcription after Bossler, 1783)

Example 8.3. Sonata in E flat major WoO 47/1, mvt. 1, Allegro cantabile, bars 30–1 (transcription after Bossler, 1783)

Beethoven's annotations in his personal copy of the sonatas provide little information about his ideas of trill notation.[38] In contrast to the many articulation marks and fingerings he added later, in only three cases was his attention drawn to the embellishments. Once he marked a missing appoggiatura in the left hand of an *unisono* passage, once he added an obviously missing *tr.* and once he put a cross near a misleadingly placed ⁓ sign.[39] Since he left rather a lot of similar places uncommented, one can conclude that the trills were obviously not Beethoven's main concern when he worked through the edition of the sonata. Thus, Beethoven did not correct even the most obvious inconsistencies in the placement of the embellishment signs, although, from the intensity of other annotations on the same pages, we can suppose that they did not remain unobserved. This circumstance suggests that he was, at the time the sonatas were being published (and possibly still at the moment when

---

[38] For a description of Beethoven's *Handexemplar* of WoO 47, see Ladenburger, "Der junge Beethoven – Komponist und Pianist," 111–12.

[39] Beethoven pointed out thirty-nine places of interest and inconsistencies on the first nine pages of the edition by means of crosses.

he annotated them), not actively working with the embellishment systems of any of the known tutors.

THE EVOLUTION AND THE PERFORMANCE OF THE SHORT TRILL SYMBOL IN BEETHOVEN'S WORK

William Newman writes that the short trill sign ∿ stands for "less than 10 percent of Beethoven's trills, most of that portion being concentrated in his early works." According to Newman, this sign had "one, unequivocal sense" as a substitute for a main-note–auxiliary-note–main-note shake ♫. This conclusion is apparently based on Beethoven's nearly consistent manner of notating it.[40] The objective of the following discussion is to challenge Newman's claim that the execution of Beethoven's short trill sign was unequivocal. As I will show, Beethoven's use of this sign did indeed eventually become restricted to a very narrow range of musical contexts. But neither the history of its interpretation in the eighteenth century nor Beethoven's early use of the sign are straightforward enough to justify a decision about its indisputable meaning.

Newman apparently did not include the sonatas WoO 47 in his statistics. As I have discussed, Beethoven used the short trill sign in various ways in these pieces. Around 60 percent of the trills in the pieces are represented by this sign. Two instances are of special interest, first of all since they both represent Beethoven's later consistent placement of the trill sign ∿ on a good beat, and also because Beethoven wrote fingerings for them. These fingerings prove that, at the time, Beethoven had not yet clearly defined the execution of the short trill. In bar 56 of the Andante of the second sonata, the fingerings suggest a short upper-note trill ♫ played with fingers 4 and 3 (Example 8.4). In contrast, Beethoven's right-hand fingering of the Finale theme of the same sonata suggests a different execution of the short trill (Example 8.5).

If we assume that the fingers 4 and 2 indeed indicate the fingers that start the trills, Example 8.5 allows for no other solution than the one that Newman actually suggests. One would have to perform a

Example 8.4. Sonata in F minor WoO 47/2, mvt. 2, Andante, bar 56 (transcription after Beethoven's *Handexemplar*)

---

[40] Newman, "The performance of Beethoven's trills," 449–50.

Example 8.5. Sonata in F minor WoO 47/2, mvt. 3, Presto, bars 1–4 (transcription after
Beethoven's *Handexemplar*)

main-note–auxiliary–main-note shake ♩♩♩ using 4–5–4 in the first case
and 2–3–2 in the others. It would be impossible to make upper-note trills
with 4–3 and 2–1 because the fingers 3 and 1 that follow the trilled note
would already be occupied.

These fingerings, as well as the appearance of the short trill throughout
WoO 47 in varying musical contexts, suggest that, early on, Beethoven
used this sign to indicate the application of various sorts of embellishments. So we are, at this stage, not discussing various realizations of one
kind of trill. The downbeat shake ♩♩♩ that Newman describes is only
one of these options, the trill from above without a turn ♩♩♩ is
another. Other occurrences (such as all the off-beat trills in my earlier
examples) seem in fact to be best served with a plain turn. Others again,
especially in passages where ⁓ and *tr.* are mixed, might require a full trill
with a turn.

Beethoven's placement of the short trill symbol became noticeably
more standardized shortly after the publication of the Sonatas WoO 47.
In the piano part of his early Concerto in E flat major (WoO 4 from 1784),
in the three Piano Quartets WoO 36, in the Trio WoO 37, as well as in the
surviving early sketches, Beethoven uses this sign in a manner consistent
with the better-known Sonatas Op. 2 and other works from his first
decade in Vienna. The ⁓ now predominantly appears in only one
context. This is a strong-beat trill on the first note of a downward
stepwise figure; the placement of the sign as shown in Examples 8.4 and
8.5 was the one that survived. Such trills can be dissonant (Piano Sonata
Op. 13, mvt. 1, bars 81–2, and parallel spots) or consonant (Piano Concerto
Op. 15, mvt. 1, bars 358–9).

At first it seems complicated to relate this strong-beat placement of
Beethoven's short trill signs to the trill discussion of his time. Discussions
about the *Pralltriller*, or *Halbtriller*, usually expressed with the sign ⁓,
appear in the majority of eighteenth-century keyboard tutors. The most
common application of the *Pralltriller*, however, is on the *second, unaccented* note of a downward resolution, or *Abzug* (or on the third note in
a group of four notes with an accented beginning if the second and third

notes or the last three notes are slurred). C. P. E. Bach, Marpurg, Löhlein (1773), Hiller (1780), Koch (1802), Clementi (1801/1803), and Müller (1804) all describe this *Abzug* short trill in various ways.[41] In this unaccented context the *Pralltriller* assumes a shape that resembles an inverted mordent, or a single upward shake starting with the main note (historical authors occasionally failed to agree entirely about this definition and the placement of the notes; I am addressing the basic shape here).[42]

If the main-note *Pralltriller*, however, occurs "suddenly," as Marpurg puts it[43] – that is, on a downbeat or a good beat – it had, in German practice, to be indicated by small notes. Bach calls this trill a *Schneller* and gives the definition of its shape as a "short mordent in contrary motion."[44] Marpurg and Türk accept this term and agree that it is expressed in small notes only, since a proper sign for this embellishment does not exist.

On the other hand, Türk points out that, instead of writing small notes, composers sometimes put a ⟋ sign where the *Schneller* would belong – that is, on accented beginnings of a figure. He demonstrates this "exception" with printed excerpts from compositions by Bach and others, and whimsically leaves the judgment of this "crime" to the critics.[45] This is in fact the placement that Beethoven eventually adopted for this sign. Even Neefe, in his sonatas from 1773, occasionally writes the ⟋ sign on strong beats instead of an *Abzug*.

Naturally, Türk's music examples are only of limited help for understanding the execution of this sign, because he reproduces them with the *Pralltriller* sign and not with a written-out example. Türk's observation must have been based on his experience of similar passages played in the way he describes. We must believe him when he says that they were actually performed as an inverted mordent (and not as a short upper-note trill). It seems, then, that in 1789, when Türk published the first edition of his *Klavierschule*, the practice had begun to establish itself of performing the *Pralltriller* sign ⟋ in such a manner that it in fact sounded like a *Schneller*. This is consistent with Beethoven's fingerings in Example 8.5 but not with Example 8.4.

[41] Bach, *Versuch über die wahre Art, das Clavier zu spielen*, part 1, 81 § 30; Marpurg, *Anleitung zum Clavierspielen*, 56, § 8 Anmerkung 2 and Tab. V 1–4; Georg Simon Löhlein, *Klavier=Schule*, Leipzig: Waisenhaus= und Fromannische Buchhandlung, 1773, 15, § 4, 4th example; Johann Adam Hiller, *Anweisung zum musikalisch=zierlichen Gesange*, Leipzig: Johann Friedrich Junius, 1780, 69–70, § 24, examples b and c; Heinrich Christoph Koch, *Musikalisches Lexikon 1802*, Kassel: Bärenreiter, 2001, 1592; Clementi, *Méthode pour le Piano Forte*, 11, line 4, 2nd example; August Eberhard Müller, *Fortepiano=Schule*, Leipzig: Carl Friedrich Peters, 1804, 282, § 19.
[42] Bach, *Versuch über die wahre Art, das Clavier zu spielen*, part 1, 81–4, § 30–6, and Tab. IV, Figs. XLV–XLIX. See Example 8.17 and my discussion below. It would seem that, in Bach's example Tab. IV, Fig. XLV, a tie between the first two notes was forgotten; however, one cannot be too sure about this. In French music of the time, the trill could have been played in either manner.
[43] Marpurg, *Anleitung zum Clavierspielen*, 57, § 8, Anmerkung 3.
[44] Bach, *Versuch über die wahre Art, das Clavier zu spielen*, part 1 section 8, 111–12.
[45] Türk, *Klavierschule*, 273–4, § 57.

Example 8.6. Klavier Quartet in C major WoO 36/3, mvt. 1, Allegro vivace, keyboard
part, bars 37–8 (autograph)[46]

Example 8.7. Sonata in C major Op. 2/3, mvt. 1, Allegro con brio, bars 37–8 (Artaria, 1796)

This practice contrasts, however, with an alternative way of playing
downbeat short trills in quick tempi, which Bach explains as follows: "In
a very fast tempo, one can sometimes, by means of appoggiaturas, comfort-
ably realize an alternative to a trill." Bach's accompanying example
shows the replacement of a trill on an eighth note with a sixteenth-note
appoggiatura.[47] It seems that Beethoven was aware of this practice as
well. In a passage from the first movement of the Klavier Quartet WoO
36/3 from 1785, Beethoven wrote a short trill (Example 8.6).

When he re-used this subject in his Sonata Op. 2/3, he chose to convert
the trill into an appoggiatura, which is equivalent to reducing the trill to
the very issue of later disagreement: its upper note beginning (Example 8.7).
Although a notated appoggiatura in Example 8.7 is in effect a different
embellishment than a trill, it nevertheless shows that an auxiliary start on
this downbeat was acceptable for Beethoven. So this could very well be an
instance where Beethoven chose to notate the effect of a trill shortened into
an appoggiatura, just as Bach had described.[48]

Our view on the further development of Beethoven's practice of treating
the short trill is largely dependent on how we interpret his relationship to
the stylistic changes of his time. Clementi, for example, gives four different
examples of the execution of the short trill in his piano school. He demonstrates both possible placements, the one on the strong beat and the one
on the second note of an *Abzug*. For Clementi, both should begin with

---

[46] Reproduced with the kind permission of the Staatsbibliothek zu Berlin – Preussischer Kulturbesitz.
    Musikabteilung mit Mendelssohn-Archiv. Mus.ms.autogr. Beethoven Artaria 126.
[47] Bach, *Versuch über die wahre Art, das Clavier zu spielen*, part I, 76, § 18, and Tab. IV, Fig. XXIX. Bach
    uses the longer trill symbol in his example, but explicitly talks about a trill in a fast tempo.
[48] See also Drake, *The Beethoven Sonatas and the Creative Experience*, 171–2.

Example 8.8. Clementi's *Méthode pour le Piano Forte* (Pleyel, *c.* 1803), p. 11[49]

Courte Cadence
Commençant par
la note même

Autres espéces
de cadences

Quelquefois indiquée
en petites notes

the main note, giving the trill the shape of an inverted mordent. Clementi also reproduces the alternative notation of the trill in small notes, in the style of Bach's *Schneller* (Example 8.8).

At the end of his life, Beethoven recommended Clementi's method to the young Gerhard von Breuning: "In the end it is still the best."[50] How long Beethoven had favored Clementi's book, and whether this included his approach to embellishments, is, however, unknown.

In a realization of the accented short trill in the finale of the "Tempest" Sonata Op. 31/2 (bars 43–6, 49; 271–4, 277), Carl Czerny uses small notes.[51] In this example, Czerny indicates more or less the same *Schneller* that Türk announced and described in 1789, with the exception of his advice to accentuate the *last* note of the inverted mordent, a remark that later writers have occasionally criticized.[52] At the time when he conceived his *Pianoforte-Schule*, Czerny had begun to favor the main-note trill, which resulted in many inconsistencies, as Kullak demonstrated very early on.[53] Nevertheless, it is quite possible that he remembered such a characteristic example as this passage from Op 31/2 correctly and provided a more or less faithful picture of Beethoven's own practice.

It is in any case possible that, at some point, Beethoven began to prefer a main-note performance of these short strong-beat trills. Initially, however, his fingerings document a mixed practice. It is impossible to know when, or even if, Beethoven ever standardized his execution of the strong-beat short trill that he expressed with the ⁓ sign.

I need to return to Examples 8.6 and 8.7 one more time. Another interpretation of these examples could be that Beethoven changed the expression from a main-note *Schneller* in Example 8.6 into an upper-note appoggiatura in Example 8.7, simply because he intended a completely different effect in Example 8.7. This interpretation would build on the preconception that the trill in Example 8.6 must be started with a main note. But as I have shown, a main-note start for this trill was initially not mandatory for Beethoven, even when he placed the ⁓ sign on a downbeat, so again, we cannot be sure whether this interpretation is correct.

[49] Reproduced with the kind permission of Giuseppe Accardi.
[50] Kerst, *Die Erinnerungen an Beethoven*, vol II, 169.   [51] Czerny, "Die Kunst des Vortrags," 48.
[52] Kullak, "Über den Triller," xxi; Newman, "The performance of Beethoven's trills," 447, 449.
[53] Kullak, "Über den Triller," xx–xxi.

Example 8.9. Sonata in E flat major Op. 7, mvt. 1, Allegro con brio, bars 109–10
(Artaria, 1797)

In order to argue for a single, unequivocal way of playing these trills, one must assume that this way came about together with their increasingly consistent downbeat placement.[54] But this would be an entirely circular argument in that the expected result is used to explain the cause.[55]

In contrast to this last interpretation, one could in many cases experiment with short upper-note trills of the shape ♩♩♩, or in fast passages with appoggiaturas such as in Example 8.7. For example, it is possible to play the downward figure in Example 8.9 with upper-note trills.

The same could apply to the trills in the Sonata Op. 13, mvt. 1, bars 81–2 and other places. These two interpretations have two factors in common, whether as a main-note inverted mordent or as a quick four-note trill with an auxiliary start. First, they are hypothetical. Second, they are both grounded in eighteenth-century practice.

In retrospect, one could easily say that the starting-note issues associated with the short trill sign ∿ were among the most important topics for eighteenth-century musical writers, and that the appearance of this trill sign in Beethoven's music is an early indicator of a "modern" trill preference because the main-note *Pralltriller* was the form that survived in the nineteenth century.[56] However, the general tendency toward main-note trill starts obscures the basic character of the *Pralltriller* as a remnant of an arbitrary practice of indicating embellishments. As such, it was perhaps occasionally welcome because it could be conveniently used in non-crucial circumstances. The variability of contemporary practice alone is confirmation enough that, when Beethoven used this sign, this indicated that he cared little how the performer dealt with it. This in turn leads us to conclude that a decision about the correct execution of Beethoven's small downbeat trill is not possible.

---

[54] Kojima, "Über die Ausführung der Verzierungen in Beethovens Klaviermusik," 145.

[55] It is, therefore, not correct to call Beethoven's short trill a *Schneller*, as Newman did (Newman, "The performance of Beethoven's trills," 446). This word indicates that a decision about the execution of this trill has already been made.

[56] In contrast, Frederik Neumann sees late eighteenth-century main-note trills as "the same old stream of the Italo-German tradition that never ceased to flow during the 17th and 18th centuries." Neumann, *Ornamentation in Baroque and Post-Baroque Music*, 386.

THE TRILLED TURN AND THE TURN
BETWEEN TWO NOTES

A new element in Beethoven's notation in the compositions from 1784 to 1785 is the compound sign of a turn and a short trill ℛ. Beethoven added this sign three times in the right hand in bar 60 of the second movement of the Concerto WoO 4 (Example 8.10).[57]

In the Adagio introduction of the E flat major Quartet WoO 36/1, Beethoven applies the same sign to the first note of a passage in thirty-second notes (Example 8.11) and at two consecutive points with similar figurations in bars 12 and 14.

In contrast to the example from the concerto, the sign here is not placed on a turn-like melody. Elsewhere in the quartets, the same sign appears over similar figurations, but also on isolated quarter notes that function as an upbeat (WoO 36/3, mvt. 1, bar 23), on the second of two repeated eighth notes (*ibid.*, bar 84), and on the second of four sixteenth notes (WoO 36/2, violin and viola parts, bar 8). Beethoven used this sign sporadically even in later works such as Op. 54 and Op. 78.

Example 8.10. Concerto in E flat major WoO 4, mvt. 2, Larghetto, bar 60[58]

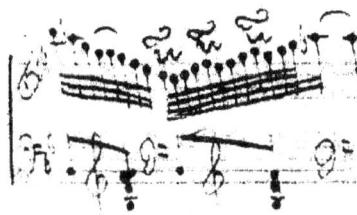

Example 8.11. Klavier Quartet in E flat major WoO 36/1, mvt. 1, Adagio assai, keyboard part, bar 10 (autograph)[59]

[57] Even at a cursory glance it is clear that its placement in this particular example is redundant, because the notes shape a turn in themselves. In other places in the concerto, the trills on similar figures are notated only with the *Pralltriller* sign ⁓.
[58] Reproduced with the kind permission of the Staatsbibliothek zu Berlin – Preussischer Kulturbesitz. Musikabteilung mit Mendelssohn-Archiv. Mus.ms.autogr. Beethoven Artaria 125.
[59] Reproduced with the kind permission of the Staatsbibliothek zu Berlin – Preussischer Kulturbesitz. Musikabteilung mit Mendelssohn-Archiv. Mus.ms.autogr. Beethoven Artaria 126.

Referring to the example from the quartet (Example 8.11), Kojima writes that Beethoven "at that time already used the sign for the *prallender Doppelschlag* ∾ only in the sense of a double turn that is based on the note itself, without a preceding appoggiatura, in contrast to the theoretical writings and [the practice of] his teacher Chr. G. Neefe. We can conclude from these observations that Beethoven was always open to new tendencies in ornamentation."[60] Newman supposed that Beethoven's use of the trilled turn, as he calls it, was inspired by Bach: "Since Beethoven (like others who used it) must have derived this type from Emanuel Bach, who claimed to have called attention to it first, there could be no reason to doubt that Bach's method of realizing it still applied."[61]

These statements present multiple problems. First of all, Kojima's observation that Beethoven's placement of the trilled turn differs from the recommendations in the theoretical literature should be more precise: it is different from what Bach writes. Bach assigns this sign a specific and somewhat elaborate execution, he indeed claims that he is the first to draw attention to it, and he explicitly states that the only correct placement of this embellishment is "after a descending second," that is, on a downward passing note.[62]

But Bach's presentation of the trilled turn is problematic in itself. It is correct that Bach was the first to indicate this specific manner of execution of a trilled turn that happens to appear on a downward passing note. He is certainly unique in that his verbal presentation, in comparison to his musical examples, is clumsy and can easily be misunderstood. However, Bach was far from the first to use this sign. François Couperin, for instance, used the same symbol in his *Pièces de Clavecin* (the first book was published in 1713), as a short symbol that in most cases indicates a *tremblement ouvert*, that is, a short trill with a turn and with an ascending resolution.[63]

Marpurg, who was well acquainted with Couperin's work, mentions the ∾ sign in his keyboard method as one of several ways to express a short upper-note trill with a two-note suffix of the basic shape ♪♪♪♪.[64] Unlike elsewhere in his book, Marpurg does not refer to Bach when describing this sign. Marpurg's application of the symbol is context-independent and, like his method in general, influenced by French practice rather than by Bach. We know from Neefe's autobiography that Neefe used

---

[60] Kojima, "Über die Ausführung der Verzierungen in Beethovens Klaviermusik," 145.

[61] Newman, "The performance of Beethoven's trills," 459–60. See also Drake, *The Beethoven Sonatas and the Creative Experience*, 174–6.

[62] Bach, *Versuch über die wahre Art, das Clavier zu spielen*, part I, 92–3, § 27 and 28, Table V, Figs. LXII–LXVIII.

[63] François Couperin, *Pièces de Clavecin, premier livre (1713)*, ed. Kenneth Gilbert, Paris: Heugel, 1973, VIII.

[64] Marpurg, *Anleitung zum Clavierspielen*, 55, § 8, and Tab. IV, 27e.

not only Bach's *Versuch* but also Marpurg's method for his self-study; Marpurg is thus not only a theorist who, in contrast to Kojima's claim, did allow the use of ∾ in unspecified contexts, but he is also highly relevant to our discussion.

This is because, in his own work, Neefe did in fact place the same sign in a variety of ways other than Bach's downward passing note, including downbeats and ascending progressions.[65] It is clear that he knew Bach's specific notation, since he uses it several times as well. Otherwise, however, Neefe's application of this sign shows that he favored a freer approach than Bach. Another advocate of a free approach was Neefe's mentor Johann Adam Hiller. In his singing school, Hiller only briefly mentions Bach's *prallender Doppelschlag* because, he says, this embellishment would probably be too difficult for many singers.[66] Hiller's alternative is the plain turn, to be placed in stepwise motion, in leaps, on repeated notes, between notes in slow tempo, and especially on the second note in an upward progression.[67] Neefe's own approach belongs to this more liberal tendency. Beethoven's application of the ∾ sign in his quartets indicates that he was, at that time, influenced by Neefe's practice in the selection and placement of his embellishments, rather than by Bach's *Versuch*.

An issue related to the trilled turn is Beethoven's placement of the simple turn (I will not discuss his occasional ambiguous placement of this sign, such as in Op. 2/3, mvt. 2, bars 45–6 and a few other places, because it has received ample attention in the literature).[68] It seems that, shortly after he moved to Vienna, Beethoven changed the notation of some of his turns. In my Examples 8.6 and 8.7, above, we can observe that in Op. 2, Beethoven notated the embellishment above the space between two notes, instead of repeating the first note and writing the turn above that note. The same difference is evident in another comparison between bars 1–5 of the Adagio con espressione in Quartet WoO 36/3 and bars 1–5 of the Adagio of Op. 2/1.[69] During the 1780s, Beethoven wrote an extra note under the turn in similar passages and never placed the symbol above a space between notes.[70] He changed this practice after he arrived in Vienna: turns over a space first appear in some of Beethoven's sketches from 1793,[71] and

---

[65] Various placements of this sign can be found, for example, in his sonatas from 1773: Sonata 2, mvt. 1, bar 4; Sonata 7, mvt. 1, bar 1; Sonata 11, mvt. 1, bars 13 and 15, and mvt. 3, bar 2.

[66] Hiller, *Anweisung zum musikalisch=zierlichen Gesange*, 75, § 27.

[67] *Ibid.*, 73–5, § 27.

[68] See, for instance, Kojima, "Über die Ausführung der Verzierungen in Beethovens Klaviermusik," 142, or Rosenblum, *Performance Practices in Classic Piano Music*, 282–3.

[69] See Examples 7.8 and 7.9 on page 196.

[70] In his sonatas from 1773, Neefe only very rarely placed a turn on a space between notes; the very few instances where it does seem to have been placed that way might even be printing mistakes.

[71] Kafka 39v. 1/4, 1/8; 42r. 15/2; 47v. 11/3. Date according to Cooper, "The ink in Beethoven's 'Kafka' sketch miscellany," 328–30.

subsequently in the sets of variations that had been partly written in Bonn but were published in 1793 (WoO 40) and 1794 (WoO 66). In this particular case it seems likely that he was influenced by Haydn, who was frequently using the same notation in his works.

This analysis of Beethoven's placement of the trilled turn and the turn over a space suggests that Beethoven was developing his notational practice along several lines. The influence of his teachers in questions such as the notation of the embellishments was probably important. On the other hand, he clearly did not adhere strictly to the tutors' more elaborate idiosyncrasies, such as Bach's *prallender Doppelschlag*. When adopting a new sign or a new notation, he was clearly guided by the notational practice of his surroundings.

TRILL STARTS, CHRONOLOGY AND FINGERINGS

Neefe's influence (or some influence from the tutors) may be evident in the consolidation of Beethoven's trill notation in the Quartets WoO 36, compared to the earlier "Kurfürsten" Sonatas WoO 47, discussed above. Furthermore, it is likely that Neefe (and later Haydn) influenced Beethoven's use and placement of some embellishment signs. There are, however, equally direct influences on Beethoven's way of playing trills that cannot be demonstrated. It is highly likely, for example, that he was exposed to various, probably even conflicting, practices among the singers and instrumentalists at the Bonn court. On the other hand, Neefe certainly must have had a clear opinion about the execution of trills. Neefe's musical education was based on C. P. E. Bach, Marpurg, and Hiller. If we accept this connection as decisive for his style, there can be no doubt that Neefe himself represented the tradition of the upper-note trill.[72]

This means that the best way to trace the development of Beethoven's own approach is to look for signs that suggest a break with this tradition of performing trills that start with the auxiliary. Apart from the possibility of some flexibility, difficult to discern today, in the tradition itself, such a break could have been caused by Beethoven's disagreement with the tradition, by his exposure to a more flexible culture, and finally by his exposure to new stylistic influences. It follows that a chronological approach is appropriate when discussing this question. In the following sections of this chapter, I will analyze several indications for Beethoven's trill execution that illustrate his relationship to the tradition, and to new developments in trill notation

[72] See Bach, *Versuch über die wahre Art, das Clavier zu spielen*, part I, 72, § 5; Marpurg, *Anleitung zum Clavierspielen*, 55, § 7; Hiller, *Anweisung zum musikalisch=zierlichen Gesange*, 68, § 26.

Example 8.12. Trill sketch from *c.* 1790–92[73]

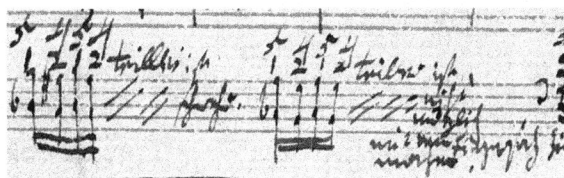

and execution. I will start by discussing seven examples of original fingerings that indicate the starting note of a trill.

Beethoven's surviving trill fingerings, when carefully analyzed, form reliable clues to the trill starts.[74] Such an analysis reveals four unequivocal upper-note starts, one main-note start and one case that has generated a dispute.

1) The first example is a sketch with two double trill beginnings in parallel sixths for the right hand from around 1790–92, featuring the experimental fingering 5–4 for the upper voice and, inverted, 1–2 for the lower voice. This figure, written out in sixteenth notes representing an upper-note start, is identified as a trill in the accompanying text, which reads for the first group, "Trill is difficult," and for the second group, "Trill cannot possibly be made with this fingering" (Example 8.12). This example is interesting for two reasons. First of all, Beethoven here provides a written-out realization which he explicitly calls a "trill." Apart from this example and his two realizations of the "Beethoven trill" at the end of the autograph of Op. 53, it is rather seldom that he realizes standard trills in this fashion in an unambiguous way (I will discuss other written-out trills below). Second, he introduces an inverted fingering in double trills, where (in the right hand) the thumb plays the top note and the second finger the lower one. This example is certainly "difficult" since it also requires that the thumb be placed on a flat. This fingering recurs in my next example and also in a late example from Op. 111 which has generated controversy in the literature. Possibly the idea of inverting the thumb and second finger in trills with sharps or flats derives from C. P. E. Bach, who recommends it for single trills in the left hand where the higher note is a sharp or a flat.[75]

2) Three sets of fingerings that indicate upper-note trills can be found at the end of the coda of the Variations WoO 40 for piano and violin, published in 1793 (Example 8.13). This example includes the "Beethoven trill" which Beethoven published to embarrass the Viennese *Klaviermeister*.

---

[73] Single sketch sheet, Beethoven-Haus Bonn, HCB Bsk 17/65c, v. 11/3. Reproduced with the kind permission of the Beethoven-Haus Bonn. The original text reads: "Triller ist schwer … Triller ist nicht möglich mit diesem Fingersatz zu machen."

[74] Newman, *Beethoven on Beethoven*, 197–8.

[75] Bach, *Versuch über die wahre Art, das Clavier zu spielen*, part 1, 74, § 12.

Example 8.13. Variations on "Se vuol ballare" from W. A. Mozart's *Le nozze di Figaro*,
WoO 40, Coda, bars 57–82[76]

A double trill in thirds in bar 59 is fingered 5–4 for the upper voice
and inverted 1–2 for the lower voice. A trill start in the left hand in
bar 60 is fingered 1–2. The trill start in bar 69 in the right hand of
the long trill with accompanying voices (first below and then above
the trill) is fingered 5–4. After the lower accompanying voice is
discontinued in bar 74 and before the upper voice enters, the fingering of the (continuing) trill is re-arranged to 2–3 instead of 5–4 in
order to free the fifth finger for the entering the top voice. The finger
to change first must naturally be the one on the lower trill note:
otherwise an awkward 5–4–3 skip would occur during the transition.
Consequently, the first changing finger is indicated here as 2, followed by 3 for the top note of the trill.

3) In the autograph of the Trio WoO 39, Beethoven fingers two right-hand
   trills in bars 8 and 103 with 4–3, indicating auxiliary starts. The trill in
   bar 8 is placed on a downward passing eighth note (in six-eight time)
   under a slur (Example 8.14); in bar 103 the slur is omitted.[77]

   The fingerings in this work, written in 1812 for the ten-year-old Maxe
   Brentano as an "encouragement in piano playing," probably have a
   pedagogical function.[78]

4) The famous triple trill in Op. 111, mvt. 2, bar 112 is, in the autograph,
   fingered 5–4 for the top voice, inverted 1–2 for the middle voice and, in
   pencil, 1–2 for the left-hand top voice.[79] The autograph with these

---

[76] Reproduced with the kind permission of the Beethoven-Haus Bonn.
[77] Elfrieda F. Hiebert, "Beethoven's fingerings in the Piano Trio in B-flat major, WoO 39," *Early Keyboard Journal* 4 (1985–86): 21. See also Rosenblum, *Performance Practices in Classic Piano Music*, 251.
[78] See also Winter, "Second thoughts on the performance of Beethoven's trills," 488–9.
[79] Description in *ibid.*, 493.

Example 8.14. Trio in B flat major WoO 39, piano part, bar 8 (transcription of autograph)

Example 8.15. Sonata in C minor Op. 111, mvt. 2, Arietta, bars 109–15
(Schlesinger, 1822/23)

fingerings dates from early 1822.[80] The two sets of fingerings for the right hand appear in small print in the Schlesinger edition from 1822/23 (Example 8.15).

It would seem that this example needs no further comment since the inverted inner fingering is the same as that for the trills in Example 8.12 and the double trill in thirds in Example 8.13. However, the question of the proper execution of these fingerings has caused some controversy. Some scholars interpret these fingerings literally and propose that the inner trill is to be played in contrary motion.[81] Others vote for an upper-note interpretation akin to Example 8.12, with the second finger playing the lower D by crossing the thumb that plays the E♭.[82] On the light action of early pianos, the fingering indicated is practicable on a parallel upper-note trill. It seems highly unlikely that Beethoven would have

---

[80] Kinsky and Halm, *Das Werk Beethovens: Thematisch-Bibliographisches Verzeichnis*, 318, no. 2.

[81] Here Newman sees an analogy to the written-out oscillations in contrary movement in Op. 90, mvt. 2, bars 48–51 (Newman, "The performance of Beethoven's trills," 442, 445), whereas Kojima gives as an example the oscillations in triplets of Op. 96, mvt. 1, bars 138–9 (Kojima, "Über die Ausführung der Verzierungen in Beethovens Klaviermusik," 150). Neither author explains why they believe that these passages with different textures and completely different harmonic contexts are comparable at all.

[82] This controversy is reviewed, for example, in Kojima, "Über die Ausführung der Verzierungen in Beethovens Klaviermusik," 150, 153, n. 29, and Rosenblum, *Performance Practices in Classic Piano Music*, 251, 458, n. 121. See also Winter, "Second thoughts on the performance of Beethoven's trills," 494.

Example 8.16. Bagatelle in C major Op. 119/7. From Friedrich Starke's *Wiener Piano-forte-Schule*, vol. III, 1821[83]

relied only on a pair of fingering notations had he wanted any of the other two trills to be played in contrary motion to the upper trill. In any case, if we keep to the indisputable facts, we can state beyond any doubt that he indicated the highest and the lowest trills with auxiliary starts.

5) A final example is the beginning of the Bagatelle Op. 119/7, bars 1–2. Here the unprepared trill is indicated 3–4 in bar 1 and 1–2 in bar 2, which points to a main-note trill (Example 8.16).[84]

Various inaccuracies in previous discussions of these examples have obscured the fact that each of them (with the possible exception of Example 8.15, depending on how it is read) is consistent in itself. Example 8.13, especially, has been misinterpreted in different ways by Newman and Rosenblum, possibly because the first edition was not accessible to them.[85] If one interprets the fingering in bar 74 as the beginning of the trill, this would indeed indicate a main-note start. In reality, all the trills in the entire passage are fingered as upper-note trills. In Example 8.14, Beethoven indicated the fingering of the trill only in the two instances mentioned. The main-note starts in a few other instances that Elfrieda Hiebert proposes in an article about these fingerings, based on tone repetition or ascending movement, are all the result of an

[83] Reproduced with the kind permission of the Beethoven-Haus Bonn.
[84] Newman lists a few more examples of fingerings that are supposed to indicate trill starts (Newman, *Beethoven on Beethoven*, 197–8). In a sketch on Kafka 132v. 7, the fingering on two bass notes, each followed by two small sixteenth notes that look like trill suffixes, is 4–3, suggesting a main-note bass trill. But Beethoven did not write trills in this example, and it remains unclear whether he intended any. This could also be a demonstration of silent finger changes, akin to the one on Kafka 39v. 1/3, where he demonstrates a silent 4–3 replacement in the right hand.
   Op. 1/1, mvt. 2, bars 69–70. The fingering, suggesting a short main-note trill with suffix, is apparently not original (Hiebert, "Beethoven's fingerings in the Piano Trio in B-flat major, WoO 39," 12, n. 18).
   Op 1/3, mvt. 1, bars 308–9. The trill on A♭ in the right hand is approached from below and the last two notes before the trill are fingered 1–2. The approach from below might make a main-note trill seem more elegant; the fingering, however, certainly does not rule out an upper-note start.
   Trio Op. 3, mvt. 2, cello part, bars 41–2. The fingering 2 in this example allows for several interpretations.
[85] Newman, *Beethoven on Beethoven*, 198; Rosenblum, *Performance Practices in Classic Piano Music*, 250.

Example 8.17. C. P. E. Bach *Versuch über die wahre Art, das Clavier zu spielen,* Tab. IV, Fig. XLV.[86]

interpretation based on rules that are unaccounted for and hence disputable (see below).[87] This survey thus offers a revised picture in comparison to Newman's claim that a full 70 percent of Beethoven's fingerings on trills indicate main-note starts. In fact we see a more even, less chronologically determined distribution of upper-note trills.

Most importantly, the "Beethoven trill" of WoO 40 (Example 8.13), a texture that abounds in Beethoven's sketches of that time, is fingered to begin with the upper note. This is noteworthy for two reasons. First of all, the non-cadential trill whose main function is to prolong a note is a typical candidate for a main-note start, or for an undecided one, as, for example, Haydn's musical clocks suggest (see above). Second, Beethoven sketched the coda with this trill when he was just becoming familiar with the musical customs of Vienna. If there was any ambivalence toward trill starts in that culture, it did not, at this particular moment, reveal itself in Beethoven's approach to the trill.

Bar 8 of WoO 39 (Example 8.14) indicates a surprisingly conservative solution. A passing trill under a slur would be tied over according to most of the tutors' descriptions of the passing *Pralltriller*. The fingering 4–3 on the trill suggests that, as late as 1814, Beethoven followed C. P. E. Bach's execution of this trill, as shown in Bach's example Tab. IV, Fig. XLV (Example 8.17). The starting note of the passing trill is actually played.

It should be noted that, in WoO 39, Beethoven indicated the trill with *tr.*, using the more modern notation that Clementi, for instance, also uses in his keyboard method.[88] Clementi tied the beginning of passing trills of this kind in descending lines and began with the main note in ascending lines (the latter was a novelty compared to other tutors).

The indisputable auxiliary start of the A♭ treble trill of Example 8.15 has three characteristics worth noting. First, it is preceded by five repeated A♭s, after which Beethoven wants the trill to start with the auxiliary. Second, it is on the seventh of a chord with a dominant function which does not directly resolve into the cadence; in other words, it does not represent the typical cadential trill of a standard shape. Third, it actually resolves into a chromatic upward trill chain that assumes a clear melodic function. All these

---

[86] From Bach, *Versuch über die wahre Art, das Clavier zu spielen*. Reproduced with the kind permission of Breitkopf & Härtel, Wiesbaden.

[87] Hiebert, "Beethoven's fingerings in the Piano Trio in B-flat major, WoO 39," 21–2.

[88] Clementi, "Cadence liée à la note précédente," in *Méthode pour le Piano Forte*, 11.

characteristics will return in my further discussion below about trills without fingerings. The lowest trill on F, which also begins with the auxiliary, is preceded by one note at the same pitch.

Example 8.16 indicates main-note trill starts. The starting trill appears on the fifth (G), clashing with the fourth (F). An upper-note trill would have obscured the 3–4 clash, weakened the dominant character of the G, and transformed this chord full of tension into a simple $\frac{6}{4}$ chord; however, these explanations of why Beethoven might have chosen to indicate a main-note trill are mine and not Beethoven's.[89] One can simply state that he wanted and indicated a main-note trill at this specific moment.

What remains is to consider Beethoven's reasons for writing these fingerings and their influence on our conclusion about the starting note of these trills. In those cases where the fingering has the function of explaining the execution of a technically difficult passage (Examples 8.12, 8.13, and 8.15), the main focus is probably not on the trill itself, so perhaps the trills are normal for Beethoven, although their fingering is daring. In a pedagogical piece (Example 8.14), one might expect an uncontroversial fingering to indicate Beethoven's idea of the most common shape of the trill.[90] In cases where the trill is part of a harmonically complex opening of a piece (Example 8.16), the fingering provides a means of indicating an unconventional trill start. However, this example perhaps shows a break with the traditional way of beginning a piece, rather than a new trill practice. If, as I stated at the beginning of this section, our understanding of Beethoven's approach is dependent on signs that suggest a break with the tradition of auxiliary trill starts, these five examples are actually of little help. Apart from in Example 8.16, we cannot see a break in Beethoven's style in any of the examples.

BEETHOVEN'S PRESCRIBED TRILL STARTS

Judging from the examples in the previous section, a normal trill for Beethoven still began with the upper note almost until his last works for piano. However, the total number of Beethoven's trill fingerings is very small and one might suspect that they do not provide a representative picture. There are two other kinds of notation that can help to illustrate Beethoven's trill practice. In the first of these Beethoven makes use of conventional practice and indicates the trill start by means of appoggiaturas. A good example of this notation is the first movement of the "Apassionata" Op. 57. In this movement, grace note prefixes indicate

---

[89] Winter, "Second thoughts on the performance of Beethoven's trills," 492 provides a similar reasoning.
[90] See *ibid.*, 489.

Example 8.18. Sonata in F minor Op. 57, mvt. 1, Allegro assai, bars 6–11
(Bureau des Arts et d'Industrie, 1807)

Example 8.19. Sonata in F minor Op. 57, mvt. 1, Allegro assai, bars 44–6

that eight trills begin with the lower auxiliary, while four trills in a specific context are indicated as upper-note trills. Twelve trills lack a prefix.

These trills fall into two groups. The first group includes those trills that end the concluding half-phrase of the main subject. Such trills also occur when the same half-phrase appears on its own. For these trills, lower auxiliary prefixes are prescribed in bars 3, 7, 9, 23, 69, 144, and 146; all the others have no prefix. Example 8.18 shows two trills with prefixes and one without.

The total distribution of grace notes in this material throughout the movement is as follows: in the exposition, four trills with a prefix and two trills without; at the beginning of the development, one trill with a prefix and three trills without; in the recapitulation, two trills with a prefix and six without. This amounts to a total of eleven trills without and seven with a prefix in similar thematic material over the entire movement.

To the second group belong the non-thematic whole-bar trills in bars 44–6 and 183–5 that are indicated with grace notes (Example 8.19).

In this group there are two issues of inconsistency. First, as can be seen in Example 8.19 (the first of these instances), the grace notes are written as eighth notes in the first edition, while in bars 183–5 they are written as sixteenth notes. One of the two must be an error. Additionally, in the autograph and the first edition, the prefix from below that occurs in bar 44 is missing in bar 183.[91] This is obviously an error too. The remaining four trills of each group are indicated by grace notes to start from above.

---

[91] My list is based on the first edition from 1807 (Bureau des Arts et d'Industrie) and on several modern critical editions.

For the performance of the trills with grace notes, eighteenth-century practice was still valid. The trill beginning with one or two lower grace notes ♪♪ or ♪♪ would invariably have had this shape ♪♪♪♪♪. This can be confirmed by consulting any of the major tutors, such as Bach, Marpurg, Türk, or Clementi.[92] In fact Beethoven's notation with one grace note is old-fashioned compared to both Türk, who of various options prefers the two-note prefix, and Clementi, who exclusively uses the two-note prefix.[93]

The performance of the remaining thematic trills in this movement that are not preceded by a grace note is entirely uncontroversial, no matter which philosophy or argument we use. The realization that Beethoven's notation of these grace-note trills is traditional would suggest that the plain trills also are to be interpreted traditionally, that is, as upper-note trills. This is not even controversial according to early Romantic practice: as already mentioned, even Czerny recommends upper-note trills if they are preceded by the same note.[94]

Two questions remain to be answered when considering the trills in the first movement of Op. 57. First, what is the motivation for the seeming inconsistency between the indicated lower-auxiliary trills and the supposed upper-auxiliary trills in the thematic trills? Second, what reason did Beethoven have for indicating the non-thematic trills in bars 45–6 and 184–5 with an *upper* auxiliary? I will discuss these questions in turn.

In his first article about Beethoven's trills, Newman expressed his puzzlement about the apparent inconsistency in this movement. Commenting on a trill in bars 21–2 that lacks a suffix, he wrote: "Thematic integrity, the need to achieve a melodic and dissonant peak, and the downward resolution all seem to favor a start on the upper note. But why, then, does Beethoven not use a grace-note prefix to indicate this starting note, as he does so carefully for the starting notes – both upper and lower – in all of the other numerous trills of this movement?"[95] Inexplicably, in this instance Newman did not account for the remaining ten thematic trills that lack a prefix, and he also made no distinction between the thematic and the non-thematic trills. Robert Winter explains in his analysis of these examples why he thinks that Beethoven often used the lower auxiliary: "The direction to begin each trill with the lower auxiliary avoids a repetitious emphasis on the apex of the second half of the phrase ... for consistency, some performers may

---

[92] Bach and Marpurg present both versions as equivalent (Bach, *Versuch über die wahre Art, das Clavier zu spielen*, part 1, 79, § 22; Tab IV, Fig. XXXIV. Marpurg, *Anleitung zum Clavierspielen*, 57 § 8, 5; Tab V, Example 10).

[93] Türk, *Klavierschule*, 267, § 48; Clementi, "Cadence preparée," in *Méthode pour le Piano Forte*, 11.

[94] See my discussion of Example 8.32, on page 256.

[95] Newman, "The Performance of Beethoven's Trills," 442.

wish to add the same lower auxiliary to measures 11 and 21."[96] In the revised version of his original article, Newman, too, advises the completion of the lower auxiliary trills for reasons of analogy. The likely error of both authors is that they suspect a notational inconsistency where Beethoven was indicating expressive diversity. It is perhaps possible that he indicated inconsistent trills in a manuscript, but it seems unlikely that he would not, at the very least, have made an attempt to correct this in an edition. Occasional engraving errors might indeed occur, as in the case of bar 183, but that he would have missed more than half of the suffixes while making the effort to indicate the remaining ones seems entirely unlikely. We should assume, then, that the difference is intentional.

We can in fact discern a slightly lopsided pattern in these starts. The trills in the first statement of the first subject, its restatement in G flat major, and the returning half-phrase in the main key begin from below. The quasi-recapitulation beginning of the development section (upbeat to bars 67–70) gets the same lower auxiliary trill. All restatements of the second half-phrase of the subject in "searching" keys (bars 11 and 71) or with a modulating function (bar 73, and bars 76, 158, 160, and 162) receive upper-note trills. The *piano* trills in bars 21 and 156 that belong to the *fortissimo* restatement of the first subject also begin on the upper note (apart from being modulating, bars 158, 160, and 162 in fact belong to this category as well). The only important deviation from this pattern is that the organ point on C at the beginning of the recapitulation provides the foundation for one "searching" trill, which now begins with the lower auxiliary (bar 146). Conversely, the first statement of the main subject in the recapitulation (bar 138), and its restatement (bar 142) on the organ points C and D♭, are changed. Here the trills no longer start from below, but from above. A third difference concerns the modulating bar 23 of the exposition, which has the lower auxiliary. This bar is, of course, replaced in the recapitulation by the longer sequence of bars 158–62 and is not directly comparable.

I should emphasize that such an attempt to find a structural pattern in these trills neglects to some degree the various possible executions and the various ways of hearing upper and lower-note trill starts. If, for instance, the thematic trills that were indicated to start from below were really meant to avoid "a repetitive emphasis on the apex of the second half of the phrase," as Winter writes, this requires a universal idea about how to play this trill and a universal listener's experience to understand its meaning. Simply put, as long as it is possible to play an upper-note trill shyly and inconspicuously, and a trill that starts from below so assertively, noisily, or expressively as to create an accent or rhetorical emphasis in the listener's experience, it is not possible to be sure what Beethoven actually wanted to avoid with his notation.

[96] Winter, "Second thoughts on the performance of Beethoven's trills," 499.

The second question is why Beethoven specially indicated the upper-note beginning of the non-thematic trills in bars 45–6 and 184–5. There are several ways to explain this. First of all, in a passage with three similar trills at different pitches, a player could in fact have been in doubt as to whether he had to play all the trills similarly. Furthermore, the second and third trills are both unprepared and unaccompanied. Winter writes, "The special context of unaccompanied trills … demands that their starting notes be spelled out."[97] More specifically, these trills could have given the impression that Beethoven wanted their pitch to be emphasized, which could most easily be accomplished by an accented start on the main note.[98] Similar consider-ations will become important in my further discussion below, since they depend on what I will call the intuition and the common sense of the player. Another possibility is that he wanted these trill starts to be especially accented, played as appoggiaturas. A final answer, however, cannot be given. We can, simply, state that, in these examples, Beethoven wanted to indicate the beginning note of the trills in an unambiguous way.

Beethoven used grace notes to indicate trill starts throughout his entire work. Most of the time he adhered to the one-note grace-note prefix; very occasionally he wrote two prefix notes as Clementi and Türk did, for example, in Op. 56, mvt. 3 cello part, bar 117.[99] As discussed above, these notations were seen as equivalent, and neither gives any further information about the shape of the ordinary trill without grace notes. I have found no case where Beethoven indicated a main-note trill with a grace note of the same pitch.[100] This specific notation is therefore traditional and shows no significant changes during Beethoven's lifetime.

WRITTEN-OUT TRILL TEXTURES IN BEETHOVEN

As mentioned, Beethoven explicitly called his early written-out double trill (Example 8.12) a "trill." However, most of Beethoven's written-out oscillat-ing textures are not trills. Before deciding whether they can serve as models for other trills that are not written out, one must discuss their function. These are, in any case, spelled-out and rhythmicized trills that are more strictly tied to the musical fabric than free trills. This means that they generally create a more formal expression in their context. Furthermore, they can be part of a notation that traditionally uses written-out oscilla-tions or they can be specifically explicatory – that is, they can show a shape

---

[97] *Ibid.*

[98] Although Beethoven sometimes used upper auxiliaries to indicate accidentals of the upper note more clearly (see, for instance, the sketch on Kafka 46r. 7/4–7/9), this seems not to be his reason for writing upper grace notes in this particular case.

[99] Cited in Newman, *Beethoven on Beethoven*, 199.

[100] The appoggiatura on the pitch of the trill note in Kafka 97r. 7 in Kerman, ed., *Ludwig van Beethoven Autograph Miscellany from ca. 1786 to 1799 (The "Kafka" Sketchbook)*, vol. II, 55, is a transcription error.

Example 8.20. Clementi's *Méthode pour le Piano Forte* (*c.* 1803, Paris: Pleyel), p. 11

Example 8.21. Türk, *Klavierschule*, p. 270[101]

that cannot be expressed conveniently in signs. Often the border between written-out trills and tremolo textures is unclear. So, for instance, on f. 61v. of the "Kafka" miscellany, we find an upper-note trill beginning in sixteenth notes marked *allegro*, which forms the lower part of a tremolo with added quarter notes a third higher.[102] On the same page, however, a sixteenth-note trill in sixths, marked *allegrissimo*, starts with the main note.[103]

The main reason for Beethoven to write out trill-like oscillations in notes was to indicate trills where the main note and the *lower* auxiliary alternate, forming several forms of extended mordents. The beginning of prolonged mordents is not strictly defined, hence various approaches are possible, such as beginning the figure on the lower auxiliary or on the main note. Example 8.20 shows Clementi's realizations of these two beginnings.

Such written-out extended mordents appear in Beethoven's music, for example, in the defined form of the anticipated trill, or "voraus geschickter Triller," as Hiller and Türk call it.[104] Beethoven's adherence to the antici-pated trill is noteworthy, since it again follows an eighteenth-century convention. In Türk's written-out realization, one can clearly see the differ-ence between the preparation and the trill itself, because he identifies the latter with the word "final trill" ("Schlußtriller") (Example 8.21).

From Türk's example (as well as comparable examples in other tutors) it is clear that, in common late eighteenth-century practice, this trill was not necessarily specially indicated. Beethoven, however, chose to be explicit and wrote out the trill anticipation (Examples 8.22 and 8.23).

The interpretation of these examples should not present a problem since we are looking at a traditional formula.[105] Beethoven continued

---

[101] Reproduced with the kind permission of Bärenreiter Verlag, Kassel.　　[102] *Ibid.*, vol. 1, f. 61v. 5/4.

[103] *Ibid.*, f. 61v. 15/5–15/7.

[104] Hiller, *Anweisung zum musikalisch=zierlichen Gesange*, 68, § 23. Türk refers to Hiller. Türk, *Klavierschule*, 270–1, § 53.

[105] Newman's interpretation that "the starting note [i.e. of the trill itself] is evidently the main note by analogy with the previous, notated trill" is clearly incorrect. Newman, *Beethoven on Beethoven*, 195, 202–3.

Example 8.22. Sonata in C major Op. 2/3, mvt. 1, Allegro con brio, end of bar 233–235

Example 8.23. Sonata in E flat major Op. 27/1, mvt. 4, bar 263 (Cappi, 1802)

using the *voraus geschickter Triller* until his middle-period works, for example, in the fourth variation of the Andante of the Violin Sonata Op 47, bar 4, or in the first movement of the Fourth Piano Concerto Op. 56, bars 109–10. However, beginning with those works that belong to his "new style," the Sonatas Op. 31 and the Variations Op. 34 and 35, he began to use more varied preparatory passages for his trills increasingly often, and even the trill suffixes sometimes became more ornamented and less standardized.

Apart from this specific trill formula, Beethoven applies free extended written-out mordents in a variety of musical environments throughout his work. We can find these textures in a thematic function (Op. 2/3, mvt. 1, first subject; later in the movement the same mordent is extended to form the beginning of a *voraus geschickter Triller*, see Example 8.22) or as part of an ornamental motif (Op. 5/1, mvt. 2, bars 54–9). They can also have the function of prolonging a tone, either with another voice (for example, in Op. 7, mvt. 1, bars 355–8; Op. 10/3, mvt. 1, bars 93–6) or on their own (for example, in Op. 10/3, mvt. 1, bars 327–32; Op. 22, mvt. 1, bars 152–60; Op. 70/1, mvt. 2, bars 31–5 and others; Op. 101, mvt. 3, bars 347–58). The important general characteristic of the extended mordent is that its starting note is not standardized, and because it includes a lower auxiliary ornament, it cannot serve as a model for trill starts that are not written out.

Occasionally, Beethoven did write out ordinary trills – that is, oscillations between the main and the upper note. One reason for writing out part of a trill was to indicate an *accelerando*. Here, a written-out slow trill start resolves into a trill indicated with a *tr.* symbol (see, for example, Kafka 90r.

Example 8.24. Sonata in E minor Op. 90, mvt. 2, Nicht zu geschwind und sehr singbar vorzutragen, bars 48–51 (Steiner, 1815)

13/18 and 15/1, or Kafka 125r. 9/5–9/7, where upper-note oscillations in eighth notes resolve into trills, and Op. 73, mvt. 3, 227–38; see below for further examples).[106]

The three remaining reasons for writing out ordinary trills are when the trill had to fit a rhythmic environment exactly, when a specific trill shape was required, and when a complex shape could not be expressed with signs. A famous case of the last kind is the double trill in contrary motion in Op. 90 (Example 8.24).

While it might be argued whether this is a trill at all because of the relatively slow tempo, the upper-note tremolos at the end of the first movement of the Fifth Piano Concerto Op. 73 (bars 561–8) certainly count as trills of this particular kind.

The most important group of written-out trills, however, includes examples of the first two kinds. In theory, their starting notes could be interpreted either as traditional or as innovative, which makes them an insecure indicator of Beethoven's trill preferences. Luckily, the reality of Beethoven's written-out trills is easier to interpret. They confirm common claims that the general stylistic change toward main-note trills did eventually influence Beethoven in his trill practice. Beethoven's early written-out trills are usually upper-note trills. From around 1809, more and more main-note trills begin to appear until finally, in the late works, Beethoven's written-out trills have as a rule become main-note trills.

So the trills in Op. 22 and Op. 26, for example, are upper-note trills (Examples 8.25 and 8.26).

In various places throughout the Fifth Piano Concerto Op. 73, written-out upper-note trills still appear. The accelerating trill in the Rondo, beginning in bar 227, is perhaps the most striking example. A similar accelerating upper-note trill appears in bars 362–72 of the first movement of the "Hammerklavier" Sonata Op. 106.

---

[106] This can even happen in a trill that moves up stepwise, as in the Polonaise Op. 89, bars 4–5. This figure can be interpreted in various ways, but most likely not as a "modernized" *voraus geschickter Triller* (compare Kojima, "Über die Ausführung der Verzierungen in Beethovens Klaviermusik," 149).

Example 8.25. Sonata in B flat major Op. 22, mvt. 4, Rondo allegretto, bars 107–11
(Hoffmeister, 1802)

Example 8.26. Sonata in A flat major Op. 26, mvt. 1, bars 197–200 (Cappi, 1802)

Example 8.27. Sonata in E flat major, Op. 81a, mvt. 3, Vivacissimamente, bars 146–7
(Breitkopf & Härtel, 1811)

However, in the finale of Sonata Op. 81a from 1809, Beethoven writes main-note trills that have an important function throughout the movement (Example 8.27).

From this point on, main-note starts become more frequent and they often appear at structurally important moments. So, for instance, the long written-out accelerating trill in octaves in the sixth variation of the Finale of Op. 109, bars 160–7, is a main-note trill. The trill that leads to the main subject in the first movement of Op. 111 (bars 16–18) is also a main-note trill.

To conclude, the overall pattern of Beethoven's written-out trills corresponds with the same development that was apparent in his trill fingerings. Considering that explicitly indicated upper-note trills survived until his last Piano Sonata Op. 111 (Example 8.15 above), whereas explicit main-note trills are apparent much earlier (Op. 81a), the most likely interpretation of these trills is that Beethoven, in his late works, added new elements to his style, instead of substituting one practice for another. At no point in his work do his explicit trill starts indicate an adherence to an upper-note trill *rule*. Upper-note trills were, however, clearly his custom well into his middle period and they might indeed also have been his preference for a long time.

Judging from his written-out trill indications, his trill practice diversified at the latest sometime around 1809.

MODERN ARGUMENTS VERSUS THE PLAYER'S INTUITION

Barry Cooper has shown that, contrary to previous claims in the literature, Beethoven's notation of appoggiaturas was based on the notational conventions of the mid-eighteenth century and remained largely consistent throughout his life.[107] The preceding discussion has suggested that, as far as we can know, even in his trill notation and in his choice of the starting note, Beethoven was traditional for a long time, or perhaps even conservative (as in the Trio WoO 39, Example 8.14).

This view is far from universally accepted. To conclude this chapter, I will provide examples of various conflicting arguments in the literature about the trill starts in Beethoven's music. At the end, I will propose that we accept ambiguity in some cases as a problem that even pianists of Beethoven's time faced, and I will argue for an intuitive approach based on simple spontaneous musical observations.

First, I will provide five examples of trills written by Beethoven that lack fingerings (Examples 8.28–8.32).

Each of these trills except the last one requires interpretation, and each one including the last one triggers further questions and comments. They also have one factor in common, namely that, according to various arguments, they could all begin with the main note instead of the auxiliary. In the following, I will present my description of the trills in question, followed by selected opinions from the literature.

The trill that begins in bar 259 of Example 8.28 is comparable to the organ point trill in WoO 40, but instead of appearing on the dominant to F, it here represents an organ point on the tonic C. Just as in WoO 40, the right-hand trill in this example is approached from the B♮ below. If one chooses an upper-note beginning, the proper execution in both examples would be to skip from the B♮ to the auxiliary D. For Newman, such a diatonic approach

Example 8.28. Sonata in C major Op. 2/3, mvt. 4, Allegro assai, bars 255–63

---

[107] Barry Cooper, "Beethoven's appoggiaturas: long or short?" *Early Music* 31/2 (2003).

Example 8.29. Sonata in C sharp minor Op. 27/2, mvt. 3, Presto agitato, bars 183–91

Example 8.30. Sonata in G major Op. 31/1, mvt. 2, Adagio grazioso, bars 1–5
(Simrock, 1803)

Example 8.31. Sonata in E flat major Op. 31/3, mvt. 1, Allegro, bars 74–80

Example 8.32. Sonata in C major Op. 53, mvt. 3, bars 47–54

from below indicates a main-note trill.[108] For Winter, the consonant trill note would without doubt indicate an auxiliary start.

The dramatic trill on the downbeat of bar 187 from the finale of the "Moonlight" Sonata (Example 8.29) on the ninth of the dominant, which is indicated by a rather small *tr.* sign in the autograph that is almost invisible in

---

[108] Newman, *Beethoven on Beethoven*, 198, Example 7/7, Op. 1/3, mvt. 1, bars 308–9.

the first edition, is approached in an *accelerando* chromatic scale from below. This trill is harmonically so unlike the usual cadential trill that it requires us to argue our case no matter which way we want to begin it. If it is played in the Baroque way, beginning from above, the cross-relation between the major third in the tenor and the minor tenth of the upper note of the trill is emphasized. Thus the traditionalist approach results in a rougher effect. If we instead respond to the *accelerando* and rush into the trill, beginning it on the main note, we would achieve a sense of drama by a horizontal effect. The trill would remain dramatic, but less shocking. However, in the autograph there is a page break, and in the first edition a new line begins before the trill, so the forward surge one might seek in the music cannot in fact be seen on the page. This trill would in either case be dissonant. In a similar example, Newman looks at the downward exit of a trill to determine its starting note (Op. 27/1, mvt. 3, bars 25–6) and concludes: "The main note has a needed downward pull that is lacking in the upper note."[109] This argument would also apply here.

Example 8.30 shows a trill on the tonic C and another one on the fifth of the dominant. The first trill is unprepared; the second is approached chromatically from below. Later in this movement, the same thematic trill is sometimes approached from above (bars 27 and 91), and in the left hand its beginning is occasionally indicated by a sixteenth-note appoggiatura an octave or a fifth below the trill (bars 9, 11, 73, and 75). The latter notation may be unique for these four instances, but the small notes could nevertheless have the function of a substitute trill start instead of the usual one, which in that case would be on the auxiliary, in accordance with eighteenth-century theory. Both trills in this example are, however, thematic, and the whole piece is written in a Rossini-esque style of the newest kind. This may suggest main-note trills. Rosenblum writes: "Both trills … begin on the main note because of their obvious melodic coloristic (rather than harmonic) function, as well as to keep the outline of the triadic motive clear."[110] Robert Winter would probably not agree with this view because of his claim that Beethoven's strong-beat trills usually had a dissonant beginning.[111]

Example 8.31 shows a typical trill on the fifth of the dominant. Thinking traditionally, this trill would certainly begin with the auxiliary. However, the approach from above would mean that the auxiliary start is a repetition of the previous note. Drake cites a similar case (Op. 54, mvt. 2, bar 160) and asserts that "Beethoven would hardly have repeated the auxiliary … in the trill."[112] Newman provides an example in a slow tempo (Op. 10/1, mvt. 2, bars 8–9), calls it a legato approach (although the beginning of the bar with

[109] Newman, *Beethoven on Beethoven*, 159–60.
[110] Rosenblum, *Performance Practices in Classic Piano Music*, 253.
[111] Winter, "Second thoughts on the performance of Beethoven's trills," 485.
[112] Drake, *The Beethoven Sonatas and the Creative Experience*, 167.

the approach to the trill lacks legato slurs) and recommends a main-note start.[113] Kojima, in a discussion of Beethoven's change of style at that time (1802), introduces the term "prepared trills," and he re-interprets notes of a small value that might precede a trill as "quasi-anticipations," that is, replacements of the grace notes that would otherwise be used in cases where a trill start was specified.[114] Of course, these quasi-anticipations would fall before the beat. Appoggiaturas that indicate the trill start fall on the beat. With his theory, Kojima has therefore either blurred the on-beat character of a trill or created an argument for main-note trills after every approach in small note values.

In Example 8.32, from the "Waldstein" Sonata, written only a year after Op. 31, a similarly uncomplicated trill start on the dominant G is also indicated with an eighth-note appoggiatura. Is this not a redundant nota-tion, since the trill would have started with the upper note anyway? Would the fact that it is preceded by repeated notes of the same pitch normally dictate a main-note start, so that Beethoven had to specifically indicate an upper-note start because he preferred it in this case? Or have we finally arrived at the moment when Beethoven expected trills to be performed with main note starts as a rule and began marking all the other trill starts with small notes? Winter discusses this example and writes, "The unfamiliarity of this type of trill (which later evolves into a 'Beethoven trill') probably prompted the composer to specify the starting note. A secondary factor may have been the repetition of the principal note directly before the trill."[115] But according to Czerny, an approach from the same note requires an upper-note start in any case.[116] Elfrieda Hiebert provides further alter-natives. If a repeated note before the trill also forms a dissonance with the bass, the trill should start with a main note. If not, an upper-note or a lower-auxiliary start is better. One could even play an extended mordent instead.[117] Newman points out, however, that "Beethoven never used a sign for trilling with the note below."[118] This observation is correct. As discussed earlier, Beethoven meticulously wrote out his extended mordents.

This catalogue of speculation shows that the modern performer, who has a whole machinery of rules, exceptions, and analogies at his disposal, and has access to Beethoven's whole oeuvre for analysis, nevertheless is often left at a loss about how to perform Beethoven's trills. Our task is to understand the character of the contemporary consensus, Beethoven's usual customs, and guidelines for exceptions to the rules. If we in addition assume that the

---

[113] Newman, "The performance of Beethoven's trills," 442–3.
[114] Kojima, "Über die Ausführung der Verzierungen in Beethovens Klaviermusik," 147.
[115] Winter, "And even more thoughts on the Beethoven trill …," 498.
[116] Czerny, *Vollständige theoretisch-praktische Pianoforte-Schule*, Part 1, 85. 17th lesson § 4b. See also Drake, *The Beethoven Sonatas and the Creative Experience*, 168 and Newman, "The Performance of Beethoven's Trills," 196.
[117] Hiebert, "Beethoven's fingerings in the Piano Trio in B-flat major, WoO 39," 22.
[118] Newman, *Beethoven on Beethoven*, 196.

"usual" trill start was at some point replaced by a "new" start, we end up in a situation where almost every single trill approach and trill placement in Beethoven's music is open to conflicting interpretations.

Many modern scholars clearly assume that all these questions were answerable for Beethoven's contemporaries. If we believe, however, that the overwhelming body of trill-start rules that dominates the discussion today was truly relevant at Beethoven's time, we have to accept another scenario. Realistically, Beethoven's contemporaries, who perhaps based their decisions on knowledge derived from a tutor or two, and on some musical education, would have been just as much at a loss about how to perform these trills as we seem to be today.

Obviously, however, pianists of Beethoven's time must have addressed this problem in some way. To solve the riddles of the previous examples they would surely have resorted to a practical blend of knowledge, intuition, and common sense. Perhaps the staccato approach in Example 8.28 triggered a different response than the *legato-accelerando* of Example 8.29, so the same pianist would play an upper note trill in the first case but not in the second. Perhaps a player performed the melody in Example 8.30 not as an example of modern Italian opera or of Beethoven's new style, but simply in her or his favorite way of playing beautiful melodies. A conservative player would have interpreted the trill in Example 8.31 as cadential and applied the standard shape with an appoggiatura from above. Someone used to Beethoven's scores would perhaps have supplied a lower-auxiliary start. A third person might have started with the main note because she or he personally found it attractive to emphasize pitch in similar situations instead of the appoggiatura, or because she or he was influenced by Hummel and thought that main-note trills were fashionable.

Of course, composers could rely at least on some general or even local consensus about trill execution. Furthermore, the music provided at least some easy-to-grasp clues for coming to quick decisions about the shape of a trill. In the sight-reading culture of Beethoven's day, such clues would have been apparent at the beginning of a trill.[119] So, for example, a lengthy approach from below, ending on the pitch of the following trill, initiates an auxiliary start for that trill. If a second approach one bar later ends on the trill itself instead, without anticipating its main note, no elaborate reasoning is required to deduce that this time perhaps a main-note start is intended (Op. 34, first variation, ends of bars 6 and 7). Finally, however, the possibility of contrasting personal responses has to be accepted not only for pianists in our time, but for pianists in Beethoven's time as well.

---

[119] Kojima's claim that a small-note continuation of a trill beginning with a restatement of the main note of the trill (Op 31/1, mvt. 2, bar 26) shows that Beethoven even intended a main-note start for that trill is in any case not correct, because in other places Beethoven indicated upper-note trill starts together with similar continuations on the trill note (for example, in Op. 73, mvt. 3, bars 227–39).

The truly important feature of all of my examples except the last, then, is that Beethoven did *not* specifically indicate how he wanted these trills to be played – even though he was otherwise more meticulous in his expressive notation than other composers of his time, and even though his trill notation was occasionally very elaborate. My analysis suggests that he himself would have started the trills with the upper note in most instances. Perhaps the younger Carl Czerny would also have done so: as Paul Badura-Skoda reports, Czerny's fingerings in his arrangement of the second move-ment of the "Kreutzer" Sonata Op. 47 from 1821 indicate upper-note trills throughout except for stepwise descending trills.[120] Beethoven, however, through his frequent less-than-clear trill notation, gave the responsibility over to the pianists. Since contemporary conventions were less rigid than the modern re-interpretation of the theorists' opinions has made them, it must be assumed that he was fully aware of the potential ambiguity of his notation. He could easily have solved the problem, but he did not. The idea that Beethoven in every case had an equally clear intention, or that he always cared to convey his intention unequivocally, must be revised. Plainly, some of his trill starts have never been easy to solve.

Finally, the appoggiatura start in Example 8.32 alerts us to the problem of an adequate performance: how clearly does the upper-note start need to be emphasized in various situations? Robert Winter writes:

If one accepts accented starts (as the sources suggest Beethoven generally meant) then the starting note affects the entire way we perceive the trill. This is an acoustical phenomenon which, although difficult to explain, is nevertheless a real part of our experience of cadential and other trills.[121]

Indeed, the whole starting note discussion would be completely superfluous were there not some truth to these words. On the other hand, the very character of embellishments as "graces," that is, as a means of personalizing musical expression, means that they can be exaggerated, whereupon they fail to convince. They can be timed inadequately, so that their effect gets lost. Finally, they can even be intentionally made ridiculous in order to show up how inadequate they actually are. It is clear that, in the end, the composer had to relinquish the responsibility of a tasteful execution of the embellishments to the performer. In his piano school, Clementi states this circumstance explicitly:

The general mark for the shake is this *tr* and composers trust chiefly to the taste and judgment of the performer.[122]

---

[120] Czerny, "Anekdoten und Notizen," 15 n.5. This is especially remarkable because the melodic trills in the fourth variation would, according to modern informed practice, be played with the main note.
[121] Winter, "Second thoughts on the performance of Beethoven's trills," 485.
[122] Muzio Clementi, *Introduction to the Art of Playing the Pianoforte*, London: Clementi, 1801, 11.

Perhaps of all Clementi's recommendations, this sentence influenced Beethoven most of all.

CONCLUSION

In his earliest works, Beethoven did not use a consistent system for notating embellishments and he performed the same symbol in various ways. When he corrected his copy of the first edition of the "Kurfürsten" Sonatas WoO 47 from 1783, he still had little interest in this particular aspect of musical notation. In the Piano Concerto WoO 4 from 1784, however, he had become more secure in handling the embellishment symbols, and in the piano quartets from 1785, his trill notation had by and large become stabilized.

One of the signs Beethoven used freely in his early works, but later only for short trills on strong beats, has been represented in the literature as a *Schneller* or inverted mordent. However, eighteenth-century theorists did not agree about its appropriate name, placement, and interpretation. Whereas Beethoven's placement of this sign is consistent in his mature work, its meaning remains ambiguous.

Beethoven occasionally indicated the starting notes and shapes of his trills by fingerings, by grace notes, or by writing out the entire trill. Most trills in the first category start with the upper auxiliary. However, there are very few examples of this kind, and they are perhaps not representative of his practice as a whole. To the second group belong trills that begin with the lower auxiliary or where the upper-auxiliary start is especially indicated. Both notations are true to eighteenth-century notational practice, and the only conclusion that can be drawn from them is that they appear in places where Beethoven clearly wanted to indicate specific trill starts. Most of Beethoven's written-out trills of the third group are in fact extended mordents of various kinds. Otherwise, we find both main-note trills and upper-auxiliary written-out trills in his works.

There is every reason to believe that, in the tradition of Beethoven's education, an upper-note trill start was the rule. A notation of a trill that does not specify the starting note might mean that Beethoven expected musicians to know about its appropriate execution. However, we are considering a time when customs were changing. Occasionally, the contemporary pianist might have had difficulties in understanding the meaning of some of Beethoven's many trills with no specifically notated beginnings. This was a risk that composers were evidently aware of. Beethoven's decision not to specify many trill starts could very well indicate that he left the responsibility of deciding about their execution to the performer.

Epilog

The main topic of this book has been the confrontation between old and new in Beethoven's world. The old shows itself in Beethoven's relationship to his teachers and to the traditional musical practices of his time. Although we know very little about Beethoven's opinion of various stylistic conventions from the time of his upbringing, many notational details do link his practice to his teachers Neefe and Haydn, and to keyboard methods such as Marpurg's or Bach's. And even when he wrote "new" music, his communication with his customers and audiences had to rely on tradition; his expressive notation was conventional most of the time, even when his music was not.

Old and new define Beethoven's piano playing as well, although in a much more problematic sense. "New" in Beethoven's playing was what was still fresh in the memory of his contemporaries and first biographers. This is the decline of his pianistic abilities, which made a clear and lasting impression and has shaped the image of Beethoven the pianist until the present day. This circumstance has obscured the "old" element of his playing: the qualities as a pianist that he might have had during his first decade in Vienna, when he was at the height of his powers and performed frequently.

Finally, his opinion of various types of pianos would also have addressed both old and new, had it not been shaped by his ever more problematic relationship to piano playing on account of his deafness. Soon after 1800, he was no longer able to fully appreciate his instruments, or to treat them well. Consequently, his criticism of the fortepiano – dating from the same time – cannot be seen as a mere matter of sound ideals. Other contemporary reports about piano building provide some help in filling the gaps of information that Beethoven's own scattered comments have left. This enables us to re-appreciate the possibilities that various kinds of early pianos have to offer for the performance of Beethoven's music.

We have to ask ourselves how the gathered information can be made useful for modern Beethoven playing. Renewed practical and artistic experience with early pianos has helped us to enhance our historical understanding of Beethoven's music. But even the fortepianist's approach is not exclusively retrospective: historical understanding becomes mixed with modern experience. Even if we play historically appropriate instruments, using an interpretive approach that might be historically adequate, we are nevertheless performing in modern halls and under modern circumstances, and we are addressing the audiences of our time.

One topic not mentioned in my discussion of the relationship between modern taste and old instruments is the relationship between relative and absolute loudness in piano playing and the related problem of audibility in various halls. An often-heard argument is that modern concert halls are bigger than the Viennese theaters and halls that Beethoven had at his disposal for performing his works and that early instruments do not match these halls.[1]

The reason I abandoned this topic is twofold. First of all, in my experience, most instrument–repertoire–hall mismatches are a matter of planning and can be prevented in practice. There is no reason to let a single fortepiano battle against a full-sized classical orchestra in a hall that suits Bruckner or Mahler. Many concert locations are perfectly suited for all sorts of fortepiano performances. This is especially relevant for the piano sonatas, which were not usually performed in front of large audiences. But even in concerto performances, an effort to match a medium-sized hall with ensembles of an appropriate size solves many problems of balance and audibility.

Second, the importance of absolute loudness for the success of the musical delivery is highly overrated in many discussions about historical instruments. After a welcoming applause from a large audience, even the *fortissimo* beginning of the "Hammerklavier" Sonata, played on a modern piano in a large hall with a good sound, sounds tiny and strained. Of course, even modern pianists are aware of this phenomenon. Edwin Fischer relates Ferruccio Busoni's solution (on the modern piano):

I once asked Busoni for the reason for his sound. He said: 'This is a very simple secret. You know, I play *mezzoforte* where the others play *forte*.' He adjusted the scale downwards. You can always reduce the *piano* further, but the *forte* has a limit.'

In the same fashion, piano concertos with *piano* solo entries "work" at least as well as the ones that start *fortissimo*. For the same reason it is possible for an audience to enjoy clavichord or lute recitals in medium-sized halls (if there is no background noise), and harpsichord recitals even in larger halls and churches. An instrument or a hall may have its limits, but the ear is adjustable – at least if the listener wants it to adjust. Of course, the total volume and the tone projection of an instrument in a given hall do have an influence on the listening experience, but this is true of all sorts of instruments. The player's task to play expressively and clearly, and to project the

---

[1] See Stephan Weinzierl, *Beethovens Konzerträume*, Frankfurt: Bochinsky, 2002.
[2] From a master class in Potsdam, 1936. Hugo Haid, ed., *Dank an Edwin Fischer*, Wiesbaden: F. A. Brockhaus, 1961, 65.

sound properly, is the same for both the fortepianist and the modern pianist. Both strive to fill a given hall with sound all the way to the corners.

A frequently heard opinion is that information on performance practice restricts the musician's creative approach. I hope I have helped to show that this is in fact a misjudgment. Historical information about Beethoven, his instruments, and his playing enhances the picture of Beethoven even for the modern performer. A knowledge of the importance of his educational background, an assessment of the possibilities of his pianos, the acknowledgment that his flexible, detailed articulation and his legato technique belong together, and the suggestion that decisions about his trills might sometimes have been difficult even for a pianist of his time, all facilitate more diverse interpretations of his music. The task of Beethoven performance practice studies is not to set aside the values of Beethoven reception history. They can, however, add to the existing picture and occasionally put right views that may be too narrow, or even incorrect.

The experience we gain is relevant for today, since performance practice research and the musicianship it informs are issues of today. However, this experience feeds directly back into our way of dealing with historical instruments. Together with her or his growing experience, a specialist in early pianos gains intuition, which can be defined as an increasingly direct access to the essential categories of knowledge and aesthetics, but which is simultaneously characterized by an essentially unhistorical element. Intuition is a spontaneous accumulation of new aesthetic preferences, in this case triggered by the historically informed framework. Playing Beethoven on old pianos is not a statement of correctness that denies the views of the modern Classical tradition; it is an opening to creativity.

Bibliography

Adlung, Jakob. *Anleitung zu der musikalischen Gelahrtheit*. Erfurt, 1758.
   Musica Mechanica Organoedi, edited by Christhard Marenholz. Kassel: Bärenreiter, 1931.

Agricola, Johann Friedrich. *Anleitung zur Singkunst 1757*, edited by Thomas Seedorf. Kassel: Bärenreiter, 2002.

Askenfeld, Anders, ed. *The Acoustics of the Piano*. Uppsala: Almqvist & Wiksell, 1991.

Bach, Carl Philipp Emanuel. *Versuch über die wahre Art, das Clavier zu spielen*, edited by Lothar Hoffmann-Erbrecht. Leipzig: Breitkopf & Härtel, 1957.

Badura-Skoda, Eva, and Paul Badura-Skoda. *Interpreting Mozart on the Keyboard*. New York: St. Martin's Press, 1962.

Badura-Skoda, Paul. "Playing the early piano." *Early Music* 12/4 (1984): 477–80.

Bannelier, Charles. "Les Instruments Historiques à l'Exposition Universelle de Vienne (1873)." *Revue et Gazette musicale de Paris*, September 5 (1875): 284.

Barth, George. *The Pianist as Orator*. Ithaca and London: Cornell University Press, 1992.

Beck, Dagmar, Karl-Heinz Köhler, and Grita Herre, eds. *Ludwig van Beethovens Konversationshefte*, 12 vols. Leipzig: VEB Deutscher Verlag für Musik, 1968–2001.

Beethoven, Ludwig van. *Briefwechsel Gesamtausgabe*, edited by Sieghard Brandenburg, 7 vols. Munich: Henle, 1996.
   The 32 Piano Sonatas, edited by Brian Jeffery. London: Tecla 1989.
   Klaviersonaten, vol. II, edited by Bertha Antonia Wallner. Munich: Henle, 1953.

Bekker, Paul. *Beethoven*. Stuttgart: Deutsche Verlags-Anstalt, 1912.

Berdux, Silke. "Johann Peter oder Philipp Jacob Milchmeyer? Biographische und bibliographische Notizen zum Autor der Hammerklavierschule 'Die wahre Art das Pianoforte zu spielen'." *Musica Instrumentalis* 2 (1999): 103–20.

Berdux, Silke, and Susanne Wittmayer. "Biographische Notizen zu Anton Walter." In *Mitteilungen der Internationalen Stiftung Mozarteum* 48/1–4, edited by Rudolph Angermüller. Salzburg: Internationale Stiftung Mozarteum, 2000, 13–106.

Biba, Otto, ed. *"Eben komme ich von Haydn." Georg August Griesingers Korrespondenz mit Joseph Haydns Verleger Breitkopf & Härtel 1799–1819*. Zürich: Atlantis, 1987.

Bilson, Malcolm. "Beethoven and the Piano." *Clavier* 12/8 (1983): 18–21.
   "The emergence of the fantasy-style in the Beethoven piano sonatas of the early and middle periods." DMA thesis, University of Illinois, 1968.

"The myth of the authentic pianoforte." *International Piano Quarterly* (July 2003): 47–53.

Bleyer, Jakob. "Historische Beschreibung der aufrechtstehenden Forte-Pianos, von der Erfindung Wachtl und Bleyers in Wien." *Intelligenz-Blatt zur Allgemeinen Musikalischen Zeitung* 17 (November 1811): 73–7.

Boßler, Heinrich Philipp. *Musikalische Real-Zeitung für das Jahr 1788.* Hildesheim: Olms, 1971.

Breitman, David. "The damper pedal and the Beethoven piano sonatas: a historical perspective." DMA thesis, Cornell University, 1993.

Brendel, Alfred. *Musical Thoughts and Afterthoughts.* London: Robson, 1976, 1998.

Brown, Clive. *Classical & Romantic Performing Practice 1750–1900.* Oxford University Press, 1999.

Bruser, Madeline. *The Art of Practicing.* New York: Bell Tower, 1997.

Burnett, Richard. "English pianos at Finchcocks." *Early Music* 13/1 (1985): 45–51.

Burney, Charles. *Tagebuch einer musikalischen Reise, trans. C. D. Ebeling 1772,* edited by Richard Schaal. Wilhelmshaven: Heinrichshofen, 1975.

Busch-Weise, Dagmar von. "Beethovens Jugendtagebuch." *Studien zur Musikwissenschaft* 25 (1962): 68–88.

Clementi, Muzio. *Introduction to the Art of Playing the Pianoforte.* London: Clementi, 1801.

Méthode pour le Piano Forte c. 1803. Rotterdam: Giuseppe Accardi, 1989.

Cooper, Barry. "Beethoven's appoggiaturas: long or short?" *Early Music* 31/2 (2003).

"Beethoven's revisions to his Fourth Piano Concerto." In Robin Stowell, ed., *Performing Beethoven.* Cambridge University Press, 1994, 23–48.

"The evolution of the first movement of Beethoven's 'Waldstein' sonata." *Music and Letters* 58 (1977): 170–91.

"The ink in Beethoven's 'Kafka' sketch miscellany." *Music and Letters* 68 (1987): 315–32.

ed. *Das Beethoven Kompendium.* Munich: Droemer Knaur, 1992.

Couperin, François. *Pièces de Clavecin, premier livre (1713),* edited by Kenneth Gilbert. Paris: Heugel, 1973.

Cramer, Carl Friedrich. *Magazin der Musik 1783–1787.* Hildesheim: Olms, 1971–74.

Czerny, Carl. "Anekdoten und Notizen über Beethoven 1852." In *Über den richtigen Vortrag der sämtlichen Beethoven'schen Klavierwerke,* edited by Paul Badura-Skoda. Vienna: Universal, 1963.

"Die Kunst des Vortrags der älteren und neueren Klavierkompositionen, zweites und drittes Kapitel." In *Über den richtigen Vortrag der sämtlichen Beethoven'schen Klavierwerke,* edited by Paul Badura-Skoda. Vienna: Universal, 1963, 24–113.

"Erinnerungen aus meinem Leben, 1842." In *Über den richtigen Vortrag der sämtlichen Beethoven'schen Klavierwerke,* edited by Paul Badura-Skoda. Vienna: Universal, 1963.

"Recollections from my life." *Music Quarterly* 42 (1956): 302–17.

Vollständige theoretisch-praktische Pianoforte-Schule in drei Theilen op. 500 (1839). Wolfenbüttel: Holle, without date.

Deiters, Hermann, and Hugo Riemann, eds. *Ludwig van Beethovens Leben, von Alexander Wheelock Thayer.* 3rd ed., vol. I. Leipzig: Breitkopf & Härtel, 1917.

DeNora, Tia. *Beethoven and the Construction of Genius*. Berkeley: University of California Press, 1995.

Drake, Kenneth. *The Beethoven Sonatas and the Creative Experience*. Bloomington: Indiana University Press, 1994.

Dreyfus, Laurence. "Early music defended against its devotees: a theory of historical performance in the twentieth century." *The Musical Quarterly* **69**/3 (1983): 297–322.

Droysen-Reber, Dagmar. "Carl Maria von Weber und sein Brodmann-Hammerflügel." In Monika Lustig, ed., *Zur Geschichte des Hammerklaviers*. Institut für Aufführungspraxis Michaelstein, 1993, 58–62.

Fischinger, Markus. "Historische Tasteninstrumente im 20. Jahrhundert am Beispiel der Restaurierung eines Hammerflügels von J. H. E. Fessel, Dresden (um 1800)." Magisterarbeit, Humboldt Universität, 2005.

Fontana, Eszter. "Ein Geschenk für Beethoven." In *Musikästhetik und Analyse, Festschrift W. Seidel zum 65. Geburtstag*. Laaber, 2002, 261–79.

Frimmel, Theodor. *Beethoven-Handbuch*. Leipzig: Breitkopf & Härtel, 1926. Reprint Hildesheim: Olms, 2003.

Neue Beethoveniana. Vienna: Carl Gerold's Sohn, 1888.

Gall, Joseph, ed. *Clavier–Stimmbuch, oder deutliche Anweisung wie jeder Musikfreund sein Clavier–Flügel, Fortepiano und Flügel–Fortepiano selbst stimmen, reparieren, und bestmöglichst gut erhalten könne*. Vienna: Carl Kupffer, 1805.

Gätjen, Bram. "Das Hammerklavier – akustisches Bindeglied zwischen Clavichord, Cembalo und modernem Flügel? Untersuchungen zur Wechselwirkung zwischen Hammer und Saite." In Monika Lustig, ed., *Zur Geschichte des Hammerklaviers*. Institut für Aufführungspraxis Michaelstein, 1993, 148–55.

Goebel-Streicher, Ute, Jutta Streicher, and Michael Ladenburger. *"Diesem Menschen hätte ich mein ganzes Leben widmen mögen": Beethoven und die Wiener Klavierbauer Nannette und Andreas Streicher*. Bonn: Beethoven-Haus, 1999.

Grundmann, Herbert, and Paul Mies. *Studien zum Klavierspiel Beethovens und seiner Zeitgenossen*. Bonn: Bouvier, 1966.

Haid, Hugo, ed. *Dank an Edwin Fischer*. Wiesbaden: Brockhaus, 1961.

Harding, Rosamond E. M. *The Piano-Forte*. 2nd edn. London: Heckscher & Co., 1933 and 1978.

Haynes, Bruce. *Pitch Standards in the Baroque and Classical Periods*. Ann Arbor, 1996.

Hiebert, Elfrieda F. "Beethoven's fingerings in the Piano Trio in B-flat major, WoO 39." *Early Keyboard Journal* **4** (1985–86): 5–27.

Hiller, Johann Adam. *Anweisung zum musikalisch=zierlichen Gesange*. Leipzig: Johann Friedrich Junius, 1780.

Huber, Alfons. "Beethovens Erard-Flügel, Überlegungen zu seiner Restaurierung." *Restauro* **3** (1990): 181–8.

Hughes, Martin. "Beethoven's piano music: contemporary performance issues." In Robin Stowell, ed., *Performing Beethoven*. Cambridge University Press, 1994, 228–39.

Hummel, Johann Nepomuk. *Anweisung zum Pianoforte-Spiele 1826*. Straubenhardt: Zimmermann, 1989.

Johnson, Douglas P. *Beethoven's Early Sketches in the "Fischhof Miscellany": Berlin Autograph 28*. 2 vols. Ann Arbor: UMI Research Press, 1980.

Johnson, Douglas P., Alan Tyson, and Robert Winter. *The Beethoven Sketchbooks: History, Reconstruction, Inventory*. Berkeley: University of California Press, 1985.

Jurgenson, William. "The case of the weak case." Paper presented at the Antwerpiano conference, Antwerp, 1993.

"The structure of the classical piano." Paper presented at the Antwerpiano conference, Antwerp, 1989.

Kalkbrenner, Frédéric. *Méthode pour apprendre le piano-forte à l'aide du guide-mains. Op. 108*. Paris, 1831.

Kann, Hans, ed. *Johann Baptist Cramer, 21 Etüden für Klavier: Nach dem Handexemplar Beethovens aus dem Besitz Anton Schindlers*. Vienna: Universal, 1974.

Kerman, Joseph, ed. *Ludwig van Beethoven Autograph Miscellany from ca. 1786 to 1799 (The "Kafka" Sketchbook)*. 2 vols. London: The Trustees of the British Museum, 1970.

Kerst, Friedrich. *Die Erinnerungen an Beethoven*. 2 vols. Stuttgart: Julius Hoffmann, 1913.

Kinsky, Georg, and Hans Halm. *Das Werk Beethovens: Thematisch-Bibliographisches Verzeichnis*. Munich: Henle, 1955.

Kite, Christopher. "Playing the early piano." *Early Music* 13/1 (1985): 54–6.

Klinke, Willibald, ed. *Johann Georg Sulzers Pädagogische Schriften*. Langensalza: Friedrich Mann, 1922.

Klöppel, Renate. *Mentales Training für Musiker*. Kassel: Gustav Bosse, 1996.

Knittel, K. M. "Wagner, deafness, and the reception of Beethoven's late style." *Journal of the American Musicological Society* 51/1 (1998): 49–82.

Koch, Heinrich Christoph. *Musikalisches Lexikon 1802*. Kassel: Bärenreiter, 2001.

Kojima, Shin Augustinus. "Über die Ausführung der Verzierungen in Beethovens Klaviermusik." In Rudolf Klein, ed., *Beethoven Kolloquium*. Kassel: Bärenreiter, 1977, 140–53.

Komlós, Katalin. *Fortepianos and their Music*. Oxford: Clarendon Press, 1995.

Koster, John. *Keyboard Musical Instruments in the Museum of Fine Arts, Boston*. Boston: Museum of Fine Arts, 1994.

Kramer, Richard. "Notes to Beethoven's education." *Journal of the American Musicological Society* 28 (1975): 72–101.

Kroll, Franz, ed. *Joh. Seb. Bachs Clavierwerke, 3. Bd. Das Wohltemperierte Clavier*. Leipzig: C. F. Peters, 1866.

Kullak, Franz. "Allgemeine Bestimmungen über den Vortrag der Beethoven'schen Klavierkonzerte." In *Beethovens Klavierkonzerte*. Leipzig: Steingräber, 1881, iv–xii.

"Über den Triller." In *Beethovens Klavierkonzerte*. Leipzig: Steingräber, 1881, xii–xxviii.

Küthen, Hans-Werner. "Ein verlorener Registerklang. Beethovens Imitation der Aeolsharfe." *Musik & Ästhetik* 34 (April 2005): 83–92.

Ladenburger, Michael. "Der junge Beethoven – Komponist und Pianist. Beethovens Handexemplar der Originalausgabe seiner Drei Klaviersonaten WoO 47." *Bonner Beethoven Studien* (2003): 107–17.

Latcham, Michael. "Alternatives to the modern piano for the performance of Mozart." Paper presented at the Institut für Aufführungspraxis, Michaelstein, 1992.

"The check in some early pianos and the development of piano technique around the turn of the 18th century." *Early Music* 21/1 (1993): 28–42.

"The development of the Streicher firm of piano builders under the leadership of Nannette Streicher, 1792–1823." In Beatrix Darmstädter, Rudolf Hopfner, and Alfons Huber, eds., *Das wiener Klavier bis 1850*. Tutzing: Schneider, 2007, 43–71.

"Franz Jakob Spath and the Tangentenflügel, an Eighteenth-Century Tradition." *Galpin Society Journal* 57 (2004): 150–70.

"Mozart and the pianos of Gabriel Anton Walter." *Early Music* 25/3 (1997): 382–400.

"Mozart and the pianos of Johann Andreas Stein." *The Galpin Society Journal* 51 (1998): 114–53.

"Soundboards Old & New." *The Galpin Society Journal* 45 (1992): 50–8.

The Stringing, Scaling and Pitch of Hammerflügel Built in the Southern German and Viennese Traditions 1780–1820. 2 vols. München-Salzburg: Katzbichler, 2000.

"Swirling from one level of the affects to another: the expressive Clavier in Mozart's time." *Early Music* 30/4 (2002): 502–20.

Lelie, Christo. *Van piano tot forte*. Kampen: Kok Lyra, 1995.

Löhlein, Georg Simon. *Klavier=Schule*. Leipzig: Waisenhaus= und Fromannische Buchhandlung, 1773.

Lohmann, Ludger. *Studien zu Artikulationsproblemen bei den Tasteninstrumenten des 16.–18. Jahrhunderts*. Regensburg: Bosse, 1986.

Lütge, Wilhelm. "Andreas und Nanette Streicher." In *Der Bär (Jahrbuch von Breitkopf & Härtel)*, 53–69, 1927.

Marpurg, Friedrich Wilhelm. *Anleitung zum Clavierspielen 1765*. New York: Broude, 1969.

Marx, Adolf Bernhard. *Anleitung zum Vortrag Beethovenscher Klavierwerke*, edited by Eugen Schmitz. Regensburg: Bosse, 1912.

Mattheson, Johann. *Der vollkommene Capellmeister 1739*, edited by Margarethe Reimann. Kassel: Bärenreiter, 1954.

Matzenauer, Sabine. "Zur Restaurierung eines Piano-Fortes von J. A. Stein – erhaltene Instrumente im Vergleich." In Monika Lustig, ed., *Zur Geschichte des Hammerklaviers*. Institut für Aufführungspraxis Michaelstein, 1993, 50–7.

Maunder, Richard. *Keyboard Instruments in Eighteenth-Century Vienna*. Oxford: Clarendon Press, 1998.

Meyers Konversations=Lexikon. Leipzig and Vienna: Bibliographisches Institut, 1896.

Milchmeyer, Johann Peter. *Die wahre Art das Pianoforte zu spielen*. Dresden: Meinhold, 1797.

Miller, Alice. *Am Anfang war Erziehung*. Frankfurt a. M.: Suhrkamp, 1980.

Das Drama des begabten Kindes. Frankfurt a. M.: Suhrkamp, 1979.

Du sollst nicht merken. Frankfurt a. M.: Suhrkamp, 1981.

Mobbs, Kenneth. "A performer's comparative study of touchweight, key-dip, keyboard design and repetition in early grand pianos, c.1770 to 1850." *The Galpin Society Journal* 54 (2001): 16–44.

Molsen, Uli. *Die Geschichte des Klavierspiels in historischen Zitaten.* Balingen: Uli Molsen, 1983.

Morrow, Mary Sue. *Concert Life in Haydn's Vienna: Aspects of a Developing Musical and Social Institution.* Stuyvesant, NY: Pendragon Press, 1989.

Moysan, Alain. "L'Erard de 1790." In *Sébastien Erard 1752–1831 ou la rencontre avec le pianoforte.* Luxeuil-Les-Bains: Publi-Lux, 1993, 28–47.

Mozart, Leopold. *Versuch einer gründlichen Violinschule 1756.* Frankfurt: Grahl, 1976.

Mozart, Wolfgang Amadeus. *Briefe und Aufzeichnungen,* edited by Ulrich Konrad. 8 vols. Munich: Deutscher Taschenbuch Verlag, 2005.

Müller, August Eberhard. *Fortepiano=Schule.* Leipzig: Carl Friedrich Peters, 1804.

Neefe, Christian Gottlob. "Christian Gottlob Neefens Lebenslauf von ihm selbst beschrieben. Nebst beigefügtem Karakter." In *Die Sammlung der UB Kiel,* 22. Bonn, 1782 and 1789. Available under the tab "fasz.II" at www.uni-kiel.de/ub/Nachlass/Cramer/ (last accessed March 2, 2009).

Zwölf Klaviersonaten 1773, edited by Jean Saint-Arroman. Bressuire: J. M. Fuzeau, 2004.

Neumann, Frederik. *Improvisation and Ornamentation in Mozart.* Princeton University Press, 1986.

Ornamentation in Baroque and Post-Baroque Music. Princeton University Press, 1978.

Newman, William S. *Beethoven on Beethoven. Playing His Piano Music His Way.* New York: Norton, 1988.

"Beethoven's pianos versus his piano ideals." *Journal of the American Musicological Society* **23**/3 (1970): 484–504.

"The Performance of Beethoven's Trills." *Journal of the American Musicological Society* **29**/3 (1976): 437–62.

"Second and one-half thoughts on the performance of Beethoven's trills." *The Musical Quarterly* **64**/1 (1978): 98–103.

Nicholson, Linda. "Playing the early piano." *Early Music* **13**/1 (1985): 52–4.

Nohl, Ludwig. *Beethoven: Nach den Schilderungen seiner Zeitgenossen.* Stuttgart: Cotta, 1877.

ed. *Musiker=Briefe.* Leipzig: Duncker und Humblot, 1873.

Parrish, Carl. "Criticisms of the piano when it was new." *The Musical Quarterly* **30**/4 (1944): 428–40.

Plantinga, Leon. *Beethoven's Concertos.* New York: Norton, 1999.

Clementi, his Life and Music. London: Oxford University Press, 1977.

Pollens, Stewart. "Gottfried Silbermann's pianos." *The Organ Yearbook* **17** (1986): 103–21.

Prod'homme, Jacques-Gabriel. "From the unpublished autobiography of Antoine Reicha." *The Musical Quarterly* **22**/3 (1936): 339–53.

Quantz, Johann Joachim. *Versuch einer Anweisung die flute traversiere zu spielen 1789,* edited by Hans-Peter Schmitz. Kassel: Bärenreiter, 1953.

Raessler, Daniel M. "Türk, touch and slurring: finding a rationale." *Early Music* **17**/1 (1989): 55–9.

Rampe, Siegbert. "Beethovens Klavier – Klangwelt und Aufführungspraxis." In Wolfram Steinbeck and Hartmut Hein, eds., *Beethovens Klaviermusik. Das Handbuch.* Laaber, in preparation.

"'*Figurieren*' und '*Fantasieren*': Improvisationen bei Beethoven." In Wolfram Steinbeck and Hartmut Hein, eds., *Beethovens Klaviermusik. Das Handbuch.* Laaber, in preparation.

Mozarts Claviermusik. Klangwelt und Aufführungspraxis. Kassel: Bärenreiter, 1995.

Reichardt, Johann Friedrich. *Briefe, die Musik betreffend,* edited by Grita Herre und Walther Siegmund-Schultze. Leipzig: Philipp Reclam, 1976.

Riethmüller, Albrecht, ed. *Beethoven. Interpretationen seiner Werke.* 2 vols. Laaber, 1996.

Ringer, Alexander. "Beethoven and the London Fortepiano School." *The Musical Quarterly* **56**/4 (1970): 742–58.

Robbins Landon, Howard C., ed. *Das Mozart Kompendium.* Munich: Droemer Knaur, 1990.

ed. *Ludwig van Beethoven. Leben und Werk in Zeugnissen der Zeit.* Zürich: Universal, 1970.

Rose, Maria. "Beethoven and his French piano: proof of purchase." *Musique, Images, Instruments* 7 (2005): 110–22.

Rosenblum, Sandra P. *Performance Practices in Classic Piano Music.* Bloomington and Indianapolis: Indiana University Press, 1988.

Rowland, David. "Beethoven's pianoforte pedalling." In Robin Stowell, ed., *Performing Beethoven.* Cambridge University Press, 1994, 49–69.

A History of Pianoforte Pedalling. Cambridge University Press, 1993.

Rück, Ulrich. "Mozarts Hammerflügel erbaute Anton Walter, Wien." *Mozart Jahrbuch* (1955): 246–62.

Rutschky, Katharina, ed. *Schwarze Pädagogik, Quellen zur Naturgeschichte der bürgerlichen Erziehung.* Munich: Ullstein, 2001.

Schiedermair, Ludwig. *Der junge Beethoven.* Leipzig: Quelle & Meyer, 1925.

Schiedmayer, Johann Lorenz, and Carl Dieudonné. *Kurze Anleitung zu einer richtigen Behandlung der Forte-Pianos 1824.* Tübingen: Gulde-Verlag, 1994.

Schindler, Anton Felix. *Beethoven as I Knew Him,* translated by Constance S. Jolly, edited by Donald MacArdle. London: Faber and Faber, 1966. Reprint Dover, 1996.

Schleuning, Peter. *Verzierungsforschung und Aufführungspraxis. Zum Verhältnis von Notation und Interpretation in der Musik des 18. Jahrhunderts, Basler Jahrbuch für historische Aufführungspraxis,* vol III. Winterthur: Amadeus, 1979.

Schleuning, Peter, and Martin Geck. *"Geschrieben auf Bonaparte" Beethovens "Eroica": Revolution, Reaktion, Rezeption.* Reinbeck: Rowohlt, 1989.

Schlosser, Johann Aloys. *Beethoven: the First Biography [1827],* translated by Reinhard G. Pauly, edited by Barry Cooper. Portland: Amadeus Press, 1996.

Schmidt-Görg, Joseph, ed. *Des Bonner Bäckermeisters Gottfried Fischer Aufzeichnungen über Beethovens Jugend.* Munich/Duisburg: Henle, 1971.

Schönfeld, Johann Ferdinand von. *Jahrbuch der Tonkunst von Wien und Prag 1796.* Munich: Katzbichler, 1976.

Skowroneck, Martin. "Cembalobauer als Kopisten." Paper presented at the Colloquium of the Ruckers Genootschap, Antwerp 1977.

Skowroneck, Tilman. "Beethoven's Erard piano: its influence on his compositions and on Viennese fortepiano building." *Early Music* **30**/4 (2002): 522–38.

"Keyboard instruments of the young Beethoven." In Scott Burnham and Michael Steinberg, eds., *Beethoven and His World*. Princeton University Press, 2000, 151–92.

Solomon, Maynard. *Beethoven*. New York: Macmillan, 1977.

Šolotová, Olga. *Antonín Rejcha*, translated by Deryck Viney. Prague: Supraphon, 1990.

Spànyi, Miklòs. "Concerning the ornaments in Carl Philipp Emanuel Bach's keyboard music." In *Carl Philipp Emanuel Bach: Sämtliche Klavierwerke*. Budapest: Könemann Music, 1999, vol. I, 156–63.

Speerstra, Joel. *Bach and the Pedal Clavichord: An Organist's Guide*. The University of Rochester Press, 2004.

Stetten, Paul von. *Kunst-, Gewerb- und Handwerks-Geschichte der Reichs-Stadt Augsburg*. Vol. II. Augsburg, 1788.

Streicher, Andreas. *Kurze Bemerkungen über das Spielen, Stimmen und Erhalten der Fortepiano, welche von Nannette Streicher, geborene Stein in Wien verfertiget warden 1801*. The Hague: Lelieveld, 1979.

Tan, Melvyn. "The technique of playing music authentically does not mean simply using the appropriate instruments." *Early Music* **12**/1 (1985): 57–8.

Thayer, Alexander Wheelock. *Life of Beethoven*, edited by Elliot Forbes. Princeton University Press, 1967.

Tomlinson, Gary. "The historian, the performer, and authentic meaning in music." In Nicholas Kenyon, ed., *Authenticity and Early Music*. Oxford University Press, 1988, 114–36.

Türk, Daniel Gottlob. *Klavierschule 1789*, edited by Erwin R. Jacobi. Kassel: Bärenreiter, 1967.

Van der Meer, John Henry. "Beethoven et le pianoforte." In *L'interprétation de la musique classique de Haydn à Schubert. Colloque International, Evry, 13–15 octobre 1977*. Paris: Minkoff, 1980, 67–85.

"Beethoven und das Fortepiano." *Musica Instrumentalis* **2** (1999): 56–82.

Van der Zanden, Jos. "Ferdinand Ries in Wien. Neue Perspektiven zu den Notizen." In Ernst Herttrich, ed., *Reihe V Bonner Beethoven-Studien*. Bonn: Verlag Beethoven-Haus, 2005, 191–212.

Van Hasselt, Luc. "Beethoven in Holland." *Die Musikforschung* **18** (1965): 181–4.

Van Oort, Bart. "The English Classical piano style and its influence on Haydn and Beethoven." DMA thesis, Cornell University, 1993.

"Haydn and the English Classical piano style." *Early Music* **28**/1 (2000): 73–89.

Wagner, Ernst David. *Musikalische Ornamentik oder die wesentlichen Verzierungs-Manieren im Vortrage der Vokal- und Instrumental-Musik*. Berlin: Schlesinger, 1869.

Wainwright, David. *Broadwood by Appointment. A history*. London: Quiller Press, 1982.

Wegeler, Franz Gerhard, and Ferdinand Ries. *Biographische Notizen über Beethoven*. Coblenz: Bädeker, 1838.

Weinzierl, Stephan. *Beethovens Konzerträume*. Frankfurt: Bochinsky, 2002.

Wetzstein, Margot, ed. *Familie Beethoven im kurfürstlichen Bonn. Neuauflage nach den Aufzeichnungen des Bonner Bäckermeisters Gottfried Fischer*. Bonn: Verlag Beethoven-Haus, 2006.

Winter, Robert. "And even more thoughts on the Beethoven trill…" *The Musical Quarterly* **65**/1 (1979): 111–16.

"Second thoughts on the performance of Beethoven's trills." *The Musical Quarterly* **63**/4 (1977): 483–504.

Index

Lightning Source UK Ltd.
Milton Keynes UK
UKOW04n2157020217

293483UK00006B/132/P

9 780521 119597